GREAT BIRDING IN THE GREAT LAKES

◆

A Guide to the 50 Best Birdwatching Sites in the Great Lakes States

By Tom Powers

Illustrated by Timm E. Rye

 Walloon Press

Author photo by Jim Bakken

All other photos are by the author
p. vi, Crab Orchard National Wildlife Refuge
p. 32, Twin Swamps Nature Preserve
p. 58, Whitefish Point
p. 100, Ottawa National Wildlife Refuge
p. 144, Point Pelee National Park
p. 156, Necedah National Wildlife Refuge

Great Birding in the Great Lakes

Walloon Press
1130 Lafayette
Flint, Michigan 48503

Printed in the United States of America
First Printing, March 1998

ISBN 0-9660068-0-1

CONTENTS

Forward ....*iv*

Introduction ....*v*

ILLINOIS

1. MONTROSE HARBOR 1

2. WOODED ISLE, JACKSON PARK 4

3. LAKE CALUMET 7

4. CHICAGO BOTANICAL GARDEN AND
   SKOKIE LAGOONS 10

5. FOREST GLEN PRESERVE 13

6. CHAUTAUQUA
   NATIONAL WILDLIFE REFUGE 16

7. PERE MARQUETTE STATE PARK AND
   MARK TWAIN NATIONAL WILDLIFE
   REFUGE 19

8. REND LAKE 23

9. CRAB ORCHARD
   NATIONAL WILDLIFE REFUGE 27

INDIANA & KENTUCKY

10. THE MIGRANT TRAP 33

11. INDIANA DUNES STATE PARK 36

12. JASPER-PULASKI FISH AND WILDLIFE
    AREA 39

13. SHADES STATE PARK 41

14. MUSCATATUCK NATIONAL WILDLIFE
    AREA 44

15. FALLS OF THE OHIO STATE PARK 47

16. HOVEY LAKE WILDLIFE AREA AND
    TWIN SWAMPS NATURE PRESERVE....51

17. JOHN JAMES AUDUBON STATE PARK ...54

MICHIGAN

18. WHITEFISH POINT 59

19. SAULT STE. MARIE 63

20. TAWAS POINT STATE PARK 66

21. NAYANQUING POINT WILDLIFE AREA .70

22. KIRTLAND'S WARBLER
    NESTING AREA 73

23. SHIAWASSEE NATIONAL WILDLIFE
    REFUGE 76

24. FISH POINT WILDLIFE AREA 79

25. PORT CRESCENT STATE PARK..........82

26. METRO BEACH METRO PARK..........85

27. LAKE ERIE METRO PARK.................88

28. POINTE MOUILLEE
    STATE GAME AREA........................91

29. BERRIEN COUNTY DUNES AND
    LAKESHORE...............................95

OHIO

30. OAK OPENINGS METRO PARK AND
    IRWIN PRAIRIE PRESERVE................101

31. MAGEE MARSH AND CRANE CREEK
    STATE PARK 105

32. OTTAWA NATIONAL WILDLIFE
    REFUGE 109

33. SHELDON MARSH
    STATE NATURE PRESERVE..............113

34. MENTOR MARSH AND HEADLANDS
    DUNES STATE NATURE PRESERVES..117

35. CUYAHOGA VALLEY
    NATIONAL RECREATION AREA........122

36. GREEN LAWN CEMETERY 126

37. CLEAR CREEK VALLEY
    METRO PARK.............................129

38. KILLDEER PLAINS WILDLIFE AREA..132

39. SPRING VALLEY WILDLIFE AREA 135

40. SHAWNEE LOOKOUT AND
    MIAMI WHITEWATER COUNTY PARKS
    AND OXBOW LAKE........................138

ONTARIO

41. POINT PELEE NATIONAL PARK 145

42. HOLIDAY BEACH
    CONSERVATION AREA....................150

43. ST. CLAIR RIVER..........................153

WISCONSIN

44. GREEN BAY..................................157

45. GEORGE W. MEAD WILDLIFE AREA ..161

46. NECEDAH NATIONAL
    WILDLIFE REFUGE 164

47. HORICON MARSH NATIONAL
    WILDLIFE REFUGE 168

48. WYALUSING STATE PARK...............172

49. TREMPEALEAU NATIONAL
    WILDLIFE REFUGE 174

50. CREX MEADOWS WILDLIFE AREA...177

Rare Bird Alert.............................183

FORWARD

Writing a book can be a humbling experience. I knew I was nowhere near to calling myself an expert birder when I began writing this book — those who read it will find I still have far to go — and instead of expertise I brought enthusiasm, some modest research skills, a willingness to learn, and a love of birding to the job. It took less than six months to discover I knew a whole lot less about birding in general, and particularly birding in the Midwest than I thought I did. But whenever and wherever I turned for help there was a birder offering assistance. This book simply could not have happened without dozens of birders and naturalists, in the field and in the office, willingly and freely giving of their time and expertise.

Much of the preliminary research for this book was done by haunting the many Rare Bird Alerts in the Midwest. For the uninitiated, these are weekly reports of birding activity in specific geographical areas that are recorded on telephone answering machines or posted on the Internet. The Rare Bird Alerts mainly report unusual or rare bird sightings, or announce the arrival of migrating species in the spring and fall. The RBAs, as birders like to call them, are invaluable to birdwatchers who are seeking rarities to add to their life lists or to let birders know when there is an influx of migrating birds at a particular location. The hours spent by dedicated birders recording and announcing bird sightings throughout the Midwest is appreciated by every avid birdwatcher, and this author is deeply indebted to them. You will find a list of Rare Bird Alert phone numbers in the back of this book.

I would like to thank the following people who responded with grace, information, and encouragement when this author intruded on their lives. They are Doug Anderson, Beth Arthur, George Bangs, Elaine T. Barnum, Krista Beck, Byron Bossenbroek, Ken Brock, Alan Bruner, Diane M. Chalfant, Paul Clyne, Nancy M. Csidor, Joan Coogan, Doug Damberg, Edward P. DeVries, Monica Essenmacher, Erica Feldkamp, Todd Funk, Sara Gilbert, Glenn Grant, Michelle Grigore, Tim Gundlach, Roger L. Hedge, James E. Hoefler, Gary Imwalle, Sharon Johnson, Ned Keller, Tom Kemp, Ron McMurray, Walter J. Marcisz, Kip Miller, Tim Smart, Wendy Smith, Leslie Sutton, Gary Wilford, Geoffrey A. Williamson, Helen Wuestenfeld, and Jerry Wykes.

I owe a special debt of gratitude to the following people: Jeff Beucking, a peerless birder, gave freely of his time, advice, and accompanied, no, led me on many birding trips. Jeff also read the manuscript of this book and saved me the embarrassment of inventing several new bird species. Charlie Hansen accepted the dauntless task of proofreading the manuscript of a grammatically challenged author. Gary Barfknecht gave me the courage to set up a publishing house. And lastly, Barb Powers put up with me for the four years it took to write this book. I suspect only the spouses of other writers can truly appreciate her accomplishment.

Tom Powers
Flint, Michigan

INTRODUCTION

Determining the 50 best bird-watching sites in the Great Lakes states was a formidable task. The hundreds of good birding sites in the Midwest were judged against the following criteria: 1) the number of species regularly seen in an area; 2) ease of accessibility and viewing; 3) the number and variety of rarities that are regularly seen at the site; 4) one-of-a-kind viewing opportunities; and 5) the natural beauty of the surroundings. The last criterion was given much less weight than the first four because in several notable cases birds seemed to favor areas that lacked any and all aesthetic values.

In pursuit of the best birding sites in the Great Lakes, I read every book I could find on birding in the states included within the scope of this book and searched out articles on birding in the Great Lakes that appeared in magazines and newspapers over the past decade. Naturalists and expert birders in each of the states were surveyed and fellow Audubon and American Birding Association members from throughout the Great Lakes were contacted for information and advice. All of the information gathered from the above sources was judged against the above criteria and all the sites were visited, many several times.

I also let the birds have a voice — so to speak — in the selection process. For two years I kept running tabs on the variety and number of bird species reported on Rare Bird Alerts from throughout the Great Lakes area. Through the volunteers who posted the sightings within their states or areas, the birds spoke volumes. A year's worth of Rare Bird Alert postings from Montrose Harbor and Jackson Park's Wooded Isle leave little doubt that both of these Chicago sites attract an incredible number and variety of birds.

A few of the sites that made it on the list of 50 best birding spots were included not because of the variety of birds found at the site but because of a single species found there. No one will argue that the Grayling/Mio area of Michigan deserves to be on the list because it is the nesting site of Kirtland's Warblers, one of the rarest birds in the world. Sandhill Cranes, on the other hand, are not among the world's rarest birds, but when virtually every Sandhill Crane east of the Mississippi River gathers in one spot, every fall, it is a sight to behold.

I expect that the inclusion or exclusion of birding sites found in this book could and will be fodder for endless discussions and differences of opinion. In the end, the sites included, in my judgment, best fit my criteria. You are more than welcome to disagree with me. Go ahead and do your own research and follow the birds from Sault Ste. Marie, Michigan to Evansville, Indiana and from Cleveland, Ohio to Bayfield, Wisconsin.

You will have the time of your life.

ILLINOIS

MONTROSE HARBOR, 1

WOODED ISLE / JACKSON PARK, 4

CHICAGO BOTANICAL GARDEN
AND SKOKIE LAGOONS, 10

FOREST GLEN PRESERVE, 13

CHAUTAUQUA
NATIONAL WILDLIFE REFUGE, 16

PERE MARQUETTE STATE PARK
AND MARK TWAIN
NATIONAL WILDLIFE REFUGE, 19

REND LAKE, 23

CRAB ORCHARD
NATIONAL WILDLIFE REFUGE, 27

Montrose Harbor

Nearly every experienced Chicago birder is familiar with Montrose Harbor, and it is probably the most extensively birded spot in the greater Chicago area. My preliminary research indicated Montrose Harbor was one of the most remarkably productive birding sites not only in Chicago but in the entire Midwest. A year's worth of checking the Chicago Rare Bird Alert, via the Internet, turned up an incredible number and variety of bird sightings at the harbor, and local birders have labeled one spot in the area "The Magic Hedge" because of its almost mystical ability to attract birds.

It seemed that Chicago not only draws huge numbers of human tourists but an equally large number of feathered travelers, and during the migration season the birding at Montrose can be simply unbelievable. On any given day throughout the course of the year the number and variety of birds is staggering. A quick check of the past year's sightings turned up 290 Forster's Terns in one day (that's 280 more of the species than I have seen in my entire life). Other tallies for a single day at Montrose Harbor include 11 different sparrow species, 195 Franklin's Gulls, 5,000 ducks, 5 Snowy Owls, and frequent sightings of more than 20 different warbler species in May, September and October.

I couldn't uncover an official bird checklist for the area, but a casual tally of the Rare Bird Alert postings for Montrose Harbor and my sightings in a two-hour visit totaled 114 species. Keep in mind that the above service does not usually list the everyday or common birds found in the area, only species of special interest. Tricolored Heron, American Avocet, Whimbrel, Mew and Kumlein's gulls, Lapland Longspur, Osprey, Northern Shrike, Palm, Cerulean and Pine warblers, Lincoln's and Sharp-tailed sparrows and a Magnificent Frigatebird will give you just a taste of the sightings at Montrose Harbor. Start adding songbirds, sparrows and other species common to Chicago, toss in the ubiquitous Herring and Ring-billed gulls and the usual waterfowl seen along the lakeshore, and the list would surely top 200.

I didn't have much time to think about it while moving bumper-to-bumper at 50 mph along Lake Shore Drive, but after exiting the four lanes of traffic (through which Chicago cabbies hurled themselves like kamikaze pilots looking for an enemy aircraft carrier), and taking Montrose Drive out onto the slim finger of land enclosing Montrose Harbor, my nerves and grip on the steering wheel relaxed enough to realize why this is such a great birding area. Migrating birds tend to follow shorelines on their semi-annual migrations, and the nearly straight north/south shoreline on either side of Lake Michigan serves as a natural highway for birds. Almost every mile of the Michigan side of the lake offers migrating birds a place to rest and feed, but when birds travel the west side of Lake Michigan and hit the Chicago area, it's the equivalent of 40 miles of expressway driving without a rest stop.

Even without leaving the car the views from Montrose Drive were exhilarating. Lake Michigan stretched to the north, south, and east for as far as I could see with the spectacular Chicago skyline hugging the lakeshore. If I found the view mesmerizing, birds must look on the area as a virtual oasis in a desert. For land birds the wide lawns, few trees, and the skimpiest of shrubbery is a welcome respite from the endless miles of highrise apartment buildings and office towers

"I asked if this was the 'Magic Hedge'. They confirmed I had found the Holy Grail of Chicago birders."

LOCATION: Chicago, Illinois.

DIRECTIONS: Take Lake Shore Drive (U.S. 41) north from downtown Chicago to Montrose and turn right (east).

HOURS: Open all year.

BEST TIMES: Spring and fall migration are best but any time of the year the area can produce extraordinary sightings.

BIRDING HIGHLIGHTS: Montrose Harbor is the most extensively birded area in Chicago and the one of the great spots for spotting migrating birds in the entire Midwest. Other areas may come close to equaling or even exceeding the number and variety of birds, but at Montrose there is virtually no cover and birds couldn't be more obvious if they carried around sandwich boards. It consistently produces rarities and unusual birds throughout the year.

"Men and women in business suits arrive at 6:30 a.m. with binoculars and bird books to spend an hour watching birds before heading to the office."

on the one hand and open water on the other. For gulls and waterfowl the snug little harbor offers shelter and a resting spot, and the wide sandy beaches lining the Lake Michigan side of the harbor acts as a magnet for shorebirds. The stark fact is that Montrose offers only minimal shelter for migrating birds, but the beckoning finger of land that juts out into Lake Michigan is an "it or nothing" proposition for several miles in either direction if birds need to rest and feed.

From the parking lot I walked down to the little harbor that is jammed with boat docks and, on that 31-degree, April morning, packed with gulls instead of boats. The harbor is a favorite spot for turning up rare and unusual gulls, and I checked off a Lesser Black-backed Gull and a Glaucous Gull but couldn't find a Thayer's Gull, which was reportedly in the harbor. The only way I'd have picked out the California Gull (seen in the area the day before) from the hundreds of Herring Gulls was if it had a surfboard tucked under a wing. Paddling in and around the docks were Common and Red-breasted mergansers, Mallards, Lesser Scaup, and a Horned Grebe.

Tired of trying to sort the wheat from the chaff among all the gulls, I turned from the harbor and went in search of the "The Magic Hedge". On the drive out to the harbor I had seen nothing but a huge expanse of grass and a few trees. After some looking I finally saw two people with binoculars standing on a slight rise of ground east of the harbor. It wasn't until I was out of the car and walking toward them that I discerned a meager line of woody vegetation on the crown of the small rise of land. If this was a hedge, it was the equivalent of *Charlie Brown's*

MONTROSE HARBOR FIELD CHECKLIST

(This checklist was compiled from the Chicago Rare Bird Alert hotline and is only an indication of the variety of birds to be seen at Montrose Harbor).

___ Common Loon	___ Piping Plover	___ Black-billed Cuckoo	___ Water Pipit	___ Vesper Sparrow
___ Horned Grebe	___ American Avocet	___ Yellow-billed Cuckoo	___ Northern Shrike	___ Lark Sparrow
___ Double-crested Cormorant	___ Willet	___ Short-eared Owl	___ Philadelphia Vireo	___ Savannah Sparrow
___ Magnificent Frigatebird	___ Spotted Sandpiper	___ Snowy Owl	___ Northern Parula	___ Grasshopper Sparrow
___ American Bittern	___ Whimbrel	___ Red-headed Woodpecker	___ Yellow Warbler	___ LeConte's Sparrow
___ Least Bittern	___ Red Knot	___ Red-bellied Woodpecker	___ Magnolia Warbler	___ Sharp-tailed Sparrow
___ Great Egret	___ Sanderling	___ Yellow-bellied Sapsucker	___ Cape May Warbler	___ Fox Sparrow
___ Tricolored Heron	___ Semipalmated Sandpiper	___ Olive-sided Flycatcher	___ Black-throated Blue Warbler	___ Lincoln's Sparrow
___ Mallard	___ Least Sandpiper	___ Western Wood-pewee	___ Yellow-rumped Warbler	___ Swamp Sparrow
___ Lesser Scaup	___ Baird's Sandpiper	___ Alder Flycatcher	___ Black-throated Green Warbler	___ White-throated Sparrow
___ Common Merganser	___ Pectoral Sandpiper	___ Willow Flycatcher	___ Pine Warbler	___ Golden-crowned Sparrow
___ Red-breasted Merganser	___ Buff-breasted Sandpiper	___ Horned Lark	___ Palm Warbler	___ White-crowned Sparrow
___ Black Scoter	___ Franklin's Gull	___ Cliff Swallow	___ Cerulean Warbler	___ Harris's Sparrow
___ White-winged Scoter	___ Bonaparte's Gull	___ Winter Wren	___ Louisiana Waterthrush	___ Lapland Longspur
___ Osprey	___ Mew Gull	___ Sedge Wren	___ Kentucky Warbler	___ Snow Bunting
___ Northern Harrier	___ Ring-billed Gull	___ Marsh Wren	___ Mourning Warbler	___ Bobolink
___ Merlin	___ California Gull	___ Golden-crowned Kinglet	___ Wilson's Warbler	___ Eastern Meadowlark
___ Peregrine Falcon	___ Herring Gull	___ Ruby-crowned Kinglet	___ Canada Warbler	___ Yellow-headed Blackbird
___ Virginia Rail	___ Thayer's Gull	___ Eastern Bluebird	___ Yellow-breasted Chat	___ Rusty Blackbird
___ Sora	___ Kumlien's Gull	___ Swainson's Thrush	___ Scarlet Tanager	___ Orchard Oriole
___ Black-bellied Plover	___ Lesser Black-backed Gull	___ Hermit Thrush	___ Indigo Bunting	___ Purple Finch
___ American Golden-plover	___ Glaucous Gull	___ Gray Catbird	___ American Tree Sparrow	___ Common Redpoll
___ Semipalmated Plover	___ Forster's Tern	___ Northern Mockingbird	___ Clay-colored Sparrow	___ House Sparrow

Christmas Tree. With more than a little skepticism I asked if this was "The Magic Hedge." They confirmed I had found the Holy Grail of Chicago birders.

I stood in awe of what is called a "hedge" in Chicago. The woody vegetation stretched in a straight line for about 40 yards, at its thickest it couldn't have been more than 10 feet wide or 5 feet high. But what really stuck me dumb was the density and thickness of the hedge. I am used to hedges you would need a chain saw to get through and dense enough to hide a deer. This was almost wispy by comparison. You could have walked through it at almost any point without hardly disturbing the widely-spaced reedy stalks. Yet it was also obvious that this poor excuse for a hedge is the only appreciable cover in the area except for a few trees. And then Joan Coogan, who lives a couple of miles from the harbor, began filling me in about her experiences over the last couple of years at the hedge, and my awe turned to pure wonderment.

Joan has been riding her bike down here almost daily for the last couple of years. She said that during the peaks of spring and fall migration, birds pack the hedge, and it's "like watching fish in a tank." Birders arrive early in the morning with lawn chairs, coffee thermoses and donuts, encircle the hedge several rows deep, and watch the show throughout the morning. Joan has seen men and women in business suits arrive at 6:30 a.m. with binoculars and bird books to spend an hour watching birds before heading to the office. Even on this cold, early April morning, the hedge produced a little magic. A Fox Sparrow sat shivering in the thin brush; an Eastern Meadowlark poked around the grassy edges of the hedge; and a Yellow-bellied Sapsucker investigated a nearby tree.

Joan said the sandy beaches also attract a numerous and surprising assortment of shorebirds throughout the year but birders have to get to the area early in the morning to catch sight of them because the open grassy lawn bordering the beach is a favorite place for nearby apartment dwellers to run their dogs. Even as she spoke, a couple of golden retrievers, a German shepherd and several smaller dogs were enjoying a run. It seems the high point of the day for many of the dogs is a run along the beach to see how many birds they can scatter. Chicago birders are liable to call Montrose's beach the "Magic Beach" if there are more days like August 6, 1996 when 164 Willets, a Marbled Godwit, a Whimbrel, 19 Stilt Sandpipers, 4 Ruddy Turnstones, assorted numbers of Pectoral Sandpipers, Short-billed Dowitchers, Semipalmated Plovers, Semipalmated Sandpipers, and peeps were all spotted along the shoreline.

"When birds travel the west side of Lake Michigan and hit the Chicago area, it's the equivalent of 40 miles of expressway driving without a rest stop."

Wooded Isle, Jackson Park

"Seeing 80 to 100 species a day is almost a common occurrence during the first three weeks in May, and as many as 130 species have been recorded in a single day."

LOCATION: Chicago, Illinois.

DIRECTIONS: From the intersection of I-55 and Lake Shore Drive (Route 41) drive south on Lake Shore approximately 3 miles to the Museum of Science and Industry. To reach Wooded Island, park on the south side of the museum and walk across Clarence Darrow Bridge.

HOURS: Open all year, but for safety's sake it is only recommended that you bird here in the morning or in groups. (See text).

BEST TIMES: The first three weeks in May can be extraordinary while the rest of spring migration is memorable. The fall can also produce good birding and area birders have reported unusual and interesting birds throughout the year.

BIRDING HIGHLIGHTS: Wooded Isle in Jackson Park is one of the prime spots in the Midwest for birding during spring migration. A daily tally of 80 to 100 species is not unusual for experienced birdwatchers. Wooded Isle is especially noted for warblers during spring migration with sightings of more than 20 species a day common during late April and early May. The record for a single observer is 32 warbler species in a day. The rest of Jackson Park, especially the Lake Michigan shoreline, yields a variety of shorebirds, marsh birds, gulls and waterfowl.

Doug Anderson, who has conducted bird walks and studied migratory patterns for over 15 years on Wooded Isle in Jackson Park, not only knows the area better than I'll ever know it, he is more succinct. He calls the 16-acre island, "the best small area to see the largest numbers of birds within 100 miles of Chicago." He estimates that over 80% of all the birds ever recorded in his state have, at one time or another, shown up at the Wooded Isle. Paul Clyne, another expert on the area, estimates that 200 species are annually recorded in Jackson Park, and his own personal checklist has reached 268 species in seven years of recordkeeping.

Based on the research for this book, I can go Anderson one better and claim that Wooded Isle, also known as the Paul O. Douglas Nature Sanctuary, is one of the best spots in the entire Midwest for birding during the peak of spring migration. Seeing 80 to 100 species a day is almost a common occurrence at Wooded Isle during the first three weeks in May, and as many as 130 species have been recorded in a single day. This, by the way, can sometimes be accomplished in little more than a two-hour walk. If that's not enough to convince you to make travel plans for early May, it is not uncommon to see more than 20 warbler species a day, and the single observer record for number of warblers in a single day is 32! And then there are the rarities that turn up with enough regularity to keep area birders constantly on the alert. In the past few years a Magnificent Frigatebird, an Anhinga, Illinois' first Townsend's Warbler, a Tricolored Heron, Brant, Yellow and Black rails, an Ash-throated Flycatcher, California Gulls, and a Brewer's Sparrow are just a few of the rarities that have called at either Wooded Isle or the nearby Lake Michigan shoreline. The park also boasts one of the largest populations of Monk Parakeets in the Midwest, and they are currently listed as a countable bird by the Illinois Ornithological Society. The fact of the matter is: birdwatching, as incongruous as it seems, should be considered one more of Chicago's fantastic tourist attractions, with Wooded Isle, Montrose Harbor, and Chicago Botanic Garden as the biggest birding draws.

Wooded Isle, by the way, was designed by Frederick Law Olmsted, the same landscape architect who designed Central Park in New York. The island was created for and held the World's Columbian Exposition of 1893. It was at the exposition that F. W. Rueckheim mixed up and sold a concoction of popcorn, peanuts, and molasses that America and the world has been munching on ever since. More than a 100 years later Wooded Isle is still a Cracker Jack spot for birdwatching. But, birders should be aware that in addition to birdwatching skills they need to practice some urban street skills when visiting the area. Although those I've talked to have never had a problem, they have all mentioned that the area can and does attract some unsavory and seedy—no pun intended—characters, especially in the late afternoon and early evening. It is perfectly safe to bird here in the morning, even birding alone, but both Anderson and Clyne suggest either avoiding the area in the afternoon or birding it with a group.

Since 1974 Anderson has been leading bird walks at the island on Wednesdays at 7:00 a.m. and Saturdays at 8:00 a.m. from March 26th through the end of the year. I planned to meet the group on a Saturday early in April—at their starting point on the Clarence Darrow Bridge, at the north entrance to the Wooded Isle—but found that closing a blues bar on Friday night is not entirely compatible with early rising on Saturday morning. It was after 10:30 a.m. when I pulled into the parking lot on the south side of the Chicago Museum of Science and Industry, grabbed bird book, binoculars, and notebook and headed for the bridge. I met the group, but they were headed back from a very productive walk that totaled over 30 species.

George Bangs of Evanston, Illinois was kind enough to share his list of morning sightings and told me that he has been birding the Wooded Isle since the 1960s and considers it, "day-in and day-out, the best birding spot in Chicago." On the lookout for the Horned Grebe, Wood Thrush, Yellow-bellied Sapsucker, Eastern Phoebe, Greater Yellowlegs, and other birds on George's list, I headed

"Birdwatching should be considered one more of Chicago's fantastic tourist attractions."

across the bridge and into the lush, overgrown and somewhat timeworn site of the 1893 Columbian Exposition. The island is a great mix of mature trees, dense shrubbery, flower beds, and grassy opening, all of which is surrounded by the waters of a lagoon. Paths and walks wind through the island and present plenty of fine views of the lagoon. I counted Red-breasted Mergansers, Mallards, Ring-necked Ducks, and Canada Geese in the lagoon and found the Greater Yellowlegs on a far bank, but my contemplation of the bird was interrupted by a Belted Kingfisher that rattled past calling for my attention. A pleasant hour's walk turned up several early migrating Wood Thrushes, George's Yellow-bellied Sapsucker, the phoebe, and a couple of wrens, for a total of 28 species.

The Lake Michigan shoreline, which marks the eastern edge of Jackson Park, is a constant producer of shorebirds, gulls, and waterfowl. Jackson Park Beach and the breakwater just south of the beach—to the east of Lake Shore Drive—is an area favored by birders. Loons and grebes are common spring visitors as are a variety of sandpipers and plovers. Viewing is best in the spring and fall when the beach is not heavily used by bathers. The area around the breakwater often remains free of ice in the winter and attracts Old-squaw, Common Goldeneyes, Buffleheads, and mergansers. In the past year a Franklin's Gull, an albino Sanderling, Willets, and a Whimbrel have also been seen here.

HOODED WARBLER

WOODED ISLE, JACKSON PARK FIELD CHECKLIST

(This is an incomplete checklist compiled from a variety of sources)

___ Common Loon	___ Sandhill Crane	___ Willow Flycatcher	___ Solitary Vireo	___ Scarlet Tanager
___ Pied-billed Grebe	___ Killdeer	___ Least Flycatcher	___ Yellow-throated Vireo	___ Northern Cardinal
___ Horned Grebe	___ Great Yellowlegs	___ Eastern Phoebe	___ Warbling Vireo	___ Rose-breasted Grosbeak
___ Eared Grebe	___ Lesser Yellowlegs	___ Ash-throated Flycatcher	___ Philadelphia Vireo	___ Indigo Bunting
___ Double-crested Cormorant	___ Solitary Sandpiper	___ Great Crested Flycatcher	___ Red-eyed Vireo	___ Dickcissel
___ American Bittern	___ Willet	___ Eastern Kingbird	___ Blue-winged Warbler	___ Rufous-sided Towee
___ Least Bittern	___ Spotted Sandpiper	___ Horned Lark	___ Golden-winged Warbler	___ American Tree Sparrow
___ Great Blue Heron	___ Whimbrel	___ Purple Martin	___ Tennessee Warbler	___ Chipping Sparrow
___ Great Egret	___ Ruddy Turnstone	___ Tree Swallow	___ Orange-crowned Warbler	___ Clay-colored Sparrow
___ Little Blue Heron	___ Sanderling	___ Northern Rough-winged Swallow	___ Nashville Warbler	___ Field Sparrow
___ Tricolored Heron	___ Semipalmated Sandpiper	___ Bank Swallow	___ Northern Parula Warbler	___ Vesper Sparrow
___ Green Heron	___ Common Snipe	___ Cliff Swallow	___ Yellow Warbler	___ Lark Sparrow
___ Black-crowned Night-heron	___ American Woodcock	___ Barn Swallow	___ Chestnut-sided Warbler	___ Savannah Sparrow
___ Yellow-crowned Night-heron	___ Franklin's Gull	___ Blue Jay	___ Magnolia Warbler	___ Grasshopper Sparrow
___ Greater White-fronted Goose	___ Bonaparte's Gull	___ American Crow	___ Cape May Warbler	___ Henslow's Sparrow
___ Snow Goose	___ Ring-billed Gull	___ Black-capped Chickadee	___ Black-throated Blue Warbler	___ Le Conte's Sparrow
___ Canada Goose	___ Herring Gull	___ Red-breasted Nuthatch	___ Yellow-rumped Warbler	___ Sharp-tailed Sparrow
___ Wood Duck	___ Glaucous Gull	___ White-breasted Nuthatch	___ Townsend's Warbler	___ Fox Sparrow
___ Northern Shoveler	___ Great Black-backed Gull	___ Brown Creeper	___ Black-throated Green Warbler	___ Song Sparrow
___ American Wigeon	___ Caspian Tern	___ Carolina Wren	___ Blackburnian Warbler	___ Lincoln's Sparrow
___ Canvasback	___ Common Tern	___ House Wren	___ Pine Warbler	___ Swamp Sparrow
___ Redhead	___ Forster's Tern	___ Winter Wren	___ Palm Warbler	___ White-throated Sparrow
___ Ring-necked Duck	___ Black Tern	___ Sedge Wren	___ Bay-breasted Warbler	___ White-crowned Sparrow
___ Greater Scaup	___ Rock Dove	___ Marsh Wren	___ Blackpoll Warbler	___ Harris' Sparrow
___ Lesser Scaup	___ Mourning Dove	___ Rock Wren	___ Cerulean Warbler	___ Dark-eyed Junco
___ Harlequin Duck	___ Black-billed Cuckoo	___ Golden-crowned Kinglet	___ Black-and-white Warbler	___ Bobolink
___ White-winged Scoter	___ Yellow-billed Cuckoo	___ Ruby-crowned Kinglet	___ American Redstart	___ Ring-winged Blackbird
___ Common Goldeneye	___ Eastern Screech-owl	___ Blue-gray Gnatcatcher	___ Prothonotary Warbler	___ Eastern Meadowlark
___ Bufflehead	___ Short-eared Owl	___ Eastern Bluebird	___ Worm-eating Warbler	___ Yellow-headed Blackbird
___ Hooded Merganser	___ Common Nighthawk	___ Veery	___ Swainson's Warbler	___ Brewer's Blackbird
___ Red-breasted Merganser	___ Whip-poor-will	___ Gray-cheeked Thrush	___ Ovenbird	___ Common Grackle
___ Ruddy Duck	___ Chimney Swift	___ Swainson's Thrush	___ Northern Waterthrush	___ Brown-headed Cowbird
___ Turkey Vulture	___ Ruby-throated Hummingbird	___ Hermit Thrush	___ Louisiana Waterthrush	___ Orchard Oriole
___ Osprey	___ Belted Kingfisher	___ Wood Thrush	___ Kentucky Warbler	___ Baltimore Oriole
___ Northern Harrier	___ Red-headed Woodpecker	___ American Robin	___ Connecticut Warbler	___ Purple Finch
___ Sharp-shinned Hawk	___ Red-bellied Woodpecker	___ Gray Catbird	___ Mourning Warbler	___ Pine Siskin
___ Cooper's Hawk	___ Yellow-bellied Sapsucker	___ Brown Thrasher	___ Common Yellowthroat	___ Evening Grosbeak
___ Red-tailed Hawk	___ Northern Flicker	___ Bohemian Waxwing	___ Hooded Warbler	___ House Sparrow
___ Merlin	___ Olive-sided Flycatcher	___ Cedar Waxwing	___ Wilson's Warbler	
___ Virginia Rail	___ Eastern Wood-pewee	___ Loggerhead Shrike	___ Canada Warbler	
___ Common Moorhen	___ Yellow-bellied Flycatcher	___ European Starling	___ Yellow-breasted Chat	
___ American Coot	___ Alder Flycatcher	___ White-eyed Vireo	___ Summer Tanager	

Lake Calumet

Lake Calumet may be—no, let's be completely up front about this—Lake Calumet has to be one of the most aesthetically dispiriting places to bird in the entire country. For anyone who loves nature and birds, a visit to this area is equal parts amazement and horror. It is an urban and ecological nightmare of junkyards, landfills, chemical treatment plants, sewage treatment lagoons and heavy industry. And if the landscape's not bad enough, there's the thick, pervasive odor of the place. It's a choking combination of eau de rust and noxious chemicals that sticks to your clothes and leaves a distinctive metallic taste in your mouth. I expected to see birds hanging onto life with respirators dangling around their necks, and thought I caught a glimpse of a Great Blue Heron flying by with only one wing flapping and the other held over its nose.

The Lake Calumet area was intended as a major harbor, but whatever the purpose it has degenerated into a holding ground for industrial offal. Scattered among the landfills, junkyards and heavy industry are extensive stretches of open water, mudflats and marshlands; many of the latter I suspect are remnants of a vast marsh that covered the area before the coming of industry. Much of this bird habitat is threatened by even more landfills. One can only hope that the move afoot to establish an urban ecological park within the area will succeed.

The horror and amazement is not just restricted to the ecological abuse but to the bird life that appears to thrive in this industrial wasteland. Lake Calumet is one of the best places in Illinois and the Midwest for shore- and marsh birds; and summer shorebird watching here, even through watering eyes, can be phenomenal. The area holds several state firsts for rare birds; and only a partial checklist, compiled from a variety of sources, contains 85 species, most of which are waterfowl, shore- or marsh birds. The area shelters the largest nesting colonies of Black-crowned Night-heron and Common Moorhens in the state. Rarities show up with some frequency, and even common shorebirds can put on a great show during July and August when fall shorebird migration peaks here. On more than one occasion in the past few years, flocks of shorebirds in excess of 1,000 have been spotted in the area's marshes and mudflats. In mid-July of 1995, 506 Least Sandpipers, 237 Lesser Yellowlegs and 161 Short-billed Dowitchers were counted among a gathering of over a thousand shorebirds in the Big Marsh area of Lake Calumet.

I must admit though, I didn't bird the area with much enthusiasm. Faced with the industrial blight and noxious odors it is not hard to imagine, even though I've not come across documentation, the waters in the Lake Calumet area must be the equivalent of a toxic stew. If a scant trace of DDT or heavy metals can turn a cormorant's bill into a pretzel, elsewhere in the Great Lakes, I shudder to think what harm could come to birds just passing through this area.

Besides the aesthetic drawbacks associated with birding at Lake Calumet is the fact that most of the good birding sites are all on private property. These are not homes where you walk up to the front door and politely ask if you can walk through the backyard. This is industrial property where trespassing is more than frowned on and can be dangerous to health and safety. As important a birding spot as this is, I was on the verge of not including it because of the numerous people who said it couldn't be birded because of the no trespassing rules and the time

"On more than one occasion in the past few years, flocks of shorebirds in excess of 1,000 have been spotted in the area's marshes and mudflats."

LOCATION: Chicago, Illinois.

DIRECTIONS: Approximately 5 miles south of the intersection of I-57 and I-94 on the south side of Chicago exit I-94 at 130th Street and drive east. See text for specific directions to sites within the Lake Calumet area.

HOURS: This is primarily birding from the roadside in a decaying urban setting. There are no posted hours.

BEST TIMES: July, August, and early September. Spring migration in May offers good counts of migrating shorebirds, but the fall migration period for shorebirds is much more productive in both numbers and species. The area is heavily hunted from September through December.

BIRDING HIGHLIGHTS: This is an extraordinary area for shore- and marsh birds, especially during fall migration periods. The area is not easy or pleasant to bird, but the results can be spectacular. Winter gull watching is very good, with rare species turning up with some regularity.

FOR MORE INFORMATION: Calumet Ecological Park Association, 12932 S. Escanaba Avenue, Chicago, IL 60633.

"For anyone who loves nature and birds, a visit is equal parts amazement and horror."

it would take to intimately familiarize myself with the area in order to even attempt to find the best vantage points from which to bird on public property. Fortunately one of the leading authorities on birding at Lake Calumet, Walter J. Marcisz of Chicago, pointed out that many of the best sites within the area can be surveyed from the roadside without entering the property, and, to prove it, sent me a copy of a detailed guide to birding Lake Calumet he wrote for *Meadowlark, A Journal of Illinois Birds*. I am also indebted to Mr. Marcisz for a detailed map of the area, showing roadside parking sites, created by the Calumet Ecological Park Association (see address, p. 7).

The following tour of birding sites at Lake Calumet, with directions, all begin on the far south side of Chicago after exiting I-94 and heading east on 130th Street.

The Thomas J. O'Brien Lock and Dam on the Calumet River is the spot for finding interesting and unusual gulls in the winter. The lock and dam is the first right after heading east from I-94. The turnoff from 130th Street to the lock is just before a bridge crossing the Calumet River. Glaucous, Thayer's, Lesser Black-backed, Iceland and Great Black-backed gulls have all been regularly seen here among the ever-present Herring and Ring-billed gulls. Much rarer sightings have been reported of California and Franklin's gulls. The marsh to the south of the parking lot often attracts a good many shorebirds from July through September. Godwits, phalaropes and American Avocets have all been seen here along with shorebirds more common to the area. Coyotes have also been seen in this area. Another excellent location for winter gull watching is Lake Calumet proper. The best access point for viewing Lake Calumet is reached by turning north on Frontage Road immediately after exiting I-94. Drive north on Frontage Road 1.7 miles to the Medusa Cement Company and park at the gate. From there, walk east to the lake. It is necessary to bring a spotting scope to identify the gulls which are often on the ice far out in the lake.

Hegewisch Marsh is not always reliable, but a trip to the area should be included in a visit because, at times, the marsh can pay off like a long overdue slot machine. Marcisz reports that Ruddy Ducks, Redheads, Pied-billed Grebes, Blue-winged Teal, coots, moorhens, and Yellow-headed Blackbirds have been observed nesting in the marsh, off and on, in the past few years. The viewing of migrant shorebirds can be fantastic in July and August if water levels are low. Hegewisch Marsh is reached by traveling east on 130th Street, crossing the bridge over the Calumet River and taking a right at Torrence Avenue. Roadside parking is available about 0.1 mile south on Torrence Avenue on the right-hand side of the road, just after crossing the railroad tracks.

Turning left (north) on Torrence Avenue from 130th Street will take you to the rest of the prime birding spots in the area. The 116th Street Marsh is reached by driving north on Torrence Avenue approximately 1.5 miles to 116th Street. Turn left on 116th Street and go about 0.1 mile to a roadside parking lot on the left-hand side of the road. The marsh to the south is a favorite stopover for migrating shorebirds in the spring. Among the species of note seen here in the past few years are White-rumped Sandpiper, Wilson's Phalarope, Dunlin, and Willet. Sora and Virginia Rails have nested in the marsh in the past, and the area can also produce large numbers of migrating shorebirds in the fall.

Indian Ridge Marsh is the surest bet in the area for spotting Black-crowned Night-heron, Great Egrets, and Common Moorhens. From the intersection of 130th Street and Torrence Avenue go north on Torrence Avenue about 1 mile to 122nd Street and turn left. A roadside parking area is located approximately a quarter-mile east of Torrence Avenue, on the north side of 122nd Street, just before crossing a set of railroad tracks. Marcisz suggests scanning the marsh and grove of cottonwoods to the north for the night-heron and egrets. Late April and early May are the best times for spotting the birds. The area also contains Yellow-headed Blackbirds. This is also the best site for witnessing the extraordinary gathering of Red-winged Blackbirds and European Starlings that occur at Lake Calumet every winter. Most of us wouldn't walk across a street to see either one of the species, but at Lake Calumet they congregate in flocks that total more than 20,000 birds in the winter months. That kind of spectacle may well entice you out of the house. The birds are best seen just before sunset when they fly into the Indian Ridge Marsh area to roost for the night.

Deadstick Pond and Big Marsh are best viewed from Stony Island Road. After leaving Indian Ridge Marsh drive west on 122nd Street about 1 mile to where it ends at Stony Island Road. Deadstick Pond lies to the south of 122nd Street and can be surveyed from a parking area on Stony Island Road just to the south of the intersection. Deadstick Pond is a proven hot spot for migrating shorebirds in the fall. In addition to egrets, heron and the more common shorebirds, Red-necked and Wilson's phalaropes, Red Knots, Black-necked Stilts, Hudsonian Godwits, and White-rumped, Curlew, Baird's and Stilt sandpipers have all put in appearances at Deadstick Pond.

The all-around best birding spot in the Lake Calumet area may well be Big Marsh on Stony Island Road to the north of 122nd Street. There is a fairly large roadside parking area 1 mile north of 122nd Street on the right hand side of the road. The reed-filled marsh supports a large colony of Black-crowned Night-heron and the state endangered Least Bittern. During fall migration the marsh attracts large numbers of shorebirds, heron and every year brings at least one unusual sighting. Over the past few years Reddish Egrets, Tricolored Heron, American Avocets, American White Pelican, Hudsonian Godwits, Willet, Least and Large-billed terns, Eurasian Wigeon, and White Ibis have been spotted in the Big Marsh. From the parking area, it is possible to walk for some distance along the side of the road and search the edges of the marsh for birds. In fact, most of the roads in the Lake Calumet area have wide shoulders to allow you to pull off and take a closer look at any interesting bird.

"The area holds several state firsts for rare birds."

LAKE CALUMET FIELD CHECKLIST

(This is an incomplete checklist compiled from a variety of sources.)

___ Pied-billed Grebe				___ Iceland Gull
___ American White Pelican	___ Northern Shoveler	___ Common Moorhen	___ Least Sandpiper	___ Lesser Black-backed Gull
___ Brown Pelican	___ Gadwall	___ American Coot	___ White-rumped Sandpiper	___ Glaucous-winged Gull
___ Double-crested Cormorant	___ Eurasian Wigeon	___ Semipalmated Plover	___ Baird's Sandpiper	___ Glaucous Gull
___ Least Bittern	___ Redhead	___ Killdeer	___ Pectoral Sandpiper	___ Great Black-backed Gull
___ Great Blue Heron	___ Lesser Scaup	___ Black-necked Stilt	___ Dunlin	___ Royal Tern
___ Great Egret	___ Common Goldeneye	___ American Avocet	___ Curlew Sandpiper	___ Least Tern
___ Snowy Egret	___ Bufflehead	___ Greater Yellowlegs	___ Ruff	___ Large-billed Tern
___ Little Blue Heron	___ Common Merganser	___ Lesser Yellowlegs	___ Short-billed Dowitcher	___ Barn Owl
___ Reddish Egret	___ Red-breasted Merganser	___ Solitary Sandpiper	___ Common Snipe	___ Snowy Owl
___ Black-crowned Night-heron	___ Ruddy Duck	___ Willet	___ Wilson's Phalarope	___ Short-eared Owl
___ Yellow-crowned Night-heron	___ American Kestrel	___ Spotted Sandpiper	___ Red-necked Phalarope	___ European Starling
___ Tricolored Heron	___ Merlin	___ Hudsonian Godwit	___ Franklin's Gull	___ Bell's Vireo
___ White Ibis	___ Peregrine Falcon	___ Marbled Godwit	___ Ring-billed Gull	___ Red-winged Blackbird
___ Canada Goose	___ Virginia Rail	___ Ruddy Turnstone	___ California Gull	___ Yellow-headed Blackbird
___ Green-winged Teal	___ Sora	___ Red Knot	___ Herring Gull	___ Brewer's Blackbird
___ Blue-winged Teal	___ Purple Gallinule	___ Semipalmated Sandpiper	___ Thayer's Gull	___ Common Grackle

Chicago Botanic Garden and Sokie Lagoon

"I couldn't have been more stunned if the bird had called out, 'Hey dummy, there isn't a poor spot for birdwatching in the entire 300-acre botanical garden.'"

LOCATION: Glencoe, Illinois.

DIRECTIONS: Chicago Botanic Garden is located 25 miles north of downtown Chicago. Take I-94 (Edens Expressway) north to Lake-Cook Road, turn right (east) and drive .5 mile to the entrance. Skokie Lagoons are reached by exiting I-94 and turning right on any of the three exits immediately south of Lake-Cook Road. Willow Road, approximately 3 miles and two exits south of Lake-Cook Road, is the most popular spot to access the lagoons.

HOURS: Chicago Botanic Gardens is open daily 8:00 a.m.-sunset. There is a small admission charge for non-members. Skokie Lagoons are open year-round.

BEST TIMES: Mid-April through mid-May and from late August through late September witness plenty of bird activity at both locations. Spring migration reaches its peak here in the second and third weeks of May.

BIRDING HIGHLIGHTS: The wide variety of habitats at both the botanic garden and the Skokie Lagoons attracts an impressive number species. This is one of the better places in the Midwest to witness spring and fall migration, and it is not uncommon to find over a 100 different species on a May trip. It is especially noted for songbirds and its ability to attract rarities.

FOR MORE INFORMATION: The Chicago Botanic Garden, P.O. Box 400, Glencoe, IL 60022. Phone: (708) 835-5440.

Sometimes the obvious just has to slap me in the face to get my attention. Entering the Visitors Center of the Chicago Botanic Garden, I walked up to the information desk and asked the volunteer on duty to suggest where there might be some good birding. She pointed me toward the Naturalistic Garden because it features landscaping ideas using plants native to the state and that attract birds. Immediately outside the Visitors Center, while crossing the short bridge leading to the gardens, in the least likely birding spot in the area, I saw the bird of the day, a Horned Grebe. I couldn't have been more stunned if the bird had called out, "Hey dummy, there isn't a poor spot for birdwatching in the entire 300-acre botanical garden."

The botanic garden serves up a fantastic smorgasbord of habitats for birds. There are loads of fruit-bearing ornamental trees and shrubs, seasonal mudflats, lots of open water of varying depths, tall and short grass prairies, marshes, native woodlands, and a variety of small formal gardens that are, in effect, micro-habitats. The result is a bird checklist tallying 249 species, of which all but a half-dozen species have been seen here within the last few years.

This is not only one of the premier birdwatching sites in Chicago and the Midwest but one of the most beautiful. Even the most dedicated birders may find their attention drifting from the pursuit of birds to enjoying the sublime beauty of the display gardens, the natural areas, and the often unique and dramatic settings. Chicago Botanic Garden has been sculpted around the northern third of the Skokie Lagoons, a flood control project built in 1933 by the Civilian Conservation Corps. The formal gardens, and even some of the natural areas, are spread over more than a half-dozen picturesque islands, connected by footbridges, lying in a long, sinuous lagoon. Water is used as a backdrop for most of the small demonstration and display gardens and dramatically frames the islands and peninsulas jutting out into the lagoon that are given over to large natural areas.

The result is a strikingly beautiful landscape with different plantings and gardens revealed around every bend of the lagoon or gravel path. And memorable bird sightings can turn up anywhere. In the past few years, King Rails were found along a service road bordering the lagoon, Worm-eating Warblers were sighted in Turnbull Woods, and Pine Warblers took up brief residence in the Japanese garden. The best birding is traditionally in the second and third weeks of May during the peak migration season. It is often possible to tally over a 100 species during a May visit to the garden, but even earlier in spring the results can be impressive. By mid-March, migrating birds begin to leak into the area, and it's not uncommon for a mid-April bird walk to uncover 50 different species.

Although the entire area promises great birding, there are several spots where Chicago Botanic Garden is more apt to keep its word than others. The Turnbull Woods Nature Trail, near the entrance on Lake-Cook Road, winds through an oak-hickory woodland favored by warblers during May. There is excellent birding throughout the length of the 1-mile trail, but the creek and pond within the woods is a notorious hotspot.

The southern end of the garden holds a couple of areas that shouldn't be overlooked by birders. Marsh Island can be particularly good for shorebirds. The island's seasonal pond, crossed by a boardwalk, is an excellent location for snipe, rails, and shorebirds. Also worth checking out is the long narrow peninsula that lies immediately to the right after crossing the bridge to the island. By midsummer the water level in the lagoon has usually fallen enough to ring the peninsula with a band of mudflats that attract a variety of shorebirds and waders. The prairie restoration area south of Marsh Island shelters 16 species of sparrows and is an excellent spot from which to observe flights of migrating birds from March through mid-May. Impressive numbers of migrating songbirds and shorebirds have all been seen from here.

And finally not to be overlooked—well, really impossible to overlook—are the numerous and picturesque ponds and small lakes created within the lagoon by the jigsaw puzzle-shaped islands. Regular spring visitors at the ponds and lakes include Wood Ducks, Northern Pintails, Northern Shovelers, American Wigeon, Canvasbacks, Buffleheads, and Ruddy Ducks. Even American White Pelicans have made at least one appearance in the garden's ponds and lakes. All together 27 species of waterfowl have been seen in the garden. A detailed map of the garden and a bird checklist, available at the Visitors Center, will lead you to all the prime birding spots.

The remaining two-thirds of the Skokie Lagoons, which lie to the south of the botanic garden, offer equally good birding in a more natural setting. The long, narrow lagoons stretch for nearly four miles along the east side of Edens Expressway and can be reached by exiting the freeway on Dundee, Tower or Willow roads. The most popular access point is from a parking lot on Willow Road, just off the expressway. From the parking lot, birders can walk the banks of the lagoon, follow trails, or hike the bridle path that winds along the west side of the lagoons.

As a counterpoint to the carefully planned botanic gardens to the north, the landscape surrounding the lower two-thirds of the lagoons has been left to nature to design. In addition to plenty of open water, large wooded areas, overgrown fields, meadows and shrubs provide plenty of cover and food for a wide variety of birds. During spring and fall migration the area seethes with warblers, vireos, thrushes, swallows, flycatchers, and sparrows.

Among the many species of special interest that have been found here are Worm-eating, Connecticut, Kentucky, Hooded, Cerulean, Canada, and Prothonotary warblers, Least Bitterns, Western Kingbirds, Scarlet Tanagers, Ospreys, and Harris', Clay-colored, and Lincoln's sparrows. As with the botanic garden to the north, the area attracts an excellent sampling of waterfowl and shorebirds. Of special note are the Yellow-crowned Night-heron that have nested in the lagoons for several years. The area is also worth checking out in the winter when Glaucous, Iceland and Thayer's gulls can sometimes be found sprinkled in among the ubiquitous Ring-billed and Herring gulls. The wooded areas are also known to hold an occasional raptor or Northern Shrike in winter.

"The formal gardens, and even some of the natural areas, are spread over more than a half-dozen picturesque islands, connected by footbridges, lying in a long, sinuous lagoon."

HORNED GREBE

CHICAGO BOTANIC GARDEN AND SKOKIE LAGOONS FIELD CHECKLIST

___ Common Loon
___ Pied-billed Grebe
___ Horned Grebe
___ Eared Grebe
___ American White Pelican
___ Double-crested Cormorant
___ American Bittern
___ Least Bittern
___ Great Blue Heron
___ Great Egret
___ Little Blue Heron
___ Cattle Egret
___ Green Heron
___ Black-crowned Night-heron
___ Yellow-crowned Night-heron
___ Tundra Swan
___ Mute Swan
___ Greater White-fronted Goose
___ Ross' Goose
___ Snow Goose
___ Barnacle Goose
___ Canada Goose
___ Wood Duck
___ Green-winged Teal
___ American Black Duck
___ Mallard
___ Northern Pintail
___ Blue-winged Teal
___ Northern Shoveler
___ Gadwall
___ American Wigeon
___ Canvasback
___ Redhead
___ Ring-necked Duck
___ Greater Scaup
___ Lesser Scaup
___ White-winged Scoter
___ Common Goldeneye
___ Bufflehead
___ Hooded Merganser
___ Common Merganser
___ Red-breasted Merganser
___ Ruddy Duck
___ Turkey Vulture
___ Osprey
___ Bald Eagle
___ Northern Harrier
___ Sharp-shinned Hawk
___ Cooper's Hawk
___ Northern Goshawk

___ Red-shouldered Hawk
___ Broad-winged Hawk
___ Red-tailed Hawk
___ Rough-legged Hawk
___ American Kestrel
___ Merlin
___ Peregrine Falcon
___ Black Rail
___ King Rail
___ Virginia Rail
___ Sora
___ American Coot
___ Sandhill Crane
___ Lesser Golden-plover
___ Semipalmated Plover
___ Killdeer
___ Greater Yellowlegs
___ Lesser Yellowlegs
___ Solitary Sandpiper
___ Willet
___ Spotted Sandpiper
___ Upland Sandpiper
___ Semipalmated Sandpiper
___ Least Sandpiper
___ White-rumped Sandpiper
___ Baird's Sandpiper
___ Pectoral Sandpiper
___ Dunlin
___ Stilt Sandpiper
___ Buff-breasted Sandpiper
___ Short-billed Dowitcher
___ Common Snipe
___ American Woodcock
___ Little Gull
___ Bonaparte's Gull
___ Ring-billed Gull
___ Herring Gull
___ Thayer's Gull
___ Glaucous Gull
___ Caspian Tern
___ Forster's Tern
___ Black Tern
___ Rock Dove
___ Mourning Dove
___ Black-billed Cuckoo
___ Yellow-billed Cuckoo
___ Eastern Screech-owl
___ Great Horned Owl
___ Short-eared Owl
___ Northern Saw-whet Owl

___ Common Nighthawk
___ Whip-poor-will
___ Chimney Swift
___ Ruby-throated Hummingbird
___ Belted Kingfisher
___ Red-headed Woodpecker
___ Red-bellied Woodpecker
___ Yellow-bellied Sapsucker
___ Downy Woodpecker
___ Hairy Woodpecker
___ Northern Flicker
___ Pileated Woodpecker
___ Olive-sided Flycatcher
___ Eastern Wood-pewee
___ Yellow-bellied Flycatcher
___ Acadian Flycatcher
___ Alder Flycatcher
___ Willow Flycatcher
___ Least Flycatcher
___ Eastern Phoebe
___ Vermilion Flycatcher
___ Great Crested Flycatcher
___ Western Kingbird
___ Eastern Kingbird
___ Scissor-tailed Flycatcher
___ Horned Lark
___ Purple Martin
___ Tree Swallow
___ Northern Rough-winged Swallow
___ Bank Swallow
___ Cliff Swallow
___ Barn Swallow
___ Blue Jay
___ American Crow
___ Black-capped Chickadee
___ Red-breasted Nuthatch
___ White-breasted Nuthatch
___ Brown Creeper
___ Carolina Wren
___ House Wren
___ Winter Wren
___ Sedge Wren
___ Marsh Wren
___ Golden-crowned Kinglet
___ Ruby-crowned Kinglet
___ Blue-gray Gnatcatcher
___ Eastern Bluebird
___ Veery
___ Gray-cheeked Thrush
___ Swainson's Thrush

___ Hermit Thrush
___ Wood Thrush
___ American Robin
___ Gray Catbird
___ Northern Mockingbird
___ Brown Thrasher
___ American Pipit
___ Bohemian Waxwing
___ Cedar Waxwing
___ Northern Shrike
___ European Starling
___ White-eyed Vireo
___ Solitary Vireo
___ Yellow-throated Vireo
___ Warbling Vireo
___ Philadelphia Vireo
___ Red-eyed Vireo
___ Blue-winged Warbler
___ Golden-winged Warbler
___ Tennessee Warbler
___ Orange-crowned Warbler
___ Nashville Warbler
___ Northern Parula
___ Yellow Warbler
___ Chestnut-sided Warbler
___ Magnolia Warbler
___ Cape May Warbler
___ Black-throated Blue Warbler
___ Yellow-rumped Warbler
___ Black-throated Green Warbler
___ Blackburnian Warbler
___ Yellow-throated Warbler
___ Pine Warbler
___ Prairie Warbler
___ Palm Warbler
___ Bay-breasted Warbler
___ Blackpoll Warbler
___ Cerulean Warbler
___ Black-and-white Warbler
___ American Redstart
___ Prothonotary Warbler
___ Worm-eating Warbler
___ Ovenbird
___ Northern Waterthrush
___ Louisiana Waterthrush
___ Kentucky Warbler
___ Connecticut Warbler
___ Mourning Warbler
___ Common Yellowthroat
___ Hooded Warbler

___ Wilson's Warbler
___ Canada Warbler
___ Yellow-breasted Chat
___ Summer Tanager
___ Scarlet Tanager
___ Northern Cardinal
___ Rose-breasted Grosbeak
___ Indigo Bunting
___ Dickcissel
___ Rufous-sided Towhee
___ American Tree Sparrow
___ Chipping Sparrow
___ Clay-colored Sparrow
___ Field Sparrow
___ Vesper Sparrow
___ Savannah Sparrow
___ Grasshopper Sparrow
___ LeConte's Sparrow
___ Sharp-tailed Sparrow
___ Fox Sparrow
___ Song Sparrow
___ Lincoln's Sparrow
___ Swamp Sparrow
___ White-throated Sparrow
___ White-crowned Sparrow
___ Harris' Sparrow
___ Dark-eyed Junco
___ Lapland Longspur
___ Snow Bunting
___ Bobolink
___ Red-winged Blackbird
___ Eastern Meadowlark
___ Western Meadowlark
___ Yellow-headed Blackbird
___ Rusty Blackbird
___ Brewer's Blackbird
___ Common Grackle
___ Brown-headed Cowbird
___ Orchard Oriole
___ Baltimore Oriole
___ Purple Finch
___ House Finch
___ Red Crossbill
___ White-winged Crossbill
___ Common Redpoll
___ Pine Siskin
___ American Goldfinch
___ Evening Grosbeak
___ House Sparrow

Forest Glen Preserve

Gary Wilford, Park Naturalist at Forest Glen Preserve, was being more than just a little humble when he allowed that Forest Glen Preserve gave a "good glimpse of Central Illinois bird life." In fact, this 1,800-acre Vermillion County park offers some of the best birding in central Illinois. The park's steep-sided, wooded ravines, five acres of restored tall grass prairie, several ponds, three miles of frontage on the Vermillion River, magnificent stands of old-growth beech-maple forest, oak-hickory uplands, marshy areas, wooded floodplains, old fields, and brushy fencerows attract 230 species of birds; and, 100 species have been recorded nesting the park.

The most interesting time of the year for birders is the last week in April and the first week in May when spring migration hits its stride at Forest Glen. The woods and fields are alive with birds, and warbler fanciers can search for the 36 species that have been recorded within the property. Early fall brings enough terns, gulls and especially shorebirds to peak interest. A good sampling of sandpipers, plovers, and dowitchers can usually be counted on to frequent the park's mudflats for a few days each fall before continuing their southward journey. In addition to the mudflats, wet fields, and ponds, the Vermillion River can also yield a pleasing variety of shorebirds including Black-bellied, Lesser Golden-, and Semipalmated plovers, both yellowlegs, Willets, and Dunlins during spring and fall migration.

Forest Glen is also an excellent spot for driving yourself crazy trying to identify fall warblers during their heavy passage through the park. If you have never tried to identify warblers in the fall when they are sporting their winter plumage, it is advisable to slip some Prozac in with the binoculars and birdbook before heading out.

If spring and fall are best, the rest of the year should not be dismissed as uninteresting. Towhees, Summer and Scarlet tanagers, Great Horned Owls, Eastern Bluebirds, and LeConte's, Savannah, Grasshopper and Henslow's sparrows all nest in the park. Included among the dozen warblers nesting here are Blue-winged, Prairie, Cerulean, Worm-eating, and Yellow-breasted Chat. Kentucky, Yellow-throated, Ovenbird and Northern Parula warblers are also thought to nest in the park but, as yet, have not been confirmed.

Wilford pointed out the Old Barn Trail and the Big Woods Trail on the park map are the two most interesting birding walks at Forest Glen. The Old Barn Trail is regularly used by park personnel in their guided bird walks and is generally regarded as the best trail for birding in the park. During spring migration, it is not uncommon to find more than a 100 species on the approximately one-mile walk. The trail borders or cuts through meadows, wetlands, ponds, upland oak-hickory, and bottomland forest. The Old Barn Trail, with its many habitats, serves as a microcosm of the entire park.

The aptly named Big Woods Trail winds through a primal forest or, as Wilford says, "as close to a primal forest as you're going to get in central Illinois," and ends at a 72-foot observation tower overlooking a beautiful, wooded valley sculpted by the Vermillion River. The trail passes some truly imposing trees and edges many wet, steep-sided ravines. The Big Woods Trail and ravines are almost sure bets for Louisiana Waterthrushes, Ovenbirds, and Kentucky Warblers; and, the lucky

"If you have never tried to identify warblers in the fall when they are sporting their winter plumage, it is advisable to slip some Prozac in with the binoculars and birdbook before heading out."

LOCATION: Westville, Illinois.

DIRECTIONS: From the junction of I-74 and Route 1 on the south side of Danville drive south on Route 1 approximately 6 miles to Westville. In Westville, turn left at the stoplight in the center of town and drive east about 8 miles to the park.

HOURS: Open daily 7 a.m.-11 p.m.

BEST TIMES: The last week in April and the first week in May finds the spring migration at full throttle at Forest Glen and consequently great birding. Birding is also good in summer and fall.

BIRDING HIGHLIGHTS: A wide diversity of habitats makes this one of the best birding spots in central Illinois. Over 230 species have been recorded in the park, and during spring migration birding here can be spectacular with The Old Barn Trail alone often yielding more than 100 species in its 1.3-mile length.

FOR MORE INFORMATION: Forest Glen County Preserve, 20301 E. 900 North Road, Westville, IL 61883. Phone: (217) 662-2142.

"Towhees, Summer and Scarlet tanagers, Great Horned Owls, Eastern Bluebirds, and LeConte's, Savannah, Grasshopper and Henslow's sparrows all nest in the park."

birder may spot Worm-eating Warblers. The area immediately surrounding the observation tower always seems to house some nesting warblers, and the entire trail is good for a wide variety of forest birds.

I arrived about three weeks in advance of the main spring migration. In fact, Wilford had just that morning seen the year's first Eastern Phoebe, but Forest Glen still proved worth a trip. Then, of course, any time I see a Pileated Woodpecker it's worth the trip. Walking the two trails recommended by Wilford yielded a pleasing variety of sparrows and woodpeckers, an Eastern Meadowlark, several thrushes, a couple of vireos, and an assortment of other birds that totaled over 30 species for the 90-minute walk. But the high point of the walk involved hoofed creatures rather than feathered ones. About a quarter-mile down the Big Woods Trail a loud snort froze me in my tracks, then five deer rose from a shallow depression not 20 feet from me and bolted down the trail. The deer hadn't gone 30 yards before they slowed to a walk and finally stopped and turned to see who had disturbed their afternoon siesta. As the deer gently picked their way down a ravine and out of sight, I slowly overcame cardiac arrest and continued down the trail to another heart-stopping view from the top of the observation tower.

In addition to the fine birding, the park offers outdoor lovers a variety of picnic areas and playgrounds, a restored pioneer homestead, two fishing ponds, an 11-mile backpacking trail and both a family campground and a primitive campground. All of which make it convenient for birders to leave their non-birding family members to enjoy other outdoor pursuits while they pursue birds.

FOREST GLEN PRESERVE FIELD CHECKLIST

___ Pied-billed Grebe
___ Horned Grebe
___ American Bittern
___ Least Bittern
___ Great Blue Heron
___ Great Egret
___ Little Blue Heron
___ Cattle Egret
___ Green Heron
___ Black-crowned Night-heron
___ Yellow-crowned Night-heron
___ Snow Goose
___ Canada Goose
___ Wood Duck
___ Green-winged Teal
___ American Black Duck
___ Mallard
___ Northern Pintail
___ Blue-winged Teal
___ Northern Shoveler
___ Gadwall
___ American Wigeon
___ Redhead
___ Ring-necked Duck
___ Lesser Scaup
___ Common Goldeneye
___ Bufflehead
___ Hooded Merganser
___ Common Merganser
___ Red-breasted Merganser
___ Ruddy Duck
___ Turkey Vulture
___ Osprey
___ Bald Eagle
___ Northern Harrier
___ Sharp-shinned Hawk
___ Cooper's Hawk
___ Northern Goshawk
___ Red-shouldered Hawk
___ Broad-winged Hawk
___ Red-tailed Hawk
___ Rough-legged Hawk
___ Golden Eagle
___ American Kestrel
___ Merlin
___ Peregrine Falcon
___ Ring-necked Pheasant

___ Wild Turkey
___ Northern Bobwhite
___ Virginia Rail
___ Sora
___ American Coot
___ Sandhill Crane
___ Black-bellied Plover
___ Lesser Golden-plover
___ Semipalmated Plover
___ Killdeer
___ Greater Yellowlegs
___ Lesser Yellowlegs
___ Solitary Sandpiper
___ Upland Sandpiper
___ Sanderling
___ Semipalmated Sandpiper
___ Least Sandpiper
___ Baird's Sandpiper
___ Pectoral Sandpiper
___ Dunlin
___ Common Snipe
___ American Woodcock
___ Bonaparte's Gull
___ Ring-billed Gull
___ Herring Gull
___ Common Tern
___ Black Tern
___ Rock Dove
___ Mourning Dove
___ Black-billed Cuckoo
___ Yellow-billed Cuckoo
___ Barn Owl
___ Eastern Screech-owl
___ Great Horned Owl
___ Barred Owl
___ Long-eared Owl
___ Short-eared Owl
___ Northern Saw-whet Owl
___ Common Nighthawk
___ Chuck-will's-widow
___ Whip-poor-will
___ Chimney Swift
___ Ruby-throated Hummingbird
___ Belted Kingfisher
___ Red-headed Woodpecker
___ Red-bellied Woodpecker
___ Yellow-bellied Sapsucker

___ Downy Woodpecker
___ Hairy Woodpecker
___ Northern Flicker
___ Pileated Woodpecker
___ Olive-sided Flycatcher
___ Eastern Wood-pewee
___ Yellow-bellied Flycatcher
___ Acadian Flycatcher
___ Alder Flycatcher
___ Willow Flycatcher
___ Least Flycatcher
___ Eastern Phoebe
___ Great Crested Flycatcher
___ Eastern Kingbird
___ Horned Lark
___ Purple Martin
___ Tree Swallow
___ Northern Rough-legged Swallow
___ Bank Swallow
___ Cliff Swallow
___ Barn Swallow
___ Blue Jay
___ American Crow
___ Black-capped Chickadee
___ Carolina Chickadee
___ Tufted Titmouse
___ Red-breasted Nuthatch
___ White-breasted Nuthatch
___ Brown Creeper
___ Carolina Wren
___ Bewick's Wren
___ House Wren
___ Winter Wren
___ Sedge Wren
___ Marsh Wren
___ Golden-crowned Kinglet
___ Ruby-crowned Kinglet
___ Blue-gray Gnatcatcher
___ Eastern Bluebird
___ Veery
___ Gray-cheeked Thrush
___ Hermit Thrush
___ American Robin
___ Gray Catbird
___ Northern Mockingbird
___ Brown Thrasher
___ American Pipit

___ Cedar Waxwing
___ Northern Shrike
___ Loggerhead Shrike
___ European Starling
___ White-eyed Vireo
___ Bell's Vireo
___ Solitary Vireo
___ Yellow-throated Vireo
___ Warbling Vireo
___ Philadelphia Vireo
___ Red-eyed Vireo
___ Blue-winged Warbler
___ Golden-winged Warbler
___ Tennessee Warbler
___ Orange-crowned Warbler
___ Nashville Warbler
___ Northern Parula
___ Yellow Warbler
___ Chestnut-sided Warbler
___ Magnolia Warbler
___ Cape May Warbler
___ Black-throated Blue Warbler
___ Yellow-rumped Warbler
___ Black-throated Green Warbler
___ Pine Warbler
___ Prairie Warbler
___ Palm Warbler
___ Palm Warbler
___ Bay-breasted Warbler
___ Blackpoll Warbler
___ Cerulean Warbler
___ Black-and-white Warbler
___ American Redstart
___ Prothonotary Warbler
___ Worm-eating Warbler
___ Ovenbird
___ Northern Waterthrush
___ Louisiana Waterthrush
___ Kentucky Warbler
___ Connecticut Warbler
___ Mourning Warbler
___ Common Yellowthroat
___ Hooded Warbler
___ Wilson's Warbler
___ Canada Warbler
___ Yellow-breasted Chat
___ Summer Tanager

___ Scarlet Tanager
___ Northern Cardinal
___ Rose-breasted Grosbeak
___ Indigo Bunting
___ Dickcissel
___ Rufous-sided Towhee
___ American Tree Sparrow
___ Chipping Sparrow
___ Field Sparrow
___ Vesper Sparrow
___ Lincoln's Sparrow
___ Savannah Sparrow
___ Grasshopper Sparrow
___ Henslow's Sparrow
___ LeConte's Sparrow
___ Fox Sparrow
___ Song Sparrow
___ Swamp Sparrow
___ White-throated Sparrow
___ White-crowned Sparrow
___ Harris' Sparrow
___ Dark-eyed Junco
___ Lapland Longspur
___ Snow Bunting
___ Bobolink
___ Red-winged Blackbird
___ Eastern Meadowlark
___ Yellow-headed Blackbird
___ Rusty Blackbird
___ Brewer's Blackbird
___ Common Grackle
___ Brown-headed Cowbird
___ Orchard Oriole
___ Baltimore Oriole
___ Purple Finch
___ House Finch
___ Red Crossbill
___ White-winged Crossbill
___ Common Redpoll
___ Pine Siskin
___ American Goldfinch
___ Evening Grosbeak
___ House Sparrow

Chautauqua National Wildlife Refuge

"I can't ever remember seeing more than two Red-headed Woodpeckers at one time, but in the next ten minutes I saw more than I'd seen in my entire life."

LOCATION: Havanna, Illinois.

DIRECTIONS: From Havana drive 6 miles north on Manito Blacktop Road and follow signs to the refuge.

HOURS: Open all year, sunrise to sunset.

BEST TIMES: Winter for Bald Eagles, fall for waterfowl with numbers peaking in mid-November, April for spring waterfowl migration, May for songbirds and warblers, and August for shorebirds.

BIRDING HIGHLIGHTS: Extraordinary concentrations of waterfowl in spring and fall with numbers reaching as high as 150,000 in the fall. Shorebird viewing can be spectacular in August and early September; nearly 200,000 waders have descended on the refuge when conditions are perfect. The refuge provides good warbler and songbird viewing in May, and wintering Bald Eagles can be usually counted as sure bets.

FOR MORE INFORMATION: Chautauqua National Wildlife Refuge, Rural Route #2, Havana, IL 62664. Phone: (309) 535-2290.

It was getting boring. Barb and I had been driving for what seemed like hours through the rich, flat — oh, so flat — farmland of central Illinois with large, well-tended farms, one after another, receding in the rear-view mirror. It didn't seem to matter whether we were on a freeway or driving on less traveled, two-lane blacktop, the farms kept appearing ahead of us with the certainty of bills in the mail. It was hard to imagine that there could be a national wildlife refuge anywhere within a 100 miles of us that featured vast expanses of open water, marshes, and woodlands; and even if there was, that waterfowl and shorebirds by the thousands, and migrating songbirds in equally impressive numbers could find this aviary needle in an agrarian haystack. We were about to be proved wrong, on both counts.

From the headquarters parking lot the refuge wasn't slow to reveal its magic. We made for the trailhead at the edge of the parking lot and slipped into a late April, still winter-bare deciduous woods and were met by a "fuss" of Red-headed Woodpeckers. I can't ever remember seeing more than two Red-headed Woodpeckers at one time, but in the next ten minutes I saw more than I'd seen in my entire life. They were flashing through the trees, ripping the air with their calls, and hammering on anything that was wood. They were in almost constant motion, flying in and out of view, making it difficult to even guess at their numbers, but there must have been at least 20, plus a couple of flickers who joined in the fun.

The cacophony from the woodpeckers lessened somewhat as the wide, level, wheelchair-accessible path approached the low bluff overlooking Lake Chautauqua. Three wooden observation decks are strung along the shore of the 3,400-acre manmade lake and from any one of them hundreds of ducks and geese could be seen sprinkled across the surface of the water. Unfortunately, most were too far away to be identified with binoculars and the spotting scope was back in the car. The second observation deck has permanently mounted binoculars, set at wheelchair height, but they didn't have any more pulling power than mine. Closer at hand, small shorebirds kept flying along the muddy transition zone between lake and dry land but they obviously had other business than landing to let us attempt to identify them.

The view from any of the platforms is impressive and made more so with the knowledge that what you are seeing is a triumph of nature over man. From prehistoric times the floodplain wetlands bordering the Illinois River have attracted huge numbers of migrating waterfowl and shorebirds. The immense richness and diversity of plant and animal life surrounding the refuge provided a year-round bounty for Native Americans and supported a large number of permanent and seasonal settlements. The area is peppered with barely visible traces of their burial grounds, seasonal hunting camps and villages. When Europeans came to the area, they looked at the rich bottomland and instead of game, saw potential cropland going to waste.

In the 1920s the floodplain was diked, dammed, drained, and planted with crops. But Mother Nature, maybe resenting man's intrusion, swept the area with one of her periodic floods and wiped out most of man's attempt to cultivate the lowlands. In 1936 the federal government purchased most of the area and created the Chautauqua National Wildlife Refuge. Levees separating the floodplain from the Illinois River were repaired and used not to drain the area but regulate the water levels in Lake Chautauqua and surrounding units to provide resting and feeding areas for waterfowl.

The results have been spectacular. In mid-November 100,000 ducks and half that many Canada, Blue and Snow geese gather in the refuge. Some just use it as a stopover on their way south while others spend the winter here. Early April witnesses another peak in the waterfowl population as migrating birds join the winter residents before they head north. Twenty-six species of ducks and geese have been seen in the refuge and though most of them are transitory; Wood Ducks, Mallards, Blue-winged Teal and Canada Geese nest in the area.

Shorebird activity can even be more spectacular, if irregular. In August and September if water levels are low enough to expose extensive areas of mudflats, shorebirds arrive in incredible numbers. In a good year more than 150,000 yellowlegs, plovers, sandpipers, dowitchers, egrets, heron and other shorebirds literally carpet the refuge. It's not unusual to see some shorebirds from spring through fall. Great Blue Heron, Green Heron, egrets, and Black-crowned Night-heron nest in the refuge, and all can be seen fishing the shallow waters throughout spring and summer. A spotting scope is a must with the waders often far out in the swallow waters.

Winter draws birders to Chautauqua for Bald Eagle viewing. Large concentrations of eagles are seen all along the Illinois River and as many as 35 have been counted in the refuge. They usually arrive in October and, if the winter is not too severe, stay until spring.

All together more than 275 species of birds have been recorded in the refuge and in a matter of a few weeks the woods along the nature trail, where the redheads were now running riot, would be full of songbirds. The refuge bird checklist lists 32 warblers, 7 vireo, and 10 flycatchers in addition to a wide variety of thrushes, wrens, and sparrows. Even in the doldrums of summer birders can look for Rose-breasted Grosbeaks, Indigo Buntings, Rufous-sided Towhees, Prothonotary Warblers, seven different woodpeckers, including Pileated Woodpeckers, Bell's and Warbling vireos, Common Moorhens, Pied-billed Grebes, and coots that all nest in the refuge.

After sweeping the lake from the last of the observation decks, Barb and I followed the trail as it turned away from the lake. As if to bid us good-bye the calls of several coyotes wafted across the lake and sent chills up and down our spines as we headed back to the parking lot. The half-mile trail packs a lot of diversity into a short walk. In addition to offering a spectacular view of the wetlands from the observation decks, the trail passes through bottomland and upland forests and a small prairie remnant.

Back in the car we retraced our steps to the entrance of the refuge headquarters and turned north on State Road 15. Following the refuge map we passed through a quiet little bulge in the road called Buzzville and followed signs to the boat launching ramp on Lake Chautauqua where we hit waterfowl pay dirt. Ducks, geese, and coots thronged the north end of the lake. A casual sweep of the binoculars turned up scores of Tundra Swans, Canvasbacks, Green- and Blue-winged Teal, Northern Shovelers, Mallards, Wood Ducks and Canada Geese. With the aid of a spotting scope American Widgeons, Ring-necked Ducks, and Lesser Scaup could be seen near the distant shore. Overhead a lone Bald Eagle and a couple of Turkey Vultures drifted across the sky. Marking a perfect end to our visit to Chautauqua National Wildlife Refuge, a male Eastern Bluebird laid claim to a fence post as we pulled back on to the road and headed south.

"As if to bid us good-bye, the calls of several coyotes wafted across the lake and sent chills up and down our spines as we headed back to the parking lot."

CHAUTAUQUA NATIONAL WILDLIFE REFUGE FIELD CHECKLIST

The checklist is compiled and published by the wildlife refuge.

___ Common Loon	___ Northern Bobwhite	___ Barred Owl	___ Northern Mockingbird	___ Vesper Sparrow
___ Pied-billed Grebe	___ King Rail	___ Short-eared Owl	___ Brown Thrasher	___ Lark Sparrow
___ Horned Grebe	___ Virginia Rail	___ Common Nighthawk	___ American Pipit	___ Savannah Sparrow
___ American White Pelican	___ Sora	___ Whip-poor-will	___ Cedar Waxwing	___ Grasshopper Sparrow
___ Least Bittern	___ Common Moorhen	___ Chimney Swift	___ Loggerhead Shrike	___ LeConte's Sparrow
___ Great Blue Heron	___ American Coot	___ Ruby-throated Hummingbird	___ European Starling	___ Sharp-tailed Sparrow
___ Great Egret	___ Sandhill Crane	___ Belted Kingfisher	___ White-eyed Vireo	___ Fox Sparrow
___ Snowy Egret	___ Black-bellied Plover	___ Red-headed Woodpecker	___ Bell's Vireo	___ Song Sparrow
___ Little Blue Heron	___ Lesser Golden-plover	___ Red-bellied Woodpecker	___ Solitary Vireo	___ Lincoln's Sparrow
___ Cattle Egret	___ Semipalmated Plover	___ Yellow-bellied Sapsucker	___ Yellow-throated Vireo	___ Swamp Sparrow
___ Green Heron	___ Piping Plover	___ Downy Woodpecker	___ Warbling Vireo	___ White-throated Sparrow
___ Black-crowned Night-heron	___ Killdeer	___ Hairy Woodpecker	___ Philadelphia Vireo	___ White-crowned Sparrow
___ Yellow-crowned Night-heron	___ American Avocet	___ Northern Flicker	___ Red-eyed Vireo	___ Harris' Sparrow
___ Tundra Swan	___ Greater Yellowlegs	___ Pileated Woodpecker	___ Blue-winged Warbler	___ Dark-eyed Sparrow
___ Greater White-fronted Goose	___ Lesser Yellowlegs	___ Olive-sided Flycatcher	___ Golden-winged Warbler	___ Lapland Longspur
___ Snow Goose	___ Solitary Sandpiper	___ Eastern Wood-pewee	___ Tennessee Warbler	___ Snow Bunting
___ Canada Goose	___ Willet	___ Yellow-bellied Flycatcher	___ Orange-crowned Warbler	___ Bobolink
___ Wood Duck	___ Spotted Sandpiper	___ Acadian Flycatcher	___ Nashville Warbler	___ Red-winged Blackbird
___ Green-winged Teal	___ Upland Sandpiper	___ Alder Flycatcher	___ Northern Parula	___ Eastern Meadowlark
___ American Black Duck	___ Hudsonian Godwit	___ Willow Flycatcher	___ Yellow Warbler	___ Rusty Blackbird
___ Mallard	___ Marbled Godwit	___ Least Flycatcher	___ Chestnut-sided Warbler	___ Common Grackle
___ Northern Pintail	___ Ruddy Turnstone	___ Eastern Phoebe	___ Magnolia Warbler	___ Brown-headed Cowbird
___ Blue-winged Teal	___ Red Knot	___ Great Crested Flycatcher	___ Cape May Warbler	___ Orchard Oriole
___ Northern Shoveler	___ Sanderling	___ Eastern Kingbird	___ Yellow-rumped Warbler	___ Baltimore Oriole
___ Gadwall	___ Semipalmated Sandpiper	___ Horned Lark	___ Pine Warbler	___ Purple Finch
___ American Wigeon	___ Western Sandpiper	___ Purple Martin	___ Bay-breasted Warbler	___ Pine Siskin
___ Canvasback	___ Least Sandpiper	___ Tree Swallow	___ Blackpoll Warbler	___ American Goldfinch
___ Redhead	___ White-rumped Sandpiper	___ Northern Rough-winged Swallow	___ Cerulean Warbler	___ Evening Grosbeak
___ Ring-necked Duck	___ Baird's Sandpiper	___ Bank Swallow	___ Black-and-white Warbler	___ House Sparrow
___ Greater Scaup	___ Pectoral Sandpiper	___ Cliff Swallow	___ American Redstart	___ Eurasian Tree Sparrow
___ Lesser Scaup	___ Dunlin	___ Barn Swallow	___ Ovenbird	
___ Black Scoter	___ Stilt Sandpiper	___ Blue Jay	___ Prothonotary Warbler	**Accidental birds**
___ Surf Scoter	___ Buff-breasted Sandpiper	___ American Crow	___ Northern Waterthrush	___ Eared Grebe
___ White-winged Scoter	___ Long-billed Dowitcher	___ Black-capped Chickadee	___ Louisiana Waterthrush	___ Trumpeter Swan
___ Common Goldeneye	___ Common Snipe	___ Tufted Titmouse	___ Kentucky Warbler	___ Mute Swan
___ Bufflehead	___ American Woodcock	___ Red-breasted Nuthatch	___ Connecticut Warbler	___ Cinnamon Teal
___ Hooded Merganser	___ Wilson's Phalarope	___ White-breasted Nuthatch	___ Mourning Warbler	___ Oldsquaw
___ Common Merganser	___ Laughing Gull	___ Brown Creeper	___ Common Yellowthroat	___ Northern Goshawk
___ Red-breasted Merganser	___ Franklin's Gull	___ Carolina Wren	___ Hooded Warbler	___ Sharp-tail Sandpiper
___ Ruddy Duck	___ Bonaparte's Gull	___ Bewick's Wren	___ Wilson's Warbler	___ Whimbrel
___ Turkey Vulture	___ Ring-billed Gull	___ House Wren	___ Canada Warbler	___ Red-necked Phalarope
___ Osprey	___ Herring Gull	___ Winter Wren	___ Yellow-throated Chat	___ Parasitic Jaeger
___ Bald Eagle	___ Sabine's Gull	___ Marsh Wren	___ Summer Tanager	___ Little Gull
___ Northern Harrier	___ Caspian Tern	___ Golden-crowned Kinglet	___ Scarlet Tanager	___ Thayer's Gull
___ Sharp-shinned Hawk	___ Common Tern	___ Ruby-crowned Kinglet	___ Northern Cardinal	___ Iceland Gull
___ Cooper's Hawk	___ Forster's Tern	___ Blue-gray Gnatcatcher	___ Rose-breasted Grosbeak	___ Glaucous Gull
___ Red-shouldered Hawk	___ Least Tern	___ Eastern Bluebird	___ Blue Grosbeak	___ Lesser Black-backed Gull
___ Broad-winged Hawk	___ Black Tern	___ Veery	___ Indigo Bunting	___ Ivory Gull
___ Red-tailed Hawk	___ Rock Dove	___ Gray-cheeked Thrush	___ Dickcissel	___ Snowy Owl
___ Rough-legged Hawk	___ Mourning Dove	___ Swainson's Thrush	___ Rufous-sided Towhee	___ Red Crossbill
___ American Kestrel	___ Black-billed Cuckoo	___ Hermit Thrush	___ American Tree Sparrow	___ White-winged Crossbill
___ Merlin	___ Yellow-billed Cuckoo	___ Wood Thrush	___ Chipping Sparrow	___ Common Redpoll
___ Peregrine Falcon	___ Eastern Screech-owl	___ American Robin	___ Clay-colored Sparrow	
___ Ring-necked Pheasant	___ Great Horned Owl	___ Gray Catbird	___ Field Sparrow	

Pere Marquette State Park and The Mark Twain National Wildlife Refuge, Calhoun Division

From the time man first encountered the mighty body of living, moving water that bisects most of the North American continent, the Mississippi River has represented more than just an imposing and awe-inspiring geographical feature. Depending on where you live, where you're going, or what you do for a living, the river has been thought of as the Gateway to the West, an untamable source of devastating floods, a huge commercial highway, an almost mystical living creature, a great playground and battleground, and an allegory for life itself. But in addition to a river of floods, commerce, and myth we should also think of the Mississippi as a river of birds. It is one of the great migratory flyways of the world. Nowhere is this more evident than at the point where the Illinois River joins the Mississippi, just north of St. Louis, where the Calhoun Division of the Mark Twain National Wildlife Refuge and the Pere Marquette State Park line either side of the Illinois River.

In any given year 5 million ducks and 50,000 geese travel up and down the Mississippi during spring and fall migration. Birds of prey also use the river as a migratory highway, and the tally of just Broad-wing Hawks passing a given point on the river can reach five figures for a single 24-hour period in October. Between January and early March, more than 700 Bald Eagles winter in the area around the refuge and park. Their presence has created a new winter tourist industry. In addition to the eagles, thousands of waterfowl make the area their winter home, including upwards of 10,000 Snow Geese. During spring migration over 20 species of ducks can be seen in the national wildlife refuge and both the refuge and the state park attract large numbers of shorebirds and songbirds. Summer birding features a good variety of nesting warblers, lots of marsh birds and shorebirds including Yellow-crowned Night-heron, and of late, Mississippi Kites. The combined bird checklist for the adjoining areas total 256 species and includes the European Tree Sparrow, which is only found in the St. Louis area.

Barb and I arrived in late March and pulled into the parking lot next to the large, rustic lodge of the Pere Marquette State Park so I could consult the park's map and decide where to start birding. With my nose buried in a map and muttering to myself about where to begin, Barb quietly suggested I get my head out of my ... aaah map — I think that's what she said — and look at the apple tree which the car's front bumper was almost touching. There, not two feet above the hood of the car was a Pileated Woodpecker with a punk rocker's haircut and dye job quietly exploring a cavity. We sat for ten minutes watching the crow-sized woodpecker patiently work the tree. It didn't even disturb the bird when we started the car and drove up to the lodge. While Barb took her knitting and a book and made herself comfortable in the lodge's magnificent lobby with its view of

"More than 700 Bald Eagles winter in the area around the refuge and park. Their presence has created a new winter tourist industry."

LOCATION: Grafton, Illinois.

DIRECTIONS: Approximately 25 miles west of Alton, Illinois on Highway 100.

HOURS: Open all year. The Visitors Center at the Calhoun District of the Mark Twain National Wildlife Refuge is open 7:30 a.m.-4:00 p.m. on weekdays.

BEST TIMES: The two adjoining areas offer great birding all year, but each season offers something special. Bald Eagle watching peaks from December 1 to March 1. Spring and fall migration heralds the arrival of enormous numbers of waterfowl, shorebirds and warblers. Summer offers good chances for spotting a variety of marsh birds and warblers.

BIRDING HIGHLIGHTS: Some of the best concentrations of Bald Eagles on the Mississippi. Great viewing of waterfowl, shorebirds, and songbirds. The combined checklist for the two areas totals 256 species.

FOR MORE INFORMATION: Mark Twain National Wildlife Refuge, Brussels District, HCR Box 107, Brussels, IL 62013. Phone: (618) 883-2524.

Pere Marquette State Park, P.O. Box 158, Grafton, IL 62037. Phone: (618) 786-2204.

"Trees more than a foot in diameter and bigger lay like match sticks all pointed in the same direction and all broken off at a uniform height of about six feet above the ground. It was as if Paul Bunyan had walked the area with a giant scythe."

the Illinois River, I went looking for birds across the river at the Calhoun District of the Mark Twain National Wildlife Refuge.

The refuge's headquarters lie on the south side of the Illinois River, and the only way across the river is via the small Brussels Ferry. It's about a 3-mile drive to the headquarters after debarking from the ferry, and for nearly the entire drive the effects of the great flood of 1993 were still evident, two years later. Much of this area had been at least 6 feet under water, and high water marks were still visible on buildings and trees. The flood also fatally weakened many of the larger trees, and with the first good wind they toppled like tenpins, but with strange effect. Trees more than a foot in diameter and bigger lay like match sticks all pointed in the same direction and all broken off at a uniform height of about six feet above the ground. It was as if Paul Bunyan had walked the area with a giant scythe. The other strange sight was an immature Bald Eagle sitting on a telephone wire as if it was a Mourning Dove. At the refuge headquarters the ranger said the flood had simply devastated the area, wiped out much of the wildlife habitat, and left a black desert of mud. Dikes and pools have been rebuilt though and the birds are returning, including a half-dozen shorebirds in the pool directly in front of the headquarter's observation deck. I was doing my best to ignore them, because they belonged to the group of small sandpipers that send my mind into gridlock when trying to identify.

At the ranger's suggestion I backtracked a mile to a refuge road that follows a dike to an observation point overlooking Swan Lake. The road bisects several moist soil units, and later in the summer this should be a prime shorebird area. The ditches beside the road were filled with American Coots and Blue-winged Teal, but the real treat came when I left the car and scanned the south end of the lake. It was packed with ducks. American Coots, teal, Bufflehead, Northern Shovelers and stately Northern Pintails blanketed the calm waters. A large contingent of Snow Geese kept to themselves near the northern shore and a scattering of Wood Ducks and American Wigeon could be spotted here and there among the larger concentrations of teal and coot. What I first took to be foam washed up on a distant shore turned out to be at least 100 White Pelicans, a fact your sharp-eyed observer didn't realize until a couple of pelicans landed in the foam, disturbing the other birds and they rearranged themselves with much flapping of wings. A few Double-crested Cormorants also watched the activity on the lake from dead trees where they were drying their wings.

Calhoun Point at the confluence of the Illinois and Mississippi Rivers regularly boasts the highest nesting count of Prothonotary Warblers in Illinois. Birders also occasionally spot Mississippi Kites and Fish Crows in the area as well as Yellow-crowned Night-heron. Although it was too early in the year to expect any warblers, I checked out several pull-offs and boat launching sites on the way back to the Brussels Ferry and was rewarded for my efforts with a Red-shouldered Hawk, Red-bellied and Red-headed woodpeckers, and a lone Mallard who evidently didn't prefer the company of the other ducks back at Swan Lake. Several crows showed themselves, but the only hope I have of recognizing a Fish Crow is to spot one with a fly rod.

The ranger at the refuge headquarters also highly recommended Gilbert Lake on the north bank of the Illinois River. The area stretches west from the Brussel Ferry dock to the lodge at the Mark Twain State Park and is accessible from a parking lot off Highway 100 across from the lodge. A service road, open only to foot traffic, begins at the parking area and leads birders through a lowland hardwood forest lying between the Illinois River and the Gilbert Lake — a long, narrow finger of water that parallels the river. The three-mile trail is the refuge's most popular birding area. The hike offers good birding for waterfowl and shorebirds, and in late April and early May the bottomland hardwoods and wetlands can hold a wide variety warblers and songbirds.

The best place for waterfowl at the state park is Stump Lake, just a couple of hundred yards west of the parking area for the Gilbert Lake Trail. The lake shelters a wide variety of waterfowl in the winter and in late March. From the boat dock and its parking lot, I could easily spot hundreds of ducks that still hadn't taken wing for the north. Among the teal, coot, Mallard and occasional Northern Shovelers were numerous Great Blue Heron, a lone Little Blue Heron, and several Great Egrets fishing the shallow waters. About a half mile northwest on Highway 100 is the Dabbs access to Stump Lake. From the parking area a wide path leads to a levee that crosses the lake and ends at the Illinois River. Yet more ducks and heron could be seen from the levee and, wonder-of-wonders, shorebirds I could identify. Probing the mudflats on either side of the levee were representatives of both yellowlegs, Spotted Sandpipers and Semipalmated Plovers.

The best area for songbirds and warblers in the state park is near the eastern edge of the park on Graham Hollow Road. The road is not graced with a sign and is easily missed from Highway 100. The narrow, two-lane blacktop road lies 0.7 mile to the east Brussels Ferry. The picturesque road follows a creek as it winds its way up a draw in the bluffs overlooking the Illinois and Mississippi rivers. Birding is good anywhere along the road with the best spot near a fork in the road where birders can pull off, park, cross the stream, and look for the Ovenbirds, Northern Parulas, Yellow-breasted Chats and Hooded and Blue-winged warblers that nest in the wooded hillsides bordering the hollow.

The bluffs with their spectacular overlooks of the Illinois and Mississippi rivers can be reached by continuing up Graham Hollow or by taking the road at the back of the park's lodge. In addition to the fine views, the heavily wooded bluffs are a great spot for observing hawks anytime of the year but especially during migration. The woods and small openings also provide good birding for a variety of songbirds.

But maybe the best way to appreciate the River of Birds is where Barb and I found ourselves after a busy and tiring day. From the comfort of a chair on the flagstone verandah in front of the Pere Marquette State Park's lodge with a drink, birdbook and binoculars close at hand, we watched the passing show. A huge flock of American White Pelicans turned and wheeled over the river. Egrets and Great Blue Heron were always somewhere in view moving over the river and wetlands, and at least 50 cormorants moved up river in a sloppy, undisciplined V that would have shamed any self-respecting flight of geese. Ducks singly and in groups of two or three continuously flew by the lodge, and a parade-ground perfect V of geese showed the cormorants how it's supposed to be done. In the hour we sat in front of the lodge, hundreds of birds moved passed our comfortable vantage point.

The Great River Road (Highway 100) from Alton to the Pere Marquette State Park is one of the best places in America to find wintering Bald Eagles. Prime viewing is between December 1 and March 1 and it's not uncommon to see a hundred of the great birds in a day trip. Bald Eagle watching has gotten so popular three different agencies presently offer eagle tours. But you can do just as well on your own by starting out from Alton early in the morning and watching for eagles fishing in the Mississippi and perched in trees along the bluffs bordering the great river. Eagle sighting gets better the closer one gets to Grafton, Illinois,

"There, not two feet above the hood of the car was a Pileated Woodpecker with a punk rocker's haircut and dye job quietly exploring a cavity."

and from Grafton to the state park along the Illinois River eagle watching can be spectacular. Eagles especially favor the Brussels Ferry because of the fish it churns up. Birders can usually count on seeing the birds perched in trees on either side of the river and even fishing in the boat's wake. For those who want to search for eagles on foot the Gilbert Lake Trail is usually rewarding.

PERE MARQUETTE STATE PARK AND MARK TWAIN NATIONAL WILDLIFE REFUGE, CALHOUN DIVISION FIELD CHECKLIST

Common Loon	Cooper's Hawk	Forster's Tern	Winter Wren	Northern Waterthrush
Pied-billed Grebe	Northern Goshawk	Least Tern	Sedge Wren	Louisiana Waterthrush
Horned Grebe	Red-shouldered Hawk	Black Tern	Marsh Wren	Kentucky Warbler
Eared Grebe	Broad-winged Hawk	Rock Dove	Golden-crowned Kinglet	Mourning Warbler
Western Grebe	Red-tailed Hawk	Mourning Dove	Ruby-crowned Kinglet	Common Yellowthroat
American White Pelican	Rough-legged Hawk	Black-billed Cuckoo	Blue-gray Gnatcatcher	Hooded Warbler
Double-crested Cormorant	Golden Eagle	Yellow-billed Cuckoo	Eastern Bluebird	Wilson's Warbler
American Bittern	American Kestrel	Eastern Screech-owl	Veery	Canada Warbler
Least Bittern	Merlin	Great Horned Owl	Gray-cheeked Thrush	Yellow-breasted Chat
Great Blue Heron	Peregrine Falcon	Barred Owl	Swainson's Thrush	Summer Tanager
Great Egret	Prairie Falcon	Long-eared Owl	Hermit Thrush	Scarlet Tanager
Snowy Egret	Ring-necked Pheasant	Short-eared Owl	Wood Thrush	Northern Cardinal
Little Blue Heron	Wild Turkey	Northern Saw-whet Owl	American Robin	Rose-breasted Grosbeak
Cattle Egret	Northern Bobwhite	Common Nighthawk	Gray Catbird	Indigo Bunting
Green Heron	King Rail	Chimney Swift	Northern Mockingbird	Dickcissel
Black-crowned Night-heron	Virginia Rail	Ruby-throated Hummingbird	Brown Thrasher	Rufous-sided Towhee
Yellow-crowned Night-heron	Sora	Belted Kingfisher	American Pipit	American Tree Sparrow
White Ibis	Common Moorhen	Red-headed Woodpecker	Cedar Waxwing	Chipping Sparrow
Glossy Ibis	American Coot	Red-bellied Woodpecker	Loggerhead Shrike	Field Sparrow
Tundra Swan	Black-bellied Plover	Yellow-bellied Sapsucker	European Starling	Vesper Sparrow
Greater White-fronted Goose	Lesser Golden-plover	Downy Woodpecker	White-eyed Vireo	Lark Sparrow
Snow Goose	Semipalmated Plover	Hairy Woodpecker	Solitary Vireo	Savannah Sparrow
Ross' Goose	Piping Plover	Northern Flicker	Yellow-throated Vireo	LeConte's Sparrow
Canada Goose	Killdeer	Pileated Woodpecker	Warbling Vireo	Sharp-tailed Sparrow
Wood Duck	American Avocet	Eastern Wood-peewee	Philadelphia Vireo	Fox Sparrow
Green-winged Teal	Greater Yellowlegs	Yellow-bellied Flycatcher	Red-eyed Vireo	Song Sparrow
American Black Duck	Lesser Yellowlegs	Acadian Flycatcher	Blue-winged Warbler	Lincoln's Sparrow
Mallard	Solitary Sandpiper	Alder Flycatcher	Golden-winged Warbler	Swamp Sparrow
Northern Pintail	Willet	Willow Flycatcher	Tennessee Warbler	White-throated Sparrow
Blue-winged Teal	Spotted Sandpiper	Least Flycatcher	Orange-crowned Warbler	White-crowned Sparrow
Northern Shoveler	Upland Sandpiper	Eastern Phoebe	Nashville Warbler	Dark-eyed Junco
Gadwall	Red Knot	Great Crested Flycatcher	Northern Parula	Lapland Longspur
American Wigeon	Semipalmated Sandpiper	Eastern Kingbird	Yellow Warbler	Bobolink
Canvasback	Western Sandpiper	Horned Lark	Chestnut-sided Warbler	Red-winged Blackbird
Redhead	Least Sandpiper	Purple Martin	Magnolia Warbler	Eastern Meadowlark
Ring-necked Duck	White-rumped Sandpiper	Tree Swallow	Cape May Warbler	Rusty Blackbird
Greater Scaup	Pectoral Sandpiper	Northern Rough-winged Swallow	Yellow-rumped Warbler	Brewer's Blackbird
Lesser Scaup	Dunlin	Bank Swallow	Black-throated Green Warbler	Common Grackle
Oldsquaw	Stilt Sandpiper	Cliff Swallow	Blackburnian Warbler	Brown-headed Cowbird
Common Goldeneye	Short-billed Dowitcher	Barn Swallow	Yellow-throated Warbler	Orchard Oriole
Bufflehead	Long-billed Dowitcher	Blue Jay	Pine Warbler	Baltimore Oriole
Hooded Merganser	Common Snipe	American Crow	Prairie Warbler	Purple Finch
Common Merganser	American Woodcock	Fish Crow	Palm Warbler	Pine Siskin
Red-breasted Merganser	Wilson's Phalarope	Black-capped Chickadee	Bay-breasted Warbler	American Goldfinch
Ruddy Duck	Red-necked Phalarope	Tufted Titmouse	Blackpoll Warbler	Evening Grosbeak
Turkey Vulture	Franklin's Gull	Red-breasted Nuthatch	Cerulean Warbler	House Sparrow
Osprey	Bonaparte's Gull	White-breasted Nuthatch	Black-and-white Warbler	European Tree Sparrow
Mississippi Kite	Ring-billed Gull	Brown Creeper	American Redstart	
Bald Eagle	Herring Gull	Carolina Wren	Prothonotary Warbler	
Northern Harrier	Caspian Tern	Bewick's Wren	Worm-eating Warbler	
Sharp-shinned Hawk	Common Tern	House Wren	Ovenbird	

Rend Lake

From the top of the observation deck I didn't need binoculars to see and identify the Great Blue Heron arrayed in stately ranks far out in the shallow waters of the lake. But nearer the platform, where water and terra firma couldn't quite make up their minds where one began and the other left off, an undisciplined army of skittering shorebirds were beyond my birding expertise without the aid of magnification, and that was out of the question today. A blustery April wind was beating against the sturdy observation platform overlooking the northern end of Rend Lake with such force that the deck underfoot trembled. The wind was also trying to dispute my right to be on the platform. It begrudgingly allowed me to stand upright, but focusing binoculars or a spotting scope was out of the question. It was an inauspicious introduction to one of the great shorebird and waterfowl gathering spots in Illinois and the entire Midwest.

Rend Lake, created by the damming of the Big Muddy River in 1965, looks like a raised fist with the thumb and first two fingers extended. Down at the base of the palm, at the dam site, the water reaches a depth of 10 feet. Up in the extended digits the dam's backwater barely covers some of the flattest land in southern Illinois. An inch or two reduction in the water level can expose acres of mud flats.

The large expanse of open water in the south, the shallows to the north, and the bottom land forest surrounding the lake has proved to be immensely appealing to birds. The area bird checklist totals a whopping 272 species with 72 species noted as commonly sighted. By late summer extensive mud flats can ring the northern end of the lake and attract a staggering number and variety of shorebirds. The checklist contains 35 species of shorebirds, and experienced birders have reported sighting 25 species in a single day.

On the southern end of the lake, the relatively deeper waters draw an equally impressive number of ducks, grebes, geese, loons, and gulls. Greater White-fronted and Ross' geese, Tundra Swans, Old Squaw, King Eider, Ruddy Duck, Gadwall, and Surf Scoter are just some of the more than 31 species of waterfowl, in addition to 10 species of gulls, seen in the area.

No, the problem at Rend lake is not finding birds nor finding a place from which to view them, but trying to decide just which of the many local birding hot spots you have time to visit. That's unless you throw up your hands at trying to see everything in a day and set up a base camp in a nearby town, or better yet camp at Wayne Fitzgerrell State Park, which occupies a peninsula that juts out into the lake, and is itself a great spot from which to bird.

For making the decision on where to go, either easier or more difficult, depending on your point of view, there is an excellent Watchable Wildlife brochure, available from the U.S. Army Corp of Engineers or from the local tourist bureau. The guide gives detailed directions with maps to a dozen prime birdwatching sites around the lake. Included in each brief description is the habitat at each locale, and the different birds and animals likely to be seen from either trails or observation platforms. Plan ahead. Send for this helpful guide before your birding expedition to Rend Lake.

The consensus among the experts and those familiar with Rend Lake point to four areas of special interest. Moving clockwise around Rend Lake, and starting

"What I first mistook for a low-flying crow identified itself as a Green Heron when it flared its wings and settled on a floating log near its larger cousin."

LOCATION: Benton, Illinois.

DIRECTIONS: Located in the southern tip of Illinois, Rend Lake is easily accessible from three exits on I-57 between Benton and Ina, Illinois. To reach the U.S. Army Corp of Engineers Visitors Center at the main dam take exit 71 from I-57 and drive west 2.5 miles on SR 14 to Rend City Road. Turn right on Rend City Road and drive north 3 miles to Main Dam Road. Turn right, cross the dam, and follow signs to the Visitors Center.

HOURS: Open year-round.

BEST TIMES: Winter for Canada Geese, gulls, and ducks. Spring through fall for shorebirds with the peak shorebird viewing in the fall. Spring and fall migration for waterfowl and songbirds.

BIRDING HIGHLIGHTS: Extraordinary opportunities for seeing shorebirds, gulls, and waterfowl. Huge concentrations of geese in the winter. An all-around great birding locale with 272 species recorded on the area checklist.

FOR MORE INFORMATION: U.S. Army Corp of Engineers, Rend Lake Management Office, R.R. #3, Benton, IL 62812. Phone: (618) 724-2493.

Southern Illinois Tourism Council, P.O. Box 40, Whittington, IL 62897. Phone: (800) 342-3100.

"Rend Lake looks like a raised fist with the thumb and first two fingers extended."

at twelve o'clock position the first area encountered is the Waterfowl Refuge Observation Stand on the first knuckle of Rend Lake's index finger, where the wind was threatening to blow me off the platform. The observation stand overlooks an area of prime mud flats for shorebirds from spring through fall, and upwards of 175,000 Canada Geese spend the winter here. Bald Eagles also frequent this area in midwinter. To reach the Waterfowl Refuge Observation Stand drive north on State Route 37 to Bonnie. In Bonnie turn west on 550N and drive approximately 1 mile to 1250E. At 1250E turn south and drive less than a half-mile to 500N where your turn west again and go about 1.5 miles to 1100E. At 1100E turn south and drive 1.5 miles to the Observation Stand.

The Rend Dam and the spillway just below it on the southern end of the lake, at the six o'clock position, is the second birding spot that shouldn't be overlooked on any visit. Main Dam Road which crosses the dam and gives access to the Rend

SHORT-BILLED DOWITCHER

Lake Visitors Center is the place to go in winter to see thousands of gulls. Among the plentiful gathering of Ring-billed Gulls, the careful and lucky observer may spot Laughing, Franklin's, Thayer's, Bonaparte's, Mew, Glaucous, and Sabine's gulls. The rare Pomarine Jaeger has also been spotted here in the winter. Ducks also frequent this area in the fall and winter. Barb and I arrived in early April and after a brief survey of the lake's wind-tossed, open waters from the dam and the Visitors Center parking lot, which netted four species of ducks, two gulls and a Pied-billed Grebe, we finally found respite from the wind below the dam where the Big Muddy River is freed from its impoundment.

River Road heads south from Main Dam Road near the spillway and dips into a bottomland forest for a short distance before ending at a parking lot next to the Big Muddy River. If winter is the best time for spotting waterfowl and gulls from the top of the dam, spring is the best time for birding the bottomland forest below the big earthen impoundment. The mingling of thick woods, flooded sloughs, and the rejuvenated river creates a small but varied pocket of ecosystems. While sitting in the car and eating a sack lunch, Barb and I were treated to the sight of Wood Ducks, a Northern Shoveler, and a Blue-wing Teal drifting among the dead trees of a small flooding. Tree and Barn swallows cut the air above the flooding while a Great Egret and Great Blue Heron stared intently into the dark waters from downed timber on the far shore. What I first mistook for a low-flying crow identified itself as a Green Heron when it flared its wings and settled on a floating log near its larger cousin. A few weeks later in the spring this bottomland with its thickets, dense trees, and water should be a prime viewing area for migrating songbirds. Directions to the Visitors Center, Rend Dam and the spillway area can be found at the end of this chapter.

Ward Branch, at the nine o'clock position, on the west side of the lake is mecca for shorebirds. Baird's, Buff-breasted, Least, and Western sandpipers as well as Short-billed Dowitchers, Ruddy Turnstones, Whimbrel, Marbled and Hudsonian godwits, American Avocets, and Red-necked Phalaropes have all been tallied here. Viewing opportunities are good in the spring but best from August through October. To reach Ward Branch turn north from State Route 154 on to 800E and drive approximately 2 miles to where 800E bears to the west and becomes 085N. Drive approximately a quarter-mile on 085N to 725E. Turn north on 725E and drive 1.1 miles to the Ward Branch Wetlands.

The best area for song and forest birds lies at the northern end of Rend Lake's middle finger at about the eleven o'clock on the clock face. Ryder's Bottom encompasses hundreds of acres of mature old growth hardwoods where Scarlet Tanagers, woodpeckers, numerous vireos, warblers, owls, and flycatchers have been found. Among the notable list of birds finding food and shelter in the trackless bottomland are Pileated Woodpeckers, Kentucky, Northern Parula, and Cerulean warblers, Yellow-crowned Night-heron, and Yellow-billed Cuckoos. There are no formal trails in the area so if you plan to venture far from the parking lot a good pair of hiking boots and a compass are a must. The parking area is found by travel east out of Waltonville on State Route 148 for 3.5 miles to 900E. Turn north and drive approximately 2.5 miles on 900E to 750N. Turn west on 750N and drive 1 mile to the parking area.

These four areas consistently produce birds, but almost anywhere along the 162 miles of shoreline and thousands of acres of fields and forests adjacent to the lake can yield a cornucopia of rewarding sightings. A map and guide, available from the addresses on page 23, are almost a necessity for finding your way around the area and getting to the prime birdwatching spots.

"Four areas consistently produce birds, but almost anywhere along the 162 miles of shoreline and thousands of acres of fields and forests adjacent to the lake can yield a cornucopia of rewarding sightings."

REND LAKE FIELD CHECKLIST

___Red-throated Loon
___Common Loon
___Pied-billed Grebe
___Horned Grebe
___Red-necked Grebe
___Eared Grebe
___Western Grebe
___American White Pelican
___Double-crested Cormorant
___American Bittern
___Least Bittern
___Great Blue Heron
___Great Egret
___Snowy Egret
___Little Blue Heron
___Cattle Egret
___Green Heron
___Black-crowned Night-heron
___Yellow-crowned Night-heron
___Tundra Swan
___Mute Swan
___Greater White-fronted Goose
___Snow Goose
___Ross' Goose
___Canada Goose
___Wood Duck
___Blue-winged Teal
___Green-winged Teal
___American Black Duck
___Mallard
___Northern Pintail
___Northern Shoveler
___Gadwall
___American Wigeon
___Canvasback
___Redhead
___Ring-necked Duck
___Greater Scaup
___Lesser Scaup
___King Eider
___Oldsquaw
___Black Scoter
___Surf Scoter
___White-winged Scoter
___Common Golden-eye
___Bufflehead
___Hooded Merganser
___Common Merganser
___Red-breasted Merganser
___Ruddy Duck
___Turkey Vulture
___Osprey
___Bald Eagle
___Golden Eagle
___Northern Harrier

___Sharp-shinned Hawk
___Copper's Hawk
___Northern Goshawk
___Red-shouldered Hawk
___Broad-winged Hawk
___Red-tailed Hawk
___Rough-legged Hawk
___American Kestrel
___Merlin
___Peregrine Falcon
___Ring-necked Pheasant
___Bobwhite
___Virginia Rail
___Sora
___Common Moorhen
___American Coot
___Sandhill Crane
___Black-bellied Plover
___Lesser Golden-plover
___Semipalmated Plover
___Piping Plover
___Killdeer
___American Avocet
___Greater Yellowlegs
___Lesser Yellowlegs
___Solitary Sandpiper
___Willet
___Spotted Sandpiper
___Upland Sandpiper
___Whimbrel
___Hudsonian Godwit
___Marbled Godwit
___Ruddy Turnstone
___Red Knot
___Sanderling
___Semipalmated Sandpiper
___Western Sandpiper
___Least Sandpiper
___White-rumped Sandpiper
___Baird's Sandpiper
___Pectoral Sandpiper
___Dunlin
___Curlew Sandpiper
___Buff-breasted Sandpiper
___Short-billed Sandpiper
___Long-billed Sandpiper
___Common Snipe
___American Woodcock
___Wilson's Phalarope
___Red-necked Phalarope
___Laughing Gull
___Franklin's Gull
___Bonaparte's Gull
___Mew Gull
___Ring-billed Gull

___California Gull
___Herring Gull
___Thayer's Gull
___Glaucous Gull
___Sabine's Gull
___Caspian Tern
___Common Tern
___Forster's Tern
___Least Tern
___Black Tern
___Rock Dove
___Mourning Dove
___Black-billed Cuckoo
___Yellow-billed Cuckoo
___Eastern Screech-owl
___Great Horned Owl
___Snowy Owl
___Barred Owl
___Long-eared Owl
___Short-eared Owl
___Common Nighthawk
___Chuck-will's-widow
___Whip-poor-will
___Chimney Swift
___Ruby-throated Hummingbird
___Belted Kingfisher
___Red-headed Woodpecker
___Red-bellied Woodpecker
___Yellow-bellied Sapsucker
___Downy Woodpecker
___Hairy Woodpecker
___Northern Flicker
___Pileated Woodpecker
___Olive-sided Flycatcher
___Eastern Wood-pewee
___Yellow-bellied Flycatcher
___Acadian Flycatcher
___Alder Flycatcher
___Willow Flycatcher
___Least Flycatcher
___Eastern Phoebe
___Great Crested Flycatcher
___Eastern Kingbird
___Purple Martin
___Tree Swallow
___Northern Rough-winged Swallow
___Bank Swallow
___Cliff Swallow
___Barn Swallow
___Horned Lark
___Blue Jay
___American Crow
___Fish Crow
___Carolina Chickadee
___Tufted Titmouse

___Red-breasted Nuthatch
___White-breasted Nuthatch
___Brown Creeper
___Carolina Wren
___House Wren
___Winter Wren
___Sedge Wren
___Marsh Wren
___Golden-crowned Kinglet
___Ruby-crowned Kinglet
___Blue-gray Gnatcatcher
___Eastern Bluebird
___Veery
___Gray-cheeked Thrush
___Swainson's Thrush
___Hermit Thrush
___Wood Thrush
___American Robin
___Gray Catbird
___Northern Mockingbird
___Brown Thrasher
___Water Pipit
___Cedar Waxwing
___Loggerhead Shrike
___Starling
___White-eyed Vireo
___Bell's Vireo
___Solitary Vireo
___Yellow-throated Vireo
___Warbling Vireo
___Philadelphia Vireo
___Red-eyed Vireo
___Blue-winged Warbler
___Golden-winged Warbler
___Tennessee Warbler
___Orange-crowned Warbler
___Nashville Warbler
___Northern Parula
___Yellow Warbler
___Chestnut-sided Warbler
___Magnolia Warbler
___Cap May Warbler
___Black-throated Blue Warbler
___Yellow-rumped Warbler
___Black-throated Green Warbler
___Blackburnian Warbler
___Yellow-throated Warbler
___Palm Warbler
___Bay-breasted Warbler
___Blackpoll Warbler
___Cerulean Warbler
___Black-and-white Warbler
___Prothonotary Warbler
___Worm-eating Warbler
___American Redstart

___Ovenbird
___Northern Waterthrush
___Louisiana Waterthrush
___Kentucky Warbler
___Connecticut Warbler
___Mourning Warbler
___Common Yellowthroat
___Hooded Warbler
___Wilson's Warbler
___Canada Warbler
___Yellow-breasted Chat
___House Sparrow
___Bobolink
___Red-winged Blackbird
___Eastern Meadowlark
___Rusty Blackbird
___Brewer's Blackbird
___Common Grackle
___Brown-headed Cowbird
___Orchard Oriole
___Baltimore Oriole
___Summer Tanager
___Scarlet Tanager
___Northern Cardinal
___Rose-breasted Grosbeak
___Blue Grosbeak
___Evening Grosbeak
___Indigo Bunting
___Dickcissel
___Rufous-sided Towhee
___American Tree Sparrow
___Chipping Sparrow
___Field Sparrow
___Vesper Sparrow
___Savannah Sparrow
___Grasshopper Sparrow
___LeConte's Sparrow
___Sharp-tailed Sparrow
___Fox Sparrow
___Song Sparrow
___Lincoln's Sparrow
___Swamp Sparrow
___White-throated Sparrow
___Dark-eyed Junco
___Lapland Longspur
___Purple Finch
___House Finch
___White-crowned Sparrow
___American Goldfinch
___Smith's Longspur
___Snow Bunting
___Pine Siskin

Crab Orchard National Wildlife Refuge

How does a national wildlife refuge manage to accommodate over a million human visitors a year while still attracting and providing refuge to more than a 100,000 migrating waterfowl? That was only the first of several questions that aroused our curiosity as Barb and I neared the huge 43,000-acre Crab Orchard National Wildlife Refuge in southern Illinois. Other no less interesting questions also came to mind. Would we have any sense of being in the neighborhood of one of the highest maximum security federal prisons in the country? What is the impact of 20 industrial plants within the refuge boundaries, making everything from sporting goods to munitions, on the primary mission of the refuge? And not necessarily last, how good was the birding going to be here this early in the spring, and where would be the best places to look?

Some of the questions were answered at the refuge's Visitors Center just inside its northern boundary on State Route 148. The ranger on duty pulled out a detailed map of the refuge and began making Xs and drawing circles around the most promising spots to check out, while filling us in on the extraordinary amount of bird life in the area.

"The primary purpose of the refuge," the ranger told us, "is to provide a winter feeding and resting area for geese and ducks." Upwards of 200,000 Canada Geese spend the winter on the refuge's three lakes and adjoining marshes and fields. Joining them are 40,000 ducks. If that's not enough of a pulse quickening spectacle for even the most jaded birder, then maybe the sight of Golden and Bald eagles that also winter here will spike their heart beat.

Like condo time-sharing in Florida or Hawaii, waterfowl and humans have divided up use of the refuge. In the summer, the refuge is an immense human playground for boaters, campers, and fishermen. It is the most visited national wildlife refuge in the United States. Picnic areas, numerous boat ramps, swimming beaches, marinas, and fishing sites ring the refuge's two smaller lakes and the western edge of Crab Orchard Lake. When the weather turns cold and the summer people depart, ducks and geese arrive to take up residence for the winter.

But Crab Orchard is more than just waterfowl. The refuge's checklist records 245 species as regular visitors and another 29 accidentals — species that have only been seen once or twice and are far outside their usual range at Crab Orchard. Included in the checklist are 20 species of ducks, 9 hawks, 25 shorebirds, 9 flycatchers, 7 vireos and over 30 warbler species. Among the 103 species that nest here are Black- and Yellow-crowned night-heron, Warbling and Bell's vireo, Prothonotary Warblers, Yellow-breasted Chats and both Summer and Scarlet tanagers. The refuge produces large numbers of Eastern Bluebirds every year, and Wild Turkeys have become so numerous that they are trapped here for reintroduction to other areas of the Midwest. And this year, the ranger happily informed us, the refuge had three active Bald Eagle nests, one of which was easily viewable from behind the refuge headquarters on Road A-3.

Not bad for an area that in the 1930s was used-up and worn-out farmland. During the Depression, the government began buying up the tired farms and

"You could close your eyes, throw a dart at a map of the refuge and hit a good birding location."

LOCATION: Carterville, Illinois.

DIRECTIONS: At the intersection of I-57 and Highway 13 in Marion, Illinois drive west 4 miles on Highway 13 to State Route 148. Turn south on State Route 148 and drive 2 miles to the Visitors Center.

HOURS: The refuge is open year-round. Office hours are 8:00 a.m.-4:30 p.m. daily.

BEST TIMES: Fall and winter for waterfowl and Bald Eagles. Spring and early summer for shorebirds and songbirds.

BIRDING HIGHLIGHTS: Spectacular waterfowl concentrations in the fall and winter that build to 200,000 geese and 40,000 ducks. Bald Eagles and the occasional Golden Eagle spend the winter here and the refuge has supported at least two active Bald Eagle nests for several years. Spring and early summer brings large flights of songbirds. Hawk and owls also nest and frequent the refuge.

FOR MORE INFORMATION: Crab Orchard National Wildlife Refuge, P.O. Box J, Carterville, IL 62918. Phone: (618) 997-3344.

CRAB ORCHARD NATIONAL WILDLIFE REFUGE FIELD CHECKLIST

___Common Loon
___Pied-billed Grebe
___Horned Grebe
___Eared Grebe
___American White Pelican
___Double-crested Cormorant
___American Bittern
___Least Bittern
___Great Blue Heron
___Great Egret
___Little Blue Heron
___Cattle Egret
___Green Heron
___Black-crowned Night-heron
___Yellow-crowned Night-heron
___Greater White-fronted Goose
___Snow Goose
___Canada Goose
___Wood Duck
___Green-winged Teal
___American Black Duck
___Mallard
___Northern Pintail
___Blue-winged Teal
___Northern Shoveler
___Gadwall
___American Wigeon
___Canvasback
___Redhead
___Ring-necked Duck
___Greater Scaup
___Lesser Scaup
___Oldsquaw
___White-winged Scoter
___Common Goldeneye
___Bufflehead
___Hooded Merganser
___Common Merganser
___Red-breasted Merganser
___Ruddy Duck
___Black Vulture
___Turkey Vulture
___Osprey
___Bald Eagle
___Northern Harrier
___Sharp-shinned Hawk
___Cooper's Hawk
___Northern Goshawk
___Red-shouldered Hawk
___Broad-winged Hawk
___Rough-legged Hawk
___Golden Eagle
___American Kestrel
___Merlin
___Wild Turkey

___Northern Bobwhite
___Virginia Rail
___Sora
___Common Moorhen
___American Coot
___Black-bellied Plover
___Lesser Golden-plover
___Semipalmated Plover
___Killdeer
___American Avocet
___Greater Yellowlegs
___Lesser Yellowlegs
___Solitary Sandpiper
___Willet
___Spotted Sandpiper
___Upland Sandpiper
___Ruddy Turnstone
___Sanderling
___Semipalmated Sandpiper
___Least Sandpiper
___White-rumped Sandpiper
___Baird's Sandpiper
___Pectoral Sandpiper
___Dunlin
___Stilt Sandpiper
___Short-billed Dowitcher
___Long-billed Dowitcher
___Common Snipe
___American Woodcock
___Wilson's Phalarope
___Franklin's Gull
___Bonaparte's Gull
___Ring-billed Gull
___Herring Gull
___Caspian Tern
___Common Tern
___Forster's Tern
___Least Tern
___Black Tern
___Rock Dove
___Mourning Dove
___Black-billed Cuckoo
___Yellow-billed Cuckoo
___Eastern Screech-owl
___Great Horned Owl
___Barred Owl
___Short-eared Owl
___Common Nighthawk
___Chuck-will's-widow
___Whip-poor-will
___Chimney Swift
___Ruby-throated Hummingbird
___Belted Kingfisher
___Red-headed Woodpecker
___Red-bellied Woodpecker

___Yellow-bellied Sapsucker
___Downy Woodpecker
___Hairy Woodpecker
___Northern Flicker
___Pileated Woodpecker
___Olive-sided Flycatcher
___Eastern Wood-pewee
___Yellow-bellied Flycatcher
___Acadian Flycatcher
___Willow Flycatcher
___Least Flycatcher
___Eastern Phoebe
___Great Crested Flycatcher
___Eastern Kingbird
___Horned Lark
___Purple Martin
___Tree Swallow
___Northern Rough-winged Swallow
___Bank Swallow
___Cliff Swallow
___Barn Swallow
___Blue Jay
___American Crow
___Carolina Chickadee
___Tufted Titmouse
___Red-breasted Nuthatch
___White-breasted Nuthatch
___Brown Creeper
___Carolina Wren
___Bewick's Wren
___House Wren
___Winter Wren
___Sedge Wren
___Marsh Wren
___Golden-crowned Kinglet
___Ruby-crowned Kinglet
___Blue-gray Gnatcatcher
___Eastern Bluebird
___Veery
___Gray-cheeked Thrush
___Swainson's Thrush
___Hermit Thrush
___Wood Thrush
___American Robin
___Gray Catbird
___Northern Mockingbird
___Brown Thrasher
___American Pipit
___Cedar Waxwing
___Loggerhead Shrike
___European Starling
___White-eyed Vireo
___Bell's Vireo
___Solitary Vireo
___Yellow-throated Vireo

___Warbling Vireo
___Philadelphia Vireo
___Red-eyed Vireo
___Blue-winged Warbler
___Golden-winged Warbler
___Tennessee Warbler
___Orange-crowned Warbler
___Nashville Warbler
___Northern Parula
___Yellow Warbler
___Chestnut-sided Warbler
___Magnolia Warbler
___Cape May Warbler
___Black-throated Blue Warbler
___Yellow-rumped Warbler
___Black-throated Green Warbler
___Blackburnian Warbler
___Yellow-throated Warbler
___Pine Warbler
___Prairie Warbler
___Palm Warbler
___Bay-breasted Warbler
___Blackpoll Warbler
___Cerulean Warbler
___Black-and-white Warbler
___American Redstart
___Prothonotary Warbler
___Worm-eating Warbler
___Swainson's Warbler
___Ovenbird
___Northern Waterthrush
___Louisiana Waterthrush
___Kentucky Warbler
___Connecticut Warbler
___Mourning Warbler
___Common Yellowthroat
___Hooded Warbler
___Canada Warbler
___Yellow-breasted Chat
___Summer Tanager
___Scarlet Tanager
___Northern Cardinal
___Rose-breasted Grosbeak
___Blue Grosbeak
___Indigo Bunting
___Dickcissel
___Rufous-sided Towhee
___American Tree Sparrow
___Chipping Sparrow
___Field Sparrow
___Vesper Sparrow
___Lark Sparrow
___Savannah Sparrow
___Grasshopper Sparrow
___Henslow's Sparrow

___LeConte's Sparrow
___Fox Sparrow
___Song Sparrow
___Lincoln's Sparrow
___Swamp Sparrow
___White-throated Sparrow
___White-crowned Sparrow
___Dark-eyed Junco
___Lapland Longspur
___Bobolink
___Red-winged Blackbird
___Eastern Meadowlark
___Rusty Blackbird
___Common Grackle
___Brown-headed Cowbird
___Orchard Oriole
___Baltimore Oriole
___Purple Finch
___Pine Siskin
___American Goldfinch
___House Sparrow

Accidentals

___Red-throated Loon
___Red-necked Grebe
___Western Grebe
___Snowy Egret
___Tundra Swan
___Brant
___Black Scoter
___Surf Scoter
___Barrow's Goldeneye
___Mississippi Kite
___Swainson's Hawk
___Sandhill Crane
___Marbled Godwit
___Western Sandpiper
___Red-necked Phalarope
___Glaucous Gull
___Great Black-backed Gull
___Common Ground Dove
___Long-eared Owl
___Black-capped Chickadee
___Vermillion Flycatcher
___Scissor-tailed Flycatcher
___Bachman's Sparrow
___Clay-colored Sparrow
___Harris' Sparrow
___Snow Bunting
___Brewer's Blackbird
___Pine Grosbeak
___Red Crossbill

slowly turning the area into a recreational and wildlife haven. Over the next 20 years over 3 million trees were planted and three lakes created. Work was interrupted by World War II when more land bordering the future refuge was purchased by the government and turned into a huge ordnance complex. By the end of the war, 10,000 workers were turning out nearly 500,000 artillery shells and 70,000 bombs a month.

After the war, the land was turned over to the U.S. Fish and Wildlife Service, and Crab Orchard National Wildlife Refuge was created in 1947. But the plants still remain and today manufacture a wide variety of products. Many of them are smack in the middle of the refuge. If this seems a little incongruous to the average human, not so to the birds. They appear to be oblivious to the pockets of industry chugging out widgets behind the cyclone fences next to where they are taking the winter sun or mating and nesting in the summer.

Armed with a handful of brochures describing, in detail, the history of the refuge and all its attractions, a bird checklist, and the ranger's notations on a refuge map, we set out to find some birds. On the advice of the ranger, we concentrated our efforts on the periphery of the extensive sanctuary on the east side of the refuge.

The first spot to receive our attention was the short, paved nature trail that begins across the parking lot from the Visitors Center. The wheelchair accessible path winds through a quiet woodland with the trees rising out of a dense understory of shrubs. In several places the path brushes the edge of a lovely pond whose still waters captured and reflected the images of newly leafing trees and slow moving clouds overhead with an absolute clarity and poetic composition rivaling Ansell Adams' best work. A Mallard drake rested, in perfect stillness, in the middle of the pond, superimposed on nature's photograph as if transfixed by the sublime beauty. In a mood nearing reverence we observed Carolina Chickadees, a Brown Creeper, a White-breasted Nuthatch, and a Northern Mockingbird in the surrounding trees and shrubs while an unidentifiable thrush teased us with the briefest of glimpses as it rummaged around the forest floor well away from the trail. The ranger had informed us that just a few weeks later and this popular birdwatching area would be packed with warblers.

Back in the car we headed south on State Route 148 crossing the eastern arm of Crab Orchard Lake on a half-mile long causeway. Most of the geese had already decamped for the north, but a few late starters could be seen loafing on the man-made lake. Just south of the causeway an observation tower and a photographic blind can be reached from the same parking lot. Both are handicapped accessible. The observation tower overlooks a large meadow that dips westward into a wetlands area. The wetlands are so distant that a spotting scope is a necessity for searching out shorebirds from the observation deck, but a paved path leads to a large wooden blind perched out over the shallow water. From the blind, even binoculars are not needed to observe the shorebirds.

But at least a modicum of expertise, sadly lacking in this instance, is required to identify what you are seeing. I was pretty sure what was standing not 20 feet from the blind and waiting patiently for me to identify, were sandpipers, but what kind? After 15 frustrating minutes of increasingly crazed concentration that involved flipping back and forth from bird to *Peterson's* and then checking the refuge's bird list, to see what could possibly be eliminated, I arrived at the startling conclusion that Crab Orchard was the home to a, hitherto, unknown species of shorebird that I proudly named the Pectoral-least-upland-solitary-

"Like condo time-sharing in Florida or Hawaii, waterfowl and humans have divided up use of the refuge."

"A Swainson's Thrush perched on a fallen log long enough for me to spot its eye-ring."

psychosis-inducing Sandpiper.

Fortunately, I lacked the courage to stop at the Visitors Center and tell the ranger of my new discovery as we drove back up State Route 148 to where A-3 Road heads west along the northern edge of the refuge. The ranger said that A-3 Road is a sure bet for Eastern Bluebirds, and we saw several from the car. After an hour of birding by car, we stopped to hike the Chamnestown Trail on A-3 Road, about a half-mile west of the intersection of State Route 148. The self-guided, pine-needle-soft trail cuts through a stand of evergreens before leading to open meadows and fields. A Northern Flicker greeted us at the trail head and a Downy Woodpecker was gently tapping a tree not 50 feet into the hike. Robins took turns walking point for us on the trail and a Swainson's Thrush perched on a fallen log long enough for me to spot its eye-ring.

Crab Orchard National Wildlife Refuge is simply too big to fully explore in even a full day. There are over 20 miles of good roads circling or, in the case of State Route 148, bisecting the sanctuary. All offer good birding opportunities. Numerous foot trails lead birders through a variety of habitats and penetrate the edge of the wilderness areas. At Crab Orchard you could close your eyes, throw a dart at a map of the refuge and hit a good birding location.

INDIANA and KENTUCKY

THE MIGRANT TRAP, 33

INDIANA DUNES STATE PARK, 36

JASPER-PULASKI
FISH AND WILDLIFE AREA, 39

SHADES STATE PARK, 41

MUSCATATUCK
NATIONAL WILDLIFE AREA, 44

FALLS OF THE OHIO STATE PARK, 47

HOVEY LAKE WILDLIFE AREA AND
TWIN SWAMPS NATURE PRESERVE, 51

JOHN JAMES AUDUBON
STATE PARK, 54

Migrant Trap

At first glance it's all but impossible to image this forlorn scrap of land edging the southern shore of Lake Michigan near the Indiana/Illinois border as one of the great birding sites in the Midwest. Ken Brock of Indiana University Northwest, the acknowledged expert on the area, admits the "Migrant Trap would certainly not receive any landscaping awards," but adds, "it is Indiana's premier passerine birding site; no other location regularly attracts the concentration of migrants found in the Trap."

The Migrant Trap is a 16-acre pocket of landfill covered by cottonwoods, long-stemmed grass and a scattering of low shrubs. For years the area was an illegal dumping ground for area residents and the only way to stretch the word "pretty" to cover the Trap was to compare it to the surrounding vista of heavy industry and urban decay. Even the broad expanse of Lake Michigan, reaching to the north as far as the eye can see, doesn't do much to ameliorate the scenic drudgery. The ironic truth is man has unwittingly conspired with nature and geography at the Migrant Trap (the name was bestowed on the area by local birders) to create an area that draws a multitude of songbirds during spring and fall migration and an impressive number of rarities.

The Migrant Trap is a perfect example of the three most important rules in real estate: location, location, location. The postage stamp-sized piece of real estate is strategically located at the southern end of Lake Michigan, and northbound birds looking for a place to rest and feed, before either heading out over the lake or following the shoreline north, funnel into the Migrant Trap in April, May, and June. The funneling effect is even greater in the fall as birds fly south along the lakeshore, or cross the open water of the great lake and look for a landfall where they can rest and feed.

You can't really appreciate the significance of this small, scrubby strip of cottonwoods bordering Lake Michigan, or understand how man has magnified its importance to migrating songbirds, until you stand on the property and take a look around. From the highest point of the Migrant Trap, I looked west and found nothing but an endless line of power plants and heavy industries smudging the skyline and perfuming the air. To the north, Lake Michigan filled the eye and to the south the Migrant Trap was bordered by acres of asphalt, small industries, businesses and the close-packed homes of Hammond. To the east, a new municipal marina brightened the landscape and the Empress, a floating casino, bordered a new building rising on the lakeshore east of the marina. For songbirds the Migrant Trap is the human equivalent of a Motel 6 and Denny's restaurant smack-dab in the middle of Death Valley.

The fecundity of the Migrant Trap during spring and fall migration is evidenced almost daily on Indiana's Rare Bird Alert. In a not-unusual-sighting, hundreds of sparrows were seen there on October 6, 1995 and in addition to the hundred-plus White-throated Sparrows, LeConte's, Grasshopper, Chipping, Field, Swamp, Fox, Savannah, Song, and Lincoln's sparrows plus Dark-eyed Juncos were also observed. On the same day ten species of warblers, a Bobolink and a Black-billed Cuckoo were also seen. A day in September that year saw Yellow-bellied and Least flycatchers, Red-breasted Nuthatches, Gray-cheeked and Swainson's thrushes, Northern Parula, Cape May, Connecticut, Mourning, Blackpoll, and

"On any given day in the spring and fall, the Migrant Trap is the best 16-acres of birding in the Midwest."

LOCATION: Hammond, Indiana.

DIRECTIONS: From the corner of Calumet Avenue and U.S. 12/20 in Hammond, turn west on U.S. 12/20 and drive approximately a quarter-mile to the sign for Empress Casino and Marina. Turn left (south) and follow the road as it circles around and over an overpass. Immediately after the overpass make a hard right onto a frontage road and follow it to the Casino parking lot. Park at the east end of the parking lot where the sanctuary is accessible. Or, from I-90 also known as the Chicago Skyway, exit on to Indianapolis Blvd, (U.S. 12/20) and drive east to the entrance to the Casino parking lot. Or from nearly any major road in the Hammond area follow signs to the Empress Casino.

HOURS: Open all year.

BEST TIMES: April through June, and August through early October.

BIRDING HIGHLIGHTS: Best spot in the state for viewing migrating songbirds. In addition to the incredible variety and numbers of songbirds the area usually yields a good assortment of shorebirds.

"The ironic truth is man has unwittingly conspired with nature and geography to create an area that draws a multitude of songbirds during spring and fall migration and an impressive number of rarities."

14 other species of warblers funneling into the trap. Another typical fall birding day found Marsh, Sedge and Winter wrens, a Yellow-crowned Night-heron, 2 Short-eared Owls, 5 Solitary Vireo, and 12 species of warblers including Orange-crowned, Wilson's, Black-throated Blue, and an Ovenbird, plus an interesting assortment of other species. The single day record for the most warblers species in the Migrant Trap occurred in May when 25 were tallied. The beach area of the Trap also attracts shore- and marsh birds with Red Knots, Soras, rails and American Woodcocks being tallied, sometimes in large numbers.

If the area is great for birds, it was not so accommodating, until lately, for birdwatchers. Up until the summer of 1996, the land was owned by the Northern Indiana Public Service Company and in the fall of 1995, after a string of malicious fires, the area was closed to the public and the company declared all trespassers subject to arrest. I arrived the next May with the hope that the no trespassing ban would soon be lifted, and at the very least I could walk up to the fence and stare through it with the same longing with which I press my cholesterol-flushed face against the windows of northern Michigan fudge shops. But road construction, associated with improving access and creating parking for a floating casino, made it impossible to even get near the site. The only bird I saw even near the Trap — a dead Yellow-rumped Warbler in the marina parking lot — epitomized the trip.

Ah, but how things can change in just a few months. Northern Indiana Public Service Company gave the Migrant Trap to the City of Hammond with deed restrictions that established the area as a bird sanctuary. The change in ownership also saw an official name bestowed on the area, The Hammond Lakefront Park and Sanctuary. The city is working with Ken Brock, the Indiana Department of Natural Resources, and other individuals and agencies to develop a long-range plan that includes new landscaping, fencing, and nature trails. And, figure the odds on this, the new casino (The Empress) has greatly facilitated getting to and on the Migrant Trap. The parking lot for the Empress borders the south side of the Migrant Trap, and all you have to do is follow signs, from practically any place in the Midwest, to the Empress and when you get to the large, busy casino parking lot, just drive to the eastern end of the pavement where there is access to the Migrant Trap.

After years of neglect and access that was at best difficult, the Migrant Trap's future, for both birds and birdwatchers, is especially bright. The rest of the birding world will soon discover what a relatively few, persistent area birders have known for years: that on any given day, in the spring and fall, the Migrant Trap is the best 16-acres of birding in the Midwest.

MIGRANT TRAP FIELD CHECKLIST

This list was compiled by Ken Brock
and includes birds seen on adjacent beaches and nearby Lake Michigan.

___ Common Loon
___ Pied-billed Grebe
___ Horned Grebe
___ Eared Grebe
___ Double-crested Cormorant
___ American Bittern
___ Least Bittern
___ Great Blue Heron
___ Great Egret
___ Green Heron
___ Black-crowned Night-heron
___ Yellow-crowned Night-heron
___ Tundra Swan
___ Mute Swan
___ Canada Goose
___ Wood Duck
___ Green-winged Teal
___ American Black Duck
___ Mallard
___ Northern Pintail
___ Blue-winged Teal
___ Northern Shoveler
___ Gadwall
___ Canvasback
___ Redhead
___ Ring-necked Duck
___ Greater Scaup
___ Lesser Scaup
___ King Eider
___ Harlequin Duck
___ Oldsquaw
___ Black Scoter
___ Surf Scoter
___ White-winged Scoter
___ Common Goldeneye
___ Bufflehead
___ Hooded Merganser
___ Common Merganser
___ Red-breasted Merganser
___ Ruddy Duck
___ Turkey Vulture
___ Osprey
___ Northern Harrier
___ Sharp-shinned Hawk
___ Cooper's Hawk
___ Northern Goshawk
___ Red-shouldered Hawk
___ Red-tailed Hawk
___ Rough-legged Hawk

___ American Kestrel
___ Merlin
___ Peregrine Falcon
___ Ring-necked Pheasant
___ Ruffed Grouse
___ Virginia Rail
___ Sora
___ American Coot
___ Sandhill Crane
___ Black-bellied Plover
___ Semipalmated Plover
___ Piping Plover
___ Killdeer
___ Greater Yellowlegs
___ Lesser Yellowlegs
___ Willet
___ Spotted Sandpiper
___ Whimbrel
___ Ruddy Turnstone
___ Redknot
___ Sanderling
___ Semipalmated Sandpiper
___ Least Sandpiper
___ Baird's Sandpiper
___ Pectoral Sandpiper
___ Purple Sandpiper
___ Dunlin
___ Short-billed Dowitcher
___ American Woodcock
___ Pomarine Jaeger
___ Parasitic Jaeger
___ Laughing Gull
___ Bonaparte's Gull
___ Ring-billed Gull
___ Herring Gull
___ Thayer's Gull
___ Lesser Black-backed Gull
___ Kelp Gull
___ Glaucous Gull
___ Greater Black-backed Gull
___ Caspian Tern
___ Common Tern
___ Forster's Tern
___ Black Tern
___ Rock Dove
___ Mourning Dove
___ Black-billed Cuckoo
___ Yellow-billed Cuckoo
___ Barn Owl

___ Great Horned Owl
___ Snowy Owl
___ Burrowing Owl
___ Long-eared Owl
___ Short-eared Owl
___ Common Nighthawk
___ Whip-poor-will
___ Chimney Swift
___ Ruby-throated Hummingbird
___ Belted Kingfisher
___ Red-headed Woodpecker
___ Red-bellied Woodpecker
___ Yellow-bellied Sapsucker
___ Downy Woodpecker
___ Hairy Woodpecker
___ Northern Flicker
___ Olive-sided Flycatcher
___ Eastern-wood Pewee
___ Yellow-bellied Flycatcher
___ Alder Flycatcher
___ Willow Flycatcher
___ Least Flycatcher
___ Eastern Phoebe
___ Great Crested Flycatcher
___ Eastern Kingbird
___ Horned Lark
___ Purple Martin
___ Tree Swallow
___ Northern Rough-winged Swallow
___ Bank Swallow
___ Cliff Swallow
___ Barn Swallow
___ Blue Jay
___ American Crow
___ Black-capped Chickadee
___ Tufted Titmouse
___ Red-breasted Nuthatch
___ White-breasted Nuthatch
___ Brown Creeper
___ Bewick's Wren
___ Carolina Wren
___ Winter Wren
___ Sedge Wren
___ Marsh Wren
___ Golden-crowned Kinglet
___ Ruby-crowned Kinglet
___ Blue-gray Gnatcatcher
___ Eastern Bluebird
___ Veery

___ Gray-cheeked Thrush
___ Swainson's Thrush
___ Hermit Thrush
___ Wood Thrush
___ American Robin
___ Gray Catbird
___ Northern Mockingbird
___ Brown Thrasher
___ American Pipit
___ Cedar Waxwing
___ Northern Shrike
___ Loggerhead Shrike
___ Eurasian Starling
___ White-eyed Vireo
___ Solitary Vireo
___ Yellow-throated Vireo
___ Warbling Vireo
___ Philadelphia Vireo
___ Red-eyed Vireo
___ Blue-winged Warbler
___ Golden-winged Warbler
___ Tennessee Warbler
___ Orange-crowned Warbler
___ Nashville Warbler
___ Northern Parula
___ Yellow Warbler
___ Chestnut-sided Warbler
___ Magnolia Warbler
___ Cape May Warbler
___ Black-throated Blue Warbler
___ Yellow-rumped Warbler
___ Black-throated Green Warbler
___ Blackburnian Warbler
___ Pine Warbler
___ Prairie Warbler
___ Palm Warbler
___ Bay-breasted Warbler
___ Blackpoll Warbler
___ Cerulean Warbler
___ Black-and-white Warbler
___ American Redstart
___ Prothonotary Warbler
___ Worm-eating Warbler
___ Ovenbird
___ Northern Waterthrush
___ Louisiana Waterthrush
___ Kentucky Warbler
___ Connecticut Warbler
___ Mourning Warbler

___ Common Yellowthroat
___ Hooded Warbler
___ Wilson's Warbler
___ Canada Warbler
___ Yellow-breasted Chat
___ Summer Tanager
___ Scarlet Tanager
___ Northern Cardinal
___ Rose-breasted Grosbeak
___ Indigo Bunting
___ Rufous-sided Towhee
___ American Tree Sparrow
___ Chipping Sparrow
___ Clay-colored Sparrow
___ Field Sparrow
___ Vesper Sparrow
___ Lark Sparrow
___ Savannah Sparrow
___ Grasshopper Sparrow
___ Henslow's Sparrow
___ LeConte's Sparrow
___ Sharp-tailed Sparrow
___ Fox Sparrow
___ Song Sparrow
___ Lincoln's Sparrow
___ Swamp Sparrow
___ White-throated Sparrow
___ White-crowned Sparrow
___ Harris' Sparrow
___ Dark-eyed Junco
___ Lapland Longspur
___ Snow Bunting
___ Bobolink
___ Red-winged Blackbird
___ Eastern Meadowlark
___ Rusty Blackbird
___ Common Grackle
___ Brown-headed Cowbird
___ Orchard Oriole
___ Baltimore Oriole
___ Purple Finch
___ House Finch
___ Common Redpoll
___ Pine Siskin
___ American Goldfinch
___ Evening Grosbeak
___ House Sparrow

Indiana Dunes State Park

"Every warbler species seen in the dune country of northern Indiana has been recorded within the park."

LOCATION: Chesterton, Indiana.

DIRECTIONS: From the intersection of I-94 and Indiana 49, drive 3 miles north on Indiana 49 to the park entrance. There is a small daily entrance fee.

HOURS: Open all year

BEST TIMES: Good year-round birding and spectacular birding in the last week of April and first two weeks of May. Fall can bring good birding for warblers, waterfowl, and shorebirds.

BIRDING HIGHLIGHTS: Indiana Dunes State Park is the crème de la crème of birding spots within a region known as the best birding area in the state. Fantastic birding during spring migration for songbirds, and very good birding for a wide variety of species throughout the rest of the year.

FOR MORE INFORMATION: Indiana Dunes State Park, 1600 N. 25E., Chesterton, IN 46304. Phone: (219) 926-1952.

My walk along the northern edge of the marsh at the Indiana Dunes State Park was barely progressing at the rate of a crawl. The state park is widely reputed to be one of the best birding spots in an area known for great birding, and there was so much bird activity along the trail suggested by the volunteer at the Nature Center that a snail could have out distanced me in the first half-hour. I had ticked off several warblers, a Wood Thrush, White-breasted and Red-breasted nuthatches, and a dozen other species within the first 15 minutes. The weight of birds lining the trail was taking an imperceptible toll on my forward motion. The final feather that brought me to a complete halt was a warbler wearing a yarmulke.

I had just spotted a Cape May Warbler and was making a note of it in my field book as I rounded a bend in the trail skirting a finger-like extension of the marsh. There flitting among the thickets lining the open water was a half-ounce ball of energy — soft yellow on the breast and belly, a warm olive-green on the back, with a skull cap perched atop a yellow face — my first Wilson's Warbler in several years. I stopped and watched the bird for at least ten minutes before dragging myself away in search of further treasures. An hour later, and a bare mile further along the trail at a platform overlooking the marsh, I met a couple who were experiencing problems similar to mine. They said they had started on the south side of the marsh and barely made three miles in three hours because of the birds calling for their attention. Their arms were weary from lifting their binoculars, and they fervently wished the birds would leave them alone long enough to get back to their car and grab a drink. Their parting advice was to stay well away from the trail on the south side of the marsh. They said I could easily OD on warblers over there.

The dune country of Indiana is one the richest birding areas in the state. More than 300 species have been reported in the 40-mile stretch of Indiana's Lake Michigan shoreline and for all around great birding on the state's northern border, Indiana Dunes State Park is regarded as the crème de la crème. Admittedly some of the park's reputation comes by default. Heavy industry and dense population centers like Gary chew up much of the birding habitat and make public access difficult. Even the Indiana Dunes National Lakeshore to the east of the state park has seen much of its original habitat disturbed. The state park, on the other hand, not only contains the largest expanse of untouched dunes in the state; but, its upland forests, swamps, marshes, dunes, and broad sandy beaches shelter the most diverse assemblage of flora and fauna in the Midwest.

The park is a mixing ground for both southern and northern species and attracts a fair share of rarities. Every warbler species seen in the dune country of northern Indiana has been recorded within the park. If the park simply bursts with birds during spring and fall migration, Wendy Smith, the naturalist for the state park, is quick to point out that birding is a four-season attraction here. More than 70 species are regularly tallied in and around the park during the Christmas Bird Count, and nesting species such as Ovenbirds, Cerulean, Hooded, and Blue-winged warblers keep things interesting in the summer. Fall can not only bring a return of warblers and waterfowl, but good numbers and varieties of shorebirds are possible.

The park's barrier dunes and lakeshore are good places to watch for gulls, waterfowl out on the lake and soaring birds of prey. Hawk migration in the spring can be heavy throughout the Indiana dunes area. But during spring migration, the places to bird are the trails encircling the large marsh lying to the east of the park's Nature Center. To the north of the marsh, Trail #10 etches a fine line between the marsh and wetlands on one side and the steeply rising, wooded dunes on the other. At roughly the two-mile mark on Trail #10, Trail #2 cuts off to the right and crosses the marsh on a long boardwalk. After crossing the marsh, Trail #2 turns to the west and eventually returns to the Nature Center via Trail #8. Hikers wishing to walk the south side first will have to take Trail #8 south from the Nature Center for a quarter-mile before it connects with Trail #2. A detailed map of the trail system is available at the Nature Center, and birders will usually have their appetite whetted by viewing all the bird activity around the Center's feeders. In the few minutes I stood at the large windows overlooking the feeding stations, I saw several Downy Woodpeckers, a dozen Tufted Titmice, a White-crowned Sparrow, a gang of raucous Blue Jays, and a single hummingbird. In the winter, the feeding stations at the Nature Center should provide hours of interesting and comfortable birding.

After pulling myself away from the Wilson's Warbler, I continued down the trail in stops and starts. Black-and-white Warblers suckered me into stopping a dozen times as they worked trees just far enough away that I couldn't identify them without getting binoculars up and focused — I'm hopeless at identifying birds by their calls. I tell my smug friends who have good ears, and even better imaginations when it comes to bird calls, that I go out to see birds, not to listen to them. I wish one of them would have been with me at the park.

A Yellow-bellied Sapsucker and a Brown Creeper broke up the monotony of the Black-and-white Warblers, and then I hit gold again with a Tennessee Warbler, an American Redstart, and a Chestnut-sided Warbler within 100 yards of each other. And just before I reached the observation platform overlooking the marsh, I nearly stumbled over an Ovenbird on the edge of the trail. At the observation platform I listened to the horror story of the couple plagued by warblers on the south side of the marsh while spotting a Great Egret, several Great Blue Heron, and a Green Heron strung along the edge of the marsh. This looked like excellent bittern and rail habitat, but a half-hour of searching by the three of us failed to turn up a single one.

After nearly two hours of walking, I finally reached Trail #2 and the boardwalk crossing the marsh. By that time I had added Blackburnian, Common Yellowthroat, Canada, and Bay-breasted warblers and a dozen other species to the day's tally, but nothing had prepared me for what I met 100 yards out on the boardwalk. I ran into a veritable swarm of Yellow-rumped Warblers. They were simply everywhere and in constant motion, darting from tree to tree. Without exaggerating, there must have been over 30 within a radius of 25 yards. I'd never seen anything like it, and I suddenly started taking seriously the warnings of the couple who said they had spent over three hours walking the 3 miles of trail edging the south side of the marsh. Already long overdue for lunch, I beat a well ordered retreat back down the trail to the Nature Center. Indiana Dunes State Park is on the top of my list for a longer and more leisurely visit in early May in the near future.

"Black-and-white Warblers suckered me into stopping a dozen times as they worked trees just far enough away that I couldn't identify them without getting binoculars up and focused."

INDIANA DUNES STATE PARK FIELD CHECKLIST

The following checklist represents the area in and around the state park.

___ Common Loon	___ Rough-legged Hawk	___ Laughing Gull	___ White-breasted Nuthatch	___ Louisiana Waterthrush
___ Red-throated Loon	___ Golden Eagle	___ Franklin's Gull	___ Red-breasted Nuthatch	___ Kentucky Warbler
___ Red-necked Grebe	___ Bald Eagle	___ Bonaparte's Gull	___ Brown Creeper	___ Connecticut Warbler
___ Horned Grebe	___ Northern Harrier	___ Little Gull	___ House Wren	___ Mourning Warbler
___ Eared Grebe	___ Osprey	___ Black-legged Kittiwake	___ Winter Wren	___ Common Yellowthroat
___ Western Grebe	___ Peregrine Falcon	___ Sabine's Gull	___ Sedge Wren	___ Yellow-breasted Chat
___ Pied-billed Grebe	___ Merlin	___ Forsters' Tern	___ Northern Mockingbird	___ Hooded Warbler
___ Double-crested Cormorant	___ American Kestrel	___ Common Tern	___ Gray Catbird	___ Wilson's Warbler
___ Great Blue Heron	___ Northern Bobwhite	___ Caspian Tern	___ Brown Thrasher	___ Canada Warbler
___ Green Heron	___ Ring-necked Pheasant	___ Black Tern	___ American Robin	___ American Redstart
___ Little Blue Heron	___ Sandhill Crane	___ Rock Dove	___ Wood Thrush	___ House Sparrow
___ Cattle Egret	___ King Rail	___ Mourning Dove	___ Hermit Thrush	___ Bobolink
___ Great Egret	___ Virginia Rail	___ Yellow-billed Cuckoo	___ Swainson's Thrush	___ Eastern Meadowlark
___ Black-crowned Night-heron	___ Sora	___ Black-billed Cuckoo	___ Gray-cheeked Thrush	___ Western Meadowlark
___ Yellow-crowned Night-heron	___ Yellow Rail	___ Eastern Screech-owl	___ Veery	___ Yellow-headed Blackbird
___ Least Bittern	___ Common Gallinule	___ Great Horned Owl	___ Eastern Bluebird	___ Red-winged Blackbird
___ American Bittern	___ American Coot	___ Snowy Owl	___ Blue-gray Gnatcatcher	___ Orchard Oriole
___ Mute Swan	___ American Avocet	___ Barred Owl	___ Golden-crowned Kinglet	___ Baltimore Oriole
___ Tundra Swan	___ Piping Plover	___ Long-eared Owl	___ Ruby-crowned Kinglet	___ Rusty Blackbird
___ Canada Goose	___ Semipalmated Plover	___ Short-eared Owl	___ American Pipit	___ Brewer's Blackbird
___ Brant	___ Killdeer	___ Northern Saw-whet Owl	___ Cedar Waxwing	___ Common Grackle
___ Snow Goose	___ Lesser Golden-plover	___ Whip-poor-will	___ Northern Shrike	___ Brown-headed Cowbird
___ Mallard	___ Black-bellied Plover	___ Common Nighthawk	___ European Starling	___ Scarlet Tanager
___ American Black Duck	___ Marbled Godwit	___ Chimney Swift	___ White-eyed Vireo	___ Northern Cardinal
___ Gadwall	___ Whimbrel	___ Ruby-throated Hummingbird	___ Yellow-throated Vireo	___ Rose-breasted Grosbeak
___ Northern Pintail	___ Ruddy Turnstone	___ Belted Kingfisher	___ Solitary Vireo	___ Indigo Bunting
___ Green-winged Teal	___ American Woodcock	___ Northern Flicker	___ Red-eyed Vireo	___ Dickcissel
___ Blue-winged Teal	___ Common Snipe	___ Red-bellied Woodpecker	___ Philadelphia Vireo	___ Evening Grosbeak
___ American Wigeon	___ Upland Sandpiper	___ Red-headed Woodpecker	___ Warbling Vireo	___ Purple Finch
___ Northern Shoveler	___ Spotted Sandpiper	___ Yellow-bellied Sapsucker	___ Black-and-white Warbler	___ Pine Grosbeak
___ Wood Duck	___ Solitary Sandpiper	___ Hairy Woodpecker	___ Prothonotary Warbler	___ American Goldfinch
___ Redhead	___ Willet	___ Downy Woodpecker	___ Worm-eating Warbler	___ Red Crossbill
___ Ring-necked Duck	___ Greater Yellowlegs	___ Eastern Kingbird	___ Golden-winged Warbler	___ White-winged Crossbill
___ Canvasback	___ Lesser Yellowlegs	___ Great Crested Flycatcher	___ Blue-winged Warbler	___ Rufous-sided Towhee
___ Greater Scaup	___ Red Knot	___ Eastern Phoebe	___ Tennessee Warbler	___ Savannah Sparrow
___ Lesser Scaup	___ Purple Sandpiper	___ Yellow-bellied Flycatcher	___ Orange-crowned Warbler	___ LeConte's Sparrow
___ Common Goldeneye	___ Pectoral Sandpiper	___ Acadian Flycatcher	___ Nashville Warbler	___ Vesper Sparrow
___ Bufflehead	___ Baird's Sandpiper	___ Alder Flycatcher	___ Northern Parula	___ Dark-eyed Junco
___ Oldsquaw	___ Least Sandpiper	___ Willow Flycatcher	___ Yellow Warbler	___ American Tree Sparrow
___ Harlequin Duck	___ Dunlin	___ Least Flycatcher	___ Magnolia Warbler	___ Chipping Sparrow
___ White-winged Scoter	___ Short-billed Dowitcher	___ Olive-sided Flycatcher	___ Cape May Warbler	___ Field Sparrow
___ Surf Scoter	___ Semipalmated Sandpiper	___ Eastern Wood-pewee	___ Black-throated Blue Warbler	___ Harris' Sparrow
___ Black Scoter	___ Sanderling	___ Horned Lark	___ Yellow-rumped Warbler	___ White-crowned Sparrow
___ Ruddy Duck	___ Buff-breasted Sandpiper	___ Tree Swallow	___ Black-throated Green Warbler	___ White-throated Sparrow
___ Hooded Merganser	___ Red Phalarope	___ Bank Swallow	___ Cerulean Warbler	___ Fox Sparrow
___ Common Merganser	___ Wilson's Phalarope	___ Northern Rough-winged Swallow	___ Blackburnian Warbler	___ Lincoln's Sparrow
___ Red-breasted Merganser	___ Parasitic Jaeger	___ Barn Swallow	___ Chestnut-sided Warbler	___ Swamp Sparrow
___ Turkey Vulture	___ Pomarine Jaeger	___ Cliff Swallow	___ Bay-breasted Warbler	___ Song Sparrow
___ Sharp-shinned Hawk	___ Glaucous Gull	___ Purple Martin	___ Blackpoll Warbler	___ Lapland Longspur
___ Cooper's Hawk	___ Greater Black-backed Gull	___ Blue Jay	___ Prairie Warbler	___ Snow Bunting
___ Red-tailed Hawk	___ Herring Gull	___ Common Crow	___ Palm Warbler	
___ Red-shouldered Hawk	___ Thayer's Gull	___ Black-capped Chickadee	___ Ovenbird	
___ Broad-winged Hawk	___ Ring-billed Gull	___ Tufted Titmouse	___ Northern Waterthrush	

Jasper-Pulaski State Fish and Wildlife Area

The sky was literally being drained of Sandhill Cranes. The great birds, in groups of half-dozen to over 50, were arriving over the large field, at a uniform altitude of about 200 feet, from every point of the compass and when they hit the invisible spot marking the drain hole every single crane broke to the right in an ever-tightening circle and settled to the ground. When two, three, or more groups all arrived at the spot simultaneously, the cranes effortlessly intermingled in a brilliant piece of improvised choreography and emptied onto the field. At times, the descending birds were so thick they clearly formed the outline of a funnel with the small end touching the earth.

Not to quibble, but the cranes need to be told to descend in a counter-clockwise circle in order to make the sink-draining illusion completely authentic. In all fairness the 50 or so spectators that I joined at the observation area of the Jasper-Pulaski State Fish and Wildlife Area were in no way upset with this small inconsistency. We were all held spellbound by this annual autumn spectacle at Jasper-Pulaski. In late October and early November, the state wildlife area witnesses the largest concentration of Sandhill Cranes east of the Mississippi with the number of birds estimated at between 12,000 and 20,000. Some wildlife experts believe nearly every Sandhill Crane east of the Mississippi passes through Jasper-Pulaski on their way to wintering grounds in Georgia and Florida. Spring also brings large numbers of the huge birds — they stand 3.5 feet tall and have wing spans approaching 7 feet — to Jasper-Pulaski but in nowhere near the numbers reached in the fall.

In either spring or fall, the cranes can easily be viewed from an observation area and tower overlooking the single large field the birds roost in every night they're in the area. The best viewing times are at dawn, when the birds decamp the field and spread out over the neighboring farm land to feed, or late afternoon when they begin returning and reconvene their annual convention.

Barb and I arrived about four o'clock in the afternoon, and while Barb stayed in the parking lot in a warm car, I started off on the quarter-mile trail to the observation area. It was the first weekend in November and the greeting calls of arriving cranes — sounding like Mourning Doves on steroids — amplified by the cold, clear air, sent chills through the down coat, wool sweater, and flannel shirt before hitting my spine and traveling south. On the walk to the observation area, flights of cranes constantly passed overhead but it wasn't until arriving at the edge of the roosting field that the impact of one of the Midwest's greatest natural phenomena was fully felt.

For the first 10 minutes after reaching the base of the observation tower, I simply stood transfixed by the sight of hundreds of elegant birds zeroing in on the middle of the field from every direction. As the flights drained from the sky they joined hundreds, if not thousands, of birds gathered in a compact mass that through the naked eye looked like a living carpet stretching for several hundred yards across the field. Through binoculars the light brown, undulating berber became individual cranes standing shoulder-to-shoulder. Binoculars also revealed

"Some experts believe nearly every Sandhill Crane east of the Mississippi passes through Jasper-Pulaski on their way to wintering grounds."

LOCATION: Medaryville, Indiana.

DIRECTIONS: From the intersection of U.S. 421 and Indiana 8 travel south on U.S. 421 about 10 miles to Indiana 143. Turn right (west) and go 1.5 miles to County Road 1650 W and turn right (north) and drive less than a quarter-mile to the observation area parking lot.

HOURS: Open all year.

BEST TIMES: Late October to early November.

BIRDING HIGHLIGHTS: The largest concentration of Sandhill Cranes east of the Mississippi, often more than 12,000 in one field.

FOR MORE INFORMATION: Jasper-Pulaski State Fish and Wildlife Area, RR #1, Box 216 Medaryville, IN 47957. Phone: (219) 843-4841.

the cause of the undulating effect and reinforced the impression of the sky being drained of cranes. The downspout through which the birds landed was centered over the mass of birds already on the ground. When birds landed in this compact assemblage, they sent out ripples as the birds moved out from the center to make room for the new arrivals. There was also a splash effect when cranes nearest the landing spot hopped in the air as they moved out of the way and when they landed sending other birds hopping out of their way.

The crowd watched in a hushed awe. Although most of us glanced toward the center of the field with some regularity, and a few in the crowd had spotting scopes aimed out in the field, most of our attention was riveted overhead as we watched the endless flow of cranes make for the top of the funnel. You could, and I'm sure many did, stand there for over an hour and still not get over the sense of wonderment the birds inspired. I don't know how long I stood there with my eyes glued to the sky, but when I finally dragged myself away, the back of my head seemed to have become permanently attached to my shoulders. The wildlife area could make a bundle from a chiropractic concession.

By the time I made it back to the parking lot, the cramps in my neck had lessened to the point where I was no longer doing a poor imitation of Alfred Hitchcock. But even with my head more-or-less back to its normal position I couldn't find the car. In my absence Barb had moved to the end of the lot, parked the car facing the roosting field, and with other motorists, was enjoying the show from a warmer, if far less intimate, viewing area.

The 8,022-acre wildlife area with its vast wetlands and upland game habitats and miles of hiking trails and two-tracks closed to vehicular traffic offers a wealth of good birding, but all of that is overshadowed by the cranes which are the chief draw. The wildlife area also contains a 51-site primitive campground nestled in deep woods near the headquarters building.

SANDHILL CRANE

Shades State Park / Pine Hills Nature Preserve

I t was the seductively photogenic Deer's Mill Covered Bridge, on the northern edge of Shades State Park, that pulled us off the road and into the adjacent parking lot, but it was the bird life that kept us rooted to the spot for the next 45 minutes. The stately, old bridge, closed to all but foot traffic, wears its age with a time-worn grace and would draw attention no matter where it was located. But it crosses Sugar Creek, one of the most beautiful streams in the state. Wooded bluffs rise on either side of the timbered span, and the youthfully exuberant water rushing under the roadbed makes for a setting that cannot be ignored. I pulled off, grabbed a camera, jumped out of the car, took a couple of steps, and immediately returned to trade in the camera for binoculars and the bird book.

Birds seemed to be everywhere. Northern Rough-winged Swallows were launching themselves from perches beneath the bridge and making passes over the stream. Hairy and Downy woodpeckers occupied adjoining trees while Carolina Chickadees, an Eastern Wood-pewee, and a pair of raucous Blue Jays worked the same patch of shrubs next to the parking lot. Nearer the water, several Yellow-rumped Warblers and a lone Yellow Warbler flitted in and out of a stream-side thicket. The spot yielded a dozen different species including additional warblers, a couple of thrushes and several members of the sparrow family, all within a half-hour.

Not bad, but still a humbling experience when compared to local birder Alan Bruner's tally on the southern edge of the park later the same year. From September 5 through 7, 1995, birding just the park road from the entrance off County Road 800S to the CCC Pond, about a half-mile to the north, Mr. Bruner counted 200 warblers representing 25 species, plus all 7 species of Indiana vireos.

The 3,000-acre park is nestled in some of the most rugged and spectacularly scenic landscape in central Indiana; and while the physical beauty lures hikers, campers, and canoeists, birds, especially warblers, draw birdwatchers. Bruner has conducted a two-year breeding bird census within the park and is working on a park checklist. He has observed 197 bird species in the park including 36 warbler species. Of the 92 species nesting in the park, 17 are warblers. Magnolia Warblers were discovered nesting here in the summer of 1995 — a state first — and from the same spot nine other warbler species could be heard including Hooded, Worm-eating, Cerulean, and Northern Parula. It's little wonder that Shades is considered one of the great spots in Indiana for warbler viewing and attracts birders from coast-to-coast.

Spring and fall migrations bring the largest number and variety of warblers and other birds, but even the summer offers good birding. The best spots to enjoy the warbler show are the open areas bordering Sugar Creek on the north near the covered bridge, and along the southern edge of the park where brushy fields meet woodland, especially the transitional zone from forest to field extending from the CCC Pond east to State Road 234. Bruner, certainly the most knowledgeable birding authority on Shades, recommends the latter as traditionally the best war-

"Even avid birders will be hard put to ignore Shades' unusual and beautiful natural setting."

LOCATION: Waveland, Indiana.

DIRECTIONS: From the intersection of U.S. 231 and State Road 234 drive west approximately 8 miles to where State Road 234 makes a sharp 90-degree turn to the north at the intersection with County Road 800S. Continue heading west on County Road 800S. The park entrance lies approximately 1 mile from the intersection on CR 800S. Continuing on 234 where it turns north will bring you to Pine Hills Nature Preserve and Deer's Mill Covered Bridge at 1 and 2 miles north of the intersection with 800S.

HOURS: Open year round 7:00 a.m.-11:00 p.m. for day use visitors. Campers can, of course, spend the night.

BEST TIMES: Spring and Fall are the best birding times, but summer offers more than enough enticements to make a visit worthwhile.

BIRDING HIGHLIGHTS: Shades State Park is one of the best warbler watching spots in Indiana. Thirty-six warbler species have been recorded of which 17 nest in the park including Worm-eating, Hooded, Cerulean, Kentucky, Louisiana Waterthrush, and Northern Parula. It is the only known nesting spot for Magnolia Warblers in the state. With 197 species listed on the checklist, it also offers good birding from spring through fall.

FOR MORE INFORMATION: Shades State Park, Route 1, Box 72, Waveland, IN 47989. Phone: (317) 435-2810. Mr Alan Bruner (317) 597-2459 graciously has offered to assist anyone wishing to visit the area.

"Magnolia Warblers were discovered nesting here in the summer of 1995 — a state first."

bler spot in the park.

Even avid birders, as I found out, will be hard put to ignore Shades' unusual and beautiful natural setting. The park is cut by steep sandstone cliffs and deep, narrow ravines. The park's many trails lead to stunning views from high promontories, weave through the bottom of steep-sided ravines no wider than a walk-in closet, pass numerous springs and a couple of waterfalls. Hidden within this rugged topography is a mature forest of eastern hemlock, yew and white pine that is totally out of place in central Indiana. It's the type of vegetation one would expect to find hundreds of miles to the north. "A hike through the park," says Steve Stockton, Assistant Park Manager at Shades, "is much like a walk in the U.P. of Michigan."

Barb and I finally pulled ourselves away from the covered bridge and headed for the heart of the park. After exploring the picturesque and very pleasant primitive campground — no electrical hookups but modern shower houses — we parked next to the CCC Pond and began exploring on foot. Bruner advises birders to work eastward from the pond, but the unique and rugged landscape north of the parking lot drew us like a magnet. From the pond north to Sugar Creek the wooded, rolling hills look like they have been lacerated by a giant French Chef's knife. Small creeks and springs have cut deeply into the hills and created a labyrinth of twisting, turning ravines that eventually head north to Sugar Creek. Near the parking lot a wooden staircase led down into one ravine, and while Barb stayed above it all, I descended to the streambed.

I wish I could tell you that I saw lots of birds in the next hour. I wish I could tell you that I was even looking for birds. The truth is the strange and surreal beauty of the 20-foot deep cleft and the ruggedness of the trail so occupied my attention a bird would have had to tap me on the shoulder to be noticed. Evidently a few did because I distinctly recall encountering a Gray Catbird, an Eastern Wood-pewee, and a Red-breasted Nuthatch somewhere along the ravine.

Looking for easier walking and a landscape that would allow me to concentrate on birds rather than the natural setting, we drove to the Pine Hills Nature Preserve which abuts the eastern edge of the park. The preserve's landscape didn't prove to be any easier to ignore than the park's. Within the preserve two creeks have cut deep, parallel gorges, in the highlands south of Sugar Creek, forming four backbone ridges. It's about a 20-minute walk on the foot trail that departs from the Pine Hills Parking lot on State Road 234 to the point where visitors are treated to their first sight of the ridges and ravines.

The trees everywhere along the trail bore the distinctively oblong, almost rectangular, holes made by Pileated Woodpeckers. And always, up ahead and just out of sight, a bird kept hammering on trees. I never caught sight of a woodpecker, but the experience reminded me of what seemed to be a game two Pileateds played with a group of us hiking Isle Royale. The woodpeckers perched on trailside trees until we were almost upon them, then took off with what sounded more like an hysterical laugh than a call and flew to another tree 50 yards up the trail. They would wait for us to draw near then take off again. The game went on for almost a half-mile. If a woodpecker was playing with me here at Shades, he soon lost interest and the drumming stopped.

I must have been less than 100 yards from the first of the humpbacked ridges when the unmistakable call of a Barred Owl broke the silence. Intently searching the trees for a glimpse of the bird I was unaware of the vista opening up before me as I came to the lip of the first great gorge. One glance and I stood transfixed by the view. The ridge fell steeply away into a broad ravine that looked to be at

SHADES STATE PARK/PINE HILLS NATURE PRESERVE FIELD CHECKLIST

Compiled by Alan Bruner

___Pied-billed Grebe
___American Bittern
___Great Blue Heron
___Green Heron
___Canada Goose
___Wood Duck
___Green-winged Teal
___American Black Duck
___Mallard
___Blue-winged Teal
___American Wigeon
___Ring-necked Duck
___Lesser Scaup
___Common Goldeneye
___Bufflehead
___Hooded Merganser
___Common Merganser
___Turkey Vulture
___Osprey
___Bald Eagle
___Northern Harrier
___Sharp-shinned Hawk
___Cooper's Hawk
___Red-shouldered Hawk
___Broad-winged Hawk
___Red-tailed Hawk
___Rough-legged Hawk
___Golden Eagle
___American Kestrel
___Merlin
___Peregrine Falcon
___Ring-necked Pheasant
___Wild Turkey
___Northern Bobwhite
___Virginia Rail
___Sora
___American Coot
___Sandhill Crane
___Lesser Golden-plover
___Killdeer

___Greater Yellowlegs
___Lesser Yellowlegs
___Solitary Sandpiper
___Spotted Sandpiper
___Pectoral Sandpiper
___Short-billed Dowitcher
___Common Snipe
___American Woodcock
___Ring-billed Gull
___Black Tern
___Rock Dove
___Mourning Dove
___Black-billed Cuckoo
___Yellow-billed Cuckoo
___Eastern Screech-owl
___Great Horned Owl
___Barred Owl
___Long-eared Owl
___Northern Saw-whet Owl
___Common Nighthawk
___Whip-poor-will
___Chimney Swift
___Ruby-throated Hummingbird
___Belted Kingfisher
___Red-headed Woodpecker
___Red-bellied Woodpecker
___Yellow-bellied Sapsucker
___Downy Woodpecker
___Hairy Woodpecker
___Northern Flicker
___Pileated Woodpecker
___Olive-sided Woodpecker
___Eastern Wood-pewee
___Yellow-bellied Flycatcher
___Acadian Flycatcher
___Willow Flycatcher
___Least Flycatcher
___Eastern Phoebe
___Great Crested Flycatcher
___Eastern Kingbird

___Horned Lark
___Purple Martin
___Tree Swallow
___Northern Rough-winged Swallow
___Bank Swallow
___Cliff Swallow
___Barn Swallow
___Blue Jay
___American Crow
___Black-capped Chickadee
___Carolina Chickadee
___Tufted Titmouse
___Red-breasted Nuthatch
___White-breasted Nuthatch
___Brown Creeper
___Carolina Wren
___House Wren
___Winter Wren
___Golden-crowned Kinglet
___Ruby-crowned Kinglet
___Blue-gray Gnatcatcher
___Eastern Bluebird
___Veery
___Gray-cheeked Thrush
___Swainson's Thrush
___Hermit Thrush
___Wood Thrush
___American Robin
___Gray Catbird
___Northern Mockingbird
___Brown Thrasher
___Cedar Waxwing
___Northern Shrike
___Loggerhead Shrike
___European Starling
___White-eyed Vireo
___Bell's Vireo
___Solitary Vireo
___Yellow-throated Vireo
___Warbling Vireo

___Philadelphia Vireo
___Red-eyed Vireo
___Blue-winged Warbler
___Golden-winged Warbler
___Tennessee Warbler
___Orange-crowned Warbler
___Nashville Warbler
___Northern Parula
___Yellow Warbler
___Chestnut-sided Warbler
___Magnolia Warbler
___Cape May Warbler
___Black-throated Blue Warbler
___Yellow-rumped Warbler
___Black-throated Green Warbler
___Blackburnian Warbler
___Yellow-throated Warbler
___Pine Warbler
___Prairie Warbler
___Palm Warbler
___Bay-breasted Warbler
___Blackpoll Warbler
___Cerulean Warbler
___Black-and-white Warbler
___American Redstart
___Prothonotary Warbler
___Worm-eating Warbler
___Ovenbird
___Northern Waterthrush
___Louisiana Waterthrush
___Kentucky Warbler
___Connecticut Warbler
___Mourning Warbler
___Common Yellowthroat
___Hooded Warbler
___Wilson's Warbler
___Canada Warbler
___Yellow-breasted Chat
___Summer Tanager
___Scarlet Tanager

___Northern Cardinal
___Rose-breasted Grosbeak
___Indigo Bunting
___Dickcissel
___Rufous-sided Towhee
___Spotted Towhee
___American Tree Sparrow
___Chipping Sparrow
___Field Sparrow
___Vesper Sparrow
___Lark Sparrow
___Savannah Sparrow
___Grasshopper Sparrow
___Henslow's Sparrow
___Fox Sparrow
___Song Sparrow
___Lincoln's Sparrow
___Swamp Sparrow
___White-throated Sparrow
___White-crowned Sparrow
___Harris' Sparrow
___Dark-eyed Junco
___Bobolink
___Red-winged Blackbird
___Eastern Meadowlark
___Rusty Blackbird
___Common Grackle
___Brown-headed Cowbird
___Orchard Oriole
___Baltimore Oriole
___Purple Finch
___House Finch
___Red Crossbill
___Pine Siskin
___American Goldfinch
___Evening Grosbeak
___House Sparrow

least 100 yards deep and more than twice that across. A Turkey Vulture cut lazy circles in the sky high above the wooded gorge and scanning the bottom of the ravine with glasses, I found myself looking down at a Red-tailed Hawk perched near the top of a tree. All the while the Barred Owl's call, "Who cooks for you? Who cooks for you-all?", drifted across the ridges and ravines. Walking back to the car in the gathering dusk, I eagerly looked forward to more birding the next morning.

First-time visitors to Shades State Park should plan on a two-day birding trip. It takes nearly a day for the birder to desensitize themselves to the spectacular and unusual scenic beauty before concentrating just on looking for birds. Unfortunately, the sky split a seam the next morning and torrential rain continued to fall all day.

In the winter Bald Eagles can often be seen flying up Sugar Creek from their winter roost on the Wabash River some twenty miles away. But park personnel caution visitors that the normally rugged trails can become very treacherous in the winter and are often under water in both winter and early spring.

Muscatatuck National Wildlife Refuge

"A Gray Catbird was practicing his imitations near the stairs leading to the wetlands, and brought our bird total for the day to 42."

LOCATION: Seymour, Indiana.

DIRECTIONS: From the intersection of U.S. 50 and I-65 drive approximately 3 miles east on U.S. 50 to the refuge.

HOURS: Sunrise to sunset year-round. Volunteers man the Visitors Center on Saturday and Sunday afternoons. Most birders avoid the refuge in December when deer hunting is allowed, and access to areas within the refuge is restricted.

BEST TIMES: Spring and fall.

BIRDING HIGHLIGHTS: Thousands of Wood Ducks, large concentrations of waterfowl in the spring and fall with upwards of 15,000 ducks and geese on hand in March. Excellent shorebirding in the fall and songbirds in the spring and summer.

FOR MORE INFORMATION: Refuge Manager, Muscatatuck NWR, 12985 E. U.S. 50, Seymour, IN 47274. Phone: (812) 522-4352.

The first bird to greet us at Muscatatuck National Wildlife Refuge either presaged a great day of birding or was going to make everything that followed anticlimactic. Less than 100 feet down the entrance road Barb spotted an unfamiliar bird in a tangle of shrubs near the roadside. During the panic stop and frantic search for the field guide the bird obliged us by staying put and in clear sight. Its black head, orangish-brown breast and rump, and prominent white wing bars let us know we'd seen our first Black-headed Grosbeak.

We had come to Indiana's only national wildlife refuge with the express purpose of seeing one of our, and James Audubon's, favorite birds — the Wood Duck. The refuge was created in 1966 with money generated by the sale of federal duck stamps, and the area along the Muscatatuck River was chosen as the site for the refuge because it has historically been a Wood Duck nesting area. Even without sighting the grosbeak the trip would have been memorable. Wood Ducks seemed to be everywhere. Singly and in pairs, we saw them overhead and on nearly every body of water within the refuge.

But in addition to Wood Ducks, the refuge turned out to offer a veritable smorgasbord of birds. More than 250 species have been sighted here, and as a relatively young preserve new birds are recorded every year. Just recently, small numbers of Sandhill Cranes have begun stopping here on their southern migration in November.

A stop at the Visitors Center really whetted our appetite when a volunteer passed on the news that earlier in the morning a birder had tallied 55 species in a two-hour tour of the refuge. After a short browse through the center's well-stocked gift shop and bookstore, checking off five species at the Center's feeding station, and collecting a map of the refuge we eagerly set out to explore the refuge's forests, floodings, marshes, lakes, and meadows.

Miles of good gravel roads, including a three-mile, self-guided auto tour, and eight easily walked hiking trails wind through the refuge's various habitats. Birding can be as good from a car as on foot. The roads border several areas that are flooded in the fall to provide waterfowl feeding and resting areas, and in the spring when the water is drawn down the exposed, muddy soil attracts shorebirds. Depending on the season, visitors can get close-up looks at a dozen species of ducks or over 20 different kinds of shorebirds without leaving their car. As our car inched along the gravel road that separated a large flooding from the northern end of Moss Lake, we spotted Blue- and Green-winged teal, Canada Geese, Northern Shovelers, an American Wigeon, several Mallards, American Coots, and a Pied-billed Grebe gliding across the shallow waters. In late summer and early fall motorists would be watching sandpipers, yellowlegs, plovers, and an occasional phalarope mining the moist soil where the waterfowl were presently feeding and resting.

After an hour of creeping along the refuge's roads in the car, it came as a nice change of pace to stretch my legs on the 0.9-mile-long Richart Lake Trail. From the parking lot the trail cuts through the edge of a lush forest, crosses a meadow,

MUSCATATUCK NATIONAL WILDLIFE REFUGE FIELD CHECKLIST

___Common Loon
___Pied-billed Grebe
___Horned Grebe
___Double-crested Cormorant
___American Bittern
___Least Bittern
___Great Blue Heron
___Great Egret
___Snowy Egret
___Little Blue Heron
___Cattle Egret
___Green Heron
___Black-crowned Night-heron
___Yellow-crowned Night-heron
___Tundra Swan
___Greater White-fronted Goose
___Snow Goose
___Canada Goose
___Wood Duck
___Green-winged Teal
___American Black Duck
___Mallard
___Northern Pintail
___Blue-winged Teal
___Northern Shoveler
___Gadwall
___American Wigeon
___Canvasback
___Redhead
___Ring-necked Duck
___Greater Scaup
___Lesser Scaup
___Common Goldeneye
___Bufflehead
___Hooded Merganser
___Common Merganser
___Ruddy Duck
___Turkey Vulture
___Osprey
___Bald Eagle
___Northern Harrier
___Sharp-shinned Hawk
___Cooper's Hawk
___Northern Goshawk
___Red-shouldered Hawk
___Broad-winged Hawk
___Red-tailed Hawk
___Rough-legged Hawk
___Golden Eagle
___American Kestrel
___Ring-necked Pheasant
___Ruffed Grouse

___Wild Turkey
___Northern Bobwhite
___King Rail
___Virginia Rail
___Sora
___Common Moorhen
___American Coot
___Sandhill Crane
___Semipalmated Plover
___Killdeer
___Greater Yellowlegs
___Lesser Yellowlegs
___Solitary Sandpiper
___Spotted Sandpiper
___Semipalmated Sandpiper
___Western Sandpiper
___Least Sandpiper
___Dunlin
___White-rumped Sandpiper
___Baird's Sandpiper
___Pectoral Sandpiper
___Short-billed Dowitcher
___Long-billed Dowitcher
___Common Snipe
___American Woodcock
___Franklin's Gull
___Ring-billed Gull
___Herring Gull
___Forster's Tern
___Black Tern
___Rock Dove
___Mourning Dove
___Black-billed Cuckoo
___Yellow-billed Cuckoo
___Eastern Screech-owl
___Great Horned Owl
___Barred Owl
___Long-eared Owl
___Short-eared Owl
___Common Nighthawk
___Chuck-will's-widow
___Whip-poor-will
___Chimney Swift
___Ruby-throated Hummingbird
___Belted Kingfisher
___Red-headed Woodpecker
___Red-bellied Woodpecker
___Yellow-bellied Sapsucker
___Downy Woodpecker
___Hairy Woodpecker
___Northern Flicker
___Pileated Woodpecker

___Olive-sided Flycatcher
___Eastern Wood-pewee
___Acadian Flycatcher
___Willow Flycatcher
___Least Flycatcher
___Eastern Phoebe
___Great Crested Flycatcher
___Eastern Kingbird
___Horned Lark
___Purple Martin
___Tree Swallow
___Northern Rough-winged Swallow
___Bank Swallow
___Cliff Swallow
___Barn Swallow
___Blue Jay
___American Crow
___Black-capped Chickadee
___Carolina Chickadee
___Tufted Titmouse
___Red-breasted Nuthatch
___White-breasted Nuthatch
___Brown Creeper
___Carolina Wren
___House Wren
___Winter Wren
___Sedge Wren
___Golden-crowned Kinglet
___Ruby-crowned Kinglet
___Blue-gray Gnatcatcher
___Eastern Bluebird
___Veery
___Gray-cheeked Thrush
___Swainson's Thrush
___Hermit Thrush
___Wood Thrush
___American Robin
___Gray Catbird
___Northern Mockingbird
___Brown Thrasher
___American Pipit
___Cedar Waxwing
___Loggerhead Shrike
___European Starling
___White-eyed Vireo
___Bell's Vireo
___Solitary Vireo
___Yellow-throated Vireo
___Warbling Vireo
___Philadelphia Vireo
___Red-eyed Vireo
___Blue-winged Warbler

___Tennessee Warbler
___Nashville Warbler
___Northern Parula
___Yellow Warbler
___Chestnut-sided Warbler
___Magnolia Warbler
___Cape May Warbler
___Black-throated Blue Warbler
___Yellow-rumped Warbler
___Black-throated Green Warbler
___Blackburnian Warbler
___Yellow-throated Warbler
___Pine Warbler
___Prairie Warbler
___Palm Warbler
___Bay-breasted Warbler
___Blackpoll Warbler
___Cerulean Warbler
___Black-and-white Warbler
___American Redstart
___Prothonotary Warbler
___Worm-eating Warbler
___Ovenbird
___Northern Waterthrush
___Louisiana Waterthrush
___Kentucky Warbler
___Connecticut Warbler
___Mourning Warbler
___Common Yellowthroat
___Hooded Warbler
___Wilson's Warbler
___Canada Warbler
___Yellow-breasted Chat
___Summer Tanager
___Scarlet Tanager
___Northern Cardinal
___Rose-breasted Grosbeak
___Blue Grosbeak
___Indigo Bunting
___Dickcissel
___Rufous-sided Towhee
___American Tree Sparrow
___Chipping Sparrow
___Field Sparrow
___Vesper Sparrow
___Savannah Sparrow
___Grasshopper Sparrow
___Henslow's Sparrow
___Fox Sparrow
___Song Sparrow
___Lincoln's Sparrow
___Swamp Sparrow

___White-throated Sparrow
___White-crowned Sparrow
___Dark-eyed Junco
___Lapland Longspur
___Snow Bunting
___Bobolink
___Red-winged Blackbird
___Eastern Meadowlark
___Rusty Blackbird
___Common Grackle
___Brown-headed Cowbird
___Orchard Oriole
___Baltimore Oriole
___House Finch
___Red Crossbill
___Pine Siskin
___American Goldfinch
___Evening Grosbeak
___House Sparrow

Accidental Birds

___Red-necked Grebe
___Eared Grebe
___Tricolored Heron
___Glossy Ibis
___Cinnamon Teal
___Oldsquaw
___Ruddy Duck
___Fulvous Whistling Duck
___Black Vulture
___American Swallow-tailed Kite
___Peregrine Falcon
___Merlin
___Black-bellied Plover
___Upland Sandpiper
___Ruddy Turnstone
___Bonaparte's Gull
___Caspian Tern
___Common Tern
___Least Tern
___Barn Owl
___Northern Saw-whet Owl
___Yellow-bellied Flycatcher
___Bewick's Wren
___Golden-winged Warbler
___Orange-crowned Warbler
___Lark Sparrow
___LeConte's Sparrow
___Harris' Sparrow
___Brewer's Blackbird
___White-winged Crossbill
___Common Redpoll

"We had come to Indiana's only national wildlife refuge with the express purpose of seeing one of our, and James Audubon's, favorite birds – the Wood Duck."

and an old farm field slowly reverting to forest. Barb, enthralled by the constant overflights of ducks, stayed in the parking lot, but I didn't lack for company on the walk to Richart Lake. As I emerged from the woods, a Brown Thrasher joined me and chattered incessantly from the tree line marking the border of an old field. A Song Sparrow, Blue Jays, a Northern Flicker, American Goldfinches, an Evening Grosbeak, a Downy Woodpecker, and a White-crowned Sparrow were added to the day's tally before reaching a covered overlook on the south shore of the lake.

Thickets edge the lake on both sides of the Harkman Overlook. As a House Wren called from the newly leafing bushes something caught my attention. It was a large, white-breasted bird perched near the top of a dead tree on the other side of the lake. My binoculars reached out and brought an Osprey into stark relief. While the majestic bird scanned the lake for fish, I was more interested in the ubiquitous Wood Ducks and geese bobbing on the lake's gentle ripples, the swallows trolling the air just above the water for insects, and the lone Great Blue Heron stalking the far shore.

Seven other foot trails in the refuge lead to bird-rich woodlands, meadows, and floodings. In addition to waterfowl and shorebirds, Muscatatuck National Wildlife Refuge is known statewide for its abundance of songbirds. By late spring the trails are alive with the calls of warblers, eight species of flycatchers, Northern Mockingbirds, vireos, and cardinals. Wild Turkeys, woodpeckers, Eastern Meadowlarks, Eastern Bluebirds, thrushes, Indigo Buntings, and Belted Kingfishers are also plentiful. There's a good chance visitors will be treated to sightings of the refuge's large deer herd and if lady luck is especially kind you may be favored with a glimpse of a river otter.

Before leaving the refuge we stopped at the Visitors Center to talk birding with the knowledgeable volunteer staff and strolled the short Chestnut Ridge Trail. The trail departs from the Visitors Center parking lot and descends into a spring-fed wetland bridged by a boardwalk. A Gray Catbird was practicing his imitations near the stairs leading to the wetlands, and brought our bird total for the day to 42.

Falls of the Ohio State Park

It was a singularly odd experience. I was hundreds of miles from the nearest tropical sea, yet I was slipping and sliding over a coral reef. Appropriately enough for exploring a reef, my shoes, socks, and shorts were drenched but I was only slightly wet from the waist up because wind-driven rain (the remnants of an early season hurricane that had pushed as far inland as the Ohio River valley) kept sneaking under my umbrella and spritzing me in the face. And instead of looking for beautiful examples of living coral and tropical fish, I continued to dry off my binoculars and glasses while searching for birds.

The Falls of the Ohio is one of the natural wonders of the Midwest. The fact that the 2.5 miles of rapids opposite Louisville, Kentucky is the only spot in the entire 981-mile length of the Ohio River with exposed bedrock marks the place as exceptional, but what truly sets this area apart from anyplace else is that the bedrock is the largest exposed coral reef in the world. Actually the rapids have pretty much disappeared as a result of the Army Corp of Engineers making the Falls of the Ohio navigable for river traffic. In place of the naturally carved 26-feet vertical drop in the river, there are now channels, locks and weir dams that ensure there will always be enough water for river traffic to make its way up and down stream.

The construction of a long weir dam that made for a narrow but deeper shipping channel also exposed (on a semi-permanent basis) a 220-acre slab of the 400-million-year-old coral reef. In the spring when the water level of the river is high, a set of gates are opened that floods the fossil bed, but by July, as the level of the Ohio River goes down, the gates are closed, diverting water into the shipping channel, ensuring that it remains navigable. With the gates closed, the coral reef is exposed, and visitors are welcome to explore the fossil rich bedrock on foot.

From the time the area was first settled in the 1770s, before all the civil engineering changed the face of the falls, people have marveled at both the fossil bed and the bird life found around the rapids. The great John James Audubon delighted in the falls when he lived in Louisville and drew more than 200 bird studies while living near the rapids. Over 260 species of birds have been recorded in the greater Falls of the Ohio area, and it is a marvelous place for either the serious or casual birder to visit.

The attraction here for birds is four-fold. The locks, dams, and river traffic make for open water on the river even during the coldest months and attract gulls and wintering waterfowl. The falls area boasts a wide variety of prime birding habitat, and it lies within the greater Mississippi flyway. Lastly, the exposed bedrock is the equivalent of a sumptuous smorgasbord for birds. Even when the gates on the weir dam are closed, enough water flows over the spillway to create shallow pools, water-filled potholes, sloughs, and fast running little rivulets on the bedrock. The Army Corp of Engineers has also cut notches in the weir dam bordering the fossil bed that diverts more river water over the bedrock. The pools, potholes, and sloughs are rich in aquatic food and attract thousands of gulls, ducks, and shorebirds. The extensive bedrock also supports a small woodland

"The great John James Audubon delighted in the falls and drew more than 200 bird studies while living near the rapids."

LOCATION: Clarksville, Indiana.

DIRECTIONS: Take exit 0 off I-65 just before crossing the Ohio River into Kentucky and follow the signs to the Falls of the Ohio State Park, about a mile west of the exit on Riverside Drive.

HOURS: Open year-round 7:00 a.m.-11:00 p.m. daily. The Interpretive Center is open 9:00 a.m.-5:00 p.m. daily.

BEST TIMES: Midsummer through fall. Good birding in late April and early May for migrating songbirds and warblers. Shorebird numbers and varieties remain high from late July through October. Gulls, waterfowl, and raptors are best seen in the fall.

BIRDING HIGHLIGHTS: The world's largest exposed coral reef attracts large numbers and varieties of shorebirds and waterfowl who come to feed on the aquatic food. The large numbers of prey birds also attract plenty of raptors, especially Peregrine Falcons that have been seen year-round in the area and whose numbers peak in the fall.

FOR MORE INFORMATION: Falls of the Ohio State Park, 201 W. Riverside Dr., Clarksville, IN 47129. Phone: (812) 280-9970.

"Things really get active with the closing of the gates controlling the flow of water over the fossil bed."

habitat, pockets of prairie grass, and several wetland communities. And along the riverbank there are mudflats, and dense woodlands. All of which makes the area damn near irresistible to birds. In 1981 the Falls of the Ohio National Wildlife Conservation Area was created to protect this valuable and unique wildlife habitat which includes two large islands, locks, weir dams, and several miles of Ohio River shoreline.

The 68-acre Falls of the Ohio State Park is only a small segment of the 1,404-acre conservation area (most of which is closed to visitors) but it is the best spot from which to search for birds and venture out on the coral reef. I arrived at the park early on a Saturday morning in September only to find the dying gasps of a tropical storm that had battered the Carolinas had beat me to the Ohio River by an hour. The parking lot was hub deep in water. You couldn't make out the river nor the corral reef for the wind-whipped rain, and it was an hour before the park's new Interpretive Center was to open. It was still raining heavily an hour later when the Falls of the Ohio Interpretive Center opened, and I barely beat a busload of kids on a field trip to the restroom.

While it continued to rain, I passed a pleasant hour exploring the exhibits and displays that tell the geological, biological, and human history of the Falls of the Ohio. I browsed the well-stocked gift shop, spent a few minutes in the wildlife observation room that overlooks a small garden with several birdfeeders, and watched a sprinkling of water-logged sparrows and an equally wet cardinal nosh on a few seeds. The rain still showed no sign of letting up by the time I discovered the observation room overlooking the coral reef. I could make out several Great Blue Heron and at least a dozen Black-crowned Night-heron camped out on the reef through the rain-streaked window. I also saw a few smaller shorebirds, probably yellowlegs, poking around the edges of some of the small pools on the reef.

With the rain still falling, I finally went in search of somebody who could tell me what I could expect at the Falls of the Ohio when a dying hurricane wasn't blowing through and met Erica Feldkamp, a naturalist with the Falls of the Ohio State Park. She confirmed that the best birding is from midsummer through fall when the Upper Tainter Gates of the weir dam are closed and the coral reef is exposed. Thirty-two species of shorebirds have been observed in the area, 26 species of waterfowl, 11 different terns and gulls, and 8 species of heron and egrets. Of special interest is the fact that Least Terns, which are seldom seen anywhere in the Midwest, are occasional visitors to the falls area from spring through fall. She also pointed out that Shippingport Island, a bird sanctuary closed to visitors, is only a stone's throw from the weir dam marking the southern edge of the park, and all the species that nest on the island spill over on to the state park's coral reef to feed. On a good day in midsummer, cormorants, Great Blue Heron, and Black-crowned Night-heron completely line the weir dam, turning it white from their droppings.

Feldkamp gave me a rundown on birding throughout the year at the Falls of the Ohio that made it perfectly clear why the spot is a favorite destination for birders and birding clubs. Although spring migration sightings are not what make the area famous, there are enough warblers and other songbirds passing through to make a trip worthwhile in late April and early May. Especially productive is the 0.75-mile Woodland Trail that loops through the woods in back of the Visitors Center and borders the Ohio River. Erica counted 20 different warbler species along the trail in the spring of 1996, and the park's bird checklist totals 35 species of warblers. There are also plenty of other species from Pileated Woodpeckers to Rufous-sided Towhees to keep things interesting. Spring also finds from 150 to 200 cormorants settling in for the summer, and by June upwards of

BLACK-CROWNED NIGHT-HERON

150 Black-crowned Night-heron can usually be seen on a daily basis.

Things really get active with the closing of the gates controlling the flow of water over the fossil bed. As the bedrock is exposed, it's like the ringing of a dinner bell for waterfowl and shorebirds. Shorebird numbers and diversity remains high from July through October. Typical Rare Bird Alert postings for early August reported Ruddy Turnstones, Sanderlings, Semipalmed Plovers, 50 Semipalmated Sandpipers, and 5 American Avocets while Buff-breasted, Baird's, and Western sandpipers were reported later in the month. There are always a few ducks in the area, but large numbers don't begin showing up until fall migration is under way. Both waterfowl and large concentrations of gulls (representing six species) often remain in the area as winter residents. All the gulls, ducks, and shorebirds attract impressive numbers of birds of prey with 11 species of raptors documented in the Falls area. The area is especially favored by Peregrine Falcons. The magnificent birds have been seen here throughout the year, but their numbers peak from fall through late winter, when the birds are often seen perched on any of the four bridges crossing the Ohio River near the Falls area.

By late morning the worst of the rain had moved on and juggling binoculars, birdbook, and umbrella I set out to explore the coral reef. Feldkamp recommended that I make my way down to the spillway and from there work my way on to the outer fossil beds. Not only is the birding often better there, but the water-worn formations (cliffs, monolithic slabs, small waterfalls, and even a natural stone arch) found in the bedrock of the outer fossil beds are a must-see. It sounded great, but what I didn't expect was just how slippery wet limestone can be and that I would have to cross a wide band of wet clay to reach the spillway. I felt like a pig on ice, especially on the wet, shoe-clinging, and very slippery clay. During brief moments of equilibrium, when the wind and umbrella canceled out the slippery down slope, I glassed the further reaches of the bedrock and found Spotted and Pectoral sandpipers, Blue-wing Teal, and Great Egrets sharing the rocky shallows with the Great Blue Heron, Black-crowned Night-heron, and Greater Yellowlegs.

Having been warned that the spillway below the gates always has some water flowing over it, I was taken aback to see what looked like a good two or three inches swiftly moving over the concrete surface with footing made even more treacherous by all the algae growing on the spillway. This was definitely a feet-are-going-to-get-wet operation, and if I wasn't careful, a lot more than feet were going to come in contact with the spillway. The slow traverse of the 100-foot-long spillway took at least five minutes and resulted in one of the most memorable hours spent researching this book. Even if it wasn't wet, the roughness of the fossil bed keeps you looking at where you're going to step next, and every time you look down your eyes encountered another wonder. Fossils of every size and description are everywhere. You simply can't move without stepping on 400-million-year-old trilobites, snails, fish, and other amazing creatures. Equally attention grabbing are the small caves, strange rock formations and the miniature grand canyons worn in the rock by the river. There is not a more amazing spot for birding in the Midwest than the limestone fossil beds at the Falls of the Ohio. To avoid sensory overload or the possibility of twisted ankles and broken bones, the area can be birded with fair success from the observation deck next to the Interpretive Center. The observation deck presents a great panoramic view of the bedrock, and birders armed with a spotting scope who aren't up to the demands of walking on the coral reef, can sight a good number of birds from the comfortable and easily accessible overlook.

"The Falls of the Ohio is one of the natural wonders of the Midwest. What truly sets this area apart is that the bedrock is the largest exposed coral reef in the world."

FALLS OF THE OHIO STATE PARK FIELD CHECKLIST

Compiled by the Falls of Ohio State Park

___ Common Loon
___ Pied-billed Grebe
___ Horned Grebe
___ Double-crested Cormorant
___ Great Blue Heron
___ Great Egret
___ Snowy Egret
___ Little Blue Heron
___ Cattle Egret
___ Green Heron
___ Black-crowned Night-heron
___ Yellow-crowned Night-heron
___ Snow Goose
___ Canada Goose
___ Wood Duck
___ Green-winged Teal
___ American Black Duck
___ Mallard
___ Northern Pintail
___ Blue-winged Teal
___ Northern Shoveler
___ Gadwall
___ American Wigeon
___ Canvasback
___ Redhead
___ Ring-necked Duck
___ Greater Scaup
___ Lesser Scaup
___ Oldsquaw
___ Black Scoter
___ Surf Scoter
___ White-winged Scoter
___ Common Goldeneye
___ Bufflehead
___ Hooded Merganser
___ Common Merganser
___ Red-breasted Merganser
___ Ruddy Duck
___ Black Vulture
___ Turkey Vulture
___ Osprey
___ Bald Eagle
___ Northern Harrier
___ Sharp-shinned Hawk
___ Cooper's Hawk
___ Red-shouldered Hawk
___ Broad-winged Hawk
___ Red-tailed Hawk
___ Rough-legged Hawk
___ American Kestrel
___ Merlin
___ Peregrine Falcon
___ Northern Bobwhite
___ Sora

___ American Coot
___ Sandhill Crane
___ Black-bellied Plover
___ Lesser Golden-plover
___ Semipalmated Plover
___ Piping Plover
___ Killdeer
___ American Avocet
___ Greater Yellowlegs
___ Lesser Yellowlegs
___ Solitary Sandpiper
___ Willet
___ Spotted Sandpiper
___ Upland Sandpiper
___ Marbled Godwit
___ Ruddy Turnstone
___ Red Knot
___ Sanderling
___ Semipalmated Sandpiper
___ Western Sandpiper
___ Least Sandpiper
___ White-rumped Sandpiper
___ Baird's Sandpiper
___ Pectoral Sandpiper
___ Dunlin
___ Stilt Sandpiper
___ Buff-breasted Sandpiper
___ Short-billed Dowitcher
___ Long-billed Dowitcher
___ Common Snipe
___ American Woodcock
___ Wilson's Phalarope
___ Red-necked Phalarope
___ Red Phalarope
___ Laughing Gull
___ Franklin's Gull
___ Bonaparte's Gull
___ Ring-billed Gull
___ Herring Gull
___ Glaucous Gull
___ Caspian Tern
___ Common Tern
___ Forster's Tern
___ Least Tern
___ Black Tern
___ Rock Dove
___ Mourning Dove
___ Black-billed Cuckoo
___ Yellow-billed Cuckoo
___ Eastern Screech-owl
___ Great Horned Owl
___ Barred Owl
___ Common Nighthawk
___ Whip-poor-will

___ Chimney Swift
___ Ruby-throated Hummingbird
___ Belted Kingfisher
___ Red-headed Woodpecker
___ Red-bellied Woodpecker
___ Yellow-bellied Sapsucker
___ Downy Woodpecker
___ Hairy Woodpecker
___ Northern Flicker
___ Pileated Woodpecker
___ Olive-sided Flycatcher
___ Eastern Wood-pewee
___ Yellow-bellied Flycatcher
___ Acadian Flycatcher
___ Alder Flycatcher
___ Willow Flycatcher
___ Least Flycatcher
___ Eastern Phoebe
___ Great Crested Flycatcher
___ Eastern Kingbird
___ Horned Lark
___ Purple Martin
___ Tree Swallow
___ Northern Rough-winged Swallow
___ Bank Swallow
___ Cliff Swallow
___ Barn Swallow
___ Blue Jay
___ American Crow
___ Carolina Chickadee
___ Tufted Titmouse
___ Red-breasted Nuthatch
___ White-breasted Nuthatch
___ Brown Creeper
___ Carolina Wren
___ House Wren
___ Winter Wren
___ Sedge Wren
___ Marsh Wren
___ Golden-crowned Kinglet
___ Ruby-crowned Kinglet
___ Blue-gray Gnatcatcher
___ Eastern Bluebird
___ Veery
___ Gray-cheeked Thrush
___ Swainson's Thrush
___ Hermit Thrush
___ Wood Thrush
___ American Robin
___ Gray Catbird
___ Northern Mockingbird
___ Brown Thrasher
___ American Pipit
___ Cedar Waxwing

___ European Starling
___ White-eyed Vireo
___ Solitary Vireo
___ Yellow-throated Vireo
___ Warbling Vireo
___ Philadelphia Vireo
___ Red-eyed Vireo
___ Blue-winged Warbler
___ Golden-winged Warbler
___ Tennessee Warbler
___ Orange-crowned Warbler
___ Nashville Warbler
___ Northern Parula
___ Yellow Warbler
___ Chestnut-sided Warbler
___ Magnolia Warbler
___ Cape May Warbler
___ Black-throated Blue Warbler
___ Yellow-rumped Warbler
___ Black-throated Green Warbler
___ Blackburnian Warbler
___ Yellow-throated Warbler
___ Prairie Warbler
___ Palm Warbler
___ Bay-breasted Warbler
___ Blackpoll Warbler
___ Cerulean Warbler
___ Black-and-white Warbler
___ American Redstart
___ Prothonotary Warbler
___ Worm-eating Warbler
___ Ovenbird
___ Northern Waterthrush
___ Louisiana Waterthrush
___ Kentucky Warbler
___ Connecticut Warbler
___ Mourning Warbler
___ Common Yellowthroat
___ Hooded Warbler
___ Wilson's Warbler
___ Canada Warbler
___ Yellow-breasted Chat
___ Summer Tanager
___ Scarlet Tanager
___ Northern Cardinal
___ Rose-breasted Grosbeak
___ Indigo Bunting
___ Rufous-sided Towhee
___ American Tree Sparrow
___ Chipping Sparrow
___ Field Sparrow
___ Vesper Sparrow
___ Savannah Sparrow
___ Fox Sparrow

___ Song Sparrow
___ Lincoln's Sparrow
___ Swamp Sparrow
___ White-throated Sparrow
___ White-crowned Sparrow
___ Dark-eyed Junco
___ Bobolink
___ Red-winged Blackbird
___ Eastern Meadowlark
___ Rusty Blackbird
___ Common Grackle
___ Brown-headed Cowbird
___ Orchard Oriole
___ Baltimore Oriole
___ Purple Finch
___ House Finch
___ Pine Siskin
___ American Goldfinch
___ House sparrow

Accidentals
___ Red-throated Loon
___ Red-necked Grebe
___ Eared Grebe
___ Western Grebe
___ American White Pelican
___ American Bittern
___ Least Bittern
___ Reddish Egret
___ Wood Stork
___ Tundra Swan
___ King Rail
___ Common Moorhen
___ Purple Sandpiper
___ Curlew Sandpiper
___ Thayer's Gull
___ Iceland Gull
___ Great Black-backed Gull
___ Black-legged Kittiwake
___ Sabine's Gull
___ Barn Owl
___ Snowy Owl
___ Bewick's Wren
___ Dickcissel
___ Lapland Longspur
___ Snow Bunting

Hovey Lake State Fish and Wildlife Area and Twin Swamps Nature Preserve

For a Northerner who rarely travels south of the Mason-Dixon Line the first sight, and even the second and third, of Hovey Lake State Fish and Wildlife Area and the nearby Twin Swamps Nature Preserve came as a shock. Not quite like eating grits for the first time, but still a shock.

Hovey Lake, in the southernmost corner of Indiana, isn't even below the Mason-Dixon Line, but the still, dark waters of the lake, the starkness of the dead trees poking up out of the black-mirrored surface, and the unfamiliar shapes of the bald cypress at nearby Twin Swamps lend an otherworldly air to the area. It was easy to imagine myself in some Louisiana bayou backwater. Adding to the strangeness was the 80-degree temperature in mid-April and the Double-crested Cormorants perched in many of the dead trees at Hovey Lake. Their hunch-shouldered posture, as they slightly spread their wings to dry, gave the appearance they were holding a contest to see who could do the best impression of Dracula.

State Road 69 borders Hovey Lake for nearly a mile before reaching the refuge headquarters. During that last mile the car seemed to slow of its own accord, and Barb and I became quiet and attentive as we snatched looks at the strange lake through the trees bordering the road. Glimpses of waterfowl teased and heightened the anticipation of exploring and birding this unique area.

A profusion of birds met us at the headquarters parking lot and broke the spell. American Goldfinches, Northern Cardinals, Eastern Meadowlarks and American Tree Swallows darted around the grounds near the headquarters building, and a Red-headed Woodpecker hammered a tree near the boat ramp. Near the shore, a Great Blue Heron fished with studied elegance and grace. Further from the shore Blue-winged Teal, Mallards, Canada Geese and Northern Shovelers coasted among the dead trees. As if needing no company, a Common Loon floated in singular solitude far out in the lake. The somber face of Hovey lake had instantly transformed itself into a birder's paradise.

Five hundred years ago Hovey Lake was part of the main channel of the Ohio River. The lake was formed when the river cut across a horseshoe bend and in straightening its channel, created a new body of water. In 1939, the State of Indiana bought the property around the 1,400-acre lake. Additional purchases in later years brought the size of the area to 4,400 acres. The state manages the area for wildlife and periodically floods sections of the lowlands to provide wildlife habitat.

Autumn brings upwards of a half-million ducks and geese who winter here until March. Several hundred thousand crows also spend the winter at Hovey

LOCATION: Mt. Vernon, Indiana.

DIRECTIONS: From Mt. Vernon in southwest Indiana drive approximately 2 miles west on State Road 62 to State Road 69. Turn south on State Road 69 and drive approximately 8 miles to Hovey Lake. State Road 69 makes a sharp right turn at the entrance to the Wildlife Area Headquarters. To reach Twin Swamps follow the right turn and go straight west one mile to a 4-way stop. Turn north and drive 1 mile to the preserve parking lot on the left-hand side of the road.

HOURS: Both areas open all year, but access to Hovey Lake Wildlife Area is controlled and limited November through January for public hunting.

BEST TIMES: February through April are the prime months for birdwatching at Hovey Lake, but these two areas provide very good birding opportunities year-round.

BIRDING HIGHLIGHTS: Hovey Lake — Great concentrations of waterfowl from November through March. Good chances of seeing Bald Eagles during the winter months. In the spring songbird and shorebird migration can be very heavy at Hovey Lake providing good birding in April and early May. Twin Swamps — Prothonotary and Yellow-throated warblers are almost sure bets. The state threatened Yellow-crowned Night-heron nests here and the area offers good warbler and shorebird watching.

FOR MORE INFORMATION: Hovey Lake State Fish and Wildlife Area, RR #5, Mt. Vernon, IN 47620. Phone: (812) 838-2927.

"Adding to the strangeness was the 80-degree temperature in mid-April and the Double-crested Cormorants perched in many of the dead trees. Their hunch-shouldered posture, as they slightly spread their wings to dry, gave the appearance they were holding a contest to see who could do the best impression of Dracula."

Lake as do hundreds of cormorants. Bald Eagles frequently settle in, in February. Property manager Mark Pochon cites February for waterfowl and March-April for other species as traditionally the best times for birdwatching at the wildlife area. There is no official checklist, but Glenn Grant from Evansville, Indiana has birded Hovey Lake and Twin Swamps for the Christmas Bird Count and as a part of the state's breeding bird atlas. He has recorded 142 species at the two nearly adjoining sites.

A first visit to the area should begin at the refuge's headquarters. The lawn and parking area adjacent to the office not only makes a great platform for viewing the open waters of Hovey Lake, but the staff can be very helpful. After one last scan of the lake and the lawn, we visited the office and picked up a map of the refuge. One worker told us where he had spotted shorebirds earlier that morning, and another suggested several other areas for us to explore. And we couldn't get out of there until another employee told of how a year ago last spring he was driving to work and spotted American White Pelicans out on the lake. It was the first and only time they have ever been seen at Hovey Lake. Campers will also find the headquarters a good place for making a base camp for extended birding visits. A small, neat, primitive campground lies across the parking lot from the office and a nearby boat ramp.

On the advice of the office staff we followed State Road 69, which makes a sharp jog around the headquarters, south for about a mile to a dike that cuts a straight line out into the wildlife area. A few minutes walk from here along the road or out on the dike leads the birder to a variety of habitats. The brushy edges of the road, vast expanse of lake seemingly staked in place by dead trees, and areas of marsh and swamp bordering stretches of the dike keep birders constantly alert for songbirds, waders, and waterfowl.

The office staff also gave us directions for getting to the eastern side of the refuge. About a mile north of the wildlife headquarters on State Road 69, Access Road takes motorists to the east side of the Hovey Lake and to a landscape in sharp contrast to the moody views from State Road 69. Access Road passes through open meadows before turning south and east on a series of narrow dirt lanes that border fields, meadows and an occasional stand of trees. In addition to the species that are usually found in meadows and fields, shorebird viewing can be very good here. Shallow fingers of water extend into the meadows from the flooded areas and attract shorebirds like a magnet.

Just two miles from Hovey Lake, Twin Swamps Nature Preserve presents an entirely different visage. Roger L. Hedge, Heritage Ecologist for the Indiana Department of Natural Resources calls it, "the best remaining example of a cypress slough in the state." I would have found it hard to argue with him if he had claimed it the most beautiful micro-ecosystem in the state. In addition to its beauty what brought me here was that both Yellow-throated and Prothonotary warblers nest in the area.

From the parking lot, I followed the trail as it slowly descended into a floodplain hardwood forest. The trail snaked for 0.75-mile through a woodland that was filled with a symphony of bird calls and songs and ended at a boardwalk that extended out into the swamp for about 50 yards. Except for a Pileated Woodpecker, I hadn't had much luck spotting birds on the walk through the forest so at the end of the boardwalk I took a seat on a bench and waited for the birds to search me out.

I didn't have to wait long. A male Northern Cardinal perched on a nearby branch, inquisitive Carolina Chickadees checked me out, and Blue-gray Gnatcatchers busied themselves among the trees. But they were all warm-up acts for the Prothonotary Warbler who came to a branch not 15 feet from the bench and began striking poses with all the self-assurance of a cover girl.

Twin Swamps Nature Preserve also attracts considerable numbers of shorebirds and the state endangered Yellow-crowned Night-heron nests here. On the walk back to the car, I spotted several warblers in the flood plain, a good sampling of sparrows, a Northern Mockingbird, and several Red-winged Blackbirds as I broke out of the woods near the parking lot.

> *"They were all warm-up acts for the Prothonotary Warbler who came to a branch not 15 feet from the bench and began striking poses with all the self-assurance of a cover girl."*

HOVEY LAKE STATE FISH AND WILDLIFE AREA AND TWIN SWAMPS NATURE PRESERVE FIELD CHECKLIST

This checklist was compiled by Glenn Grant of Evansville, Indiana and is a result of years of birding both areas.

___ Common Loon	___ Red-tailed Hawk	___ Acadian Flycatcher	___ Northern Mockingbird	___ Dickcissel
___ Pied-billed Grebe	___ Rough-legged Hawk	___ Willow Flycatcher	___ Brown Thrasher	___ Rufous-sided Towhee
___ American White Pelican	___ American Kestrel	___ Eastern Phoebe	___ Water Pipit	___ American Tree Sparrow
___ Great Blue Heron	___ Northern Bobwhite	___ Great Crested Flycatcher	___ Cedar Waxwing	___ Chipping Sparrow
___ Great Egret	___ Virginia Rail	___ Eastern Kingbird	___ Loggerhead Shrike	___ Field Sparrow
___ Little Blue Heron	___ American Coot	___ Horned Lark	___ European Starling	___ Vesper Sparrow
___ Cattle Egret	___ Killdeer	___ Purple Martin	___ White-eyed Vireo	___ Fox Sparrow
___ Green Heron	___ Greater Yellowlegs	___ Tree Swallow	___ Yellow-throated Vireo	___ Song Sparrow
___ Yellow-crowned Night-heron	___ Common Snipe	___ Northern Rough-winged Swallow	___ Warbling Vireo	___ Swamp Sparrow
___ Canada Goose	___ Ring-billed Gull	___ Cliff Swallow	___ Philadelphia Vireo	___ White-throated Sparrow
___ Wood Duck	___ Herring Gull	___ Blue Jay	___ Red-eyed Vireo	___ White-crowned Sparrow
___ American Black Duck	___ Rock Dove	___ American Crow	___ Nashville Warbler	___ Dark-eyed Junco
___ Mallard	___ Mourning Dove	___ Carolina Chickadee	___ Northern Parula	___ Lapland Longspur
___ Blue-winged Teal	___ Yellow-billed Cuckoo	___ Tufted Titmouse	___ Yellow-rumped Warbler	___ Red-winged Blackbird
___ Northern Shoveler	___ Eastern Screech-owl	___ Red-breasted Nuthatch	___ Prairie Warbler	___ Eastern Meadowlark
___ Gadwall	___ Great Horned Owl	___ White-breasted Nuthatch	___ Palm Warbler	___ Rusty Blackbird
___ American Wigeon	___ Barred Owl	___ Brown Creeper	___ Cerulean Warbler	___ Brewer's Blackbird
___ Lesser Scaup	___ Common Nighthawk	___ Carolina Wren	___ Prothonotary Warbler	___ Common Grackle
___ Common Goldeneye	___ Chimney Swift	___ House Wren	___ Ovenbird	___ Brown-headed Cowbird
___ Hooded Merganser	___ Ruby-throated Hummingbird	___ Winter Wren	___ Louisiana Waterthrush	___ Orchard Oriole
___ Ruddy Duck	___ Belted Kingfisher	___ Golden-crowned Kinglet	___ Common Yellowthroat	___ Baltimore Oriole
___ Turkey Vulture	___ Red-headed Woodpecker	___ Ruby-crowned Kinglet	___ Canada Warbler	___ Purple Finch
___ Osprey	___ Yellow-billed Sapsucker	___ Blue-gray Gnatcatcher	___ Yellow-breasted Chat	___ House Finch
___ Bald Eagle	___ Downy Woodpecker	___ Eastern Bluebird	___ Summer Tanager	___ Pine Siskin
___ Northern Harrier	___ Hairy Woodpecker	___ Hermit Thrush	___ Scarlet Tanager	___ American Goldfinch
___ Sharp-shinned Hawk	___ Common Flicker	___ Wood Thrush	___ Northern Cardinal	___ House Sparrow
___ Cooper's Hawk	___ Pileated Woodpecker	___ American Robin	___ Rose-breasted Grosbeak	
___ Red-shouldered Hawk	___ Eastern Wood-pewee	___ Gray Catbird	___ Indigo Bunting	

John James Audubon State Park

"The museum's crowning possession is a copy of the original Birds of America."

A trip to John James Audubon State Park, just across the Ohio River from Evansville, Indiana, isn't so much a birding trip as a pilgrimage. The park luxuriates in birds and even a short walk along its beautiful nature trails rewards the visitor with a wealth of sightings. But the thrill here is just not spotting a Cape May Warbler, Palm Warbler, or any of the other 169 birds found in the park. It's spotting the birds on the same wooded hills and picturesque ravines where the great James Audubon spent so many pleasant hours doing the very same thing, and it's immersing yourself in a fascinating collection of the famed naturalist's memorabilia and art work in the park's museum. Even though this site is technically outside the geographic scope of this book, it is a must for inclusion. For birders it's like crossing the Jordan — in this case, the Ohio — River and visiting the Promised Land.

James Audubon arrived in Henderson, Kentucky in 1810 and with his partner, Ferdinand Rozier, opened a small store. For the next nine years Audubon tried to become a successful businessman. He invested in a steamboat and poured uncounted sums into the building of a grist mill. He was actually drawn to the area not because of its business potential but because it was on the great Mississippi flyway and attracted large numbers of birds.

If birding was good in Henderson, business was not. The succeeding years saw Audubon digging himself out from under one financial disaster only to be buried by another. Business was so bad that he had plenty of time to indulge his pastime. An avid naturalist and painter of birds, he spent hours and days roaming the nearby hills collecting specimens, studying nature, and painting birds. Audubon Park, located just north of Henderson, was one of his favorite haunts. In 1819 Audubon went bankrupt and left Henderson. Less than 20 years later he would be recognized as one of the world's great wildlife artists and naturalists.

It was at Henderson that he decided to make his living as a naturalist and painter of birds and conceived of the bold and unheard of idea to paint a life-sized portrait of every bird in America and publish them in a book. Audubon's masterpiece, *Birds of America*, was published in 1838 and contained several portraits completed while he lived in Henderson.

So, Barb and I came to Audubon State Park to walk in the footsteps of a naturalist and artist who revolutionized the way we look at the natural world. But what monopolized my attention and stroked my imagination was not the nature trails and birdwatching opportunities but the park's magnificent museum which houses the largest collection of Audubon memorabilia and one of the largest collections of his art work in the world.

With my first step into the large room devoted to interpreting and recounting Audubon's life, I was swept up in the drama and excitement of his accomplishments. Letters, drawings, memorabilia, paintings, and detailed historical displays, all seamlessly tied together with a minimum of narrative text, tell the fascinating story of a French youth who came to this country and achieved fame as one of the world's great naturalists. It was hard to decide which was more impressive, the

LOCATION: Henderson, Kentucky.

DIRECTIONS: From Evansville, Indiana, drive a half-mile south of the Ohio River on U.S. 41.

HOURS: Open year-round. The museum is open 10:00 a.m.-5:00 p.m. daily.

BEST TIMES: Spring and fall migrations offer the best birding.

BIRDING HIGHLIGHTS: Great area for woodland birds. Over 30 species of warblers have been seen in the park. The park's bird checklist totals over 160 species.

FOR MORE INFORMATION: James John Audubon State Park, P.O. Box 576, Henderson, Kentucky 42420. Phone: (502) 826-2247.

many original paintings and drawings that caused such a sensation in the art world over 150 years ago and still leaves the viewer in awe today, or the audaciousness of Audubon's dream.

In 1819, he was flat broke and even spent a night in debtor's prison. Yet during the next 19 years he painted and drew nearly every bird east of the Mississippi and many found only west of the river. He sailed to England, found an engraver who could faithfully translate his work into engravings, sold the proposed book by subscription before it went to press, and published what has become recognized as one of the great art books of all time. The museum's crowning possession is a copy of the original *Birds of America*, the huge folio collection of 435 life-sized, hand-painted lithographs published by Audubon over a 14-year period ending in 1838. The exhibits and paintings held me in their grip for over an hour, and I left the room itching to walk the same ground Audubon had so many years ago. But other attractions in the museum tugged at my sleeve and called for my attention.

The museum's Nature Center features an observation room with wraparound windows overlooking a sheltered feeding station the envy of any backyard birder. Next to the windows are binoculars, birding guides, and mounted specimens to help even the fledgling birdwatcher identify birds that, at times, mob the feeders. The Discovery Center is housed in another big room and features a fascinating array of exhibits and hands-on displays explaining bird behavior and biology. The most impressive exhibit is a human-sized bird's nest that visitors are encouraged to climb into and explore. And I still couldn't get out the door. The museum's gift shop is unavoidable when either entering or leaving the building and lures visitors with fine reproductions of Audubon's work and a wide selection of books, jewelry, and gift items with a nature motif.

Barb and I finally made it outside and on to one of the park's 5.5-miles of trails only slightly encumbered by an Audubon biography, a mug, a canvas tote bag sporting Audubon's painting of a Great Blue Heron, a trail map, bird checklist, wildflower checklist, and a list of the park's trees, shrubs, and ferns. The trails meander through a lush upland forest and vary in length from the quarter-mile Museum Trail to the more than 1.5-mile Back Country Trail.

Spring and fall bring large numbers of migrants including over 30 species of warblers to the woodlands, while Wilderness Lake nestled in the heart of the bird sanctuary attracts a surprising variety of waterfowl. As expected, the park offers good viewing opportunities for a wide number of woodland birds throughout the year. While hiking the trails and looking for birds, I couldn't help but feel just a little envy steal into my bones. When Audubon trod this area he saw Ivory-billed Woodpeckers and Whooping Cranes, the first extinct or nearly so and the latter only recently saved from extinction. Instead I saw House Sparrows, House Finches, and European Starlings. It was hardly consoling that Audubon would not have seen any of the three because they were introduced to America long after he left Henderson.

The park offers several enticements to make it a vacation destination instead of a one-day trip. A pleasant campground contains 69 grassy, shaded sites and five tourist cottages, all rented by the night. The park also has a large swimming beach and a 9-hole golf course.

"It was at Henderson that Audubon decided to make his living as a naturalist and painter of birds and conceived of the bold and unheard of idea to paint a life-sized portrait of every bird in America."

AUDUBON STATE PARK FIELD CHECKLIST

___ Horned Grebe	___ Greater Yellowlegs	___ Horned Lark	___ Solitary Vireo	___ Canada Warbler
___ Pied-billed Grebe	___ Lesser Yellowlegs	___ Purple Martin	___ Yellow-throated Vireo	___ Yellow-breasted Chat
___ Double-crested Cormorant	___ Solitary Sandpiper	___ Tree Swallow	___ Warbling Vireo	___ Summer Tanager
___ American Bittern	___ Spotted Sandpiper	___ Northern Rough-winged Swallow	___ Philadelphia Vireo	___ Scarlet Tanager
___ Great Blue Heron	___ Semipalmated Sandpiper	___ Cliff Swallow	___ Red-eyed Vireo	___ Northern Cardinal
___ Little Blue Heron	___ Pectoral Sandpiper	___ Barn Swallow	___ Blue-winged Warbler	___ Rose-breasted Grosbeak
___ Green Heron	___ Common Snipe	___ Blue Jay	___ Tennessee Warbler	___ Indigo Bunting
___ Black-crowned Night-heron	___ American Woodcock	___ Crow	___ Nashville Warbler	___ Rufous-sided Towhee
___ Snow Goose	___ Rock Dove	___ Black-capped Chickadee	___ Northern Parula	___ American Tree Sparrow
___ Canada Goose	___ Mourning Dove	___ Carolina Chickadee	___ Yellow Warbler	___ Chipping Sparrow
___ Wood Duck	___ Black-billed Cuckoo	___ Tufted Titmouse	___ Chestnut-sided Warbler	___ Field Sparrow
___ Green-winged Teal	___ Yellow-billed Cuckoo	___ Red-breasted Nuthatch	___ Magnolia Warbler	___ Fox Sparrow
___ American Black Duck	___ Eastern Screech-owl	___ White-breasted Nuthatch	___ Cape May Warbler	___ Song Sparrow
___ Mallard	___ Great Horned Owl	___ Brown Creeper	___ Yellow-rumped Warbler	___ Swamp Sparrow
___ Northern Pintail	___ Barred Owl	___ Carolina Wren	___ Black-throated Green Warbler	___ White-throated Sparrow
___ Blue-winged Teal	___ Northern Saw-whet Owl	___ Bewick's Wren	___ Blackburnian Warbler	___ White-crowned Sparrow
___ Canvasback	___ Common Nighthawk	___ House Wren	___ Yellow-throated Warbler	___ Dark-eyed Junco
___ Lesser Scaup	___ Whip-poor-will	___ Winter Wren	___ Pine Warbler	___ Lapland Longspur
___ Bufflehead	___ Chimney Swift	___ Golden-crowned Kinglet	___ Prairie Warbler	___ Red-winged Blackbird
___ Hooded Merganser	___ Ruby-throated Hummingbird	___ Ruby-crowned Kinglet	___ Palm Warbler	___ Eastern Meadowlark
___ Red-breasted Merganser	___ Belted Kingfisher	___ Blue-gray Gnatcatcher	___ Bay-breasted Warbler	___ Brewer's Blackbird
___ Black Vulture	___ Red-headed Woodpecker	___ Eastern Bluebird	___ Blackpoll Warbler	___ Common Grackle
___ Turkey Vulture	___ Red-bellied Woodpecker	___ Veery	___ Cerulean Warbler	___ Brown-headed Cowbird
___ Northern Harrier	___ Yellow-bellied Sapsucker	___ Gray-cheeked Thrush	___ Black-and-white Warbler	___ Orchard Oriole
___ Red-shouldered Hawk	___ Downy Woodpecker	___ Swainson's Thrush	___ American Redstart	___ Baltimore Oriole
___ Broad-winged Hawk	___ Hairy Woodpecker	___ Hermit Thrush	___ Prothonotary Warbler	___ Purple Finch
___ Red-tailed Hawk	___ Northern Flicker	___ Wood Thrush	___ Worm-eating Warbler	___ House Finch
___ Rough-legged Hawk	___ Pileated Woodpecker	___ American Robin	___ Swainson's Warbler	___ Red Crossbill
___ American Kestrel	___ Eastern Wood-pewee	___ Gray Catbird	___ Ovenbird	___ Pine Siskin
___ Peregrine Falcon	___ Acadian Flycatcher	___ Northern Mockingbird	___ Northern Waterthrush	___ American Goldfinch
___ Northern Bobwhite	___ Least Flycatcher	___ Brown Thrasher	___ Louisiana Waterthrush	___ Evening Grosbeak
___ American Coot	___ Eastern Phoebe	___ Cedar Waxwing	___ Kentucky Warbler	___ House Sparrow
___ Semipalmated Plover	___ Great Crested Flycatcher	___ Starling	___ Common Yellowthroat	
___ Killdeer	___ Eastern Kingbird	___ White-eyed Vireo	___ Hooded Warbler	

MICHIGAN

WHITEFISH POINT, 59

SAULT STE. MARIE, 63

TAWAS POINT STATE PARK, 66

NAYANQUING POINT
WILDLIFE AREA, 70

KIRTLAND'S WARBLER
NESTING AREA, 73

SHIAWASSEE
NATIONAL WILDLIFE REFUGE, 76

FISH POINT WILDLIFE AREA, 79

PORT CRESCENT STATE PARK, 82

METRO BEACH METROPARK, 85

LAKE ERIE METRO PARK, 88

POINTE MOUILLEE
STATE GAME AREA, 91

BERRIEN COUNTY
DUNES AND LAKESHORE, 95

Whitefish Point

When I left Flint on April 27th, and headed for Whitefish Point, spring was well established in the southern half of the Lower Peninsula. But in the Upper Peninsula there was still plenty of snow on the ground, and as I drove north of Paradise and neared the point, snow was piled as high as 5 feet along the shoulder of the road. The shock was even greater when I reached the Whitefish Point Bird Observatory and walked out to the beach. The Superior shoreline was locked in ice. But this was no giant skating rink. The ice rose in jumbled ridges running parallel to the shore or sat in huge chunky piles looking like the ancient ruins of some prehistoric temple. Here and there in the ice field, long fingers of open water shimmered coldly in the April sun. Raising my eyes from the frozen expanse of shoreline, I looked across the lake at the mesmerizing sight of the snow shrouded Canadian highlands standing out in stark relief against the blue sky. I almost started looking for penguins.

It took a moment of mental readjustment to remember that I was at one of the most important spring migration sites for birds of prey in North America. Adding to the allure of this cold, windswept piece of real estate are the hordes of migrating shorebirds, waterfowl, and songbirds observed at the point every spring and fall. Whitefish Point juts out into Lake Superior like a funnel aimed at the Canadian highlands on the north shore of Whitefish Bay. In the spring the point's sharply converging shorelines naturally herd northbound land birds to the tip of the peninsula where they must either make up their mind to cross the open water or turn back and follow the shore to a crossing point more to their liking. Waterfowl follow the coast as they head north and pass the point before heading out across Lake Superior. In the fall Whitefish Point is the first landfall for birds crossing the great lake.

To simply say that birding at Whitefish Point is spectacular is an understatement. It has been recognized as one of the most important spring raptor migration highways in North America. It is one of the best owl-watching locations in the country and is the best place in the Midwest for sighting boreal species that are usually found farther north. Recognizing that the point is one of the most significant migration sites in North America, the Whitefish Point Bird Observatory (WPBO) was established here in 1978 to "study and document birds of the Great Lakes, with a special emphasis on migration." In a typical spring the volunteers and staff of WPBO count 15,000 to 20,000 raptors, 10,000 Common Loons, over 500 Red-throated Loons, 700 plus Sandhill Cranes, band 2 or 3 dozen owls, and keep records on thousands of other birds observed on or near the point.

In the fall the number of birds calling at Whitefish Point (except for raptors who file a different flight plan for their return trip) is even greater. As many as 80,000 waterbirds have been tallied by WPBO workers in the fall; in good years 10,000 Red-necked Grebes alone pass the point with as many as 3,000 seen in a single day. Warblers, flycatchers, thrushes, and other songbirds pass through on their southward journey in September and often pack the woods near the tip of the point. Also in September, Whitefish Point offers the long-shot chance of seeing all three jaeger species. In late October, large numbers of Snow Buntings frequently touch down at the beach followed by Merlins who have trailed this moveable feast south. Birders willing to brave the cold winds blowing off Superior in

"Whitefish Point has been recognized as one of the most important spring raptor migration highways in North America. It is one of the best owl-watching locations in the country and is the best place in the Midwest for sighting boreal species that are usually found farther north."

LOCATION: Paradise, Michigan.

DIRECTIONS: Twelve miles north of Paradise, Michigan on Whitefish Point Road.

HOURS: Open year-round. The Visitors Center hours are from 10:00 a.m to 6:00 p.m. daily from April 1 through October 15.

BEST TIMES: Late April to early June and September to early November.

BIRDING HIGHLIGHTS: Whitefish Point is one of the most important spring raptor migration spots in North America with upwards of 20,000 birds moving through from late March to May. It is **THE SPOT** to see owls. The point also offers spectacular birding during spring and fall migration for waterfowl and songbirds. It is also the place to see rarities from gulls, jaegers, and Red-throated Loons to Boreal Chickadees.

FOR MORE INFORMATION: Whitefish point Bird Observatory, HC 48 Box 115, Paradise, MI 49768. Phone: (906) 492-3596.

"Serious birders don't get up at the crack of dawn, they get up before there are even any stress fractures in the night sky."

November will be rewarded by finding redpolls, Pine Siskins, and crossbills.

And then there are the vagrants. Only in the birding world are vagrants not only sought after but welcome. In birding, vagrants aren't out-of-work birds looking for a handout. Instead, they are birds that have wandered outside their usual migration range, or are normally non-migrating birds who have migrated because of food shortages in their home range. Whitefish Point collects more than its fair share of vagrants, and every year sees a couple of rarities added to its checklist. I missed seeing an Ivory Gull — only the second of its species seen in Michigan — by about 15 minutes.

If the fall brings more birds, I picked spring to visit because I wanted to experience the hawk migration and hopefully get a crack at seeing some owls. Also, WPBO holds an annual Member's Weekend in late April when raptor migration kicks into high gear, waterfowl tallies begin mounting, and some songbirds start appearing. Additional attractions pulling me north on Members' Weekend were the many programs, workshops, and guided tours, and the wealth of birding experience present to help a less than expert hawk watcher nail down iffy identifications.

After a rather stunned look at the beach and all the ice, I wandered over to the

WHITEFISH POINT FIELD CHECKLIST

___ Red-throated Loon	___ American Wigeon	___ Rough-legged Hawk	___ Red Knot	___ Glaucous Gull
___ Arctic/Pacific Loon	___ Canvasback	___ Golden Eagle	___ Sanderling	___ Great Black-backed Gull
___ Common Loon	___ Redhead	___ American Kestrel	___ Semipalmated Sandpiper	___ Ivory Gull
___ Pied-billed Grebe	___ Ring-necked Duck	___ Merlin	___ Western Sandpiper	___ Black-legged Kittiwake
___ Horned Grebe	___ Greater Scaup	___ Peregrine Falcon	___ Least Sandpiper	___ Sabine's Gull
___ Red-necked Grebe	___ Lesser Scaup	___ Gyrfalcon	___ White-rumped Sandpiper	___ Caspian Tern
___ Eared Grebe	___ King Eider	___ Prairie Falcon	___ Baird's Sandpiper	___ Common Tern
___ American White Pelican	___ Harlequin Duck	___ Spruce Grouse	___ Pectoral Sandpiper	___ Arctic Tern
___ Double-crested Cormorant	___ Oldsquaw	___ Ruffed Grouse	___ Purple Sandpiper	___ Forster's Tern
___ American Bittern	___ Black Scoter	___ Sharp-tailed Grouse	___ Dunlin	___ Ancient Murrelet
___ Least Bittern	___ Surf Scoter	___ Yellow Rail	___ Buff-breasted Sandpiper	___ Rock Dove
___ Great Blue Heron	___ White-winged Scoter	___ Virginia Rail	___ Short-billed Dowitcher	___ White-winged Dove
___ Great Egret	___ Common Goldeneye	___ Sora	___ Long-billed Dowitcher	___ Mourning Dove
___ Snowy Egret	___ Bufflehead	___ American Coot	___ Common Snipe	___ Common Ground Dove
___ Tricolored Heron	___ Hooded Merganser	___ Sandhill Crane	___ American Woodcock	___ Black-billed Cuckoo
___ Cattle Egret	___ Common Merganser	___ Black-bellied Plover	___ Wilson's Phalarope	___ Yellow-billed Cuckoo
___ Green Heron	___ Red-breasted Merganser	___ Lesser Golden-plover	___ Red-necked Phalarope	___ Great Horned Owl
___ Black-crowned Night-heron	___ Turkey Vulture	___ Semipalmated Plover	___ Red Phalarope	___ Snowy Owl
___ Tundra Swan	___ Osprey	___ Piping Plover	___ Pomarine Jaeger	___ Northern Hawk Owl
___ Snow Goose	___ Mississippi Kite	___ Killdeer	___ Parasitic Jaeger	___ Barred Owl
___ Brant	___ Bald Eagle	___ Greater Yellowlegs	___ Long-tailed Jaeger	___ Great Gray Owl
___ Canada Goose	___ Northern Harrier	___ Lesser Yellowlegs	___ Laughing Gull	___ Long-eared Owl
___ Wood Duck	___ Sharp-shinned Hawk	___ Solitary Sandpiper	___ Franklin's Gull	___ Short-eared Owl
___ Green-winged Teal	___ Cooper's Hawk	___ Willet	___ Little Gull	___ Boreal Owl
___ American Black Duck	___ Northern Goshawk	___ Spotted Sandpiper	___ Bonaparte's Gull	___ Northern Saw-whet Owl
___ Mallard	___ Red-shouldered Hawk	___ Upland Sandpiper	___ Ring-billed Gull	___ Common Nighthawk
___ Northern Pintail	___ Broad-winged Hawk	___ Whimbrel	___ Herring Gull	___ Whip-poor-will
___ Blue-winged Teal	___ Swainson's Hawk	___ Hudsonian Godwit	___ Thayer's Gull	___ Chimney Swift
___ Northern Shoveler	___ Red-tailed Hawk	___ Marbled Godwit	___ Iceland Gull	___ Ruby-throated Hummingbird
___ Gadwall	___ Ferruginous Hawk	___ Ruddy Turnstone	___ Lesser Black-backed Gull	___ Belted Kingfisher

hawk watching dune and joined a dozen or so birders on the large observation deck built to protect the fragile dunes from foot traffic. It was midafternoon on a sunny day with thermal-riding raptors dotting the sky. Singly, in pairs, and in small kettles, Red-tailed and Sharp-shinned hawks cut lazy circles in the sky above the point as they drifted toward Superior. There was always something drawing our attention and spiking our interest. Loons often winged passed the deck; occasional Bald Eagles, usually immature, stood out from the smaller birds of prey in the sky like 6-foot slabs of flying 2´ x 10´ planks; and everybody's heartbeat soared as a flight of 13 Sandhill Cranes flew directly over the observation deck and out over the lake.

I headed down to a program on hawk identification in one of the old lighthouse buildings on the point and with the rest of the overflow crowd was treated to a succinct and informative lecture on hawk identification. The star of the program was a Sharp-shinned Hawk that had been captured and tagged in a mist nest just a few moments before the program began. Before driving back to the motel and resting for the evening programs, I headed out to the beach for a last look around and was rewarded with the sight of a few loons flying up the coast line and a Sharp-shinned Hawk that came in low off the lake and settled into a

"In the spring the point's sharply converging shorelines naturally herd northbound land birds to the tip of the peninsula where they must either make up their mind to cross the open water or turn back and follow the shore to a crossing point more to their liking."

___ Red-headed Woodpecker
___ Red-bellied Woodpecker
___ Downy Woodpecker
___ Three-toed Woodpecker
___ Black-backed Woodpecker
___ Northern Flicker
___ Pileated Woodpecker
___ Olive-sided Flycatcher
___ Eastern Wood-pewee
___ Yellow-bellied Flycatcher
___ Alder Flycatcher
___ Willow Flycatcher
___ Least Flycatcher
___ Eastern Phoebe
___ Say's Phoebe
___ Great Crest Flycatcher
___ Western Kingbird
___ Eastern Kingbird
___ Scissor-tailed Flycatcher
___ Horned Lark
___ Purple Martin
___ Tree Swallow
___ Northern Rough-winged Swallow
___ Bank Swallow
___ Cliff Swallow
___ Barn Swallow
___ Gray Jay
___ Blue Jay
___ American Crow
___ Common Raven
___ Clark's Nutcracker

___ Black-capped Chickadee
___ Boreal Chickadee
___ Red-breasted Nuthatch
___ White-breasted Nuthatch
___ Brown Creeper
___ Rock Wren
___ House Wren
___ Winter Wren
___ Sedge Wren
___ Marsh Wren
___ Golden-crowned Kinglet
___ Ruby-crowned Kinglet
___ Blue-gray Gnatcatcher
___ Northern Wheateater
___ Eastern Bluebird
___ Townsend's Solitare
___ Veery
___ Gray-cheeked Thrush
___ Swainson's Thrush
___ Hermit Thrush
___ Wood Thrush
___ American Robin
___ Gray Catbird
___ Northern Mockingbird
___ Sage Thrasher
___ Brown Thrasher
___ American Pipit
___ Sprague's Pipit
___ Bohemian Waxwing
___ Cedar Waxwing
___ Northern Shrike

___ Loggerhead Shrike
___ European Starling
___ White-eyed Vireo
___ Solitary Vireo
___ Yellow-throated Vireo
___ Warbling Vireo
___ Philadelphia Vireo
___ Red-eyed Vireo
___ Blue-winged Warbler
___ Golden-winged Warbler
___ Tennessee Warbler
___ Orange-crowned Warbler
___ Nashville Warbler
___ Northern Parula
___ Yellow Warbler
___ Chestnut-sided Warbler
___ Magnolia Warbler
___ Cape May Warbler
___ Black-throated Blue Warbler
___ Yellow-rumped Warbler
___ Black-throated Green Warbler
___ Blackburnian Warbler
___ Pine Warbler
___ Prairie Warbler
___ Palm Warbler
___ Bay-breasted Warbler
___ Blackpoll Warbler
___ Cerulean Warbler
___ Black-and-white Warbler
___ American Redstart
___ Ovenbird

___ Northern Waterthrush
___ Connecticut Warbler
___ Common Yellowthroat
___ Wilson's Warbler
___ Canada Warbler
___ Yellow-breasted Chat
___ Scarlet Tanager
___ Northern Cardinal
___ Rose-breasted Grosbeak
___ Indigo Bunting
___ Dickcissel
___ Rufous-sided Towhee
___ American Tree Sparrow
___ Chipping Sparrow
___ Clay-colored Sparrow
___ Field Sparrow
___ Vesper Sparrow
___ Lark Sparrow
___ Black-throated Sparrow
___ Lark Bunting
___ Savannah Sparrow
___ Grasshopper Sparrow
___ Henslow's Sparrow
___ LeConte's Sparrow
___ Sharp-tailed Sparrow
___ Fox Sparrow
___ Song Sparrow
___ Lincoln's Sparrow
___ Swamp Sparrow
___ White-throated Sparrow
___ White-crowned Sparrow

___ Harris' Sparrow
___ Dark-eyed Junco
___ McCown's Longspur
___ Lapland Longspur
___ Smith's Longspur
___ Chestnut-collared Longspur
___ Snow Bunting
___ Bobolink
___ Red-winged Blackbird
___ Eastern Meadowlark
___ Western Meadowlark
___ Yellow-headed Blackbird
___ Rusty Blackbird
___ Brewer's Blackbird
___ Common Grackle
___ Brown-headed Cowbird
___ Orchard Oriole
___ Baltimore Oriole
___ Pine Grosbeak
___ Purple Finch
___ Red Crossbill
___ White-winged Crossbill
___ Common Redpoll
___ Hoary Redpoll
___ Pine Siskin
___ American Goldfinch
___ Evening Grosbeak
___ House Sparrow

NORTHERN SAW-WHET OWL

tree where it could be examined up-close with binoculars.

After the evening program in Paradise, the crowd was invited to meet at the hawk platform back at the point to look for migrating owls. By the time we had all gathered at the top of the dune, it was well past dusk, and looking for owls from the platform was like trying to spot stealth bombers. The sharp-eyed and experienced birders picked out the elusive birds coming silently over the distant tree line and called out directions in hushed voices to the less experienced who attempted, with only limited success, getting glasses on the fleeting shadows.

The high point of the next day took place at 6:30 a.m. outside the WPBO headquarters on the point. Let this be a warning to neophyte birdwatchers. Serious birders don't get up at the crack of dawn, they get up before there are even any stress fractures in the night sky. The owl banders keep a few of the owls caught in the hour or so just before sunrise and display them for those brave souls who can drag themselves out of bed and out to the point by 6:30 a.m. I arrived to find a crowd of at least 30 people admiring a Boreal, a Northern Saw-whet, and a Long-eared owl held by WPBO banders. Each of the banders gave a brief talk about the owl they were holding as the crowd took pictures, and within ten minutes the birds were released and flew into nearby trees. The banders stressed the importance of leaving the birds alone and not chasing them into the trees for more pictures.

After coffee and cinnamon rolls in the gift shop, group tours took off in several directions as other birders headed off to bird alone. I joined a group watching the activity at the bird feeders behind the gift shop. American Tree, Fox, Savannah, White-throated, Swamp, and Song sparrows were everywhere. Jason, a 14-year-old, pointed out a Vesper Sparrow in among the crowd at the feeders. There were also plenty of Common Redpolls, Brown-headed Cowbirds, and Purple Finches visiting the feeders and the same teenager helped me find a Pine Siskin. The staff informed the crowd that the feeder also attracts Sharp-shinned Hawks who dart in occasionally to make a meal from the easy pickings.

By the time I wandered out to the point, a line of birders and spotting scopes were scouring the sky for waterfowl and birds of prey. It was community birdwatching with the experts calling out birds and their quadrants to the less experienced. There was also an outpouring of lamentations from the latecomers like myself who had missed an Ivory Gull, an exceedingly rare sighting, which had passed over the point within the last half-hour. The sight of a Merlin zooming past the point and out over the water salved some of our hurt. A couple dozen pairs of binoculars watched the Merlin get about 200 yards off-shore before it thought better of the attempted crossing and make a sharp U-turn and come coasting back to the point where it landed in a stunted pine in plain view of everybody on the beach. Bird activity was steady all morning long on the beach, and by early afternoon the day had heated up enough that soaring hawks and eagles made things interesting at the hawk-watching platform.

The WPBO gift shop has an excellent selection of bird watching guides: a wide variety of classy looking T-shirts and sweatshirts; and a Whitefish Point bird checklist with tips on where and when to see various species at the point and other productive nearby locations. You also can't go wrong by becoming a member of WPBO. Members get a quarterly newsletter filled with a wealth of information on the human and bird activity throughout the course of the year on the Point. My membership entitled me to 10% off a great looking hooded sweatshirt that kept Lake Superior's icy drafts off the back of my neck.

Sault Ste. Marie "The Soo"

This wasn't birding at its finest. It was 7:45 a.m. in the Soo, still nearly pitch dark with the thermometer claiming it was in the high teens, practically balmy for Michigan's Upper Peninsula in mid-January, but the stiff breeze funneling down the river and off Lake Superior was doing its best to freeze dry ears, noses, and fingers. Eight of us from the Genesee County Audubon Chapter had arrived before dawn at the Edison Power Plant on the St. Mary's River with Dickensian expectations of seeing the most magnificent of all falcons, the Gyrfalcon. So we stood for nearly an hour with our backs to the Arctic blasts, watched the sky slowly lighten, searched the window ledges of the huge plant, kept a nervous eye on the cupola, one of the bird's favorite perches, and felt the cold mercilessly creep into our bones. You've got to want to hurt a little to bird Michigan's eastern Upper Peninsula in the winter.

Our trip to one of the coldest birding hot spots in the United States had gotten off to a great start the day before when we tallied two Rough-legged Hawks and a Northern Shrike just outside of Rudyard, about 20 miles south of Sault Ste. Marie. A dozen miles and a few minutes later on the outskirts of the town, we followed directions taken from the Soo birding hotline and drove to the spot where a Northern Hawk Owl had been reported. As we drove up White Road to the wooded ravine where the owl had repeatedly been sighted, it flew into the top of a conifer as if keeping an appointment with us. The bird calmly kept its perch and watched eight excited birders pile out of their cars and set up three spotting scopes. It was still there when we left 25 minutes later as another carload of birders tumbled out of their vehicle and scrambled for scopes and binoculars.

The Gyrfalcon, which usually keeps office hours at the Edison Power Plant, was not as accommodating either that evening or the next morning. Gyrfalcons spend their summers in the Arctic tundra and in the winter a few of them wander into southern Canada and the northernmost tier of the United States. The largest of all falcons, it is considered rare throughout its summer range and in the winter only a bare few are seen in the United States. The largest eruption of Gyrfalcons in southern Canada and along the northern edge of the United States occurred in the winter of 1970-71 when roughly 60 were seen from Maine to British Columbia. If there is anything like a sure bet for spotting this exceedingly rare bird it is at Sault Ste. Marie. For the last few years a Gyrfalcon has regularly spent the winter at the Soo and is most often seen either in the morning or late afternoon perched in one of the window ledges of the Edison Power Plant or overlooking its domain from the cupola on the roof. Even in the coldest winters the water around the plant stays ice-free attracting gulls and overwintering ducks on which the Gyrfalcon dines.

The Gyrfalcon's regularity and almost continuous presence on the Soo birding hot line brings people from all over North America. Our party took five rooms at a local motel and the desk clerk told us that another half-dozen rooms were oc-

"Going to the Soo without calling the Sault Birding Hot Line or the Michigan Rare Bird Alert is like going to Hollywood to find the homes of movie stars and not buying a map to their homes."

LOCATION: Sault Ste. Marie, Michigan.

DIRECTIONS: Sault Ste. Marie lies at the end of I-75 on the border with Canada. The I-75 Business Loop leads to numerous motels and merges into Ashmun Street which runs to Portage Avenue. To reach the Edison Power Plant turn right at the intersection of Ashmun Street and Portage Avenue.

HOURS: Open all year.

BEST TIMES: January and February.

BIRDING HIGHLIGHTS: One of the best places in the Midwest and the United States for winter birding. Boreal species such as Northern Hawk Owl, Snowy Owl, Gyrfalcon, Great Gray Owl, Northern Shrike, Boreal Chickadee, Spruce and Sharp-tailed grouse and winter finches are all regular winter visitors to the area.

FOR MORE INFORMATION: Sault Convention and Visitors Bureau, 2581 I-75 Business Spur, Sault Ste. Marie, MI 49783. Phone: (906) 632-3301.

Whitefish Point Winter Birding Tours: C/O Whitefish Point Bird Observatory, Michigan Audubon Society, 6011 W. St. Joseph, Suite 403, P.O. Box 80527, Lansing, MI 48908-0527.

Sault Ste. Marie Birding Hot Line: (705) 256-2790.

Michigan Rare Bird Alert: (616) 477-1360.

"The Gyrfalcon's regularity and almost continuous presence on the Soo birding hot line brings people from all over North America. The City of Sault Ste. Marie ought to present the bird with a key to the city."

cupied by people who had come to see the Gyrfalcon. The City of Sault Ste. Marie ought to present the bird with a key to the city.

During the long, cold, futile wait for the falcon to make an appearance on Sunday morning, I kept thinking about the birder who went about this much more sensibly. He rented a fourth-floor room in the Holiday Inn on the Canadian side of the Soo, set up his spotting scope, and watched the bird from the comfort of his room.

Even if the Gyrfalcon eludes birders, there are plenty of rare and unusual birds to salve the disappointment. The Soo area likes to boast that its owl central each winter. This does not mean owls are hanging from area trees like Christmas ornaments, but there are always enough owls and other winter specialties listed on the Soo birding hot line to make birders eager to brave temperatures that can get as low as 20-degrees below zero for a chance to see Great Gray Owls, Northern Hawk Owls, the highly allusive Boreal Owl, Short-eared Owls, Snowy Owls, Harlequin Ducks, Boreal Chickadees, Snow Buntings, both crossbills, Bohemian Waxwings, Northern Shrikes, Black-backed Woodpeckers, Pine Grosbeaks, Sharp-tailed and Spruce grouse, and both redpolls. It is almost guaranteed that birders will find something memorable.

After missing the Gyrfalcon Saturday night, we capped the day with the spotting of a Snowy Owl just south of town on Five Mile Road. The next morning, after giving up again on the falcon, the group took the ferry to Sugar Island in search of a Three-toed Woodpecker, reported on the birding hot line, and Great Gray Owls. Sugar Island and, just below it, Neebish Island are prime areas for Great Grays. We missed the woodpecker at a bird feeder by an hour, didn't see a single owl, but did have the pleasure of seeing plenty of Pine Grosbeaks, two Bald Eagles on the ice near the ferry dock, and a Northern Shrike dining on a vole it had impaled in a shrub just off the road.

Back on the mainland we crisscrossed the farmland to the south of the city in search of crossbills, grouse, owls, and anything else of interest. Shrikes and Common Ravens became so commonplace they hardly seemed worth mentioning until we witnessed a raven practicing barrel rolls in the stiff breeze. Every bird feeder held Black-capped Chickadees, Snow Buntings and Common Redpolls, an occasional Red-breasted or White-breasted nuthatch, but the only woodpecker to be seen was a Hairy.

A birding trip to Sault Ste. Marie in the winter necessitates at least a minimum of planning. The better part of two days should be set aside for birding, most of which will be spent riding from one spot to another and standing out in the cold scanning a snow swept field waiting for a bird to show. The wind-chill factor is often low enough to turn uncovered fingers into popsicles within minutes. Warm clothes and boots are a must. And going to the Soo without calling the Sault Birding Hot Line or the Michigan Rare Bird Alert is like going to Hollywood to find the homes of movie stars and not buying a map to their homes.

Once in the Soo, and after checking out any specific locations mentioned on the birding hot line, there are several spots that deserve a birder's attention. First and foremost is the Edison Power Plant on the St. Mary's River. The huge brick building is to the east of I-75 and the International Bridge on Portage Avenue. A park on the east side of the plant provides parking and a good spot from which to search the building for the Gyrfalcon and sweep the open water near the plant for Glaucous Gulls, Common Mergansers, Common Goldeneye and the rare Barrow's Goldeneye, Oldsquaw and Harlequin Ducks. The best place in the area to see the latter is on the Canadian side of the Soo in the power channel to the west of the International Bridge. The Edison Power Plant always collects birders in the morning and evening in hopes of spotting the Gyrfalcon and is a good place to exchange news of other sightings with birders.

East 1.6 miles on Portage from the Edison plant is the ferry dock for Sugar Island. The island is one of the prime owl watching areas in the UP with Great Gray, Snowy and Northern Hawk owls all seen here in recent years. Both crossbills, Rough-legged Hawks, Northern Shrikes, Pine Grosbeaks are also commonly sighted. Most of the island is in private hands and closed to the public, but driving the island's many roads and searching the tree lines and fences posts is as productive as tramping the fields. The ferry leaves for Sugar Island at a quarter to and a quarter after each hour.

The open farmlands just to the south of Sault Ste. Marie hold at least one or two Snowy Owls each winter and Sharp-tailed Grouse are often found feeding among birch, poplar and spruce trees in the morning. Ravens, Northern Hawk Owls, winter finches, Rough-legged Hawks and woodpeckers are only some of the birds seen in the open fields, and patches of woods. Quartering the countryside on Three, Five, Six, and Seven Mile roads which run east and west and on Ridge, Shunk, Seymour, Maple and Piche roads which run north and south usually produce a variety of birds. Be sure and check any bird feeders found along the roads, especially the feeders in front of the house at the corner of Piche Road and Six Mile Road and the feeders 200 yards east of Shunk Road on Three Mile Road.

A final spot to check, especially in the early winter, is Dafter Dump which often attracts Glaucous, Thayer's, and Iceland gulls as well as Rough-legged and Red-tailed hawks. Dafter Dump can be reached by traveling south from Sault Ste. Marie on Mackinaw Trail (H-63) to 12 Mile Road. Turn right on 12 Mile Road and travel approximately 0.3 mile and turn right on the first road after crossing the railroad tracks.

For those who want to concentrate on birds instead of trying to find their away around the countryside, the Whitefish Point Bird Observatory conducts winter birding tours of the area on weekends in January and February.

"As we drove to the wooded ravine where the owl had repeatedly been sighted, it flew into the top of a conifer as if keeping an appointment with us."

SAULT STE. MARIE FIELD CHECKLIST

(Winter birds)

Mallard	Bald Eagle	Short-eared Owl	Common Raven	Pine Grosbeak
American Black Duck	Red-tailed Hawk	Boreal Owl	Black-capped Chickadee	House Finch
Harlequin Duck	Rough-legged Hawk	Red-bellied Woodpecker	Boreal Chickadee	Red Crossbill
Oldsquaw	Gyrfalcon	Downy Woodpecker	Red-breasted Nuthatch	White-winged Crossbill
Common Goldeneye	Spruce Grouse	Hairy Woodpecker	White-breasted Nuthatch	Common Redpoll
Barrow's Goldeneye	Sharp-tailed Grouse	Three-toed Woodpecker	Bohemian Waxwing	Hoary Redpoll
Common Merganser	Great Horned Owl	Black-backed Woodpecker	Cedar Waxwing	Pine Siskin
Iceland Gull	Snowy Owl	Pileated Woodpecker	Northern Shrike	American Goldfinch
Glaucous Gull	Northern Hawk Owl	Gray Jay	House Sparrow	Evening Grosbeak
Sabine's Gull	Great Gray Owl	American Crow	Snow Bunting	

Tawas Point State Park

"The tip of the peninsula concentrates birds like the small end of a funnel."

If I was told that I had to draw a 100-foot diameter circle somewhere in Michigan's Lower Peninsula, and that circle, other than my yard, was the only place from which I could watch birds, my choice, without a second thought, would be the tip of Tawas Point in Tawas Point State Park. Nearly every May I find myself drawn to this sandy peninsula jutting out into Saginaw Bay to wonder anew at the variety and number of birds to be seen here. The last time I visited the point I sat on the large stones marking the end of the sandy spit of land and watched Cliff, Barn, and Tree swallows skimming the water only a few feet from my resting spot. Earlier that day another birder reported seeing, in a matter of a few minutes, all five swallows common to Michigan from the same spot I had staked out.

A fellow birder, sitting several feet away who knew gulls, pointed out a few Bonaparte's and Great Black-backed gulls mixed with the large gathering of Herring and Ring-billed gulls lining the edge of a small island and sandbar only a few dozen yards off the end of the peninsula. A single Great Blue Heron stalked fish at the other end of the island from the gulls, and a Mallard and a Bufflehead glided across the protected water between the peninsula and the sandbar. Further offshore a Common Loon, several Greater Scaup, and small rafts of Red-breasted Mergansers bobbed in the big lake's gentle swells with occasional cormorants flying air cover over the ducks. Mew, Laughing, Little, and Lesser Black-backed gulls have been spotted on the sandbars and small islands capping the tip of the peninsula. Out on the lake a wide variety of ducks, Horned Grebes, and large concentrations of Oldsquaws are regularly seen in spring and fall. The sandbars are also good bets for spotting some of the 30 different species of shorebirds listed on the park's checklist.

Turning my back on the water and walking a few steps inland, I saw a House Wren chattering away from the brush near the foghorn while American Goldfinches, a Gray Catbird, Rose-breasted Grosbeak, and a couple of Yellow-rumped Warblers danced through the thickets and shrubs crowding the end of the peninsula. With just a few steps to the right I could look down the long stretch of beach edging the eastern side of the peninsula. A Spotted Sandpiper could be seen skittering along the beach, and both Common and Caspian Terns patrolled the shore in loose ranks as they flew north along the coastline. As I headed back down the peninsula, but still within a hundred feet of the point, I glimpsed a Brown Thrasher and a Yellow Warbler in adjoining thickets. Up ahead of me on the trail a Northern Flicker feasted on ants.

The peninsula is one of the finest collector of birds in the Midwest, and the tip of the peninsula concentrates them like the small end of a funnel. Tawas Point State Park boasts more than 250 species on its checklist, and it often seems that most, if not all, of these species can be seen, at one time or another, on or from the last 100 feet of the peninsula. In the spring, migrating birds work their way north by following the Lake Huron shoreline. Many even follow the coastline as it bends to the southeast on the north side of Tawas Bay and end up at the tip of Tawas Point. On reaching the end of the point they may rest, feed, or consult the equivalent of a bird road map before heading north up the east side of the peninsula and along the Lake Huron shore. Those birds not averse to crossing open

LOCATION: East Tawas, Michigan.

DIRECTIONS: On U.S. 23 about a half-mile north of downtown East Tawas turn right on to Tawas Beach Road. Follow the road for 2.25 miles to the park entrance.

HOURS: Open year-round.

BEST TIMES: Mid-April through May and late August through September for songbirds. Spring and October through November for waterfowl.

BIRDING HIGHLIGHTS: Tawas Point is one of the finest migrant traps in the Midwest and presents superlative birding in both spring and fall. More than 250 species have been counted in the park. In addition to great chances of seeing numerous varieties of songbirds, waterfowl, shorebirds, and gulls the park regularly produces rarities.

FOR MORE INFORMATION: Tawas Point State Park, 686 Tawas Beach Road, East Tawas, MI 48730. Phone: (517) 362-5041.

water strike out across Tawas Bay or even Saginaw Bay with the former almost always making Tawas Point their first landfall. Many of the latter also make the tip of the peninsula their first touchdown point after a long flight over open water.

In the fall, southbound birds following the edge of Lake Huron are naturally funneled into the peninsula and on reaching the tip must decide to either cross open water or head back up north in order to circle the bay. The right weather conditions can drastically improve birding in the park. Strong south winds in the spring or heavy north winds in the fall can bring the equivalent of aviary gridlock as the winds push the birds out onto the point. A spell of nasty weather in the spring after a stretch of good flying weather will leave large numbers of migrants hunkered down in the trees, shrubs, and protected waters of the bay waiting for good weather to return. For all the above reasons, Tawas Point is recognized as one of the finest migrant traps in the Midwest.

But the rest of the 175-acre park shouldn't be ignored in a rush to get to the end of the peninsula. The entire park offers extraordinary birding. Just think of the tip of the peninsula as the frosting on the cake. In fact, good birding opportunities present themselves before you're in the park. The park's fishing access site, located a few hundred feet north of the park entrance off Tawas Beach Road, is a prime viewing area for ducks and gulls, especially in the spring and fall when boating activity has subsided. Red-necked and Horned grebes, Canvasbacks, scaups and scoters have been found here and on rare occasions Harlequin Ducks, as well as Little and Franklin's gulls.

On the Saturday morning of my latest trip to Tawas Point, White-throated and White-crowned Sparrows had greeted me as I stepped outside the motorhome in the park's comfortable and, at that time of the year, little used campground. Before finishing my coffee and heading toward the end of the peninsula, a Blue Jay, some Common Grackles, and a Downy Woodpecker had joined the crowd around the campsite. Walking toward the point along a trail that starts at the south end of the campground, Nashville and Palm warblers could be seen busily searching for breakfast in thickets and amid the pine trees just west of the lighthouse.

The trail from the campground brought me to the large day-use parking lot and a choice of three routes to the tip of the peninsula. Foot trails follow both the east and west shorelines, and a pedestrian-only work road cuts a nearly straight line down the middle of the peninsula. The eastern trail features several extensive boardwalks built on the crest of low dunes. The boardwalks give good views of the ponds in back of the dunes and are probably the best place to park a spotting scope and probe the big lake for ducks, gulls, and loons at rest out on the water or moving up or down the lake during migration. The boardwalks also provide good views of the wide sandy beaches facing Lake Huron which should be checked for shorebirds.

The western trail closely edges the bay side of the peninsula and leads to sheltered and secluded patches of beach that frequently hold shorebirds. The calmer waters of the bay are often easier to search for waterfowl and resting gulls than Lake Huron. The trail also passes close to low clumps of vegetation and shrubs that can usually be counted on to contain birds. Both trails give overviews of the interior of the peninsula.

The service road only rarely offers views of the lake or bay but can be very good for sparrows, blackbirds, and usually some surprises. On that day the surprises were an American Kestrel perched near the top of a tall shrub at the beginning of the road and a Northern Harrier lazily quartering the landscape well

"Strong south winds in the spring or heavy north winds in the fall can bring the equivalent of aviary gridlock as the winds push the birds out onto the point. A spell of nasty weather in the spring after a stretch of good flying weather will leave large numbers of migrants hunkered down in the trees, shrubs, and protected waters of the bay waiting for good weather to return."

TAWAS POINT STATE PARK FIELD CHECKLIST

Assembled from a variety of sources.

___ Red-throated Loon	___ Lesser Golden-plover	___ Common Nighthawk	___ Hermit Thrush	___ Scarlet Tanager
___ Common Loon	___ Wilson's Plover	___ Whip-poor-will	___ Wood Thrush	___ Western Tanager
___ Pied-billed Grebe	___ Semipalmated Plover	___ Chimney Swift	___ American Robin	___ Northern Cardinal
___ Horned Grebe	___ Piping Plover	___ White-collared Swift	___ Gray Catbird	___ Rose-breasted Grosbeak
___ Red-necked Grebe	___ Killdeer	___ Ruby-throated Hummingbird	___ Northern Mockingbird	___ Black-headed Grosbeak
___ American White Pelican	___ American Avocet	___ Belted Kingfisher	___ Brown Thrasher	___ Indigo Bunting
___ Double-crested Cormorant	___ Greater Yellowlegs	___ Red-headed Woodpecker	___ American Pipit	___ Dickcissel
___ American Bittern	___ Lesser Yellowlegs	___ Red-bellied Woodpecker	___ Bohemian Waxwing	___ Rufous-sided Towhee
___ Least Bittern	___ Solitary Sandpiper	___ Yellow-bellied Sapsucker	___ Cedar Waxwing	___ American Tree Sparrow
___ Great Blue Heron	___ Willet	___ Downy Woodpecker	___ Northern Shrike	___ Chipping Sparrow
___ Little Blue Heron	___ Spotted Sandpiper	___ Hairy Woodpecker	___ Loggerhead Shrike	___ Clay-colored Sparrow
___ Green Heron	___ Upland Sandpiper	___ Black-backed Woodpecker	___ European Starling	___ Field Sparrow
___ Black-crowned Night-heron	___ Whimbrel	___ Northern Flicker	___ White-eyed Vireo	___ Vesper Sparrow
___ Mute Swan	___ Ruddy Turnstone	___ Pileated Woodpecker	___ Solitary Vireo	___ Lark Sparrow
___ Brant	___ Red Knot	___ Olive-sided Flycatcher	___ Yellow-throated Vireo	___ Savannah Sparrow
___ Canada Goose	___ Sanderling	___ Eastern Wood-pewee	___ Warbling Vireo	___ Henslow's Sparrow
___ Wood Duck	___ Semipalmated Sandpiper	___ Yellow-bellied Flycatcher	___ Philadelphia Vireo	___ Grasshopper Sparrow
___ Green-winged Teal	___ Western Sandpiper	___ Acadian Flycatcher	___ Red-eyed Vireo	___ LeConte's Sparrow
___ American Black Duck	___ Least Sandpiper	___ Alder Flycatcher	___ Blue-winged Warbler	___ Fox Sparrow
___ Mallard	___ White-rumped Sandpiper	___ Willow Flycatcher	___ Golden-winged Warbler	___ Song Sparrow
___ Northern Pintail	___ Baird's Sandpiper	___ Least Flycatcher	___ Tennessee Warbler	___ Lincoln's Sparrow
___ Blue-winged Teal	___ Pectoral Sandpiper	___ Eastern Phoebe	___ Orange-crowned Warbler	___ Swamp Sparrow
___ Northern Shoveler	___ Dunlin	___ Say's Phoebe	___ Nashville Warbler	___ White-throated Sparrow
___ American Wigeon	___ Short-billed Dowitcher	___ Great Crested Flycatcher	___ Northern Parula	___ White-crowned Sparrow
___ Greater Scaup	___ Common Snipe	___ Western Kingbird	___ Yellow Warbler	___ Harris' Sparrow
___ Lesser Scaup	___ Red-necked Phalarope	___ Eastern Kingbird	___ Chestnut-sided Warbler	___ Dark-eyed Junco
___ Oldsquaw	___ Red Phalarope	___ Scissor-tailed Flycatcher	___ Magnolia Warbler	___ Lapland Longspur
___ Black Scoter	___ Laughing Gull	___ Horned Lark	___ Cape May Warbler	___ Snow Bunting
___ Surf Scoter	___ Little Gull	___ Purple Martin	___ Black-throated Blue Warbler	___ Bobolink
___ White-winged Scoter	___ Bonaparte's Gull	___ Tree Swallow	___ Black-throated Green Warbler	___ Red-winged Blackbird
___ Common Goldeneye	___ Mew Gull	___ Northern Rough-winged Swallow	___ Blackburnian Warbler	___ Eastern Meadowlark
___ Bufflehead	___ Ring-billed Gull	___ Bank Swallow	___ Pine Warbler	___ Western Meadowlark
___ Hooded Merganser	___ Herring Gull	___ Cliff Swallow	___ Kirtland's Warbler	___ Yellow-headed Blackbird
___ Common Merganser	___ Thayer's Gull	___ Barn Swallow	___ Prairie Warbler	___ Rusty Blackbird
___ Red-breasted Merganser	___ Iceland Gull	___ Blue Jay	___ Palm Warbler	___ Brewer's Blackbird
___ Turkey Vulture	___ Lesser Black-backed Gull	___ American Crow	___ Bay-breasted Warbler	___ Common Grackle
___ Northern Harrier	___ Glaucous Gull	___ Black-capped Chickadee	___ Blackpoll Warbler	___ Brown-headed Cowbird
___ Sharp-shinned Hawk	___ Great Black-backed Gull	___ Tufted Titmouse	___ Cerulean Warbler	___ Orchard Oriole
___ Cooper's Hawk	___ Caspian Tern	___ Red-breasted Nuthatch	___ Black-and-white Warbler	___ Baltimore Oriole
___ Red-shouldered Hawk	___ Common Tern	___ White-breasted Nuthatch	___ American Redstart	___ Pine Grosbeak
___ Rough-legged Hawk	___ Black Tern	___ Brown Creeper	___ Prothonotary Warbler	___ Purple Finch
___ Golden Eagle	___ Mourning Dove	___ Carolina Wren	___ Ovenbird	___ House Finch
___ American Kestrel	___ Black-billed Cuckoo	___ House Wren	___ Northern Waterthrush	___ Red Crossbill
___ Merlin	___ Yellow-billed Cuckoo	___ Winter Wren	___ Connecticut Warbler	___ White-winged Crossbill
___ Peregrine Falcon	___ Eastern Screech-owl	___ Golden-crowned Kinglet	___ Mourning Warbler	___ Common Redpoll
___ Ring-necked Pheasant	___ Great Horned Owl	___ Ruby-crowned Kinglet	___ Common Yellowthroat	___ Hoary Redpoll
___ Virginia Rail	___ Snowy Owl	___ Blue-gray Gnatcatcher	___ Hooded Warbler	___ Pine Siskin
___ Sora	___ Barred Owl	___ Eastern Bluebird	___ Wilson's Warbler	___ American Goldfinch
___ American Coot	___ Long-eared Owl	___ Veery	___ Canada Warbler	___ House Sparrow
___ Sandhill Crane	___ Short-eared Owl	___ Gray-cheeked Thrush	___ Yellow-breasted Chat	
___ Black-bellied Plover	___ Northern Saw-whet Owl	___ Swainson's Thrush	___ Summer Tanager	

"The boardwalks give good views of the ponds in back of the dunes and are probably the best place to park a spotting scope and probe the big lake for ducks, gulls, and loons."

away from the parking area. About 100 yards north of the end of the point the two trails join the service road which continues on to the end of the peninsula. The intersection of the three trails is a traditional hot spot. I was greeted by a Savannah Sparrow, a Brown Thrasher, a Black-and-white Warbler, and a Blue-gray Gnatcatcher. On extraordinarily good birding days, the last 100 yards of the service road and the point itself can make you think there isn't a better place to bird in the entire Midwest.

No matter where you walk in the park during migration periods every clump of trees and shrubs should be checked for birds. More than 250 species have been spotted within, or from, the park. The checklist includes 11 species of flycatchers, 34 warblers, 11 different gulls, and 23 from the waterfowl family. Among the rarities seen in the park are American Avocet, Say's Phoebe, Scissor-tailed Flycatcher, Western Kingbird, Loggerhead Shrike, Black-headed Grosbeak, Orange-crowned Warblers, Red Phalarope, White-collared Swift, the state's only recorded sighting of a Wilson's Plover, and a number of other birds that if spotted can make a birdwatcher's day.

Nayanquing Point State Wildlife Area

"Though couch-potato birders will see a lot of birds, those who get off their duffs will see a lot more."

LOCATION: Pinconning, Michigan.

DIRECTIONS: From I-75 north of Bay City take exit 173 (Linwood Rd.) and go east on Linwood Road approximately 1.5 miles to M-13 and turn north (left). Drive 3 miles on M-13 to Kitchen Road and turn right (east) and drive 1.5 miles to the wildlife area.

HOURS: Open year-round, but it is difficult if not foolhardy to try and watch birds during waterfowl hunting season.

BEST TIMES: Spring and fall for waterfowl and shorebirds but the number and variety of nesting birds and the propensity of rarities to stop here make birding attractive spring through fall.

BIRDING HIGHLIGHTS: The large numbers and variety of waterfowl in spring and fall that can be easily viewed from the area's roads and wildlife observation tower making birding easy and interesting. Good numbers and variety of shorebirds and marsh birds have also made this a favorite birding spot throughout mid-Michigan. The area also has a much-deserved reputation for attracting an unusual number of rarities.

FOR MORE INFORMATION: Nayanquing Point Wildlife Area, 1570 Tower Beach Road, Pinconning, MI 48650.

On a good day, Nayanquing Point is a lazy man's birding paradise. But, if you're of the moral persuasion that insists time, effort, and sweat must be endured before reaping your reward it will comfort you to know that Nayanquing Point has plenty of dikes to tramp in search of a choice bird. And while you trudge the miles of dikes you can cast a disdainful eye at birders like myself who drive up to the observation tower, climb the few steps to the top, set up their spotting scopes, and start tallying birds.

The observation tower presents birders with a 360-degree view of marshes, water-filled ditches, open pools and a wide expanse of Saginaw Bay. Looking west from the tower, from due north to due south, birders have a bird's-eye view of Nayanquing Point Wildlife Area's refuge. Visitors are only allowed into the refuge with special permission, but from the top of the tower birders with binoculars and spotting scopes can search out the many waterfowl, and shorebirds that frequent the refuge. Be sure and check any open pools in the refuge for Wilson's Phalarope, which are suspected of breeding in the refuge. Facing south, birders have an uninterrupted view of Saginaw Bay which is often dotted with gulls, and numerous ducks during spring and fall migration. To the northeast of the tower lies a pool that regularly attracts large numbers of waterfowl and due east is a small hook of land jutting out into the bay. This hook is one of the few areas at Nayanquing Point supporting trees and tall shrubs and is an excellent spot for songbirds in the spring and especially the fall. As an added dividend, shorebirds are often spotted along the sandy shore of the point.

In spring and fall Canada Geese, Snow Geese and Tundra Swans gather in large concentrations at the wildlife area and the observation tower serves as a perfect grandstand from which to enjoy the spectacle. Twenty species of ducks have been recorded in the wildlife area and with Gadwall, Northern Shoveler, Northern Pintail, American Black Ducks, Redheads, and American Wigeon all nesting in the area, it's unusual not to find something of interest from spring through fall. Other nesters of special interest include American and Least bitterns, King and Virginia rails, Sora, Black and Forster's terns, Marsh Wrens, and Yellow-headed Blackbirds. The area also gets more than its fair share of rarities with Tricolored Heron, Piping Plovers, American Avocets, Hudsonian and Marbled godwits, American White Pelicans, Cinnamon Teal, Long-tailed Jaegers, Arctic Terns, and Peregrine Falcons turning up irregularly.

The bad news for the terminally lazy birder is that you do have to decamp from the tower and actually put out a little effort to see a good variety of the non-waterfowl species. The good news is it can be as easy as driving around the wildlife area's roads and stopping to glass birds. Or, you can follow the example of the perversely persistent birders who walk the dikes with the moral certainty of seeing more species for their efforts than those who take a more relaxed and sedentary approach. Ultimately it must be admitted that even though couch-potato birders will see a lot of birds at Nayanquing, those who get off their duffs will see a lot more.

One of the best dikes to walk in the entire wildlife area is reached by driving to the southern end of Tower Beach Road, leaving your car and continuing south on a walkable dike. The dike cuts a straight line due south for about a half-mile before connecting with a trail that circles a large cattail pond. The pond and trail is an excellent area for wading birds, rarities, waterfowl and Yellow-headed Blackbirds. The area is also posted as a no-entry wildlife refuge, but birders have been granted permission to walk the trails. If you wish to bird this area get permission first from the manager.

A shouldn't-be-missed spot for both the car birder and those looking to hike the dikes is on Kitchen Road a half-mile past Tower Beach Road. There is a parking area on Kitchen Road at the spot where it makes a hard right and heads toward the observation platform another half-mile to the south. The parking area offers a grand view of a large, shallow pool that regularly attracts large numbers of waterfowl, gulls, terns, and shorebirds. The pool is so vast that a spotting scope is needed to identify the birds near the far shore. The marshy edges should be checked for heron, egrets and shorebirds. In April the field to the west of the parking lot often holds Short-eared Owls. Birders report the best time to glass the field in search of the owls is just before sunset.

A system of walkable dikes heading north from the parking lot takes birdwatchers through an area that has proven to be fairly dependable for sparrows, songbirds and rails. After approximately a mile the dike ends at a east/west dike. The fields and pool north of the east/west dike often holds bitterns and is a favorite haunt for Ospreys and Bald Eagles. Turning right or east on the dike will take the birder to Saginaw Bay. On reaching the bay, it's possible to walk the shoreline south all the way to the observation tower and then back up Kitchen Road to the parking area, but it is a several mile-long walk.

The northern edge of the wildlife area, along Erickson Road, also holds some prime birding sites. To reach Erickson Road turn north from Kitchen Road on Tower Beach Road and drive 1 mile to Erickson and turn right. There is a parking lot at the end of Erickson Road that gives immediate access to the Saginaw Bay. Walking south from the parking lot, along the shoreline, the birder has a great view of the bay and close-up views of a series of small, brush and cattail-ringed ponds lying just inland from the low dunes fronting the bay. The late spring morning I was there, I was rewarded with the sight of a stately raft of Tundra Swans out on the big water and Wood Ducks and Green-winged Teal coasting across the quiet waters of an inland pond. A couple of Great Blue Heron stood poised amid the cattails and a Great Egret speared a fish from a tree limb that dipped into the pond. As I turned back to the parking lot, a Belted Kingfisher crossed the pond heading south.

The last half-mile of Erickson Road before it ends at the bay has a well deserved reputation for songbirds during migration. I was there too early in the spring to expect to see any, but I did spot a Ring-necked Pheasant crossing the road. The road can be either walked or driven slowly in search of birds. It's also possible to pull off the road nearly anywhere, when or if something promising turns up. It's also worth driving any of the roads in or bordering the wildlife refuge. I've parked beside a drainage ditch and watched from less than 20 feet away as a Forster's Tern hovered in the air like a kestrel before tucking its wings and cannonading head first into the water after a fish.

"Be sure and check any open pools in the refuge for Wilson's Phalarope, which are suspected of breeding in the refuge."

NAYANQUING POINT STATE WILDLIFE AREA FIELD CHECKLIST

This is an incomplete checklist gathered from a number of sources but
primarily relies on Jeff Buecking's years of birding the area.

___ Red-throated Loon	___ Black Scoter	___ Willet	___ Eastern Screech-owl	___ Brown Thrasher
___ Common Loon	___ Surf Scoter	___ Hudsonian Godwit	___ Great Horned Owl	___ American Pipit
___ Pied-billed Grebe	___ White-winged Scoter	___ Marbled Godwit	___ Snowy Owl	___ Cedar Waxwing
___ Horned Grebe	___ Common Goldeneye	___ Ruddy Turnstone	___ Short-eared Owl	___ Yellow Warbler
___ Red-necked Grebe	___ Bufflehead	___ Red Knot	___ Common Nighthawk	___ Magnolia Warbler
___ American White Pelican	___ Hooded Merganser	___ Sanderling	___ Chimney Swift	___ Cape May Warbler
___ American Bittern	___ Common Merganser	___ Semipalmated Sandpiper	___ Ruby-throated Hummingbird	___ Black-throated Blue Warbler
___ Least Bittern	___ Red-breasted Merganser	___ Western Sandpiper	___ Belted Kingfisher	___ Blackburnian Warbler
___ Great Blue Heron	___ Ruddy Duck	___ Least Sandpiper	___ Redheaded Woodpecker	___ Palm Warbler
___ Great Egret	___ Turkey Vulture	___ White-rumped Sandpiper	___ Red-bellied Woodpecker	___ Blackpoll Warbler
___ Snowy Egret	___ Osprey	___ Baird's Sandpiper	___ Downy Woodpecker	___ Black-and-white Warbler
___ Little Blue Heron	___ Bald Eagle	___ Pectoral Sandpiper	___ Hairy Woodpecker	___ Scarlet Tanager
___ Tricolored Heron	___ Northern Harrier	___ Dunlin	___ Northern Flicker	___ Indigo Bunting
___ Cattle Egret	___ Sharp-shinned Hawk	___ Stilt Sandpiper	___ Eastern Wood-pewee	___ Northern Cardinal
___ Green Heron	___ Cooper's Hawk	___ Buff-breasted Sandpiper	___ Yellow-bellied Flycatcher	___ American Tree Sparrow
___ Black-crowned Night-heron	___ Red-shouldered Hawk	___ Ruff	___ Willow Flycatcher	___ Chipping Sparrow
___ White Ibis	___ Broad-winged Hawk	___ Short-billed Dowitcher	___ Least Flycatcher	___ Field Sparrow
___ Glossy Ibis	___ Red-tailed Hawk	___ Long-billed Dowitcher	___ Eastern Phoebe	___ Vesper Sparrow
___ White-faced Ibis	___ Rough-legged Hawk	___ Common Snipe	___ Great Crested Flycatcher	___ Savannah Sparrow
___ Tundra Swan	___ American Kestrel	___ Wilson's Phalarope	___ Western Kingbird	___ Grasshopper Sparrow
___ Mute Swan	___ Merlin	___ Red-necked Phalarope	___ Eastern Kingbird	___ Fox Sparrow
___ Greater White-fronted Goose	___ Peregrine Falcon	___ Long-tailed Jaeger	___ Horned Lark	___ Song Sparrow
___ Ross' Goose	___ Ring-necked Pheasant	___ Laughing Gull	___ Purple Martin	___ Lincoln's Sparrow
___ Snow Goose	___ King Rail	___ Franklin's Gull	___ Tree Swallow	___ Swamp Sparrow
___ Canada Goose	___ Virginia Rail	___ Little Gull	___ Northern Rough-winged Swallow	___ White-throated Sparrow
___ Wood Duck	___ Sora	___ Bonaparte's Gull	___ Bank Swallow	___ White-crowned Sparrow
___ Green-winged Teal	___ Common Moorhen	___ Ring-billed Gull	___ Cliff Swallow	___ Harris' Sparrow
___ American Black Duck	___ American Coot	___ Herring Gull	___ Barn Swallow	___ Dark-eyed Junco
___ Mallard	___ Sandhill Crane	___ Thayer's Gull	___ Blue Jay	___ Lapland Longspur
___ Northern Pintail	___ Black-bellied Plover	___ Lesser Black-backed Gull	___ American Crow	___ Snow Bunting
___ Blue-winged Teal	___ Lesser Golden-plover	___ Glaucous Gull	___ Black-capped Chickadee	___ Bobwhite
___ Cinnamon Teal	___ Semipalmated Plover	___ Great Black-backed Gull	___ White-breasted Nuthatch	___ Red-winged Blackbird
___ Northern Shoveler	___ Piping Plover	___ Caspian Tern	___ Brown Creeper	___ Eastern Meadowlark
___ Gadwall	___ Killdeer	___ Common Tern	___ House Wren	___ Yellow-headed Blackbird
___ American Wigeon	___ American Avocet	___ Arctic Tern	___ Sedge Wren	___ Rusty Blackbird
___ Canvasback	___ Greater Yellowlegs	___ Forster's Tern	___ Marsh Wren	___ Common Grackle
___ Redhead	___ Lesser Yellowlegs	___ Black Tern	___ Golden-crowned Kinglet	___ Brown-headed Cowbird
___ Ring-necked Duck	___ Solitary Sandpiper	___ Rock Dove	___ Ruby-crowned Kinglet	___ Baltimore Oriole
___ Tufted Duck	___ Spotted Sandpiper	___ Mourning Dove	___ Blue-gray Gnatcatcher	___ American Goldfinch
___ Greater Scaup	___ Upland Sandpiper	___ Black-billed Cuckoo	___ American Robin	___ House Sparrow
___ Lesser Scaup	___ Whimbrel	___ Yellow-billed Cuckoo	___ Gray Catbird	

Kirtland's Warbler Nesting Area

It's strange how suddenly one's perspective can change. I've passed through Grayling, Michigan too many times to count and although not a habituate of Holiday Inns I've been in enough of them to feel more than comfortable. So there I was on a Friday morning in a small conference room of the Grayling Holiday Inn feeling very ordinary when my world went from everyday to exotic faster than a Stephen Speilberg movie. From the conversation going on around me, it became evident that I was sitting in a room with a dozen paying customers of a world-famous nature tour company. I'd seen ads for this company-with-two-first-names inviting potential customers to explore some of the most exotic and remote places on earth from the jungles of Borneo to a birding trip up the Amazon.

It was almost with disbelief that I realized that in addition to treks in distant Nepal and guided trips to Central American rain forests the company-with-two-first-names offered the public a guided exploration into the heart of darkness that is central Michigan. And as I contemplated Grayling in a new and exotic light it dawned on me how fearless and independent this author must be for mounting a solo and unsupported expedition into the distant land found north of Higgins Lake. I sat up straighter in my chair, threw my shoulders back, and felt almost Indiana Jones-ish.

The prize that the clients of the company-with-two-first-names, I, and a few other intrepid adventurers to Grayling had come in search of was the Kirtland's Warbler, one of the rarest birds in the world. Their total population presently hovers around 1,400, and their sole nesting grounds are the jack pine forests of nine counties in northern Michigan. If 1,400 doesn't impress you as scarce, think of them this way: At roughly a half-ounce each, the total weight of all the Kirtland's Warblers in the world comes to about forty pounds. That's the equivalent of two California Condors, or a big bag of dog food.

Kirtland's Warblers were one of the first birds listed as endangered after the passage of the 1973 Endangered Species Act and at one time the total number of Kirtland's Warblers dipped as low as 500. The bird's scarcity is due in part to their extraordinary fussiness about their nesting habitat. They will only nest in young jack pine forests that are between 5- and 16-feet tall, and the trees must be spaced far enough apart to let sunlight through to the ground where they build their nests. A further preference is that the jack pine stands be at least 80 acres in size. What further complicates things is that cones of the jack pine only open and release their seeds after being burned. Forest fires, of course, are frowned upon by modern man. With the coming of Europeans to northern Michigan most of the jack pine forests were cut down, and forest fires were no longer allowed to burn through vast tracts of northern Michigan. The warblers need large tracts of jack pine scattered across their nesting range that mature, succumb to forest fires, and through fire, regenerate new jack pine stands. Man was pushing the little bird to the brink of existence until the U.S. Forest Service and the Michigan Department of Natural Resources began managing tracts of jack pine as nesting habitat for the

"The prize that the clients of the company-with-two-first-names, I, and a few other intrepid adventurers had come in search of was the Kirtland's Warbler, one of the rarest birds in the world."

LOCATION: Grayling and Mio, Michigan.

DIRECTIONS: The Grayling Holiday Inn is on the southern I-75 Business Loop. The Mio Ranger District Office of the U.S. Forest Service is on the corner of 4th Street and M-33 in Mio. Prior reservations are not needed except for large groups.

HOURS: Tours from the Mio Ranger District Office are at 7:00 a.m. Wednesday through Friday and 7:00 a.m. and 11:00 a.m. on Saturday and Sunday. Tours from Grayling Holiday Inn depart at 7:00 a.m. and 11:00 a.m. daily.

BEST TIMES: The only time the tours are available are from mid-May through the first week in July.

BIRDING HIGHLIGHTS: Fairly good chance of seeing one the rarest birds in the world.

FOR MORE INFORMATION: For Grayling tour information contact, U.S. Fish and Wildlife Service, East Lansing Field Office, 2651 Coolidge, East Lansing, MI 48823. Phone: (517) 351-2555.

For Mio tours contact, U.S. Forest Service, Mio Ranger District, Mio MI 48647. Phone: (517) 826-3252.

"Kirtland's Warbler parents fed the bigger, more aggressive cowbird chick while their own chicks died."

birds. Timber harvests, tree planting, and controlled burns are all employed to maintain the birds' nesting grounds.

The birds faced another threat to their survival when the Brown-headed Cowbird spread from the Great Plains into Michigan. In the West, the bird is known as the buffalo bird because it literally lived by following the buffalo. Because of their nomadic life female cowbirds lay eggs in nests of other birds leaving their young to be raised by adoptive parents. When Brown-headed Cowbirds spread to Michigan, they parasitized Kirtland's Warbler nests with the result that Kirtland's Warbler parents fed the bigger, more aggressive cowbird chick while their own chicks died. A vigorous program of trapping cowbirds found in Kirtland's Warbler nesting areas and destroying the parasitic birds has helped bring the warbler species back from the edge of extinction.

The nesting areas managed by the government are not open to the public, and it is against the law to trespass on the posted nesting grounds. But the U.S. Forest Service, Fish and Wildlife Service and the Michigan Department of Natural Resources lead regularly scheduled tours into nesting areas from mid-May through the first week in July. The tours depart from the Grayling Holiday Inn at 7:00 a.m. and 11:00 a.m. daily and from the U.S. Forest Service, Mio Ranger District office at 7:00 a.m. Wednesday through Friday, and 7:00 a.m.and 11:00 a.m. Saturdays and Sundays.

I was at the Grayling Holiday Inn on the second day of tours in the spring of 1997 and had the uncomfortable feeling that I might have pushed my luck arriving so early in the season. Grayling had received two inches of snow two nights before my arrival. My spirits slipped even lower when I overheard a ranger remark to another birder that the Mio area usually has more warblers and that the previous day's tour from Grayling had failed to turn up a single Kirtland's Warbler.

The tours generally take from 90 minutes to 2 hours depending on the weather conditions and sightings. All tours are guided by expert wildlife professionals and begin with an informative, ten-minute slide show detailing the natural history of the bird, its dependence on jack pine stands for nesting habitat, and conservation efforts to ensure the survival of the species. Neither dogs nor taped birding calls are permitted on the tour.

After the slide show the rangers led a caravan of cars and the two vans carrying the nature tour's paying customers south of Grayling to a remote dirt road bisecting large stands of jack pines. We all piled out of the vehicles and followed the ranger into the pines for about a hundred yards and then stood around in a large silent group as the ranger and the more expert birders listened for the call of a Kirtland's Warbler. It was a long, quiet wait. After 25 minutes we trooped back to the road and listened some more. We were rewarded not with a Kirtland's Warbler but by the songs of Lincoln and Vesper sparrows. The only other bird of note seen on the tour was a Wild Turkey that narrowly escaped with its life when it contested the right-of-way with the car in front of me. After a fruitless hour of listening and a short walk to see a cowbird trap, the tour broke up with the cars and two vans going their separate ways. I was only mildly disappointed that I didn't get to see the elusive little warbler (I'll mount a second expedition to the wilds of northern Michigan either later in June or next spring) but could appreciate the disappointment suffered by the people on the tour who had come from as far away as Seattle, Texas, Florida and Alabama for a glimpse of the bird.

The tour took place on Friday morning and I learned later that it wasn't until the following Monday that a Kirtland's Warbler finally showed in the Grayling area. The birds had even missed the annual festival held in their honor every year in Roscommon, Michigan at Kirtland Community College. The festival features bird watching and nature tours, photo contests, art and craft vendors, wildlife and environmental workshops, and entertainment. The festival usually takes place in mid-May. For more information call 1-517-275-5121, ext. 347. Or go online to the Internet at http://www.kirtland.cc.mi.us/~warbler/. There is also a 48-mile, self-guided auto tour through Kirtland's Warbler country south and east of Mio. The tour takes motorists to pleasant and dramatic scenery. The many interpretive signs, at designated parking areas along the tour route, are filled with both general interest wildlife information and specific information on Kirtland's Warbler. An informative brochure and a detailed map of the auto tour is available from the U.S. Forest Service, Mio Ranger District in Mio. There is, however, little or no chance of seeing a Kirtland's Warbler on the tour.

"The total weight of all the Kirtland's Warblers in the world comes to about forty pounds. That's the equivalent of two California Condors, or a big bag of dog food."

KIRTLAND'S WARBLER

Shiawassee National Wildlife Refuge

LOCATION: Saginaw, Michigan.

DIRECTIONS: The headquarters of the Shiawassee National Wildlife Refuge and the trailhead for the Ferguson Bayou Trail are on Curtis Road. Approximately 5 miles south of Saginaw on M-13 turn west on Curtis Road and drive 1 mile to the refuge headquarters or 4 miles to Ferguson Bayou Trailhead. To reach the Woodland Trail cross the Saginaw River in downtown Saginaw on M-46 and drive west approximately 2.5 miles to Center Road. Turn south on Center Road and drive 2 miles to Stroebel Road which is on the south side of the Tittabawassee river. At Stroebel turn left and drive a short distance to the trailhead parking lot.

HOURS: Open 8:00 a.m.-4:30 p.m. daily. In the fall, trail closures vary from year to year to accommodate hunters. Typically the Ferguson Bayou trail is closed until 1:00 p.m. for 3 weeks in August for goose hunting, and in November and December the trails are closed on alternate days to accommodate deer hunters.

BEST TIMES: Mid-March and October and November for waterfowl. Mid-May for songbirds. Good birding opportunities year-round.

BIRDING HIGHLIGHTS: One of the best places in Michigan to see huge numbers of waterfowl. Very good birding for warblers, songbirds, and shorebirds in spring and good birding all year. Winter months offer good chances of seeing Snowy Owls and wintering Bald Eagles.

FOR MORE INFORMATION: Shiawassee National Wildlife Refuge, 6975 Mower Road, Saginaw, MI 48601. Phone: (517) 777-5930.

What a way to say good-bye to winter! On an unseasonably warm day, less than 24 hours before the vernal equinox marked the beginning of spring, I stood on the observation tower, at the midway point of the Ferguson Bayou Trail, in the Shiawassee National Wildlife Refuge, and looked out over several square miles of fields, pools, and marsh. The huge expanse of landscape was in itself impressive, but what kept a family of four, who drove here from Lansing, and myself absolutely spellbound for the better part of an hour were the thousands of Canada Geese standing almost shoulder to shoulder in the huge wildlife arena. From near the foot of the tower the geese spread out for as far as the naked eye could pick them out, and in the distance where the individual geese began to blur and blend with their neighbors it looked like a living carpet covered the land. Sweeping the field with the 10X spotting scope mounted on the tower or with a pair of binoculars, we were delighted to discover the massive gathering of Canada Geese was seasoned with large numbers of Blue and Snow geese and Northern Pintails.

This spectacle is repeated at Shiawassee National Wildlife Refuge every spring and fall as thousands of ducks and geese stop here to feed and rest during migration. From late February through mid-April 15,000 geese and upwards of 6,000 ducks call at the refuge and during the first two weeks of November, 23,000 geese and 25 to 30,000 ducks flood the fields, marshes, and pools of the refuge. I wasn't about to attempt a count of the waterfowl spread out before me on this surprisingly warm March afternoon, but by any definition, even biblical, there was a host of birds present. Except for the Northern Pintails there were few ducks to be seen. In previous years on visits later in the spring I'd encountered large numbers of teal, Mallards, Northern Shovelers, Wood Ducks, American Black Ducks, and Common Mergansers. Less common, but often seen in spring and fall, are Greater and Lesser scaup, Ruddy Ducks, Redheads, Canvasbacks, and Bufflehead. To make up for the lack of ducks, the five of us were treated to the sight of two immature Bald Eagles soaring over the refuge.

Within the refuge four major rivers that drain one-sixth of the Lower Peninsula join to form the Saginaw River, which flows only a short distance to the north before emptying into Saginaw Bay. The refuge and much of the adjoining land is low, marshy, frequently flooded, and has historically been a gathering ground for migrating waterfowl. The refuge was established in 1953 "as an inviolate sanctuary, or for any other management purpose, for protecting migratory birds" from encroaching industrial and agricultural development. In preserving and maintaining the area as a haven for waterfowl, diked pools have been added to enhance a habitat of lowland hardwoods, swamps, bayous and marshland. Area farmers are also allowed to plant corn, wheat, barley and soybeans on 1,200 acres of the refuge with the understanding that they will leave one-third of the crop standing as food for the wildlife. This program of not only protecting and creating habitat attractive to waterfowl and other wildlife, but also setting out a banquet for them, has made the refuge one of the premier wildlife viewing areas in

Michigan.

If staggering numbers of waterfowl are the main attraction for many of the refuge visitors, there is plenty of other good birding to keep other birders happy and content throughout the year. Waterfowl begin arriving by late February and continue to pass through on their northward journey until mid-April. Mixed in with the geese and ducks are an estimated 7,000 Tundra Swans that call at the refuge between mid-March to mid-April. As the waterfowl become relatively scarce, warblers and other songbirds begin to show up at Shiawassee with their numbers peaking in mid-May. In the third and fourth week of May large numbers of shorebirds are often numerous in the muddy areas of the refuge. I once spent nearly a half-day trying fruitlessly to identify more than a dozen different small shorebirds poking around in a muddy field within sight of the parking lot.

In the summer months marsh birds are plentiful. It was along one of Shiawassee's many brush-shrouded dikes that I saw my first Sora. The refuge supports a colony of 1,500 nesting Great Blue Heron and Virginia Rails also nest here. Among birds of prey Northern Harriers, Red-tailed, and Red-shouldered hawks are all commonly seen and Bald Eagles nest in the refuge. By mid-September, ducks and geese begin to pass through the refuge and continue to show up through December. In winter, Snow Buntings, Horned Larks and occasional Snowy Owls are found in the refuge, along with as many as 20 wintering Bald Eagles. No matter what time of the year, visitors will most likely find themselves sharing a trail with deer, woodchucks, and if they're lucky, catch sight of the numerous foxes that live in the area.

Two long trails provide the public access to the refuge. Ferguson Bayou Trail, beginning on the south side of the refuge, follows the tops of dikes in a 4.5-mile loop through wooded swamps, marshes, and fields. There are two cutoffs that make for a shorter hike, but in the spring and fall the main point of walking the trail is to reach the observation tower overlooking the vast area where the waterfowl rest and feed. The tower is at the halfway point of the trail, and both cutoffs head back to the trailhead before reaching the tower.

On the last day of winter when I visited the refuge, ice still choked the swamps and ditches. Later in the year the weed-filled ditches next to trails and the woods would be alive with birds, but on this day only Red-winged Blackbirds and Blue Jays were about in any numbers. A few robins and sparrows proceeded me up the trail, with an occasional crow and a Red-tailed Hawk keeping me company overhead until I gained the observation deck and was bowled over by the vast congregation of geese. A mountain or dirt bike would make the trip from the parking lot to the observation deck and back much quicker as long as the trail is not too wet and muddy. It wouldn't have been a problem that day, but after the first serious thaw, or heavy rain, even the tops of the dikes can be soft and very muddy in spots.

On the north side of the refuge, The Woodland Trail leads birders through a bottomland forest lying between the confluence of the Tittabawassee and Shiawassee rivers. The 4-mile-long trail and a shorter 1.5-mile loop cuts through some prime songbird areas. The trail follows an old railroad grade through forest wetlands for part of the way and nearly the entire trail is prone to flooding during high water. You can call the refuge headquarters for trail conditions.

"The program of not only protecting and creating habitat attractive to waterfowl and other wildlife, but also setting out a banquet for them, has made the refuge one of the premier wildlife viewing areas in Michigan."

SHIAWASSEE NATIONAL WILDLIFE REFUGE FIELD CHECKLIST

___ Pied-billed Grebe
___ Horned Grebe
___ American White Pelican
___ Double-crested Cormorant
___ American Bittern
___ Great Blue Heron
___ Great Egret
___ Cattle Egret
___ Green Heron
___ Black-crowned Night-heron
___ Tundra Swan
___ Greater White-fronted Goose
___ Snow Goose
___ Canada Goose
___ Wood Duck
___ Green-winged Teal
___ American Black Duck
___ Mallard
___ Northern Pintail
___ Blue-winged Teal
___ Northern Shoveler
___ Gadwall
___ American Wigeon
___ Canvasback
___ Redhead
___ Ring-necked Duck
___ Greater Scaup
___ Lesser Scaup
___ Common Goldeneye
___ Bufflehead
___ Hooded Merganser
___ Common Merganser
___ Red-breasted Merganser
___ Ruddy Duck
___ Turkey Vulture
___ Osprey
___ Bald Eagle
___ Northern Harrier
___ Sharp-shinned Hawk
___ Cooper's Hawk
___ Northern Goshawk
___ Red-shouldered Hawk
___ Broad-winged Hawk
___ Red-tailed Hawk
___ Rough-legged Hawk
___ Golden Eagle
___ American Kestrel
___ Merlin
___ Peregrine
___ Ring-necked Pheasant

___ Ruffed Grouse
___ Virginia Rail
___ Sora
___ Common Moorhen
___ American Coot
___ Sandhill Crane
___ Black-bellied Plover
___ Lesser Golden-plover
___ Semipalmated Plover
___ Killdeer
___ American Avocet
___ Greater Yellowlegs
___ Lesser Yellowlegs
___ Solitary Sandpiper
___ Spotted Sandpiper
___ Upland Sandpiper
___ Hudsonian Godwit
___ Marbled Godwit
___ Red Knot
___ Sanderling
___ Semipalmated Sandpiper
___ Least Sandpiper
___ Western Sandpiper
___ White-rumped Sandpiper
___ Baird's Sandpiper
___ Pectoral Sandpiper
___ Dunlin
___ Stilt Sandpiper
___ Short-billed Dowitcher
___ Long-billed Dowitcher
___ Common Snipe
___ American Woodcock
___ Wilson's Phalarope
___ Red-necked Phalarope
___ Bonaparte's Gull
___ Ring-billed Gull
___ Herring Gull
___ Caspian Tern
___ Common Tern
___ Forster's Tern
___ Black Tern
___ Rock Dove
___ Mourning Dove
___ Black-billed Cuckoo
___ Yellow-billed Cuckoo
___ Eastern Screech-owl
___ Great Horned Owl
___ Snowy Owl
___ Barred Owl
___ Short-eared Owl

___ Common Nighthawk
___ Chimney Swift
___ Ruby-throated Hummingbird
___ Belted Kingfisher
___ Red-headed Woodpecker
___ Red-bellied Woodpecker
___ Yellow-bellied Sapsucker
___ Downy Woodpecker
___ Hairy Woodpecker
___ Northern Flicker
___ Pileated Woodpecker
___ Olive-sided Flycatcher
___ Eastern Wood-pewee
___ Willow Flycatcher
___ Least Flycatcher
___ Eastern Phoebe
___ Great Crested Flycatcher
___ Eastern Kingbird
___ Horned Lark
___ Tree Swallow
___ Northern Rough-winged Swallow
___ Bank Swallow
___ Barn Swallow
___ Blue Jay
___ American Crow
___ Black-capped Chickadee
___ Tufted Titmouse
___ Red-breasted Nuthatch
___ White-breasted Nuthatch
___ Brown Creeper
___ House Wren
___ Winter Wren
___ Sedge Wren
___ Marsh Wren
___ Golden-crowned Kinglet
___ Ruby-crowned Kinglet
___ Blue-gray Gnatcatcher
___ Eastern Bluebird
___ Veery
___ Gray-cheeked Thrush
___ Swainson's Thrush
___ Hermit Thrush
___ Wood Thrush
___ American Robin
___ Gray Catbird
___ Brown Thrasher
___ American Pipit
___ Cedar Waxwing
___ Northern Shrike
___ European Starling

___ Solitary Vireo
___ Yellow-throated Vireo
___ Warbling Vireo
___ Philadelphia Vireo
___ Red-eyed Vireo
___ Blue-winged Warbler
___ Golden-winged Warbler
___ Tennessee Warbler
___ Orange-crowned Warbler
___ Nashville Warbler
___ Northern Parula
___ Yellow Warbler
___ Chestnut-sided Warbler
___ Magnolia Warbler
___ Cape May Warbler
___ Black-throated Blue Warbler
___ Yellow-rumped Warbler
___ Black-throated Green Warbler
___ Blackburnian Warbler
___ Palm Warbler
___ Bay-breasted Warbler
___ Blackpoll Warbler
___ Cerulean Warbler
___ Black-and-white Warbler
___ American Redstart
___ Prothonotary Warbler
___ Ovenbird
___ Northern Waterthrush
___ Connecticut Warbler
___ Mourning Warbler
___ Common Yellowthroat
___ Wilson's Warbler
___ Canada Warbler
___ Scarlet Tanager
___ Northern Cardinal
___ Rose-breasted Grosbeak
___ Indigo Bunting
___ Rufous-sided Towhee
___ American Tree Sparrow
___ Chipping Sparrow
___ Field Sparrow
___ Vesper Sparrow
___ Savannah Sparrow
___ Fox Sparrow
___ Song Sparrow
___ Lincoln's Sparrow
___ Swamp Sparrow
___ White-throated Sparrow
___ White-crowned Sparrow
___ Dark-eyed Junco

___ Lapland Longspur
___ Snow Bunting
___ Bobolink
___ Red-winged Blackbird
___ Yellow-headed Blackbird
___ Eastern Meadowlark
___ Rusty Blackbird
___ Brewer's Blackbird
___ Common Grackle
___ Brown-headed Cowbird
___ Baltimore Oriole
___ Purple Finch
___ Common Redpoll
___ Pine Siskin
___ American Goldfinch
___ Evening Grosbeak
___ House Sparrow

Incidentals

___ Common Loon
___ Snowy Egrets
___ White Ibis
___ Glossy Ibis
___ Mute Swan
___ Ross' Goose
___ Barnacle Goose
___ Oldsquaw
___ White-winged Scoter
___ King Rail
___ Willet
___ Buff-breasted Sandpiper
___ Glaucous Gull
___ Great Black-backed Gull
___ Long-eared Owl
___ Whip-poor-will
___ Yellow-bellied Flycatcher
___ Acadian Flycatcher
___ Purple Martin
___ Cliff Swallow
___ Carolina Wren
___ Northern Mockingbird
___ Bohemian Waxwing
___ Pine Warbler
___ Prairie Warbler
___ Yellow-breasted Chat
___ Dickcissel
___ Pine Grosbeak

Fish Point Wildlife Area

I suspect that the only people who wouldn't enjoy the view from atop the observation deck overlooking Fish Point Wildlife Area would be air traffic controllers. It was a week before duck hunting season, and the airspace above the refuge and wildlife area was filled with waterfowl. Chevrons of Canada Geese flew across the area and settled into the open waters of the refuge and surrounding fields from all directions in precise military formations while the less disciplined ducks, singly and in pairs, entered and departed the airspace with all the decorum of Keystone Cops. The sight might remind an air traffic controller of his worst nightmare, but for myself and the two duck hunters, who were desperately trying to figure out how to get off work for opening day, it was a stirring and unforgettable show. It is also typical of the sights to be seen at Fish Point each spring and fall.

The enormous concentrations of waterfowl and the ease with which visitors can watch them make Fish Point Wildlife Area one of the premier waterfowl viewing areas in Michigan. In mid-March a huge assemblage of Canada Geese, ducks, and upwards of 3,000 Tundra Swans settle into the area's open ponds, marshes, farm fields, and the adjacent, shallow waters of Saginaw Bay to rest and feed before continuing north or dispersing to less crowded breeding areas. From the top of the observation deck or by driving Gotham, Ringle, Clark roads and Sea Gull Lane, which crisscross the wildlife area, birders are treated to awe inspiring views of the congregating waterfowl. Among the hordes of geese, ducks, and swans, Greater White-fronted and Snow geese can often be picked out. On rare occasions Brant and Barnacle geese have been seen. Ducks regularly spotted in both the spring and fall include American Black Ducks, Mallards, both Green- and Blue-winged teal, Northern Pintail, Redhead, Canvasback, Hooded Mergansers, and Northern Shoveler. Lucky birders have spotted occasional Surf Scoters, White-winged Scoters, Cinnamon Teal, Eurasian Wigeon, and Oldsquaw. Mid-March also brings flights of migrating raptors. Fall migration numbers are usually lower than spring but the viewing is still spectacular.

Leaving the duck hunters endlessly arguing over the best excuses to try on their bosses, I took the 1.1-mile hiking trail that begins at the base of the platform. The path borders a drainage ditch marking the southern end of the wildlife area's refuge before inscribing a long loop through a brush choked field and wetlands to the south of the refuge. I kicked up several Mallards and a Blue-winged Teal from the ditch, and as I neared the point where the trail cut away from the refuge, the Vs of geese entering the refuge passed so close overhead I was tempted to jump up and try to touch a flight leader.

The brush and shrubs lining the trail where it turns south and away from the refuge were saturated with sparrows. Chasing a pair into a bush with my binoculars, I was treated to both a Savannah and a Swamp sparrow within the Bushnell's field of vision. For the next hundred yards I waded through sparrows. They proceeded me down the trail, cut back and forth in front of me from shoelace to eye-level and were constantly underfoot. Even with my limited powers of discernment, I was able to pick out Song, American Tree and a few White-throated sparrows in addition to the Swamp and Savannah sparrows. The surrounding fields were packed with Canada Geese feeding on corn stubble. As I headed back

"From the top of the observation deck or by driving roads that crisscross the wildlife area, birders are treated to awe-inspiring views of the congregating waterfowl."

LOCATION: Sebewaing, Michigan.

DIRECTIONS: From the center of Unionville, drive 3 miles west on M-25 to Ringle Road. Turn north on Ringle and drive approximately 3 miles to the headquarters. The observation tower and nature trail are 0.6 miles north of the headquarters.

HOURS: Open all year, but birdwatchers will probably not want to visit during waterfowl season.

BEST TIMES: From mid-March to mid-May is best with fall being a close second.

BIRDING HIGHLIGHTS: One of the finest waterfowl viewing areas in Michigan. Also good for shorebirds in spring and fall. Warbler and songbird migration can be heavy in early May. Although there is no official bird checklist for the area, an incomplete checklist totals over140 species and indicates good all-around birding.

FOR MORE INFORMATION: Department of Natural Resources, 503 N. Euclid Avenue, Suite 1, Bay City, MI 48706.

"Lucky birders have spotted occasional Surf Scoters, White-winged Scoters, Cinnamon Teal, Eurasian Wigeon, and Oldsquaw."

to the tower, what I at first mistook for the largest flock of starlings I'd ever seen rose into the sky over a field far to the north. A glimpse through the binoculars revealed a huge swarm of at least 500 Canada Geese wheeling and turning in the air before settling back down in a far-off field.

In both spring and fall driving a car slowly along the roads bisecting the wildlife area can prove to be more productive than hiking the trail or climbing the observation tower. A slow moving car does not disturb the huge flocks of geese resting and feeding in the fields, and several of the roads also border ditches where ducks can be observed. Especially productive are Gotham and Ringle Roads. The fields bordering Gotham Road, which runs east and west, usually attracts the largest concentrations of geese. Ringle Road cuts through the center of the wildlife area and, just north of the observation tower, runs along side of the refuge. From spring through fall geese, ducks, and shorebirds can often be seen only feet from the car in the marsh bordering the road. Pied-billed Grebes, Wood Ducks, both bitterns, Yellow-headed Blackbirds, and American Coots are all regularly sighted here. Rarer birds seen in and around the marsh include Cattle Egrets, Little Blue Heron, and American White Pelicans. Following Ringle Road further north leads to private residences and duck camps bordering Saginaw Bay. Although there is no public access to the bay, good views are available from the road.

A better view of the bay can be had from the end of a nameless road that heads to the west about a half-mile north of the observation tower on Ringle Road. The road ends in a parking lot about 200 yards from Ringle Road and a wide, well-trod path leads a few yards to the west for a great view of the saucer-shallow waters of Saginaw Bay and good shorebird, gull, and waterfowl viewing opportunities. Fish Point also attracts sizable numbers of migrating passerines and warblers in May. Although any clump of trees or thicket in the wildlife area holds the promise of warblers, the neighborhood surrounding this parking lot and the trail leading from it to the southwest are especially good.

Fish Point is also worth checking out in winter with Snowy Owls, Lapland Longspurs, and Northern Shrikes sometimes in residence along with the more common Horned Larks and Snow Buntings. Once again, they can be found from both the observation platform and by driving the roads within the wildlife area. No matter what time of year you plan to visit, writing ahead for a map will help first-time visitors thoroughly explore every nook and cranny of this great bird-watching area.

FISH POINT WILDLIFE AREA FIELD CHECKLIST

Compiled from a variety of sources.

___ Pied-billed Grebe
___ American White Pelican
___ Double-crested Cormorant
___ American Bittern
___ Least Bittern
___ Great Blue Heron
___ Snowy Egret
___ Cattle Egret
___ Black-crowned Night-heron
___ Glossy Ibis
___ Tundra Swan
___ Greater White-fronted Goose
___ Snow Goose
___ Ross' Goose
___ Brant
___ Barnacle Goose
___ Canada Goose
___ Wood Duck
___ Green-winged Teal
___ American Black Duck
___ Mallard
___ Northern Pintail
___ Blue-winged Teal
___ Cinnamon Teal
___ Northern Shoveler
___ Eurasian Wigeon
___ American Wigeon
___ Canvasback
___ Redhead
___ Ring-necked Duck

___ Greater Scaup
___ Lesser Scaup
___ Oldsquaw
___ Surf Scoter
___ White-winged Scoter
___ Hooded Merganser
___ Common Merganser
___ Red-breasted Merganser
___ Ruddy Duck
___ Turkey Vulture
___ Osprey
___ Bald Eagle
___ Northern Harrier
___ Northern Goshawk
___ Red-shouldered Hawk
___ Broad-winged Hawk
___ Red-tailed Hawk
___ Rough-legged Hawk
___ Gyrfalcon
___ Peregrine Falcon
___ Merlin
___ American Kestrel
___ Ring-necked Pheasant
___ Virginia Rail
___ Sora
___ American Coot
___ Black-bellied Plover
___ Lesser Golden-plover
___ Killdeer
___ Greater Yellowlegs

___ Lesser Yellowlegs
___ Willet
___ Spotted Sandpiper
___ Upland Sandpiper
___ Whimbrel
___ Hudsonian Godwit
___ Ruddy Turnstone
___ Least Sandpiper
___ Semipalmated Sandpiper
___ Baird's Sandpiper
___ Pectoral Sandpiper
___ Dunlin
___ Buff-breasted Sandpiper
___ Ruff
___ Common Snipe
___ Wilson's Phalarope
___ Red-necked Phalarope
___ Ring-billed Gull
___ Herring Gull
___ Iceland Gull
___ Common Tern
___ Forster's Tern
___ Black Tern
___ Rock Dove
___ Mourning Dove
___ Snowy Owl
___ Short-eared Owl
___ Belted Kingfisher
___ Yellow-bellied Flycatcher
___ Acadian Flycatcher

___ Willow Flycatcher
___ Least Flycatcher
___ Great Crested Flycatcher
___ Eastern Kingbird
___ Horned Lark
___ Sedge Wren
___ Marsh Wren
___ Blue-gray Gnatcatcher
___ American Robin
___ Gray Catbird
___ American Pipit
___ Cedar Waxwing
___ Northern Shrike
___ Loggerhead Shrike
___ European Starling
___ White-eyed Vireo
___ Philadelphia Vireo
___ Red-eyed Vireo
___ Warbling Vireo
___ Solitary Vireo
___ Tennessee Warbler
___ Orange-crowned Warbler
___ Nashville Warbler
___ Yellow Warbler
___ Chestnut-sided Warbler
___ Cape May Warbler
___ Yellow-rumped Warbler
___ Kirtland's Warbler
___ Palm Warbler
___ Black-and-white Warbler

___ American Redstart
___ Common Yellowthroat
___ Canada Warbler
___ Northern Cardinal
___ Dickcissel
___ American Tree Sparrow
___ Chipping Sparrow
___ Field Sparrow
___ Vesper Sparrow
___ Savannah Sparrow
___ Henslow's Sparrow
___ Fox Sparrow
___ Song Sparrow
___ Swamp Sparrow
___ White-throated Sparrow
___ White-crowned Sparrow
___ Lapland Longspur
___ Snow Bunting
___ Bobolink
___ Red-winged Blackbird
___ Yellow-headed Blackbird
___ Rusty Blackbird
___ Brewer's Blackbird
___ Common Grackle
___ Common Redpoll
___ American Goldfinch

Port Crescent State Park

"I got so excited I forgot not only to write down what I saw but to identify most of them."

LOCATION: Port Austin, Michigan.

DIRECTIONS: Port Crescent State Park is 2 miles west of Port Austin on M-25. To reach the Wilderness Arboretum drive approximately 5 miles west of Port Austin on M-25 to Oak Beach Road. Turn south (left) and drive 0.5 miles to Loosemore Road. Turn left and drive 0.5 miles to entrance.

HOURS: Park and arboretum open dawn-dusk year-round.

BEST TIMES: Spring and fall for songbirds and waterfowl. March through May for hawk watching.

BIRDING HIGHLIGHTS: An undiscovered birding gem that features hawkwatching that may come to rival Whitefish Point. Excellent birding for other species during spring and fall migration. Of the 158 species on the park checklist, 53 are confirmed nesters and another 40 are suspected, so birding can be profitable from spring through fall.

FOR MORE INFORMATION: Huron Audubon Club, 3088 Port Austin Road, Port Austin, MI 48467.

Port Crescent State Park, 1775 Port Austin Road, Port Austin, MI 48467. Phone: (517) 738-8663.

Normally I'm no more paranoid than the next person, but within minutes of arriving at Port Crescent State Park I was sure the dozen or so birdwatchers at the park's new hawk-watching tower had spotted me for an absolute novice, and had instantaneously concocted a deviously clever plan to make me the butt of a practical joke. OK, OK, maybe I am a little more paranoid than the next person, but hear me out.

Port Crescent State Park had just been recently discovered as a great spot for witnessing the spring migration of hawks, and I arrived primed for my first hawk-watching experience. The Huron Audubon Society had begun a hawk migration observatory here in 1990 with volunteer help, and their results have been impressive. In 1994 the volunteers counted over 10,000 hawks in only 173 hours of documented observation, and in one four-hour period 4,000 Broad-winged Hawks had passed over the tip of Michigan's Thumb heading north across Lake Huron. So I was ready and eager to experience this annual natural wonder.

I climbed the steps to the top of the observation platform and exchanged friendly nods with the other birders and waited for something to happen. Within minutes one of the binoculared watchers sweeping the horizon broke through the low murmur of conversation to tell the crowd he saw two "sharpies" to the north, over the tree line. Along with everyone else in attendance, I expectantly swept my binoculars in the direction of his outthrust arm. Nothing. The azure blue sky was empty except for a scattering of cottony clouds. Somebody else called out that there were two more "sharpies" due east and an Osprey above and behind them. Someone else murmured, "good bird." What the hell was going on here, I didn't see a thing. Nothing, nada, zilch, zip, zero. I slowly lowered my glasses as my paranoia meter rose. Carefully I stole looks at the other birders. Were there smirks behind the binoculars? Was someone going to glance over at the novice and see how he was reacting to being put-on? Was this the equivalent of a country boy going to the big city and being told, and believing, that he had to buy a ticket to ride the elevator?

Maddeningly, the minutes dragged by with more sightings. Sets of glasses continued to sweep in unison back and forth over Lake Huron, the tree line on the other side of the Pinnebog River, and inland towards the knuckle of the Thumb. Finally, after dismissing my self-induced paranoia that all these people were having a whale of a time making me the butt of a fantastic joke, what I first took for a speck of dust on my eyeglasses I captured in my binoculars. With nearly unbelieving eyes I saw a bird with a long tail heading north on fluttering and intermittent wing beats. "What's that?" I exclaimed. I should have asked for help sooner because a dozen experienced hawk watchers began tutoring me on the fine points of identifying the specks of dust. Within minutes I knew the rudiments of telling the difference between a Sharp-shinned Hawk, "sharpie," and a Broad-winged Hawk. In the course of the next hour, I thrilled to the sight of several Ospreys, several dozen "sharpies," Broad-winged Hawks, and a Cooper's Hawk that darted across the sky just above the tree line. And within a half-hour of finally getting the hang of hawk spotting, the bird of the day appeared. A clearly identifiable Bald Eagle drifted by cutting lazy circles, high over the Pinnebog River. Eighty hawks were tallied in the next hour. Golden Eagles, Merlin's and Peregrine

Falcons have also been recorded at the observatory, but none were seen that day.

Huron Audubon Society members have the happy expectation that the hawk migration here at the tip of Michigan's thumb may rival the numbers that are regularly posted at the nationally famous Whitefish Point Observatory in Michigan's Upper Peninsula. Starting in late March and continuing through the first part of June, there is every indication that Port Crescent witnesses a steady flow of raptors heading north to their summer breeding grounds. A hundred or so hours of observation only gives a hint of the potential. As volunteer hours increase, Port Crescent may garner the reputation as one of the great observation points for watching hawks during spring migration.

My experience proves rank amateurs can enjoy the show as much as the old hands. And for those who want to learn the skills of hawk watching or stand next to an experienced watcher in hopes that some knowledge will rub off, the Huron Audubon Club holds a hawk-watch festival on the last Saturday of each April. Besides the thrill of watching the great birds of prey, the day also includes lectures, demonstrations, and a potluck lunch. For more information contact the Huron Audubon Club.

The park and the surrounding area also offer fine opportunities for watching waterfowl and songbirds, especially during spring and fall migration. Two Saturdays after the hawk festival, I was back to tramp the woods, marshes, and shoreline of the park looking for warblers, waterbirds, and anything else that would hold still long enough to be identified. Unlike the hawk festival, I didn't run into another birder the whole day. A 90-minute pleasant stroll alongside the backwaters of the Pinnebog River netted 45 birds, and another half-dozen warblers, vireos, and waterfowl I couldn't nail down. Included in the list were nine warblers, a Swainson's Thrush, and a near-certain spotting of a Prairie Warbler that's not even on the park's bird checklist.

There are several excellent spots that are readily accessible and easily walked that abound in birds. Just to the left of the entrance road to the park's campground is a small wooded area that is bordered by a backwater of the Pinnebog River, a small stream, M-25, and the entrance road. The little pocket of woods consistently produces warblers. The grassy area and thickets edging the woods and river contain White-throated and White-crowned sparrows, Northern Cardinals, Gray Catbirds, Eastern Kingbirds, swallows, and a host of other species. And often as not, a Great Blue Heron or egret can be seen fishing in the old river channel.

At Port Crescent State Park "warbler central" is the trail bordering the north bank of the old river channel. The trail can be reached from the beach at the campground or by crossing a pedestrian-only bridge where Port Crescent Road intersects with M-25 about a mile south of the park headquarters. Warblers seem to naturally congregate in the thickets and evergreens bordering the old channel.

Birding is also very good in the park's day-use area. This area contains swatches of oak-covered ridges, large grassy areas, the backwaters, and the main channel of the Pinnebog River and the Huron lakeshore. All are accessible from hiking and nature trails or by simply stepping out of your car. Within a half-mile walk, the birder can go from watching a Mourning Warbler or vireo near the park entrance on M-25 to spotting a Wood Duck or a Belted Kingfisher on the river to catching sight of a Great Black-backed Gull, Caspian Tern, or Red-breasted Merganser from the park's sandy beach.

The bottom line is that there is not a bad birding spot in the park. Although the park's bird checklist only records 158 species, it lists another 12 that have

"For those who want to learn the skills of hawk watching or stand next to an experienced watcher in hopes that some knowledge will rub off, the Huron Audubon Club holds a hawk-watch festival on the last Saturday of each April."

been sighted regularly in areas surrounding the park. Even this total of 170 is probably low, the compiler of the list (Monica Essenmacher of the Huron Audubon Club) expects new species will be added regularly. The checklist also gives valuable tips on where to look for what within the park.

A birding trip to Port Crescent State Park should not be considered complete without a visit to the Huron County Nature Center Wilderness Arboretum. Just five minutes away by car from the park, the area is a genuine hotspot for warblers, flycatchers, and numerous other species. Ron Weeks, the author of *Birds and Birding Finding in the Saginaw Bay Area*, considers the Wilderness Arboretum one of the least known but best migrant traps in the Saginaw Bay area. I quickly discovered why. After leaving the car in a gravel parking lot, I made my solitary way toward the back of the arboretum on the Long Loop Trail. Vireos, thrushes, Tufted Titmice, and chickadees dogged my steps until the magical moment when I reached a small, marsh marigold-blessed wetlands with a little foot bridge that crossed it. Birds seemed to be everywhere. Almost simultaneously in an arc of less than 90-degrees, I spotted a Palm Warbler, Hairy Woodpecker, Nashville Warbler, and a Blue-gray Gnatcatcher. All were close enough to identify without binoculars. Every few minutes brought a new supply of birds. I got so excited I forgot not only to write down what I saw but to identify most of them. It seemed a great climax for a near-perfect day. Without a backward glance, I turned and headed for the car.

PORT CRESCENT STATE PARK FIELD CHECKLIST

(checklist of bird species)

Metro Beach Metropark

Birding and Metro Beach Metropark are, on first impression, completely incongruous. It's true, the divided parkway leading into the heavily used outdoor playground, administered by the Huron-Clinton Metropolitan Authority, cuts through a marsh; but, after a brief glimpse of the wetlands, the parkway culminates in a huge, circular asphalt parking lot one would expect to find next to a shopping mall or a major league sports complex. Surrounding this virtual sea of asphalt are two sprawling marinas, a par 3 golf course, ball fields, grassy picnic grounds, a water slide, bathhouse, shuffleboard and tennis courts, a dance pavilion, a swimming pool large enough to float a yacht, and the ultimate shrine from which to commune with nature — a 18-hole putt-putt golf course.

Arrive here in midsummer and this 770-acre park is swarming with people who've come to picnic, swim, rotisserie themselves on the 3,000 feet of manmade beach facing Lake St. Clair, and play on, in, or at one of the recreation facilities. But there is more to this park than an asphalt replica of a black hole encircled by low-tech family amusements. The park is bordered on two sides by the remnants of the vast marsh that, at one time, covered much of Lake St. Clair's shoreline. A nature study area on the west side of the parking lot contains a large pocket of woods and a pond. The sheltered waters of two marinas and the open waters of Lake St. Clair mark the park's south and east boundaries. This oasis of diverse habitat, placed in the midst of a heavily built-up suburban residential area and on a major north/south migration route for waterfowl and songbirds, holds more than just the potential for good birding.

More than 250 bird species have been recorded either in the park or on the surrounding waters. The area attracts a good sampling of nearly every bird family with warblers, shorebirds, and waterfowl being the most heavily represented. Red-throated Loons, Red-necked Grebes, Tundra Swans, American Pipits, Loggerhead Shrikes, Northern Parula, Cerulean and Prothonotary warblers, Lapland Longspurs, Snowy Owls, a Magnificent Frigatebird, and Glaucous, California, Iceland, Franklin's, Lesser Black-backed and Heerman's gulls are just a few of the more interesting and rare species sighted here by birders. At Metro Beach birders can strike out in any direction from the parking lot and find great birding opportunities.

I arrived on an unseasonably warm Sunday early in April. The dozen or so birders, including a married couple from Great Britain, were not seriously outnumbered by the few joggers, skateboarders, and inline skaters enjoying the weather and getting some exercise. A birder's first stop should be the Nature Activity Center on the west side of the parking lot. In addition to a map of the park and a bird checklist, the modern building houses a collection of nature exhibits and a frequently updated board listing the most current bird sightings in the park. A three-quarter-mile trail departs from the front of the building and loops through a study area featuring towering cottonwoods, willow thickets, swampy areas, and a long, brushy transition zone where the adjoining ball fields run up to the wilderness area. At the back of the nature study area, the trail edges a pool and the large South Metro Marsh. A spur trail cuts off from the main trail at the southern end of the loop for further exploration of the wetlands.

Although it was too early in the spring to expect much in the way of warblers,

"A large bucket had been jammed into the crotch and from this regal, galvanized nest, two Great Horned Owls could be seen surveying their realm beyond the pail."

LOCATION: Mt. Clemens, Michigan.

DIRECTIONS: From I-94 north of St. Clair Shores take exit 236 (Metropolitan Parkway) and drive east 2 miles to park entrance.

HOURS: Open daily from 8 a.m.-dusk.

BEST TIMES: Spring and fall are the best times, but a trip anytime of the year can prove rewarding.

BIRDING HIGHLIGHTS: Excellent for migrating waterfowl and songbirds in spring and fall. Good shorebird numbers when low water exposes mud flats. The park also attracts a surprising variety of gulls with rare species being sighted every year.

FOR MORE INFORMATION: Metro Beach Metropark, 31300 Metro Parkway, P.O. Box 1037, Mt. Clemens, MI 48046. Phone: (810) 463-4332.

"One of the best ways of birding the area is by boat or canoe."

Red-wing Blackbirds were out in force and the half-hour walk turned up an Eastern Phoebe, a Brown Creeper, American Goldfinches, Black-capped Chickadees, House Finches, a Yellow-bellied Sapsucker, a single Golden-crowned Kinglet, two Downy Woodpeckers, and a Common Snipe. Just a few weeks later in the year and this area would be bursting with warblers. Thirty-six species have been spotted in the park and most, if not all, can be found in the woods, shrubs, and edges of the marsh within the nature study area.

The most unusual sighting of the day, the month, even the year occurred about halfway along the trail. A older couple had been preceding me down the trail for most of the walk when they paused to glass something in the woods. Instead of taking a look and then moving on as they had done for the entire walk, they kept their glasses aimed at one spot, then looked at each other, and from 50 yards away I heard them laugh. They glassed the spot again, then with big smiles creasing their faces, waited for me to join them. As I came up to them they could hardly contain themselves as they pointed to a large tree off in the woods and told me to aim my binoculars at the tree's first big fork. I found myself looking at a bucket of owls! A large bucket had been jammed into the crotch and from this regal, galvanized nest, two Great Horned Owls could be seen surveying their realm beyond the pail.

With absolutely no expectations of topping the owls, I drove over to the North Marina and the parking lot which forms a narrow peninsula between the boat basin and the large wetlands of the North Metro Marsh. The open water of the marsh was dotted with geese, ducks, and an occasional Tundra Swan. Wood Ducks, Green- and Blue-winged teal, Gadwall, a couple of Ruddy Ducks, and a small raft of Canada Geese lolled in the still waters. With the aid of binoculars I pulled in Bufflehead and numerous Common Mergansers further out in the water and spotted a double-crested Cormorant drying its wings on a dead tree poking out of some distant cattails. There were even more birds dotting the far reaches of the pool, but a spotting scope was needed for identification. The North Marsh also attracts Least Bitterns, Sora, and rails plus a good selection of other shorebirds, including sandpipers and plovers, when low water uncovers the mud flats. Forster's and Black terns are also found in the marsh along with Green Heron and Black-crowned Night-heron. One of the best ways of birding the area is by boat or canoe. A boat ramp is located at the end of the parking lot making for easy access.

The swimming beach stretching along Lake St. Clair on the south side of the park also offers good birding in the spring and a fall. Park personnel report that the viewing from the boardwalk bordering the beach can be exceptional in October and especially in November when more than 5,000 diving ducks gather in the waters off the beach. The beach can also produce a variety of shorebirds in May and September when swimmers and sunbathers are scarce. Fall often brings a rare gull or two to the park.

The last stop of the day at Metro Beach was Huron Point. It's better than a half-mile walk from the parking lot to the tip of this finger of land reaching out into Lake St. Clair. In the summer, a trackless train takes visitors from the parking lot to the picnic area perched on the tip of the peninsula, but no trains were running this early in the season. It was a pleasant walk along the edge of the sea wall beside Black Creek which marks the eastern edge of the point. A few ducks paddled about in the sheltered water of the creek, and an occasional gull flew up the waterway. Off the end of the point a Common Loon and a few Red-breasted Mergansers were taking turns slipping under the waters in search of food. In the half-hour of standing at the tip, six loons winged passed with their characteristic heads down flight profile, making them look like Concorde jets coming in for a landing.

Huron Point offers the best birding in the park during early spring and late fall when waterfowl by the hundreds congregate in the waters off the tip of the peninsula. Even in midwinter there is usually open water near the tip which attracts ducks and geese. The tip is also a sure bet for viewing migrating loons in April.

I tallied 43 birds in the three hours spent at the park with a Forster's Tern and a Winter Wren not seen, but listed on the Nature Activity Center's grease board.

METRO BEACH METROPARK FIELD CHECKLIST

___ Common Loon	___ Rough-legged Hawk	___ Heerman's Gull	___ Carolina Wren	___ Louisiana Waterthrush
___ Red-throated Loon	___ Bald Eagle	___ Forster's Tern	___ Marsh Wren	___ Kentucky Warbler
___ Red-necked Grebe	___ Golden Eagle	___ Common Tern	___ Sedge Wren	___ Connecticut Warbler
___ Horned Grebe	___ Northern Harrier	___ Caspian Tern	___ Brown Thrasher	___ Mourning Warbler
___ Pied-billed Grebe	___ Osprey	___ Black Tern	___ Gray Catbird	___ Cerulean Warbler
___ Double-crested Cormorant	___ American Kestrel	___ Rock Dove	___ American Robin	___ Common Yellowthroat
___ Great Blue Heron	___ Merlin	___ Mourning Dove	___ Wood Thrush	___ Yellow-breasted Chat
___ Green Heron	___ Peregrine Falcon	___ Yellow-billed Cuckoo	___ Hermit Thrush	___ Hooded Warbler
___ Little Blue Heron	___ Northern Bobwhite	___ Black-billed Cuckoo	___ Swainson's Thrush	___ Wilson's Warbler
___ Cattle Egret	___ Ring-necked Pheasant	___ Great Horned Owl	___ Gray-cheeked Thrush	___ Canada Warbler
___ Great Egret	___ King Rail	___ Snowy Owl	___ Veery	___ American Redstart
___ Snowy Egret	___ Virginia Rail	___ Long-eared Owl	___ Eastern Bluebird	___ House Sparrow
___ Black-crowned Night-heron	___ Sora	___ Northern Saw-whet Owl	___ Blue-gray Gnatcatcher	___ Bobolink
___ Least Bittern	___ Common Moorhen	___ Short-eared Owl	___ Golden-crowned Kinglet	___ Eastern Meadowlark
___ American Bittern	___ American Coot	___ Eastern Screech-owl	___ Ruby-crowned Kinglet	___ Red-winged Blackbird
___ Mute Swan	___ Piping Plover	___ Whip-poor-will	___ American Pipit	___ Orchard Oriole
___ Tundra Swan	___ Semipalmated Plover	___ Common Nighthawk	___ Cedar Waxwing	___ Baltimore Oriole
___ Canada Goose	___ Killdeer	___ Chimney Swift	___ Northern Shrike	___ Rusty Blackbird
___ Snow Goose	___ Lesser Golden-plover	___ Ruby-throated Hummingbird	___ Loggerhead Shrike	___ Common Grackle
___ Mallard	___ Black-backed Plover	___ Belted Kingfisher	___ Starling	___ Brown-headed Cowbird
___ American Black Duck	___ Ruddy Turnstone	___ Northern Flicker	___ White-eyed Vireo	___ Scarlet Tanager
___ Gadwall	___ American Woodcock	___ Red-bellied Woodpecker	___ Bell's Vireo	___ Summer Tanager
___ Northern Pintail	___ Common Snipe	___ Red-headed Woodpecker	___ Yellow-throated Vireo	___ Northern Cardinal
___ Green-winged Teal	___ Hudsonian Godwit	___ Yellow-bellied Sapsucker	___ Solitary Vireo	___ Rose-breasted Grosbeak
___ Blue-winged Teal	___ Spotted Sandpiper	___ Hairy Woodpecker	___ Red-eyed Vireo	___ Indigo Bunting
___ Eurasian Wigeon	___ Solitary Sandpiper	___ Downy Woodpecker	___ Philadelphia Vireo	___ Evening Grosbeak
___ American Wigeon	___ Greater Yellowlegs	___ Eastern Kingbird	___ Warbling Vireo	___ House Finch
___ Northern Shoveler	___ Lesser Yellowlegs	___ Great Crested Flycatcher	___ Black-and-white Warbler	___ Purple Finch
___ Wood Duck	___ Red Knot	___ Eastern Phoebe	___ Prothonotary Warbler	___ Common Redpoll
___ Redhead	___ Upland Sandpiper	___ Yellow-bellied Flycatcher	___ Golden-winged Warbler	___ Pine Siskin
___ Ring-necked Duck	___ Pectoral Sandpiper	___ Acadian Flycatcher	___ Blue-winged Warbler	___ American Goldfinch
___ Canvasback	___ White-rumped Sandpiper	___ Willow Flycatcher	___ Tennessee Warbler	___ Rufous-sided Towhee
___ Greater Scaup	___ Baird's Sandpiper	___ Alder Flycatcher	___ Orange-crowned Warbler	___ Savannah Sparrow
___ Lesser Scaup	___ Least Sandpiper	___ Least Flycatcher	___ Nashville Warbler	___ Vesper Sparrow
___ Common Goldeneye	___ Dunlin	___ Eastern Wood-pewee	___ Northern Parula	___ Dark-eyed Junco
___ Barrow's Goldeneye	___ Semipalmated Sandpiper	___ Olive-sided Flycatcher	___ Yellow Warbler	___ American Tree Sparrow
___ Bufflehead	___ Sanderling	___ Horned Lark	___ Magnolia Warbler	___ Chipping Sparrow
___ Oldsquaw	___ Short-billed Dowitcher	___ Tree Swallow	___ Cape May Warbler	___ Clay-colored Sparrow
___ Black Scoter	___ Long-billed Dowitcher	___ Bank Swallow	___ Black-throated Blue Warbler	___ Field Sparrow
___ Surf Scoter	___ Stilt Sandpiper	___ Northern Rough-winged Swallow	___ Yellow-rumped Warbler	___ White-crowned Sparrow
___ White-winged Scoter	___ Ruff	___ Barn Swallow	___ Black-throated Green Warbler	___ White-throated Sparrow
___ Ruddy Duck	___ Wilson's Phalarope	___ Cliff Swallow	___ Blackburnian Warbler	___ Fox Sparrow
___ Hooded Merganser	___ Glaucous Gull	___ Purple Martin	___ Yellow-throated Warbler	___ Lincoln's Sparrow
___ Common Merganser	___ Great Blacked-backed Gull	___ Blue Jay	___ Chestnut-sided Warbler	___ Swamp Sparrow
___ Red-breasted Merganser	___ Lesser Black-backed Gull	___ American Crow	___ Bay-breasted Warbler	___ Song Sparrow
___ Turkey Vulture	___ Herring Gull	___ Tufted Titmouse	___ Blackpoll Warbler	___ Snow Bunting
___ Northern Goshawk	___ Ring-billed Gull	___ Black-capped Chickadee	___ Pine Warbler	___ Lapland Longspur
___ Sharp-shinned Hawk	___ Laughing Gull	___ White-breasted Nuthatch	___ Kirtland's Warbler	
___ Cooper's Hawk	___ Franklin's Gull	___ Red-breasted Nuthatch	___ Prairie Warbler	
___ Red-tailed Hawk	___ Bonaparte's Gull	___ Brown Creeper	___ Palm Warbler	
___ Red-shouldered Hawk	___ Little Gull	___ House Wren	___ Ovenbird	
___ Broad-winged Hawk	___ California Gull	___ Winter Wren	___ Northern Waterthrush	

Lake Erie Metro Park

LOCATION: Rockwood, Michigan.

DIRECTIONS: From I-75 south of Detroit take exit 29 (Gibraltar Road.) and drive east on Gibraltar Road 2 miles to Jefferson Road. Turn south (right) on Jefferson Road and drive approximately 2 miles to park entrance.

HOURS: Open all year, 6:00 a.m.-10:00 p.m.

BEST TIMES: Mid-September to mid-November. For greatest diversity visit in October. For greatest number of birds visit from September 15 through 20.

BIRDING HIGHLIGHTS: One of the three best fall hawk-watching spots in North America. And in numbers counted, it is the premier site east of the Mississippi.

FOR MORE INFORMATION: Lake Erie Metropark, 32481 West Jefferson, P.O. Box 120, Rockford, MI 48173. Phone:1-800-477-3189.

Quite simply, Lake Erie Metropark is one of the three best hawk-watching sites in North America, and in numbers counted it is the top spot east of the Mississippi. And when we're talking numbers we are talking about incredible, unbelievable, staggering numbers. What can you say to 76,000 or 97,000 or even 228,000 Broad-winged Hawks seen in one day or 56,000 Broad-winged Hawks counted in one hour and 25,000 tallied in 15 minutes. Well I don't know about you, but what I say is, "Damn, damn, damn, why oh why couldn't I have been there on any one of those days."

On a cold, windy, mid-October Saturday a small contingent of the Genesee Audubon Club trekked to the metropark in hopes of a good day of hawk watching. Mid-October was picked for the trip because traditionally a greater variety of raptors are seen then rather than in September when larger numbers but fewer species are seen. All of us knew that Lake Erie Metropark had a well-deserved reputation as a great hawk-watching spot, but not all of us were aware of the huge numbers of raptors that annually pass the park. The tally board inside the park's nature center quickly set us straight. The count to date for the year totaled 268,329 raptors. The total included 6,789 Sharp-shinned Hawks; 239,778 Broad-winged Hawks; 3 Golden Eagles; 31 Peregrine Falcons; 68 Ospreys; and 189 Cooper's Hawks. Those kind of numbers warmed us better than electric socks, and we headed over to the parking lot next to the wave pool, the traditional place to watch for hawks, and began scanning the skies.

A quick glance at a map shows that Lake Erie Metropark, located at the mouth of the Detroit River where it empties into Lake Erie, sits smack dab in the middle of a major intersection for southbound fall raptors. All the southbound hawks following the eastern and western shores of Lake Huron are funneled into the Detroit River corridor and pass the metropark. Add to that huge stream of birds, the raptors that have tacked west along the northern edge of Lake Erie (see Holiday Beach) until they cross the Detroit River and head south once again, and you've got the makings for some great birding. Lake Erie Metropark is the turnstile through which pass raptors from nearly half the continent east of the Mississippi.

A seven-member-strong family of Amish, from grandfather to grandsons, had beat us to the parking lot and reported that hawk movement had been slow; but they expected it to pick up as the day warmed and the birds started riding thermals. The Amish were clothed in beautifully tailored, homemade denim pants, and lined denim jackets. All of them, even the three grandchildren, sported binoculars while their fathers and grandfather were peering through very expensive spotting scopes. I was idly wondering if I could afford one of their spotting scopes, if Barb made all my clothes, when one of them pointed out a Sharp-shinned Hawk winging by directly overhead. It was as if the rest of the birding world was waiting for the Sharp-shinned to get things started. In the next couple of hours there was a steady stream of raptors with Rough-legged, Sharp-shinned, and Red-tailed hawks wheeling by at regular intervals. Less common were the American Kestrels, Red-shouldered and Cooper's hawks. The high point of the morning was the passage of two mature Bald Eagles who drifted by at such a low altitude that you could make out details without using binoculars.

The Amish family became our resident experts at identification. They were grouped around a picnic table about 20 feet away and could be heard speaking, what I took for, German and when one of us spotted something we couldn't immediately identify we'd call over our shoulder, "What's that?" with a wave of the arm in the general direction of the bird. The friendly reply usually came almost immediately, as if they'd already seen and identified the bird. And if they spotted something of interest — a Red-shouldered Hawk, a Cooper's Hawk, or a Bald Eagle — they pointed it out to us, usually before we spotted it. As the day wore on more than a dozen birders took up station around the Amish family and fed off their expertise.

Mid-October sees the heaviest flights of Turkey Vultures moving south, and we were puzzled for most of the morning by their absence. Just two days prior to our visit 5,728 had been counted passing over the park. Once again, it was one of the Amish who came to the rescue by spotting large kettles of Turkey Vultures building up well east of us, on the Canadian side of the Detroit River, with the birds breaking out of the top of the kettles, cutting across the northwest corner of Lake Erie, and making landfall well to the south of us. We were to learn later the counter for Southeastern Michigan Raptor Research had headed to Pointe Mouillee State Game Area, which was south of us, to count birds that day. We also learned that the boat launching ramp, rather than the parking lot next to the wave pool, was the spot from which the Southeastern Michigan Raptor Research made its count. All the above information was learned from a visit to the Nature Center where we picked up an identification guide to the 16 species of raptors that fly over the park each fall and walked through an exhibit and interpretive room that displayed the story of duck hunting and natural history of the area.

All morning long we'd heard the distant bark of shotguns. On a drive around the park and out to the beach, we saw several sets of decoys strung across the cold edge of the Lake Erie. Each spread of decoys ended at a wide, shallow duck boat. The closest boat held two duck hunters laid out shoulder-to-shoulder with shotguns across their chests. The hunters lay still as death in the boat, staring skyward waiting for ducks to fly within range. They looked like the work of an obliging undertaker who was launching a couple of fanatical duck hunters into the great hereafter. When an unlucky duck did come to investigate the spread of decoys, the hunters popped upright like a pair of resurrected jack-in-the-boxes and let fly.

Well away from the laid out duck hunters, huge rafts of waterfowl bobbed in Lake Erie's swells. Over 30 species of ducks and geese have been recorded in the waters lapping the park or in the shallow pools and wetlands scattered within the park. Green- and Blue-winged teal, American Wigeons, Mallards, American Black Ducks, and Wood Ducks were everywhere. Off shore, numerous Ruddy Ducks could be picked out in large rafts of American Coots. At the southern end of the park, at the point where the channel for the metropark's sheltered marina gives access to Lake Erie, a dozen birders were scanning the sky and scoping the huge rafts of ducks, geese, and gulls looking to see if the Eurasian Wigeon that had been seen earlier in the week, in amongst a group of coots and American Wigeons, was still in the area.

On returning home I found the trip had only whetted my appetite for hawk watching and I called Tim Smart, coordinator of the Southeastern Michigan Raptor Research. He invited me down any Sunday in November to join him at the boat launch for some raptor counting and, if I was lucky, a glimpse of a Golden Eagle. My neighbor Jeff Jones, a sometime birder and outdoor photographer, was lured along by the possibility of also seeing a Golden Eagle. We arrived on the Saturday before Thanksgiving to find the park buried under a dense cloud cover

"One flock of crows seen passing over the park was three miles long and contained 10,000 birds."

"The high point of the morning was the passage of two mature Bald Eagles who drifted by at such a low altitude that you could make out details without using binoculars."

so low you could almost stick your finger in a cloud by pointing at the sky. Clearly, hawk watching was out of the question so Jeff and I met Tim Smart and Jerry Wykes, Curator/Supervising Interpreter for Lake Erie Metropark at the Nature Center and talked about hawk watching at the park.

Smart and Wykes were full of information and stories about hawk watching and quickly had Jeff and me looking forward to next September. The odds for being on hand for one of those memorable big-day events are really pretty good. The largest passage of Broad-winged Hawks usually happen between September 15 and 20 with the 18th and 19th traditionally being big days at the park. Smart gave me a thick sheaf of papers that tallied all raptor sightings at the park from 1983. A quick look revealed that on September 18th 35,000 Broad-winged Hawks were counted in 1993; 20,000 in 1994; and 114,000 in 1995. On the 19th 34,000 were seen in 1993; 228,000 in 1995; and 97,000 in 1996. Other big days are scattered throughout September but there is generally a sharp decrease in the number of Broad-winged Hawks after the 20th. Smart said that anytime in September when winds were out of the north could bring good numbers of hawks.

The tally sheets also pinpointed the major flights of Sharp-shinned Hawks in late September along with Bald Eagles, Osprey, and American Kestrels. Turkey Vultures, Cooper's Hawks, Red-shouldered, Red-tailed and Rough-legged hawks dominate the skies in October. I had noticed a lot of crows on my first visit and mentioned the fact that I wasn't aware that crows migrated. Smart and Wykes again had Jeff and me with our jaws resting on our chests when they told us of one flock of crows seen passing over the park that was 3 miles long and contained 10,000 birds. Wykes encouraged us to return, as if Jeff and I needed any encouragement, during the park's Hawk Fest which is held on the third weekend of September and usually coincides with the best Broad-winged Hawk period. In 1996, Wykes said that over 4,000 people attended the festival and got some basic instruction in raptor identification, saw demonstrations on bird banding, and went on guided hawk watching tours.

Jerry also said the park offers better than average songbird and warbler viewing in May, has more than enough marsh birds in spring and summer to pique interest, and is worth a winter visit when Tundra Swans along with a dozen Bald Eagles sometimes present. Jeff and I made a circuit of the park before heading home and spotted a Red-tailed Hawk perched in a tree, and counted plenty of Hooded Mergansers, Canvasback, Redheads, Gadwall, and Buffleheads in the marshes as well as on the Detroit River and counted hundreds of Ruddy Ducks and coots in Lake Erie.

LAKE ERIE METROPARK FIELD CHECKLIST

This checklist contains only raptors and waterfowl. For a complete checklist see Pointe Mouille State Game Area, p. 91. The two areas have published a joint checklist.

Tundra Swan	Blue-winged Teal	Ruddy Duck	Rough-legged Hawk
Trumpeter Swan	Cinnamon Teal	White-winged Scoter	Ferruginous Hawk
Mute Swan	Eurasian Wigeon	Hooded Merganser	Golden Eagle
Snow Goose	American Wigeon	Red-breasted Merganser	Bald Eagle
Canada Goose	Northern Shoveler	Common Merganser	Northern Harrier
Greater White-fronted Goose	Wood Duck	Turkey Vulture	Osprey
Ross' Goose	Redhead	Sharp-shinned Hawk	Gyrfalcon
Mallard	Ring-necked Duck	Cooper's Hawk	Peregrine Falcon
American Black Duck	Canvasback	Northern Goshawk	Merlin
Gadwall	Greater Scaup	Red-tailed Hawk	American Kestral
Northern Pintail	Lesser Scaup	Red-shouldered Hawk	
Green-winged Teal	Common Goldeneye	Broad-winged Hawk	
	Bufflehead	Swainson's Hawk	

Pointe Mouillee State Game Area

Pointe Mouille State Game Area is undoubtedly the finest shorebird viewing area in Michigan and one of the best in the Midwest. Not only does the place regularly host an impressive number and variety of plovers and sandpipers, but it's a sure bet that each year several rarities and even extreme rarities will show up and stay long enough to have birders from around the Midwest flocking to the wildlife area's dikes in hopes of adding a new bird to their life list.

But for all that, this is no place for the inexperienced birdwatcher who has little patience, can't drag along a library of bird identification books, lacks a spotting scope, and is not blessed with the gift of having a discerning eye for minute detail. Add slightly overweight, over fifty, and balding to the above description, and you have a fairly accurate description of this author. I have in fact visited Pointe Mouillee several times in the past because of an interest in shorebirds and been defeated by the enormity of the area and the almost perverse similarity between many shorebird species.

Pointe Mouillee is a huge complex of wetlands, diked marshes, river bayous, and a three-mile-long, man-made barrier island (called The Banana); all of which, was created as a rest stop for migrating waterfowl. Pointe Mouillee is also a marsh restoration project, and one of the best ways of encouraging marsh plants to grow is lowering the water level and leaving exposed mudflats. Not only does this stimulate plant growth but the exposed mudflats lure large numbers of shorebirds who view exposed mud as a huge smorgasbord. The wildlife area has been wildly successful in attracting waterfowl as well as a wide variety of other birds. More than 250 species have been recorded at Pointe Mouillee and the list includes birds you have little or no chance of seeing anywhere else in the Midwest. If that's not enough of a pull, shorebird viewing at Pointe Mouillee starts to heat up within weeks of the spring migration cooling down. It's not unusual having early fall shorebird migrants showing up in late June, and by August the fall migration of shorebirds can make things very interesting at the wildlife area. A Rare Bird Alert for the first week in August reported that in addition to a White-faced Ibis, Snowy Egrets, and a Tricolored Heron, Pointe Mouillee also boasted Curlew Sandpipers, Long-billed Dowitchers, Red-necked Phalaropes, Buff-breasted Sandpipers, Stilt Sandpipers, and Hudsonian Godwits.

I am fascinated by shorebirds, not so much for their relative rarity in the Midwest, but because of where they've been and where they're going. Most of these birds spend a short breeding season on the northern edge of our continent before heading for the Gulf Coast and points south, some as far as the southern tip of South America. I can't look at these birds of the far northern latitudes without envy. I'll probably never see and experience the vast herds of musk ox and reindeer found north of the Brooks Range along the edge of the Beaufort Sea. Nor will I ever feel the hairs at the back of my neck rise at the sight of a polar bear near Hudson Bay, spy an arctic fox lopping over the tundra in the Northwest Territories, nor catch sight of a whale off Baffin Island, but the shorebirds who call at Pointe Mouillee are a part of that world. The Arctic Circle may well be hun-

"Each unit seems to have its own personality and is favored by certain species."

LOCATION: Rockwood, Michigan.

DIRECTIONS: From I-75 south of Detroit take exit #27 (Huron River Drive). Turn left on Huron River Drive and go approximately 2 miles to W. Jefferson. Turn right on Jefferson (also known as Dixie Highway and U.S. Turnpike) and drive 2.5 miles to Sigler Road. Turn left Sigler Road and drive 0.25 mile to the parking lot.

HOURS: Open all year but birding is not recommended from September 15 through December 1 when much of the area is heavily hunted.

BEST TIMES: From early spring through May for waterfowl, and from late June through September for shorebirds.

BIRDING HIGHLIGHTS: Best site in Michigan and one of the best in the Midwest for shorebirds. Great waterfowl concentrations in early spring and fall. Good year-round birding.

FOR MORE INFORMATION: Pointe Mouille State Game Area, 37205 Mouillee Road, Rockwood, MI 48173.

"We all brought bikes so we not only wouldn't have to hump all the equipment around on our backs but also could move with relative speed on the six to eight miles of dike-topped roads."

dreds of miles north of Flint on any map you care to look at, but when a Buff-breasted Sandpiper or a Ruddy Turnstone is only a couple of dozen yards away from me, as if by magic, I'm suddenly only a couple of dozen yards away from the far north.

So for my third visit I came armed with expertise in the persons of Tim Gundlach and Jeff Buecking. Both are far more knowledgeable birders than I, and Jeff is a frequent visitor to Pointe Mouillee. This is a guy who knows shorebirds and still he brought along specialized shorebird identification guides, and both he and Tim lugged spotting scopes. At Jeff's suggestion, we all brought bikes so we not only wouldn't have to hump all the equipment around on our backs but could move with relative speed around the wildlife area on the six to eight miles of dike-topped roads in a matter of a few hours instead of all day. On Saturday, August 25, 1996, with backpacks stuffed with binoculars, spotting scopes, a half-dozen books, lukewarm pop, and assorted candy bars, we peddled out onto Pointe Mouillee with the fall migration of shorebirds well underway. It would be one of this author's most memorable days of birding with the sighting of ten species I had never seen before. And to be perfectly honest more than half of those species I will never be able to identify again without the aid of a very good birder.

The Sigler Road entrance is the favored starting point for most birders. Once past the gate that prohibits motor vehicle traffic on the dikes, birders quickly come to the Nelson Unit. It is one of several distinct and separate units within the wildlife area encircled by dikes which allows park personnel to raise and lower the unit's water level independent of the other units. Each unit seems to have its own personality and is favored by certain species. Write to the address on page 91 for a map.

The Nelson unit is really no longer a marsh and in midsummer is often planted with crops. Still, in the spring, it is often wet enough to attract shorebirds and it was here that I saw my first Dunlin earlier in the year. Pectoral and Least sandpipers as well as both species of yellowlegs are also often found here in the spring. Jeff said it was a good spot to find Bobolinks and within the next dozen steps pointed one out. To the right of the dike and opposite the Nelson Unit is the mouth of the Huron River. Forster's and Common terns were perched on snags hanging over the water. A Great Blue Heron lazily flapped across the water, and Tim spotted a Osprey perched on a tree on the north side of the river near the headquarters building.

The Nelson Unit is separated from the next unit, Long Pond, by a long double dike that runs due south for almost a mile. The Long Pond Unit usually has a large pond in the northwest corner which is favored by heron and egrets. We picked out a Black-crowned Night-heron, and both Jeff and Tim unlimbered their spotting scopes and began sorting through a busy scattering of shorebirds poking in the mud on the pond's far shore. After a few minutes of quiet study Jeff motioned me over to his spotting scope and began my shorebird education by zeroing in the scope on Pectoral, Semipalmated, Least and Stilt sandpipers. While I was looking at each species or a grouping of birds, Jeff ticked off their most important field marks. Frankly in some cases I don't know how the birds, let alone humans, can tell the differences between species.

The Long Pool Unit proved to be one of the most productive spots of the day, and the longer Jeff and Tim spent looking through their spotting scopes the more species they kept picking out on the pond's distant shore. Jeff isolated a Semipalmated Plover in his spotting scope, then a Lesser Yellowlegs and topped it off by spotting a distant group of Short-billed Dowitchers. My contribution to the day's list at this stop was finding a Double-crested Cormorant and Northern Harrier. As we mounted our bikes and started to move onto the next unit, Tim picked out a Common Snipe probing the mud only 20 yards away from us. The Long Pond Unit didn't give up a King Rail on that day, but the unit is reputedly the best place in the state for spotting the species.

The Vermet Unit, the next unit to the east, is separated from Lake Erie on the north end by a long causeway that reaches to the north end of the Banana. Large numbers of waterfowl crowd into the unit every spring and it's almost a sure bet for finding Tundra Swans and occasionally Greater White-fronted Geese here in late winter as soon as the unit is ice free. The elusive Least Bittern is sometimes seen here. On those occasions when Vermet's water level is lowered in the summer the mudflats can be simply blanketed in shorebirds. On our visit the entire unit was covered with water and we carefully searched the fringes of the open pools in hopes of spotting the American White Pelicans that had been reported in the wildlife area for most of the summer.

By the time we reached the end of the causeway and set foot on the north end of the Banana, we had biked more than two miles of dike. The north end of the Banana has a long pond fringed with rushes and marsh grass. The area around the pond and the whole north end of the Banana is known as Cell 5. By midsummer the edges of the pond often attract shorebirds and American Avocets, rare Midwest visitors, have been found here more than once in past years. The area also regularly produces the rare gull or tern. You can usually count on Cell 5 to surprise you and it lived up to its reputation. Our only sighting was a Ruby-throated Hummingbird.

From the top of the Banana we began pedaling south, stopping every 50 yards or so to scope the open water and marshy edges of the Vermet unit on our right and the occasional patches of open water in the Banana to our left. We added a Greater Black-backed Gull to the day's total before arriving at the Middle Causeway which separates the Vermet and Long Pond Units from the large Lead Unit on the south side of the causeway. Before heading up the causeway we pedaled 50 yards further south on the Banana and searched the open waters of the Lead Unit and two small islands in the middle of the unit for the pelicans and the odd gull. We found nothing out in the water but Jeff and Tim came up with a Ruddy Turnstone and a Black-bellied Plover on the muddy edges of the Lead Unit and my shorebird education continued.

As we worked our way up the Middle Causeway we hit another hot spot on the southern edge of the Long Pond Unit. Jeff's sharp eyes and experience turned up a Marbled Godwit and while I was admiring it through his spotting scope, Tim discovered both Wilson's and Red-necked phalaropes in a nearby puddle. The mouth of Mouillee Creek empties into the north end of the Lead Unit and is often a most productive place to look for birds. A Black Tern, Mute Swans, and American Coots were the only birds of interest we could spot. As we turned and headed north along the double dike separating the Nelson Unit from the Long Point Unit, Jeff called a halt to the parade by finding a White-rumped Sandpiper in a pool beside the dike. The remainder of the mile-long bike ride up the dike produced no birds until we neared the pool found in the northwest corner of the Long Pond Unit. Once again, Tim and Jeff bent to work over their scopes but couldn't find anything that we hadn't already seen. The White-rumped Sandpiper proved to be our last bird of the day and the 16th shorebird out of a total of 45 species for the day.

For those who don't mind braving cold temperatures and wind-swept vistas

"I am fascinated by shorebirds, not so much for their relative rarity in the Midwest, but because of where they've been and where they're going."

the wildlife area can prove interesting in the winter. Snowy Owls, Short-eared Owls, Bald Eagles, Snow Buntings and the occasional Northern Shrike shows up at Pointe Mouillee in the winter. Large numbers of waterfowl often winter over here and the wildlife area usually contributes 40 or so species to the Rockwood Christmas Bird Count.

POINTE MOUILLEE STATE GAME AREA FIELD CHECKLIST

This is a combined bird checklist for Lake Erie Metropark (p. 88) and Pointe Mouillee Game Area published in October 1996 with more recent additions from Rare Bird Alert postings.

___ Red-throated Loon	___ Common Merganser	___ Pectoral Sandpiper	___ Horned Lark	___ Black-throated Green Warbler
___ Common Loon	___ Red-breasted Merganser	___ Dunlin	___ Purple Martin	___ Blackburnian Warbler
___ Pied-billed Grebe	___ Ruddy Duck	___ Curlew Sandpiper	___ Tree Swallow	___ Pine Warbler
___ Horned Grebe	___ Turkey Vulture	___ Stilt Sandpiper	___ Northern Rough-winged Swallow	___ Palm Warbler
___ Red-necked Grebe	___ Osprey	___ Buff-breasted Sandpiper	___ Bank Swallow	___ Black-and-white Warbler
___ American White Pelican	___ Bald Eagle	___ Short-billed Dowitcher	___ Cliff Swallow	___ American Redstart
___ Brown Pelican	___ Northern Harrier	___ Long-billed Dowitcher	___ Barn Swallow	___ Prothonotary Warbler
___ American Bittern	___ Sharp-shinned Hawk	___ Common Snipe	___ Blue Jay	___ Ovenbird
___ Least Bittern	___ Cooper's Hawk	___ American Woodcock	___ American Crow	___ Northern Waterthrush
___ Great Blue Heron	___ Northern Goshawk	___ Wilson's Phalarope	___ Black-capped Chickadee	___ Common Yellowthroat
___ Great Egret	___ Red-shouldered Hawk	___ Red-necked Phalarope	___ Tufted Titmouse	___ Wilson's Warbler
___ Snowy Egret	___ Broad-winged Hawk	___ Franklin's Gull	___ Red-breasted Nuthatch	___ Canada Warbler
___ Little Blue Heron	___ Swainson's Hawk	___ Little Gull	___ White-breasted Nuthatch	___ Scarlet Tanager
___ Tricolored Heron	___ Red-tailed Hawk	___ Bonaparte's Gull	___ Brown Creeper	___ Northern Cardinal
___ Cattle Egret	___ Ferruginous Hawk	___ Ring-billed Gull	___ Carolina Wren	___ Rose-breasted Grosbeak
___ Green Heron	___ Rough-legged Hawk	___ Herring Gull	___ House Wren	___ Indigo Bunting
___ Black-crowned Night-heron	___ Golden Eagle	___ Iceland Gull	___ Winter Wren	___ Rufous-sided Towhee
___ Yellow-crowned Night-heron	___ American Kestrel	___ Lesser Black-backed Gull	___ Sedge Wren	___ American Tree Sparrow
___ Glossy Ibis	___ Merlin	___ Glaucous Gull	___ Marsh Wren	___ Chipping Sparrow
___ White-faced Ibis	___ Peregrine Falcon	___ Great Black-backed Gull	___ Golden-crowned Kinglet	___ Field Sparrow
___ Tundra Swan	___ Gyrfalcon	___ Caspian Tern	___ Ruby-crowned Kinglet	___ Vesper Sparrow
___ Trumpeter Swan	___ Ring-necked Pheasant	___ Common Tern	___ Blue-gray Gnatcatcher	___ Savannah Sparrow
___ Mute Swan	___ Northern Bobwhite	___ Arctic Tern	___ Eastern Bluebird	___ LeConte's Sparrow
___ Greater White-fronted Goose	___ King Rail	___ Forster's Tern	___ Veery	___ Fox Sparrow
___ Snow Goose	___ Virginia Rail	___ Black Tern	___ Swainson's Thrush	___ Song Sparrow
___ Ross' Goose	___ Sora	___ Rock Dove	___ Hermit Thrush	___ Lincoln's Sparrow
___ Brant	___ Purple Gallinule	___ Mourning Dove	___ Wood Thrush	___ Swamp Sparrow
___ Canada Goose	___ Sandhill Crane	___ Black-billed Cuckoo	___ American Robin	___ White-throated Sparrow
___ Wood Duck	___ Black-bellied Plover	___ Yellow-billed Cuckoo	___ Gray Catbird	___ White-crowned Sparrow
___ Green-winged Teal	___ Lesser Golden-plover	___ Eastern Screech-owl	___ Northern Mockingbird	___ Harris' Sparrow
___ American Black Duck	___ Snowy Plover	___ Great Horned Owl	___ Brown Thrasher	___ Lapland Longspur
___ Mallard	___ Killdeer	___ Snowy Owl	___ American Pipit	___ Snow Bunting
___ Northern Pintail	___ American Avocet	___ Long-eared Owl	___ Cedar Waxwing	___ Bobolink
___ Blue-winged Teal	___ Greater Yellowlegs	___ Short-eared Owl	___ Northern Shrike	___ Red-winged Blackbird
___ Cinnamon Teal	___ Lesser Yellowlegs	___ Northern Saw-whet Owl	___ Loggerhead Shrike	___ Eastern Meadowlark
___ Northern Shoveler	___ Solitary Sandpiper	___ Common Nighthawk	___ European Starling	___ Western Meadowlark
___ Gadwall	___ Willet	___ Ruby-throated Hummingbird	___ White-eyed Vireo	___ Yellow-headed Blackbird
___ Eurasian Wigeon	___ Spotted Sandpiper	___ Belted Kingfisher	___ Solitary Vireo	___ Common Grackle
___ American Wigeon	___ Upland Sandpiper	___ Red-headed Woodpecker	___ Warbling Vireo	___ Brown-headed Cowbird
___ Canvasback	___ Hudsonian Godwit	___ Red-bellied Woodpecker	___ Philadelphia Vireo	___ Baltimore Oriole
___ Redhead	___ Marbled Godwit	___ Downy Woodpecker	___ Red-eyed Vireo	___ Purple Finch
___ Ring-necked Duck	___ Ruddy Turnstone	___ Hairy Woodpecker	___ Blue-winged Warbler	___ House Finch
___ Greater Scaup	___ Red Knot	___ Northern Flicker	___ Tennessee Warbler	___ Common Redpoll
___ Lesser Scaup	___ Sanderling	___ Eastern Wood-pewee	___ Nashville Warbler	___ Pine Siskin
___ Oldsquaw	___ Semipalmated Sandpiper	___ Willow Flycatcher	___ Yellow Warbler	___ American Goldfinch
___ White-winged Scoter	___ Western Sandpiper	___ Least Flycatcher	___ Magnolia Warbler	___ House Sparrow
___ Common Goldeneye	___ Least Sandpiper	___ Eastern Phoebe	___ Cap May Warbler	
___ Bufflehead	___ White-rumped Sandpiper	___ Great Crested Flycatcher	___ Black-throated Blue Warbler	
___ Hooded Merganser	___ Baird's Sandpiper	___ Eastern Kingbird	___ Yellow-rumped Warbler	

Berrien County Dunes and Lakeshore

If there is a patron saint of lost causes, I was going to need all his or her help. Realistically, Wile E. Coyote stands a better chance of eventually catching the Roadrunner than I did of having any success, and I was without the assistance of those nifty, if sometimes tragically flawed, gadgets supplied by the Acme Co. Every May since 1988, three-member teams, composed of some of the best birders in the Midwest, come to Berrien County for the Annual Southwest Michigan Team Birdathon Competition. For 15 hectic hours the teams hike and motor throughout Berrien County in a contest to see which team can tally the most bird species. I arrived in the county the same weekend to test my limited birding skills against the cream of Midwest birders. Just call me a Don Quixote with binoculars.

While the teams searched for birds throughout the county, I limited myself to four proven hot spots and birded for the entire weekend instead of a mad 15 hours. The teams were allowed to identify species by calls which was an enormous advantage over this birder. With my tin ear for bird calls, I even have trouble assigning the call, "Polly wants a cracker," to a family of birds without first seeing the thing.

Why Berrien County for this contest? The county lies in a transition zone and acre-for-acre it is one of the great birding areas in the Midwest. Shoehorned into Michigan's southwest corner and blessed with a variety of habitats — Lake Michigan shoreline, heavily wooded dunes, marshes, secluded little lakes, open fields, and swatches of virtually undisturbed woodlands — the county straddles the northernmost range of many traditionally southern birds and the southernmost range of many species more characteristically found in northern forests. Additionally, the Lake Michigan shoreline is a major north-south pipeline for migrating birds. The county bird checklist totals 357 species and includes a large serving of rarities and accidentals. Just a few of the rarities seen in the past ten years include Western Grebe, Magnificent Frigatebird, Glossy Ibis, Mew Gull, Sandwich Tern, Mississippi Kite, Burrowing Owl, Rufous Hummingbird, and Blue Grosbeak. It hardly seems that a week goes by without an unusual bird noted in Berrien County on Michigan's Rare Bird Alert.

But calling an entire county a birding hot spot seemed well beyond the definition of a spot, in geographical terms. Kip Miller of Love Creek Nature Center, an expert birder and an expert on birding in Berrien County, helped narrow the available choices to a manageable few that both made coherent geographical sense and included most of the premier birding sites in the county. So while 23 bleary-eyed, bird-hungry teams scoured every corner of the county, I concentrated on the Grand Mere State Park, Warren Dunes State Park, and the beaches and harbors at New Buffalo and St. Joseph that together stretch in a north-south line along the Lake Michigan shore. Collectively they contain a fair representation of the many habitats found in the county, and the great majority of the birds on the

LOCATION: Berrien County, Michigan.

DIRECTIONS: Warren Dunes State Park is reached by taking exit 16 from I-94 and driving 3 miles south to the park entrance.

For Grand Mere State Park take exit 22 on I-94 and go 0.25 miles west to Thorton Road. Turn left on Thorton and drive 0.5 miles to the park entrance. To get to Middle and North Lakes of the state park continue west past Thorton Rd. for about 1 mile until you reach the lakes.

The New Buffalo Harbor area is reached by following U.S. 12 into town and turning right at the stoplight on Whittaker. Follow Whittaker to the harbor area.

The starting point for reaching all beaches in the St. Joseph area is from M-63 in the center of town. To reach Silver Beach County Park and Lions Park Beach on the south side of the river mouth follow the directional signs in downtown St. Joseph on Main St. (M-63). To get to Tiscornia Beach and the pier on the north side of the St. Joseph River drive north on M-63 from the center of town and turn right onto the Upton Drive exit immediately after crossing the bridge over the river. After driving down the exit ramp and turning right onto Upton Drive, drive across the railroad tracks and turn left onto Prospect Street. Follow the signs to the beach.

HOURS: Open all year.

BEST TIMES: Good year-round birding with superior birding in May and from late July through January.

BIRDING HIGHLIGHTS: Berrien County lies in a transitional zone in which southern and northern species both nest. Very good for a variety of songbirds and warblers. The area lies within a major north/south migratory flyway. Year after year large numbers and varieties of waterfowl, gulls, birds of prey, and shorebirds are recorded while passing through. It is also one of the best places in the Midwest for spotting rare and unusual birds. The county checklist tallies an incredible 357 species, most of which have been observed at the four above sites.

"The county bird checklist totals 357 species and includes a large serving of rarities and accidentals."

county's checklist have been seen at one or more of the sites. More importantly, each of the four sites is a great birding area.

My base camp for the attempt at scaling the heights of birding was Warren Dunes State Park. You can hardly turn around in the park without spotting birds, and I ticked off a half-dozen species from the comfort of a lawn chair in the campground before heading north to one of the park's great birding areas. Floral Lane heads west toward Lake Michigan from Red Arrow Highway, 1.5 miles north of the park entrance. The dirt road ends at a small turnaround at the base of the dunes, and I arrived there to find the end of the road lined with cars and several teams combing the area for birds. The park's best birding trail begins at the end of Floral Lane and heads north along the base of the dunes and passes through a variety of habitats rich in birds. I counted over 30 species along the trail and added seven more by walking the trail that heads south from the turnaround, and learned weeks later that I was about the only person not to see a Prairie Warbler in this area. My count did include a Rufous-sided Towhee, a Great Crested

BERRIEN COUNTY DUNES AND LAKESHORE FIELD CHECKLIST

Includes all of Berrien County.

Red-throated Loon	Harlequin Duck	Common Moorhen	Wilson's Phalarope	Short-eared Owl
Common Loon	Oldsquaw	American Coot	Red-necked Phalarope	Northern Saw-whet Owl
Pied-billed Grebe	Black Scoter	Sandhill Crane	Red Phalarope	Common Nighthawk
Horned Grebe	Surf Scoter	Black-bellied Plover	Pomarine Jaeger	Whip-poor-will
Red-necked Grebe	White-winged Scoter	Lesser Golden-plover	Parasitic Jaeger	Chimney Swift
Eared Grebe	Common Goldeneye	Semipalmated Plover	Laughing Gull	Ruby-throated Hummingbird
Double-crested Cormorant	Bufflehead	Piping Plover	Franklin's Gull	Belted Kingfisher
American Bittern	Hooded Merganser	Killdeer	Little Gull	Red-headed Woodpecker
Least Bittern	Common Merganser	American Avocet	Bonaparte's Gull	Red-bellied Woodpecker
Great Blue Heron	Red-breasted Merganser	Greater Yellowlegs	Ring-billed Gull	Yellow-bellied Sapsucker
Great Egret	Ruddy Duck	Lesser Yellowlegs	California Gull	Downy Woodpecker
Cattle Egret	Turkey Vulture	Solitary Sandpiper	Herring Gull	Hairy Woodpecker
Green Heron	Osprey	Willet	Thayer's Gull	Northern Flicker
Black-crowned Night-heron	Bald Eagle	Upland Sandpiper	Iceland Gull	Pileated Woodpecker
Yellow-crowned Night-heron	Northern Harrier	Whimbrel	Lesser Black-backed Gull	Olive-sided Flycatcher
Tundra Swan	Sharp-shinned Hawk	Hudsonian Godwit	Glaucous Gull	Eastern Wood-pewee
Mute Swan	Cooper's Hawk	Marbled Godwit	Great Black-backed Gull	Yellow-bellied Flycatcher
Snow Goose	Northern Goshawk	Ruddy Turnstone	Black-legged Kittiwake	Acadian Flycatcher
Canada Goose	Red-shouldered Hawk	Red Knot	Sabine's Gull	Alder Flycatcher
Wood Duck	Broad-winged Hawk	Sanderling	Caspian Tern	Willow Flycatcher
Green-winged Teal	Red-tailed Hawk	Semipalmated Sandpiper	Common Tern	Least Flycatcher
American Black Duck	Rough-winged Hawk	Western Sandpiper	Arctic Tern	Eastern Phoebe
Mallard	Golden Eagle	Least Sandpiper	Forster's Tern	Great Crested Flycatcher
Northern Pintail	American Kestrel	White-rumped Sandpiper	Black Tern	Eastern Kingbird
Blue-winged Teal	Merlin	Baird's Sandpiper	Rock Dove	Horned Lark
Northern Shoveler	Peregrine Falcon	Pectoral Sandpiper	Mourning Dove	Purple Martin
Gadwall	Ring-necked Pheasant	Purple Sandpiper	Black-billed Cuckoo	Tree Swallow
American Wigeon	Ruffed Grouse	Dunlin	Yellow-billed Cuckoo	Northern Rough-winged Swallow
Canvasback	Wild Turkey	Stilt Sandpiper	Eastern Screech-owl	Bank Swallow
Redhead	Northern Bobwhite	Buff-breasted Sandpiper	Great Horned Owl	Cliff Swallow
Ring-necked Duck	King Rail	Short-billed Dowitcher	Snowy Owl	Barn Swallow
Greater Scaup	Virginia Rail	Common Snipe	Barred Owl	Blue Jay
Lesser Scaup	Sora	American Woodcock	Long-eared Owl	American Crow

Flycatcher, three different thrushes, a couple of vireos (everyone else counted five species), and over a dozen warbler species.

If Floral Lane can usually be relied on to yield the most prodigious numbers, almost anywhere else in the park is worth a look-see, including the campground, the several picnic areas, the nature trail near the campground, and any and all of the park's winding roads. A not-to-be-missed area is the park's magnificent beach. Not only is the view of Lake Michigan and the towering dunes lining the back of the beach parking lot one of the great scenic views in the state, but the pavilion/beachhouse overlooking the beach is a ready-made observation point for seeking out the numerous gulls, waterfowl, terns, and shorebirds flying up and down the coast.

After a thorough search of the park, I headed north to the beaches and pier at St. Joseph with high expectations. The St. Joseph waterfront is justifiably famous for the numbers and varieties of shorebirds, gulls, and waterfowl seen while resting on the beaches on either side of the mouth of the St. Joseph River or glimpsed

"In several places, steep, sandy trails climb the dunes for panoramic vistas of Lake Michigan; and the top of the dunes make excellent platforms for observing birds of prey."

___ Black-capped Chickadee	___ Red-eyed Vireo	___ Wilson's Warbler	___ Brewer's Blackbird	___ Ruff
___ Tufted Titmouse	___ Blue-winged Warbler	___ Canada Warbler	___ Common Grackle	___ Long-billed Dowitcher
___ Red-breasted Nuthatch	___ Golden-winged Warbler	___ Yellow-breasted Chat	___ Brown-headed Cowbird	___ Long-tailed Jaeger
___ White-breasted Nuthatch	___ Tennessee Warbler	___ Summer Tanager	___ Orchard Oriole	___ Common Black-headed Gull
___ Brown Creeper	___ Orange-crowned Warbler	___ Scarlet Tanager	___ Baltimore Oriole	___ Mew Gull
___ Carolina Wren	___ Nashville Warbler	___ Northern Cardinal	___ Pine Grosbeak	___ Sandwich Gull
___ House Wren	___ Northern Parula	___ Rose-breasted Grosbeak	___ Purple Finch	___ Least Tern
___ Winter Wren	___ Yellow Warbler	___ Indigo Bunting	___ House Finch	___ Black Vulture
___ Sedge Wren	___ Chestnut-sided Warbler	___ Dickcissel	___ Red Crossbill	___ Mississippi Kite
___ Marsh Wren	___ Magnolia Warbler	___ Rufous-sided Towhee	___ White-winged Crossbill	___ Swainson's Hawk
___ Golden-crowned Kinglet	___ Cape May Warbler	___ American Tree Sparrow	___ Common Redpoll	___ Gyrfalcon
___ Ruby-crowned Kinglet	___ Black-throated Blue Warbler	___ Chipping Sparrow	___ Hoary Redpoll	___ Band-tailed Pigeon
___ Blue-gray Gnatcatcher	___ Yellow-rumped Warbler	___ Clay-colored Sparrow	___ Pine Siskin	___ Groove-billed Ani
___ Eastern Bluebird	___ Black-throated Green Warbler	___ Field Sparrow	___ American Goldfinch	___ Barn Owl
___ Veery	___ Blackburnian Warbler	___ Vesper Sparrow	___ Evening Grosbeak	___ Burrowing Owl
___ Gray-cheeked Thrush	___ Yellow-throated Warbler	___ Savannah Sparrow	___ House Sparrow	___ Chuck-will's-widow
___ Swainson's Thrush	___ Pine Warbler	___ Grasshopper Sparrow		___ Rufous Hummingbird
___ Hermit Thrush	___ Prairie Warbler	___ Henslow's Sparrow		___ Western Kingbird
___ Wood Thrush	___ Palm Warbler	___ Fox Sparrow	**Accidentals**	___ Black-billed Magpie
___ American Robin	___ Bay-breasted Warbler	___ Song Sparrow	(Seen less than three times in the past 10 years)	___ Boreal Chickadee
___ Gray Catbird	___ Blackpoll Warbler	___ Lincoln's Sparrow	___ Western Grebe	___ Bewick's Wren
___ Northern Mockingbird	___ Cerulean Warbler	___ Swamp Sparrow	___ Northern Gannet	___ Mountain Bluebird
___ Brown Thrasher	___ Black-and-white Warbler	___ White-throated Sparrow	___ American White Pelican	___ Varied Thrush
___ American Pipit	___ American Redstart	___ White-crowned Sparrow	___ Brown Pelican	___ Bohemian Waxwing
___ Cedar Waxwing	___ Prothonotary Warbler	___ Harris' Sparrow	___ Magnificent Frigatebird	___ Blue Grosbeak
___ Northern Shrike	___ Worm-eating Warbler	___ Dark-eyed Junco	___ Little Blue Heron	___ Painted Bunting
___ Loggerhead Shrike	___ Ovenbird	___ Lapland Longspur	___ Snowy Egret	___ Lark Sparrow
___ European Starling	___ Northern Waterthrush	___ Snow Bunting	___ Glossy Ibis	___ Lark Bunting
___ White-eyed Vireo	___ Louisiana Waterthrush	___ Bobolink	___ Greater White-fronted Goose	___ LeConte's Sparrow
___ Bell's Vireo	___ Kentucky Warbler	___ Red-winged Blackbird	___ Brant	___ Sharp-tailed Sparrow
___ Solitary Vireo	___ Connecticut Warbler	___ Eastern Meadowlark	___ Eurasian Wigeon	
___ Yellow-throated Vireo	___ Mourning Warbler	___ Western Meadowlark	___ Cinnamon Teal	
___ Warbling Vireo	___ Common Yellowthroat	___ Yellow-headed Blackbird	___ King Eider	
___ Philadelphia Vireo	___ Hooded Warbler	___ Rusty Blackbird	___ Barrow's Goldeneye	
			___ Yellow Rail	

"Shoehorned into Michigan's southwest corner and blessed with a variety of habitats — Lake Michigan shoreline, heavily wooded dunes, marshes, secluded little lakes, open fields, and swatches of virtually undisturbed woodlands — the county straddles the northernmost range of many traditionally southern birds and the southernmost range of many species more characteristically found in northern forests."

in flight as they funnel up or down the lakeshore. An added advantage at St. Joseph is the pier that juts far out into the lake bringing birders closer to birds flying by offshore. My only problem was I discovered I arrived about six hours too late. Silver Beach to the south of the river mouth and Tiscornia Beach to the north were littered not with birds but people. The unseasonably warm, 92-degree weather had people flocking to the lakeshore.

I'd forgotten one of the most important birding axioms for the St. Joseph waterfront: Get there before the crowds arrive and drive off the birds. From the pier, a large congregation of Common Terns and gulls could be made out far down the beach, well past the last sunbather and sandcastle builder. Through a spotting scope, a Caspian Tern stood head and shoulders above his smaller cousins making the only new species added to my weekend list. In spite of the sparsity of birds on the day I was there, the St. Joseph area and the New Buffalo waterfront further south draw experienced birders from early May through January who come in hopes of being on hand when the irregular parade of species rare to the Great Lakes passes by. Four species of grebes, all three phalaropes, Red-throated Loons, hundreds of migrating Common Loons, King Rails, American Avocets, Harlequin Ducks, and a veritable who's who of rare gulls from Black-legged Kittiwakes to Sabine's Gulls have electrified lucky and persistent birders at both locations.

The morning of day two found me at Grand Mere State Park. This relatively undeveloped 1,200-acre park features forested dunes, three small quiet lakes, extensive Lake Michigan shoreline, and during the height of migration, a cornucopia of birds. When I arrived the woods surrounding the parking lot were overrun with Gray Catbirds, White-throated Sparrows, and a variety of warblers, including a masked band of Common Yellowthroats. The parking lot is even more famous for the numbers of birds to be found there in mid-September during fall migration. From the parking lot, a paved path curves around the northwest edge of South Lake. To the south of the pavement the wet, marshy woods bordering the lake are only a foot-sopping step away, and on the other side steep-rising, heavily forested barrier dunes wall in the trail. At periodic breaks in the dense foliage, I spied a Great Blue Heron and a Great Egret stalking the edges of the lake but it was hard to draw my eyes away from the show being put on by warblers, vireos, and other songbirds on either side of the trail. I added Wilson's and Nashville warblers to the weekend list as well as a Yellow-billed Cuckoo. Unfortunately, I didn't tally three species for which the park is famous: White-eyed Vireos, Worm-eating Warblers, and Summer Tanagers.

In several places, steep, sandy trails climb the dunes for panoramic vistas of Lake Michigan; and the top of the dunes make excellent platforms for observing birds of prey, especially during spring and fall migration. In addition to the view, my reward for the climb was a Red-tailed Hawk. In the more spectacular category, Peregrine Falcons, Bald Eagles, and Merlins have also been seen from the dunes. The park's three small lakes are prime spots for catching sight of ducks, loons (even an occasional Red-throated Loon), cormorants, and heron. Good views of North and Middle Lakes can be had from Grand Mere Road which passes between the two lakes and from a small municipal park bordering the road. Scanning North Lake and looking for the unusual, I discovered I had been overlooking the mundane and added a Canada Goose, American Coot, and a Mallard to my tally.

The last stop of the weekend was the New Buffalo Harbor, and I'd no more than driven into the parking area bordering the mouth of the Galien River when I saw a Ruddy Turnstone and, belying its name, a Solitary Sandpiper keeping the turnstone close company. The New Buffalo Harbor over the past years has turned up an amazing number of rarities, especially among gulls, waterfowl, and shore-birds. And back from the beach and harbor is an extensive marsh that constantly pays off birders with good sightings. All three scoters, Little Blue Heron, rare sandpipers, and Parasitic Jaegers as well as good numbers of thrushes, warblers, and rails have all been seen either out over the lake or in the marsh. Scanning the shore and beach turned up a Black Tern, Cliff and Bank swallows and a Spotted Sandpiper. The marsh area, a quarter-mile north of the river mouth, is not as easy to view because most of it is surrounded by private property. The easiest accessible viewing area is reached by turning right on to East Water Street just before Whittaker Street crosses the Galien River. Drive to the end of East Water Street, park near the New Buffalo Water Building, and walk to the end of the street where there is a break in the shrubs that takes you around the fenced marina (trespassing on the marina is a big no-no!) The woody edges of the marsh were rife with warblers and thrushes, and a Black-crowned Night-heron stood solitary vigil over a distant corner of the marsh.

My grand total for the weekend came to 63 species. The winning team, I should say my winning team, because I'd pledged $20 to the Whitefish Point Bird Observatory team, totaled 154 species while a total of 201 species were recorded by the 23 teams in the competition.

"For 15 hectic hours, teams hike and motor throughout Berrien County in a contest to see which team can tally the most bird species."

OHIO

OAK OPENINGS METRO PARK, 101

MAGEE MARSH AND
CRANE CREEK STATE PARK, 105

OTTAWA NATIONAL WILDLIFE
REFUGE, 109

SHELDON MARSH
STATE NATURE PRESERVE, 113

MENTOR MARSH AND
HEADLANDS DUNES
STATE NATURE PRESERVES, 117

CUYAHOGA VALLEY
NATIONAL RECREATION AREA, 122

GREEN LAWN CEMETERY, 126

CLEAR CREEK VALLEY
METRO PARK, 129

KILLDEER PLAINS
WILDLIFE AREA, 132

SPRING VALLEY WILDLIFE AREA, 135

SHAWNEE LOOKOUT AND
MIAMI WHITEWATER
COUNTY PARKS
AND OXBOW LAKE, 138

Oak Openings Preserve Metropark and Irwin Prairie State Nature Preserve

Oak Openings Preserve Metropark is one of those enchanted places you fall in love with at first sight. As I drove through the middle of the park at 25 mph, every 30 seconds or so I passed from one picture-perfect micro-habitat to another. Blink, and the pine plantation changed to dense, wooded swamp. Top a small rise, and the oak forest abruptly gives way to a open meadow or bare, windswept dunes. Instead of a box of samplers from Whitman's, this is a box of samplers from Mother Nature.

This remarkable landscape is the legacy of ancient, ice-age lakes that laid down a line of low sand dunes that are roughly 5-miles wide and run for 25 miles through southeastern Michigan and northwest Ohio. The area got its name from the widely spread white and black oak that took root on the top of the dunes and sandy plateaus. The widely spaced oaks, through which you could easily drive a wagon, had an almost park-like appearance that was enhanced by ferns and wildflowers covering the forest floor.

If the area got its name from the stately, open stands of oak covering the higher elevations, what makes the area so unique is the variety and diversity of habitats nestled next to each other like chocolates in a box. Some of the dunes are only covered with grass while others are simply heaps of barren sand moved about at whim by the wind. It contains the state's only living sand dunes, regardless of the fact that they are a good 15 miles from Lake Erie. Between the dunes, densely timbered swamps, bogs, or wet meadows lie in sharp contrast to the dryer elevations, sometimes, only a few feet away.

As one would suspect by the diversity of habitat, Oak Openings holds a wider assortment of flora and fauna than any other area in Ohio. Many of the state's rarest plants and animals can only be found in the Oak Openings. Much of this rare landscape has been drained and farmed, but Oak Openings Preserve Metropark shelters one of the largest untouched parcels, and the nearby Irwin Prairie State Nature Preserve holds one of the largest untouched wet prairies in the Oak Openings and in the state.

Lastly, add great birding to all the other superlatives associated with Oak Openings. In spring and summer knowledgeable birdwatchers find the area irresistible. Good numbers of spring migrants are seen in the area, but it is the more than 100 nesting species that really attract birders. Nineteen species of warblers and six vireo species nest in the park along with nine species of sparrows. The

LOCATION: Toledo, Ohio.

DIRECTIONS: To reach Oak Openings Preserve Metropark drive west from Toledo on State Route 2. Approximately 10 miles west of I-475 on SR 2 turn south on Girdham Road. Girdham Road leads through the heart of the park. To reach Irwin Prairie State Nature Preserve, drive approximately 3.5 miles west of I-475 on State Route 2 to Crissey Road. Turn right (north) on Crissey and drive 3.5 miles to Brancroft Street. Turn left (west) on Bancroft and drive 1.4 miles to the Irwin Prairie parking lot on the south side of Bancroft Road and a quarter-mile west of Irwin Road.

HOURS: Open year-round.

BEST TIMES: May and June.

BIRDING HIGHLIGHTS: The unique landscape and diversity of habitat found in the Oak Openings supports and shelters a extraordinary variety of breeding birds including many rare to the area. Nineteen species of warblers, six species of vireos, a wide variety of other songbirds, woodpeckers, owls, sparrows and marsh birds are among the more than 100 species that nest in the area.

FOR MORE INFORMATION: Oak Openings Preserve Metropark, 4139 Girdham Rd., Swanton, OH 43558. Phone: (419) 826-6463.

"Oak Openings holds a wider assortment of flora and fauna than any other area in Ohio. Many of the state's rarest plants and animals can only be found in the Oak Openings."

chance of seeing Chestnut-sided, Golden-winged, Blue-winged, Mourning, Prairie, Hooded, and Kentucky warblers, and the hybrids, Brewster's and Lawrence's warblers are only part of the enticement. Add Blue Grosbeaks, Whip-poor-wills, Long-eared Owls, Henslow's, Lark, LeConte's, and Sharp-tailed sparrows, both bitterns, King and Virginia rails, Scarlet Tanagers, a nice mix of fly-catchers, a dash of buntings and Eastern Bluebirds, a good selection of hawks, then season with occasional migrants like Golden Eagles and Kirtland's Warblers, and you have a recipe that draws birdwatchers like cash draws politicians.

The birding at Oak Openings Preserve Metropark can be so good from the car that you can easily become a traffic hazard. I was coasting south on Girdham Road at a bare 25 mph with the radio off and the windows open. I can't identify many birds by their call, but I was listening for anything while my eyes roved the roadside cover. The entire length of Girdham Road from Airport Highway on the north to where Girdham Road ends at Oak Openings Parkway on the south is good birding. For that matter, so is every other road in the metropark.

You can write ahead for a map and outline your own tour of the park. I had consulted the map and planned to cut through the heart of the park. Heading south on Girdham Road from Airport Highway (SR 2), my first planned stop was at the Park Ranger and Maintenance Complex about a mile south of Airport Highway on Girdham Road. Both Blue- and Golden-winged warblers have been seen there as well as several kinds of vireos. Further south at the intersection of Girdham and Monclova roads, I headed west 0.75 mile to where Swan Creek crosses the road. The forest floor on either side of the creek held Hermit and Wood thrushes; and I tallied Palm, Hooded, and Yellow-rumped warblers flitting through the woods.

Back on Girdham Road, I continued south to the railroad tracks and just as I was pulling off the road, I spotted an Eastern Bluebird occupying a post next to the railroad crossing. The area south of the tracks is noted for Lark Sparrows and Prairie Warblers as well as Eastern Bluebirds. I had found one of the three before leaving the car. At the junction of Girdham Road and Oak Openings Parkway, I turned east on the Parkway and headed towards the best all-around birding spot in the park, but not before checking out the trees and meadows around the intersection for hawks.

A quarter-mile east of Girdham Road on the Parkway, I pulled into the parking area next to the picnic grounds overlooking Mallard Lake. The lake and the surrounding forest is probably the best birding spot in the entire park. The area is noted for Kentucky and Hooded warblers with Cerulean Warblers and Barred Owls also often seen in the area. The Mallard Lake parking lot gives access to a long, complex trail system that webs the entire park. I didn't have much luck with warblers but found both Hairy and Downy woodpeckers, an Eastern Wood-pewee, a Eastern Phoebe, a Rufous-sided Towhee, and an Ovenbird on the trails circling the lake.

Just down the parkway from Mallard Lake is the park's lodge. The area surrounding the lodge, as well as Wilkins Road which heads north from the Parkway, directly opposite the lodge, can usually be counted on for Pine Warblers and Solitary Vireos. But not today. Instead the woods were alive with both nuthatches, Blue-gray Gnatcatchers, thrushes, Brown Creepers, and Red-eyed Vireos.

By the time I left the park and headed north to Irwin Prairie, I added a couple more sparrows for a total of six different species (no Lark Sparrows), caught a male American Redstart crossing the road, spied a Green Heron in a small wetlands, and felt pretty confident in claiming a Red-shouldered Hawk.

Irwin Prairie State Nature Preserve, a few miles to the north of the Metropark, lies within the sandy Oak Openings region and is not so much a prairie as a wet meadow. A band of clay underlying the thin layer of sand at Irwin Prairie does not allow water to drain from the sand, creating a wet meadow filled with sedges and wetland grasses. From the parking lot, a 2-mile long boardwalk cuts through woods and brush before taking visitors into the heart of the wetlands.

The woods, brush, and open wetlands of Irwin Prairie hold an amazing variety of birds. Sora and Virginia Rails are common. King and Yellow rails are occasionally seen, and the rare Black Rail has been seen at least once in the preserve. It's a great spot to watch the courtship flights of American Woodcock and Common Snipe in March and April. Among the more interesting birds commonly seen are Barred Owl, Great Horned Owl and Eastern Screech-owl, White-eyed and Bell's vireo, Yellow-breasted Chats, and Blue-winged Warblers. Western Meadowlarks, Mourning Warblers, Marsh and Sedge wrens, and LeConte's Sparrows sometimes show up. Secor Metropark lies just across the road from Irwin Prairie, and if you have the time it is very good for warblers and woodpeckers.

"The birding at Oak Openings can be so good from the car that you can easily become a traffic hazard."

OAK OPENINGS PRESERVE METROPARK AND IRWIN PRAIRIE STATE NATURE PRESERVE FIELD CHECKLIST

This checklist was compiled by Tom Kemp of Whitehouse, Ohio and is based on years of experience birding the Oak Opening area.

___ Common Loon
___ Pied-billed Grebe
___ Eared Grebe
___ Double-crested Cormorant
___ American Bittern
___ Least Bittern
___ Great Blue Heron
___ Great Egret
___ Little Blue Heron
___ Green Heron
___ Black-crowned Night-heron
___ Tundra Swan
___ Snow Goose
___ Canada Goose
___ Wood Duck
___ American Black Duck
___ Mallard
___ Blue-winged Teal
___ Gadwall
___ American Wigeon
___ Canvasback
___ Redhead
___ Ring-necked Duck
___ Lesser Scaup
___ Surf Scoter
___ Common Goldeneye
___ Bufflehead
___ Hooded Merganser
___ Turkey Vulture
___ Osprey
___ Mississippi Kite
___ Bald Eagle
___ Northern Harrier
___ Sharp-shinned Hawk
___ Cooper's Hawk
___ Northern Goshawk
___ Red-shouldered Hawk
___ Broad-winged Hawk
___ Red-tailed Hawk
___ Rough-legged Hawk
___ Golden Eagle
___ American Kestrel
___ Merlin
___ Peregrine Falcon
___ Ring-necked Pheasant
___ Northern Bobwhite
___ Yellow Rail

___ Black Rail
___ King Rail
___ Virginia Rail
___ Sora
___ Common Moorhen
___ American Coot
___ Sandhill Crane
___ Black-bellied Plover
___ Semipalmated Plover
___ Killdeer
___ Greater Yellowlegs
___ Lesser Yellowlegs
___ Solitary Sandpiper
___ Spotted Sandpiper
___ Upland Sandpiper
___ Pectoral Sandpiper
___ Common Snipe
___ American Woodcock
___ Bonaparte's Gull
___ Ring-billed Gull
___ Herring Gull
___ Common Tern
___ Black Tern
___ Rock Dove
___ Mourning Dove
___ Black-billed Cuckoo
___ Yellow-billed Cuckoo
___ Eastern Screech-owl
___ Great Horned Owl
___ Barred Owl
___ Long-eared Owl
___ Northern Saw-whet Owl
___ Common Nighthawk
___ Whip-poor-will
___ Chimney Swift
___ Ruby-throated Hummingbird
___ Belted Kingfisher
___ Red-headed Woodpecker
___ Red-bellied Woodpecker
___ Yellow-bellied Sapsucker
___ Downy Woodpecker
___ Hairy Woodpecker
___ Northern Flicker
___ Pileated Woodpecker
___ Olive-sided Flycatcher
___ Eastern Wood-pewee
___ Yellow-bellied Flycatcher

___ Acadian Flycatcher
___ Alder Flycatcher
___ Willow Flycatcher
___ Least Flycatcher
___ Eastern Phoebe
___ Great Crested Flycatcher
___ Eastern Kingbird
___ Horned Lark
___ Purple Martin
___ Tree Swallow
___ Northern Rough-winged Swallow
___ Bank Swallow
___ Cliff Swallow
___ Barn Swallow
___ Blue Jay
___ American Crow
___ Black-capped Chickadee
___ Tufted Titmouse
___ Red-breasted Nuthatch
___ White-breasted Nuthatch
___ Brown Creeper
___ Carolina Wren
___ House Wren
___ Winter Wren
___ Sedge Wren
___ Marsh Wren
___ Golden-crowned Kinglet
___ Ruby-crowned Kinglet
___ Blue-gray Gnatcatcher
___ Eastern Bluebird
___ Townsend's Solitaire
___ Veery
___ Gray-cheeked Thrush
___ Swainson's Thrush
___ Hermit Thrush
___ Wood Thrush
___ Gray Catbird
___ Northern Mockingbird
___ Brown Thrasher
___ American Pipit
___ Cedar Waxwing
___ Northern Shrike
___ Loggerhead Shrike
___ European Starling
___ White-eyed Vireo
___ Bell's Vireo
___ Solitary Vireo

___ Yellow-throated Vireo
___ Warbling Vireo
___ Philadelphia Vireo
___ Red-eyed Vireo
___ Blue-winged Warbler
___ Golden-winged Warbler
___ Tennessee Warbler
___ Orange-crowned Warbler
___ Nashville Warbler
___ Northern Parula
___ Yellow Warbler
___ Chestnut-sided Warbler
___ Magnolia Warbler
___ Cape May Warbler
___ Black-throated Blue Warbler
___ Yellow-rumped Warbler
___ Black-throated Green Warbler
___ Blackburnian Warbler
___ Yellow-throated Warbler
___ Pine Warbler
___ Kirtland's Warbler
___ Prairie Warbler
___ Palm Warbler
___ Bay-breasted Warbler
___ Blackpoll Warbler
___ Cerulean Warbler
___ Black-and-white Warbler
___ American Redstart
___ Worm-eating Warbler
___ Ovenbird
___ Northern Waterthrush
___ Louisiana Waterthrush
___ Kentucky Warbler
___ Connecticut Warbler
___ Mourning Warbler
___ Common Yellowthroat
___ Hooded Warbler
___ Wilson's Warbler
___ Canada Warbler
___ Yellow-breasted Chat
___ Summer Tanager
___ Scarlet Tanager
___ Northern Cardinal
___ Rose-breasted Grosbeak
___ Black-headed Grosbeak
___ Blue Grosbeak
___ Indigo Bunting

___ Dickcissel
___ Rufous-sided Towhee
___ Bachman's Sparrow
___ American Tree Sparrow
___ Chipping Sparrow
___ Clay-colored Sparrow
___ Field Sparrow
___ Vesper Sparrow
___ Lark Sparrow
___ Savannah Sparrow
___ Grasshopper Sparrow
___ Henslow's Sparrow
___ LeConte's Sparrow
___ Fox Sparrow
___ Song Sparrow
___ Lincoln's Sparrow
___ Swamp Sparrow
___ White-throated Sparrow
___ White-crowned Sparrow
___ Dark-eyed Junco
___ Lapland Longspur
___ Snow Bunting
___ Bobolink
___ Red-winged Blackbird
___ Western Meadowlark
___ Yellow-headed Blackbird
___ Rusty Blackbird
___ Common Grackle
___ Brown-headed Cowbird
___ Orchard Oriole
___ Baltimore Oriole
___ Gray-crowned Rosy Finch
___ Pine Grosbeak
___ Purple Finch
___ House Finch
___ Red Crossbill
___ White-winged Crossbill
___ Common Redpoll
___ Pine Siskin
___ American Goldfinch
___ Evening Grosbeak
___ House Sparrow

Magee Marsh Wildlife Area and Crane Creek State Park

The average recreational jogger could run a marathon in less time than the average birdwatcher takes to walk the quarter-mile Magee Marsh Bird Trail during the height of spring migration. It is undoubtedly the slowest-walked trail in the Midwest, and by my watch it took me 15 minutes shy of three hours to walk the trail, and I was in a hurry! The reason for the glacial speed of the visitors at the Magee Marsh Bird Trail is birds. Simply put, in late April and early May this is the best quarter-mile of birding in the state and is only one of the reasons why the combined Magee Marsh Wildlife Area/Crane Creek State Park area is generally considered the best all-around birding spot in Ohio.

Songbirds are often as hesitant in flying over Lake Erie, or any large body of water, as I am about flying, period. When the northward bound migrants hit the south shore of Lake Erie they stop, rest, feed, or wait for northward moving warmfronts before attempting a crossing of the lake. Surrounded by thousands of acres of marsh and meadows that is only occasionally dotted with small stands of trees, Magee Marsh's seven acres of heavily wooded swamp bordering Lake Erie is a classic migrant trap. The trap's mature cottonwoods, dense brush, and thickets attract woodland birds like a mud puddle attracts two-year-olds. More than 150 species of songbirds including 36 warbler species have been documented at the wildlife area, and it's not uncommon during spring migration to see over 20 species of warblers and over 20 warblers of one species on the Magee Marsh Bird Trail.

All the advance reading I had done about the area had me primed for a great day of songbird and warbler watching, and as I turned into Magee Marsh Wildlife Area, off State Route 2, I was determined to hit the boardwalk first. I made it past the Sportsmen's Migratory Bird Center and a small pond sporting a Great Egret without stopping, but as the road eased onto the causeway bisecting the vast marsh the car seemed to stop of its own accord. Maybe the car was as enthralled as I was by the countless shorebirds and waterfowl spread across the huge wetlands, lining the ditches on either side of the causeway, and even walking on the shoulder of the road. Redheads, American Coots, Great Egrets, Northern Shovelers, Blue-winged Teal, Green Heron, and Great Blue Heron could be seen in any and every direction. The marsh is also a prime spot for bitterns, King and Virginia rails, Sora, and a plethora of shorebirds.

The water level in the marsh varies from year to year and with the seasons; and although the marsh always collects shorebirds, they only come in great numbers when the water level is to their liking. What you can count on is that every spring and fall the wetlands attract huge numbers of waterfowl sometimes reaching as many as 100,000 birds. Twenty-nine species of ducks and four species of geese have been seen here, and one of the great sights every spring is the arrival of large

"Muffled, mittened, and booted, I joined dozens of birders who were not so much walking the trail as doing the Magee Marsh Bird Trail Line Dance."

LOCATION: Oak Harbor, Ohio.

DIRECTIONS: On Ohio State Route 2, either 16 miles east of Toledo or 17 miles west of Port Clinton.

HOURS: Open year-round from dawn to dusk except from early October to Thanksgiving during waterfowl season when the Marsh is open to the general public on Sundays only. The Sportsmen's Migratory Bird Center is open year-round Monday through Friday 8:00 a.m.-5:00 p.m. From March to November, it is open Saturday and Sunday noon-6:00 p.m., and in April and May on Saturdays 8:00 a.m.-5:00 p.m.

BEST TIMES: Great year-round birding and spectacular birding during spring and fall migration.

BIRDING HIGHLIGHTS: Best all-around birding spot in Ohio. The marsh can hold fantastic numbers of waterfowl in both spring and fall as well as an equally impressive variety of shorebirds. The Magee Marsh Bird Trail is one of the great spots in the Midwest for viewing warblers and other songbirds during spring and fall migration.

FOR MORE INFORMATION: Area Manager, Magee Marsh Wildlife Area, 133229 West State Route 2, Oak Harbor, Ohio 43449. Phone: (419) 898-0960.

"The trap's mature cottonwoods, dense brush, and thickets attract woodland birds like a mud puddle attracts two-year-olds."

numbers of Tundra Swans. If that's not tempting enough, the marsh has sheltered such rarities as American Avocets, both godwits, Willets, Tricolored Heron, and Wilson's and Red-necked phalaropes. The number and variety of birds either stopped me dead in the middle of the road, or like a half-dozen cars ahead of me, kept my forward motion to a dead crawl. March/April and October/November are the best times for seeing large numbers of waterfowl, but even in early May there are still plenty of ducks, geese, and goslings mixed in with a fascinating array of marsh birds and shorebirds.

It took me nearly an hour to make my way across the approximately mile-wide marsh, and I had tallied over 20 species before pulling into the parking lot of Crane Creek State Park. The state park is really just a slim strip of land separating Magee Marsh from Lake Erie, and access to the park is only through Magee Marsh. The park has a great beach, picnic area, and parking lot next to the bird trail which is actually in Magee Marsh. The popularity and fame of the place was attested to by the many out-of-state license plates, even on what was a cold,

MAGEE MARSH WILDLIFE AREA AND CRANE CREEK STATE PARK FIELD CHECKLIST

Compiled by the Magee Marsh Wildlife Area.

___ Common Loon	___ American Black Duck	___ Broad-winged Hawk	___ Upland Sandpiper	___ Black-legged Kittiwake
___ Red-necked Grebe	___ Gadwall	___ Rough-legged Hawk	___ Spotted Sandpiper	___ Franklin's Gull
___ Horned Grebe	___ Northern Pintail	___ Golden Eagle	___ Solitary Sandpiper	___ Laughing Gull
___ Eared Grebe	___ Green-winged Teal	___ Bald Eagle	___ Willet	___ Bonaparte's Gull
___ Pied-billed Grebe	___ Blue-winged Teal	___ Northern Harrier	___ Greater Yellowlegs	___ Little Gull
___ American White Pelican	___ Cinnamon Teal	___ Osprey	___ Lesser Yellowlegs	___ Forster's Tern
___ Double-crested Cormorant	___ Eurasian Wigeon	___ Gyrfalcon	___ Red Knot	___ Common Tern
___ Great Blue Heron	___ American Wigeon	___ Peregrine Falcon	___ Ruff	___ Least Tern
___ Green Heron	___ Northern Shoveler	___ Merlin	___ Pectoral Sandpiper	___ Caspian Tern
___ Little Blue Heron	___ Wood Duck	___ American Kestrel	___ White-rumped Sandpiper	___ Black Tern
___ Cattle Egret	___ Redhead	___ Northern Bobwhite	___ Baird's Sandpiper	___ Mourning Dove
___ Great Egret	___ Ring-necked Duck	___ Ring-necked Pheasant	___ Least Sandpiper	___ Rock Dove
___ Snowy Egret	___ Canvasback	___ Sandhill Crane	___ Dunlin	___ Yellow-billed Cuckoo
___ Tricolored Heron	___ Greater Scaup	___ King Rail	___ Short-billed Dowitcher	___ Black-billed Cuckoo
___ Black-crowned Night-heron	___ Lesser Scaup	___ Virginia Rail	___ Long-billed Dowitcher	___ Groove-billed Ani
___ Yellow-crowned Night-heron	___ Common Goldeneye	___ Sora	___ Stilt Sandpiper	___ Barn Owl
___ Least Bittern	___ Bufflehead	___ Yellow Rail	___ Semipalmated Sandpiper	___ Eastern Screech-owl
___ American Bittern	___ Oldsquaw	___ Black Rail	___ Western Sandpiper	___ Great Horned Owl
___ Glossy Ibis	___ King Eider	___ Common Moorhen	___ Buff-breasted Sandpiper	___ Snowy Owl
___ White-faced Ibis	___ White-winged Scoter	___ American Coot	___ Marbled Godwit	___ Barred Owl
___ Mute Swan	___ Surf Scoter	___ American Avocet	___ Hudsonian Godwit	___ Long-eared Owl
___ Tundra Swan	___ Black Scoter	___ Black-necked Stilt	___ Sanderling	___ Short-eared Owl
___ Canada Goose	___ Ruddy Duck	___ Semipalmated Plover	___ Red Phalarope	___ Northern Saw-whet Owl
___ Brant	___ Hooded Merganser	___ Piping Plover	___ Wilson's Phalarope	___ Whip-poor-will
___ Barnacle Goose	___ Common Merganser	___ Wilson's Plover	___ Red-necked Phalarope	___ Common Nighthawk
___ Bar-headed Goose	___ Red-breasted Merganser	___ Killdeer	___ Parasitic Jaeger	___ Chimney Swift
___ Greater White-fronted Goose	___ Turkey Vulture	___ Lesser Golden-plover	___ Great Skua	___ Ruby-throated Hummingbird
___ Snow Goose	___ Northern Goshawk	___ Black-bellied Plover	___ Glaucous Gull	___ Belted Kingfisher
___ Snow Goose (blue form)	___ Sharp-shinned Hawk	___ Ruddy Turnstone	___ Iceland Gull	___ Northern Flicker
___ Ross' Goose	___ Cooper's Hawk	___ American Woodcock	___ Great Black-backed Gull	___ Pileated Woodpecker
___ Fulvous Whistling-duck	___ Red-tailed Hawk	___ Common Snipe	___ Herring Gull	___ Red-bellied Woodpecker
___ Mallard	___ Red-shouldered Hawk	___ Whimbrel	___ Ring-billed Gull	___ Red-headed Woodpecker

damp, and dreary day more suited for March than early May.

Muffled, mittened, and booted, I joined dozens of birders who were not so much walking the trail as doing the Magee Marsh Bird Trail Line Dance. I'd never done any line dancing before but found myself picking it up effortlessly as I stepped on the boardwalk and took my place at the end of a long line of birders. Generally speaking, the Magee Marsh Bird Trail Line Dance, hereafter known as the MMBTLD, consists of taking ten steps forward, stopping to bring up your binoculars and sweeping the trees and shrubs, spotting a bird and raising your hand to point it out to your neighbor in the line. You stand in one spot for about five minutes looking and pointing out birds then take another ten steps forward. This creates a birders' telegraph so that you know what is being seen 20 or even 40 yards up the trail as the word is passed down that there is a Yellow-breasted Chat just around the next bend. You can even measure your progress in the MMBTLD as word comes down the line that you're now only 20 yards, then 10 yards from the Yellow-breasted Chat. Through the course of the morning I knew

"Magee Marsh Wildlife Area and Crane Creek State Park offer spectacular birding on almost a year-round basis."

___ Yellow-bellied Sapsucker
___ Hairy Woodpecker
___ Downy Woodpecker
___ Eastern Kingbird
___ Western Kingbird
___ Great Crested Flycatcher
___ Eastern Phoebe
___ Yellow-bellied Flycatcher
___ Acadian Flycatcher
___ Willow Flycatcher
___ Least Flycatcher
___ Eastern Wood-pewee
___ Olive-sided Flycatcher
___ Horned Lark
___ Tree Swallow
___ Bank Swallow
___ Northern Rough-winged Swallow
___ Barn Swallow
___ Cliff Swallow
___ Purple Martin
___ Blue Jay
___ Black-billed Magpie
___ American Crow
___ Black-capped Chickadee
___ Tufted Titmouse
___ White-breasted Nuthatch
___ Red-breasted Nuthatch
___ Brown Creeper
___ House Wren
___ Winter Wren
___ Bewick's Wren
___ Carolina Wren
___ Marsh Wren

___ Sedge Wren
___ Northern Mockingbird
___ Gray Catbird
___ Brown Thrasher
___ American Robin
___ Hermit Thrush
___ Swainson's Thrush
___ Gray-cheeked Thrush
___ Veery
___ Eastern Bluebird
___ Blue-gray Gnatcatcher
___ Golden-crowned Kinglet
___ Ruby-crowned Kinglet
___ American Pipit
___ Bohemian Waxwing
___ Cedar Waxwing
___ Northern Shrike
___ Loggerhead Shrike
___ European Starling
___ White-eyed Vireo
___ Yellow-throated Vireo
___ Solitary Vireo
___ Red-eyed Vireo
___ Philadelphia Vireo
___ Warbling Vireo
___ Black-and-white Warbler
___ Prothonotary Warbler
___ Worm-eating Warbler
___ Golden-winged Warbler
___ Blue-winged Warbler
___ Tennessee Warbler
___ Orange-crowned Warbler
___ Nashville Warbler

___ Northern Parula
___ Yellow Warbler
___ Magnolia Warbler
___ Cape May Warbler
___ Black-throated Blue Warbler
___ Yellow-rumped Warbler
___ Black-throated Green Warbler
___ Cerulean Warbler
___ Blackburnian Warbler
___ Yellow-throated Warbler
___ Chestnut-sided Warbler
___ Bay-breasted Warbler
___ Blackpoll Warbler
___ Pine Warbler
___ Kirtland's Warbler
___ Ovenbird
___ Northern Waterthrush
___ Louisiana Waterthrush
___ Kentucky Warbler
___ Connecticut Warbler
___ Mourning Warbler
___ Common Yellowthroat
___ Yellow-breasted Chat
___ Hooded Warbler
___ Wilson's Warbler
___ Canada Warbler
___ American Redstart
___ Bobolink
___ Eastern Meadowlark
___ Western Meadowlark
___ Yellow-headed Blackbird
___ Red-winged Blackbird
___ Orchard Oriole

___ Baltimore Oriole
___ Rusty Blackbird
___ Brewer's Blackbird
___ Common Grackle
___ Brown-headed Cowbird
___ Scarlet Tanager
___ Summer Tanager
___ Northern Cardinal
___ Rose-breasted Grosbeak
___ Indigo Bunting
___ Dickcissel
___ Rufous-sided Towhee
___ Savannah Sparrow
___ Grasshopper Sparrow
___ LeConte's Sparrow
___ Henslow's Sparrow
___ Sharp-tailed Sparrow
___ Vesper Sparrow
___ Lark Sparrow
___ Dark-eyed Junco
___ American Tree Sparrow
___ Chipping Sparrow
___ Clay-colored Sparrow
___ Field Sparrow
___ Harris' Sparrow
___ White-crowned Sparrow
___ White-throated Sparrow
___ Fox Sparrow
___ Lincoln's Sparrow
___ Swamp Sparrow
___ Song Sparrow
___ Lapland Longspur
___ Snow Bunting

___ Evening Grosbeak
___ Purple Finch
___ Pine Grosbeak
___ Hoary Redpoll
___ Common Redpoll
___ Pine Siskin
___ American Goldfinch
___ House Sparrow

The following species have been seen in the vicinity of Magee Marsh Wildlife Area, but not on it.

___ Red-throated Loon
___ Sooty Shearwater
___ Northern Gannet
___ Wood Stork
___ Greater Flamingo
___ Barrow's Goldeneye
___ Harlequin Duck
___ Common Eider
___ Purple Sandpiper
___ Long-tailed Jaeger
___ Boreal Chickadee
___ Townsend's Warbler
___ Black-headed Grosbeak
___ Bachman's Sparrow
___ Red Crossbill
___ White-winged Crossbill
___ Northern Wheatear

"What you can count on is that every spring and fall the wetlands attract huge numbers of waterfowl sometimes reaching as many as 100,000 birds."

I was going to see an American Woodcock, Louisiana and Northern water-thrushes, a Scarlet Tanager, and several warblers long before they came into view.

The MMBTLD is of course done without music, except for bird calls, and there is a lot less regimentation than you find in the average country/western bar. It is socially acceptable to jump ahead or fall back in the line or even stand still and let the line slowly pass you by. Another unique feature of the MMBTLD that further sets it apart from the run-of-the-mill line dance is the unexpected way in which the line will dissolve in a controlled mad rush to a spot further up the boardwalk with the shouted news that a really extraordinary bird has been spotted. After the crush of birders have all gotten a view of the bird, the line reforms and the ten steps forward, raise the binoculars, sweep the woods, point out birds for five minutes, then ten steps forward dance continues. This, by the way, is a wonderful way for beginning birders to learn warblers and songbirds.

The boardwalk is famous for more than just warblers and songbirds. Northern Saw-whet, Eastern Screech- and Great Horned owls are commonly spotted along the trail. Rusty and Brewer's blackbirds are also seen in adjacent fields. Where the boardwalk brushes the edges of the vast marsh, birders can usually count on tallying some shore- and marsh birds. Spring is when the largest number of birds are seen along the trail, but fall migration also brings very good numbers as birds pull into the forested swamp to rest and feed after crossing the lake.

The beach at Crane Creek State Park should not be ignored in spite of all the hoopla over the boardwalk. Shorebirds can often be seen busily working the edge of the water. In spring and fall, large rafts of ducks and geese are usually just off-shore. During the peak of migration you can also stand on the beach and watch flights of songbirds head north out over the lake.

Thoroughly tuckered out from nearly three hours of line dancing, I climbed back in the car and headed for the Sportsmen Migratory Bird Center. It was still tough to ignore all the birds to be seen from the causeway, and on the return trip I added a Sora and a passing Osprey to the day's tally. The Sportsmen Migratory Bird Center is filled with displays and exhibits of area wildlife, conservation, and wildlife management information. It also houses an impressive collection of antique decoys and guns. What I couldn't keep my eyes off of though was the bird feeding stations just outside the Center's windows. There were a few sparrows and a chickadee or two flying off with seeds, but what kept me coming back to the windows were the bold-as-brass rats feeding at the foot of the feeders. Outside and well away from the feeders — thank you very much — I strolled around the ponds searching for wrens and sparrows and, instead, disturbed a Green Heron.

A hawk watching tower stands near the Center, and a nearby tally board testified to the impressive number of raptors that pass through here every spring. As of May 3 more than 10,000 birds of prey representing 18 species had been counted from the observation platform. I climbed the tower more for the panoramic view than for the hawk watching and was rewarded with not only a great view of the vast marsh and Lake Erie but the sighting of a couple of Red-tailed Hawks circling overhead.

Anyway you look at it, Magee Marsh Wildlife Area and Crane Creek State Park offer spectacular birding on almost a year-round basis. The area attracts birds from both the Mississippi and Atlantic flyways, and among the 303 species seen within the area are a wealth of rarities. I hated to leave. You could easily bird here from dawn to dusk. The only thing that finally drew me away from Magee Marsh was that right next door is Ottawa National Wildlife Refuge, an equally fine birding area.

YELLOW-BREASTED CHAT

Ottawa National Wildlife Refuge

Ottawa National Wildlife Refuge caught me by surprise. I expected to see lots of marsh, lots of birds, and do lots of walking on the miles of dikes separating the various units of the vast refuge. What I didn't expect was to become caught up in the history of the area. But somewhere on the Blue Heron Trail, which passes through a remnant of one of the Midwest's greatest swamps, while watching late spring arrivals in the great tide of birds that ebb and flow biannually through refuge, I couldn't help but feel the pull of history and the timeless, unchanging rhythm pervading the refuge.

Before the coming of European settlers, the 300,000-acre Black Swamp stretched in an unbroken, nearly impenetrable line along the southwestern coast of Lake Erie from Sandusky to Detroit. For years it stood as a major roadblock to land transportation around the western end of Lake Erie. But what took nature hundreds of years to create and had stood for thousands of years after the passing of the Ice Age, man managed to nearly wipe out in 100 years. The swamp was drained and cultivated, and by the 1950s less than 15,000 acres remained.

If the swamp was a roadblock to human advancement, it served as a huge rest and refueling stop for thousands upon thousands of waterfowl during the spring and fall migration. Birds from both the Atlantic and Mississippi flyways have piled into the swamp since time immemorial and like God's metronome beat time to the changing seasons. As I stood overlooking a fragment of the Black Swamp and watched ducks, who must certainly carry the genes of ducks who've been returning to this area for thousands of years, a sense of timelessness radiated from the water, woods, and waterfowl.

On the other hand, if I'd been here during the peak of fall migration in late October, I would have been simply overawed by the spectacle of 100,000 ducks crowded in the refuge with 25,000 Canada Geese and a few Greater White-fronted Geese joining in the party. The 8,316 acres of marsh, grasslands, and forest comprising the refuge make it one of the great birdwatching spots in Ohio, especially for waterfowl and wading birds. When combined with Magee Marsh Wildlife Area, which is right next door, the two areas make for one of the best birding destinations in the Midwest.

But where visitors to Magee Marsh can bird from the comfort of their car or confine most of their walking to a quarter-mile, warbler-rich birding trail, birders at Ottawa are in for a bit of exercise. Seven miles of hiking trials lie atop dikes that quarter a large portion of the refuge located behind the headquarters building. The shortest trail is roughly a quarter-mile long and circles through a woodlot just west of the parking lot. The trail presents good views of wetlands that can hold waterfowl and shorebirds, but in addition to length what sets this trail apart from most of the other trails in the refuge is the warbler viewing in May. The little pocket of woods through which the trail cuts and then circles is often packed

"The 8,316 acres of marsh, grasslands, and forest comprising the refuge make it one of the great birdwatching spots in Ohio, especially for waterfowl and wading birds."

LOCATION: Oak Harbor, Ohio.

DIRECTIONS: Fifteen miles east of Toledo or 18 miles west of Port Clinton on State Route 2.

HOURS: Open daily sunrise-sunset.

BEST TIMES: Good year-round birding and spectacular birding during spring and fall migration.

BIRDING HIGHLIGHTS: Huge concentrations of waterfowl in the fall and slightly fewer but still impressive flights in the spring. One of the best sites in the Midwest for waterfowl and wading birds. Good songbird and hawk watching in the spring. Shorebirds can turn up in the spring, but are more probable visitors from late July through October. If conditions are right the refuge can host huge flights of shorebirds. Bald eagles are common year-round.

FOR MORE INFORMATION: Refuge Manager, Ottawa National Wildlife Refuge, 14000 West State Route 2, Oak harbor, OH 43449. Phone: (419) 898-0014.

"Birds from both the Atlantic and Mississippi flyways have piled into the swamp since time immemorial and like God's metronome beat time to the changing seasons."

with all manner of songbirds and warblers during spring migration and, to a lesser extent, fall migration.

The next shortest trail is a major jump in length to the approximately two-mile long Blue Heron Trail. The trail circles a large wetlands area, passes through a small relic of the original Black Swamp, and boasts an elevated platform from which to scope the surrounding marshes, pools, and wet soil units for waterfowl and wading birds. A spotting scope is almost a must here as well as everywhere else in the refuge. The tops of the dikes, by the way, make nearly as good a platform on which to set up a spotting scope as the observation deck.

Swan Loop, Yellowlegs Loop, and Mallard Loop lead birders into the far reaches of the refuge with Mallard Loop, the longest, stretching for 4.5 miles through the refuge and bordering Crane Creek for almost a mile before heading back to the trailhead. If you're looking for an intermediate hike that can pay off with good sightings, you may want to walk the main dike that runs in a straight line

OTTAWA NATIONAL WILDLIFE REFUGE FIELD CHECKLIST

Compiled by Ottawa National Wildlife Refuge.

___ Common Loon	___ Northern Shoveler	___ Peregrine Falcon	___ Baird's Sandpiper	___ Long-eared Owl
___ Pied-billed Grebe	___ Gadwall	___ Gyrfalcon	___ Pectoral Sandpiper	___ Short-eared Owl
___ Horned Grebe	___ American Wigeon	___ Ring-necked Pheasant	___ Dunlin	___ Northern Saw-whet Owl
___ Red-necked Grebe	___ Canvasback	___ Northern Bobwhite	___ Stilt Sandpiper	___ Common Nighthawk
___ Eared Grebe	___ Redhead	___ King Rail	___ Buff-breasted Sandpiper	___ Whip-poor-will
___ American White Pelican	___ Ring-necked Duck	___ Virginia Rail	___ Ruff	___ Chimney Swift
___ Double-crested Cormorant	___ Greater Scaup	___ Sora	___ Short-billed Dowitcher	___ Ruby-throated Hummingbird
___ American Bittern	___ Lesser Scaup	___ Common Moorhen	___ Long-billed Dowitcher	___ Belted Kingfisher
___ Least Bittern	___ Oldsquaw	___ American Coot	___ Common Snipe	___ Red-headed Woodpecker
___ Great Blue Heron	___ Black Scoter	___ Sandhill Crane	___ American Woodcock	___ Red-bellied Woodpecker
___ Great Egret	___ Surf Scoter	___ Black-bellied Plover	___ Wilson's Phalarope	___ Yellow-bellied Sapsucker
___ Snowy Egret	___ White-winged Scoter	___ Lesser Golden-plover	___ Red-necked Phalarope	___ Downy Woodpecker
___ Little Blue Heron	___ Common Goldeneye	___ Semipalmated Plover	___ Red Phalarope	___ Hairy Woodpecker
___ Tricolored Heron	___ Bufflehead	___ Piping Plover	___ Franklin's Gull	___ Northern Flicker
___ Cattle Egret	___ Hooded Merganser	___ Killdeer	___ Bonaparte's Gull	___ Olive-sided Flycatcher
___ Green Heron	___ Common Merganser	___ American Avocet	___ Ring-billed Gull	___ Eastern Wood-pewee
___ Black-crowned Night-heron	___ Red-breasted Merganser	___ Greater Yellowlegs	___ Herring Gull	___ Yellow-bellied Flycatcher
___ Yellow-crowned Night-heron	___ Ruddy Duck	___ Lesser Yellowlegs	___ Iceland Gull	___ Acadian Flycatcher
___ Glossy Ibis	___ Turkey Vulture	___ Solitary Sandpiper	___ Glaucous Gull	___ Willow Flycatcher
___ White-faced Ibis	___ Osprey	___ Willet	___ Great Black-backed Gull	___ Least Flycatcher
___ Tundra Swan	___ Bald Eagle	___ Spotted Sandpiper	___ Caspian Tern	___ Eastern Phoebe
___ Mute Swan	___ Northern Harrier	___ Upland Sandpiper	___ Common Tern	___ Great Crested Flycatcher
___ Greater White-fronted Goose	___ Sharp-shinned Hawk	___ Whimbrel	___ Forster's Tern	___ Eastern Kingbird
___ Snow Goose	___ Cooper's Hawk	___ Hudsonian Godwit	___ Black Tern	___ Horned Lark
___ Brant	___ Red-shouldered Hawk	___ Marbled Godwit	___ Rock Dove	___ Purple Martin
___ Canada Goose	___ Broad-winged Hawk	___ Ruddy Turnstone	___ Mourning Dove	___ Tree Swallow
___ Wood Duck	___ Swainson's Hawk	___ Red Knot	___ Black-billed Cuckoo	___ Northern Rough-winged Swallow
___ Green-winged Teal	___ Red-tailed Hawk	___ Sanderling	___ Yellow-billed Cuckoo	___ Bank Swallow
___ American Black Duck	___ Rough-legged Hawk	___ Semipalmated Sandpiper	___ Barn Owl	___ Cliff Swallow
___ Mallard	___ Golden Eagle	___ Western Sandpiper	___ Eastern Screech-owl	___ Barn Swallow
___ Northern Pintail	___ American Kestrel	___ Least Sandpiper	___ Great Horned Owl	___ Blue Jay
___ Blue-winged Teal	___ Merlin	___ White-rumped Sandpiper	___ Snowy Owl	___ American Crow

from the headquarters north to Crane Creek. This dike marks the eastern side of Blue Heron Trail and Swan and Yellowlegs Loops. It will provide birders with plenty of opportunities for scanning marsh, pools, and moist soil units. The dike ends at the wooded banks of Crane Creek; and this area has a reputation for warblers, other songbirds, Wood Ducks, and a variety of heron.

The refuge's bird checklist totals 274 species seen on a regular basis and another 49 that are listed as rare or accidentals. More than 100 species nest on the refuge. Bald Eagles, Scarlet Tanagers, four species of wrens, Prothonotary Warblers, Wilson's Phalaropes, American Bittern, both rails, Red-shouldered and Cooper's hawks are just a few of the more interesting species that have nested on the refuge. Bald Eagles are already tending their nests when ducks and geese begin showing up in March and Tundra Swans appear in April. April and May see the arrival of songbirds, warblers, and a variety of wading birds. Spring hawk watching can be very good at the refuge with good numbers seen from March through

"Even when winter grips the refuge birding can often prove interesting."

___ Black-capped Chickadee	___ Philadelphia Vireo	___ Connecticut Warbler	___ Red-winged Blackbird	___ Clay-colored Sparrow
___ Tufted Titmouse	___ Red-eyed Vireo	___ Mourning Warbler	___ Eastern Meadowlark	___ Smith's Longspur
___ Red-breasted Nuthatch	___ Blue-winged Warbler	___ Common Yellowthroat	___ Western Meadowlark	___ Gannet
___ White-breasted Nuthatch	___ Golden-winged Warbler	___ Hooded Warbler	___ Yellow-headed Blackbird	___ Ross' Goose
___ Brown Creeper	___ Tennessee Warbler	___ Wilson's Warbler	___ Rusty Blackbird	___ Trumpeter Swan
___ Carolina Wren	___ Orange-crowned Warbler	___ Canada Warbler	___ Brewer's Blackbird	___ Harlequin Duck
___ House Wren	___ Nashville Warbler	___ Yellow-breasted Chat	___ Common Grackle	___ King Eider
___ Winter Wren	___ Northern Parula	___ Summer Tanager	___ Brown-headed Cowbird	___ Wilson's Plover
___ Sedge Wren	___ Yellow Warbler	___ Scarlet Tanager	___ Orchard Oriole	___ Pomarine Jaeger
___ Marsh Wren	___ Chestnut-sided Warbler	___ Northern Cardinal	___ Baltimore Oriole	___ Little Gull
___ Golden-crowned Kinglet	___ Magnolia Warbler	___ Rose-breasted Grosbeak	___ Purple Finch	___ Least Tern
___ Ruby-crowned Kinglet	___ Cape May Warbler	___ Indigo Bunting	___ House Finch	___ Western Kingbird
___ Blue-gray Gnatcatcher	___ Black-throated Blue Warbler	___ Dickcissel	___ Common Redpoll	___ Boreal Chickadee
___ Eastern Bluebird	___ Yellow-rumped Warbler	___ Rufous-sided Towhee	___ Pine Siskin	___ Blue Grosbeak
___ Veery	___ Black-throated Green Warbler	___ American Tree Sparrow	___ American Goldfinch	___ Red Crossbill
___ Gray-cheeked Thrush	___ Blackburnian Warbler	___ Chipping Sparrow	___ Evening Grosbeak	___ Lark Sparrow
___ Swainson's Thrush	___ Yellow-throated Warbler	___ Field Sparrow	___ House Sparrow	___ Common Black-headed Gull
___ Hermit Thrush	___ Pine Warbler	___ Vesper Sparrow		___ Wood Stork
___ Wood Thrush	___ Kirtland's Warbler	___ Savannah Sparrow	**Accidentals**	___ Cinnamon Teal
___ American Robin	___ Prairie Warbler	___ Grasshopper Sparrow	___ Red-throated Loon	___ Bohemian Waxwing
___ Gray Catbird	___ Palm Warbler	___ Henslow's Sparrow	___ American Flamingo	___ Yellow Rail
___ Northern Mockingbird	___ Bay-breasted Warbler	___ Sharp-tailed Sparrow	___ Fulvous Whistling Duck	___ Purple Sandpiper
___ Brown Thrasher	___ Blackpoll Warbler	___ Fox Sparrow	___ Eurasian Wigeon	___ Long-tailed Jaeger
___ American Pipit	___ Cerulean Warbler	___ Song Sparrow	___ Barrow's Goldeneye	___ Lesser Black-backed Gull
___ Cedar Waxwing	___ Black-and-white Warbler	___ Lincoln's Sparrow	___ Black Rail	___ Groove-billed Ani
___ Northern Shrike	___ American Redstart	___ Swamp Sparrow	___ Black-necked Stilt	___ Harris' Sparrow
___ Loggerhead Shrike	___ Prothonotary Warbler	___ White-throated Sparrow	___ Black-legged Kittiwake	___ Bewick's Wren
___ European Starling	___ Worm-eating Warbler	___ White-crowned Sparrow	___ Barred Owl	___ Townsend's Warbler
___ White-eyed Vireo	___ Ovenbird	___ Dark-eyed Junco	___ Black-billed Magpie	___ Pine Grosbeak
___ Solitary Vireo	___ Northern Waterthrush	___ Lapland Longspur	___ Townsend's Solitaire	___ White-winged Crossbill
___ Yellow-throated Vireo	___ Louisiana Waterthrush	___ Snow Bunting	___ Black-headed Grosbeak	___ Bachman's Sparrow
___ Warbling Vireo	___ Kentucky Warbler	___ Bobolink	___ Hoary Redpoll	

GREAT BIRDING IN THE GREAT LAKES

"Ottawa National Wildlife Refuge is probably the best spot in Ohio for finding 'southern' species such as Snowy Egret, Little Blue Heron, and Tricolored Heron."

May. Ottawa National Wildlife Refuge is probably the best spot in Ohio for finding "southern" heron species such as Snowy Egret, Little Blue Heron, and Tricolored Heron.

Shorebirds also make an appearance here in May. Dunlin, Short-billed Dowitchers, both yellowlegs, several varieties of sandpipers, Ruddy Turnstones, and a good sampling of plovers have all been seen in the refuge. Many species of shorebirds spend a surprisingly short breeding season along the northern edge of the continent before heading south, some as early as late July. By mid-August and on through September and October, flights of shorebirds can become huge, if conditions at Ottawa are right. Winds from the southwest can expose extensive mudflats that attract thousands of shorebirds. If the wind is coming from the opposite direction, the mudflats will be underwater and the birds will head for more promising feeding areas elsewhere.

Fall sees the greatest concentration of waterfowl with numbers peaking in October and November. Close behind the waterfowl come numerous eagles who cull the weak from the enormous flights of ducks and geese. Even when winter grips the refuge birding can often prove interesting. If there is any open water you can usually spot goldeneyes, mergansers, scaup, and Canvasback. Snow Buntings are common, and if you're lucky you could stumble across a Lapland Longspur or a Snowy Owl.

Sheldon Marsh State Nature Preserve

As a parent I'd walked, no make that, I'd been dragged through the entrance of Cedar Point Amusement Park in Sandusky, Ohio by my two children more times than I care to remember. For years the entrance to Cedar Point meant paying a goodly sum of money to stand in long lines, board amusement rides that made me physically ill or spiked my fear of heights, and slowly cook in the midsummer heat on the world's largest asphalt frying pan. In spite of the carping, the trips were worth every uncomfortable minute, because a trip to Cedar Point was the high point of the kids' summer.

The memories of those long ago visits came flooding back as I walked through Cedar Point's ornate gates on a Saturday morning in May. There were no crowds, no long lines, no charge, and most importantly, I was as excited as my kids used to be. The difference being that the gates I walked through marked the original auto entrance to Cedar Point. Motorists would drive through the gates, follow the straight, paved road to the shores of Lake Erie, and drive along the beach to Cedar Point. Storms constantly swept the road away, and decades ago the owners of the amusement park moved the entrance westward to its present location. Today, the gates I was walking through led to Sheldon Marsh State Nature Preserve, one of the finest birding spots in Ohio and the Midwest.

The Sheldon Marsh Preserve safeguards a remnant of the once vast forest-marsh-lake ecosystem that stretched for miles along the southern shoreline of Lake Erie. The preserve not only protects some of the last remaining footage of undeveloped shoreline in Sandusky Bay but includes a variety of habitats. Wooded swamp, cattail marshes, old fields, a creek estuary, hardwood forest, and a barrier sand beach are all sheltered within the 450-acre preserve.

And then, there are the birds. The wide diversity of habitats attracts an incredible variety of birdlife. The nature preserve's bird checklist (available at the entrance) numbers over 300 species. Shorebirds are plentiful in spring and fall along the preserve's beach and a mile-long sand spit. When winds are out of the south, water in the marsh is blown out into Lake Erie exposing mudflats that can draw huge numbers of shorebirds. Regular visitors among the 36 species of shorebirds recorded at the preserve include both yellowlegs, Stilt, Buff-breasted, Pectoral, and Semipalmated sandpipers, Willet, Wilson's and Red-necked phalaropes, and a host of others. Red Knot, Marbled Godwit, and Ruff can't be counted on every year but do make special appearances at the nature preserve. Shorebirds are most numerous in the fall, but they show up in enough numbers and variety in spring and summer to make a trip to Sheldon Marsh worthwhile.

Waterfowl and gulls are just as numerous. Thirty-two species of ducks and geese and 20 different gulls and terns have been found in the preserve. Add to those numbers both Red-throated and Common loons, four species of grebes, and the rare Northern Gannet. The gulls and terns are usually best seen from the preserve's beach and mile-long sand spit, and it's not uncommon for gulls to nest on the sand spit. If the gulls, terns, and waterfowl aren't found on the beach or waters of the big lake, there's a good chance that they have found shelter and food

"The Sheldon Marsh Preserve safeguards a remnant of the once vast forest-marsh-lake ecosystem that stretched for miles along the southern shoreline of Lake Erie."

LOCATION: Huron, Ohio.

DIRECTIONS: From Huron, Ohio drive 3 miles west on U.S. 6.

HOURS: Open daily 8 a.m.-dusk.

BEST TIMES: From mid-April to early June, and August to October.

BIRDING HIGHLIGHTS: One of the finest spots in the Great lakes for enjoying spring and fall migration. The area checklist contains more than 300 species and is notable for the wide variety of species. Waterfowl, hawks, shorebirds, marsh birds, and songbirds all pass through the area in great numbers.

"The wide diversity of habitats attracts an incredible variety of birdlife."

in the preserve's extensive marsh that features both plenty of open water and lots of vegetation in which to hide and feed. Birding the marshes can get exciting when you add egrets, heron, and rails to the mix.

Among all this potential for outstanding birding, you can't forget warblers and other neotropical migrants. During spring migration, the preserve's forest and wooded swamps are packed with these colorful, active, Ritalin-starved birds. Thirty-seven warbler species have been counted in Sheldon Marsh, along with seven species each of vireos and thrushes, and ten different flycatchers. This long recitation of names and numbers is not a subconscious effort on my part to fulfill a long suppressed urge to be a CPA but to bolster the claim that during spring and fall migration, and to a lesser extent even on a good day in the summer, you can walk nearly anywhere in Sheldon Marsh, turn to any point of the compass, and have a fair chance of finding an interesting bird.

SHELDON MARSH STATE NATURE PRESERVE FIELD CHECKLIST

This checklist was prepared by the Ohio Department of Natural Resources,
Division of Natural Areas and Preserves.

___ Red-throated Loon	___ Gadwall	___ American Kestrel	___ Least Sandpiper	___ Black-legged Kittiwake
___ Common Loon	___ American Wigeon	___ Merlin	___ White-rumped Sandpiper	___ Sabine's Gull
___ Pied-billed Grebe	___ Canvasback	___ Peregrine Falcon	___ Baird's Sandpiper	___ Caspian Tern
___ Horned Grebe	___ Redhead	___ Ring-necked Pheasant	___ Pectoral Sandpiper	___ Common Tern
___ Red-necked Grebe	___ Ring-necked Duck	___ Northern Bobwhite	___ Purple Sandpiper	___ Forster's Tern
___ Eared Grebe	___ Greater Scaup	___ King Rail	___ Dunlin	___ Least Tern
___ Northern Gannet	___ Lesser Scaup	___ Virginia Rail	___ Stilt Sandpiper	___ Black Tern
___ Double-crested Cormorant	___ King Eider	___ Sora	___ Buff-breasted Sandpiper	___ Rock Dove
___ American Bittern	___ Harlequin Duck	___ Common Moorhen	___ Ruff	___ Mourning Dove
___ Least Bittern	___ Oldsquaw	___ American Coot	___ Short-billed Dowitcher	___ Black-billed Cuckoo
___ Great Blue Heron	___ Black Scoter	___ Sandhill Crane	___ Long-billed Dowitcher	___ Yellow-billed Cuckoo
___ Great Egret	___ Surf Scoter	___ Black-bellied Plover	___ Common Snipe	___ Barn Owl
___ Snowy Egret	___ White-winged Scoter	___ Lesser Golden-plover	___ American Woodcock	___ Eastern Screech-owl
___ Little Blue Heron	___ Common Goldeneye	___ Semipalmated Plover	___ Wilson's Phalarope	___ Great Horned Owl
___ Cattle Egret	___ Bufflehead	___ Piping Plover	___ Red-necked Phalarope	___ Snowy Owl
___ Green Heron	___ Hooded Merganser	___ Killdeer	___ Red Phalarope	___ Barred Owl
___ Black-crowned Night-heron	___ Common Merganser	___ American Avocet	___ Pomarine Jaeger	___ Long-eared Owl
___ Yellow-crowned Night-heron	___ Red-breasted Merganser	___ Greater Yellowlegs	___ Parasitic Jaeger	___ Short-eared Owl
___ Tundra Swan	___ Ruddy Duck	___ Lesser Yellowlegs	___ Laughing Gull	___ Northern Saw-whet Owl
___ Mute Swan	___ Turkey Vulture	___ Solitary Sandpiper	___ Franklin's Gull	___ Common Nighthawk
___ Greater White-fronted Goose	___ Osprey	___ Willet	___ Little Gull	___ Whip-poor-will
___ Snow Goose	___ Bald Eagle	___ Spotted Sandpiper	___ Common Black-headed Gull	___ Chimney Swift
___ Brant	___ Northern Harrier	___ Upland Sandpiper	___ Bonaparte's Gull	___ Ruby-throated Hummingbird
___ Canada Goose	___ Sharp-shinned Hawk	___ Whimbrel	___ Ring-billed Gull	___ Belted Kingfisher
___ Wood Duck	___ Cooper's Hawk	___ Hudsonian Godwit	___ California Gull	___ Red-headed Woodpecker
___ Green-winged Teal	___ Northern Goshawk	___ Marbled Godwit	___ Herring Gull	___ Red-bellied Woodpecker
___ Blue-winged Teal	___ Red-shouldered Hawk	___ Ruddy Turnstone	___ Thayer's Gull	___ Yellow-bellied Sapsucker
___ American Black Duck	___ Broad-winged Hawk	___ Red Knot	___ Iceland Gull	___ Downy Woodpecker
___ Mallard	___ Red-tailed Hawk	___ Sanderling	___ Glaucous Gull	___ Hairy Woodpecker
___ Northern Pintail	___ Rough-legged Hawk	___ Semipalmated Sandpiper	___ Great Black-backed Gull	___ Northern Flicker
___ Northern Shoveler	___ Golden Eagle	___ Western Sandpiper	___ Lesser Black-backed Gull	___ Pileated Woodpecker

All of these birds and the many that nest in the area can all be observed via a flat, level trail that even when the asphalt gives out is accessible by wheelchair. The trail begins at the small parking lot off U.S. 6 and heads north. The first quarter-mile or so is paved and bordered on either side by a row of trees. On the east side of the pavement the single row of trees gives way to a open meadow while on the other side of the old road dense shrubs crowd the trees. On the May morning I walked the trail with a couple from Norwalk, Ohio, we counted troops of White-crowned and White-throated sparrows skulking about under the thickets on the west side of the road. A couple of male Baltimore Orioles called loudly from the trees lining the road, and we spotted a Yellow-bellied Flycatcher moving about the top of a tree.

Just before the pavement turns to compacted dirt, the trail passes a small pond on the right. A few steps from the trail brought the entire circumference of the

> *"A Spotted Sandpiper walked the edge of the pond while an Eastern Kingbird surveyed his realm from the top of a stunted tree near the pond."*

___ Olive-sided Flycatcher	___ Ruby-crowned Kinglet	___ Chestnut-sided Warbler	___ Scarlet Tanager	___ Common Grackle
___ Eastern Wood-pewee	___ Blue-gray Gnatcatcher	___ Magnolia Warbler	___ Northern Cardinal	___ Brown-headed Cowbird
___ Yellow-bellied Flycatcher	___ Eastern Bluebird	___ Cape May Warbler	___ Rose-breasted Grosbeak	___ Orchard Oriole
___ Acadian Flycatcher	___ Veery	___ Black-throated Blue Warbler	___ Indigo Bunting	___ Baltimore Oriole
___ Alder Flycatcher	___ Gray-cheeked Thrush	___ Yellow-rumped Warbler	___ Dickcissel	___ Pine Grosbeak
___ Willow Flycatcher	___ Swainson's Thrush	___ Black-throated Green Warbler	___ Rufous-sided Towhee	___ Purple Finch
___ Least Flycatcher	___ Hermit Thrush	___ Blackburnian Warbler	___ American Tree Sparrow	___ House Finch
___ Eastern Phoebe	___ Wood Thrush	___ Yellow-throated Warbler	___ Chipping Sparrow	___ Red Crossbill
___ Great Crested Flycatcher	___ American Robin	___ Pine Warbler	___ Clay-colored Sparrow	___ White-winged Crossbill
___ Eastern Kingbird	___ Gray Catbird	___ Kirtland's Warbler	___ Field Sparrow	___ Common Redpoll
___ Horned Lark	___ Northern Mockingbird	___ Prairie Warbler	___ Vesper Sparrow	___ Hoary Redpoll
___ Purple Martin	___ Brown Thrasher	___ Palm Warbler	___ Grasshopper Sparrow	___ Pine Siskin
___ Tree Swallow	___ American Pipit	___ Bay-breasted Warbler	___ Henslow's Sparrow	___ American Goldfinch
___ Northern Rough-winged Swallow	___ Cedar Waxwing	___ Blackpoll Warbler	___ LeConte's Sparrow	___ Evening Grosbeak
___ Bank Swallow	___ Northern Shrike	___ Cerulean Warbler	___ Sharp-tailed Sparrow	___ House sparrow
___ Cliff Swallow	___ Loggerhead Shrike	___ Black-and-white Warbler	___ Fox Sparrow	
___ Barn Swallow	___ European Starling	___ American Redstart	___ Song Sparrow	Accidentals
___ Blue Jay	___ White-eyed Vireo	___ Prothonotary Warbler	___ Lincoln's Sparrow	___ Brown Pelican
___ American Crow	___ Bell's Vireo	___ Worm-eating Warbler	___ Swamp Sparrow	___ American White Pelican
___ Black-capped Chickadee	___ Solitary Vireo	___ Ovenbird	___ White-throated Sparrow	___ Yellow Rail
___ Tufted Titmouse	___ Yellow-throated Vireo	___ Northern Waterthrush	___ White-crowned Sparrow	___ Heerman's Gull
___ Red-breasted Nuthatch	___ Warbling Vireo	___ Louisiana Waterthrush	___ Dark-eyed Junco	___ Spotted Redshank
___ White-breasted Nuthatch	___ Philadelphia Vireo	___ Kentucky Warbler	___ Lapland Longspur	___ Tricolored Heron
___ Brown Creeper	___ Red-eyed Vireo	___ Connecticut Warbler	___ Snow Bunting	___ Blue Grosbeak
___ Carolina Wren	___ Blue-winged Warbler	___ Mourning Warbler	___ Bobolink	___ Harris' Sparrow
___ Bewick's Wren	___ Golden-winged Warbler	___ Common Yellowthroat	___ Red-winged Blackbird	___ Eurasian Wigeon
___ House Wren	___ Tennessee Warbler	___ Hooded Warbler	___ Eastern Meadowlark	___ Brewster's Warbler
___ Winter Wren	___ Orange-crowned Warbler	___ Wilson's Warbler	___ Western Meadowlark	___ Lawrence's Warbler
___ Sedge Wren	___ Nashville Warbler	___ Canada Warbler	___ Yellow-headed Blackbird	
___ Marsh Wren	___ Northern Parula	___ Yellow-breasted Chat	___ Rusty Blackbird	
___ Golden-crowned Kinglet	___ Yellow Warbler	___ Summer Tanager	___ Brewer's Blackbird	

"During spring and fall migration — and to a lesser extent even on a good day in the summer — you can walk nearly anywhere in Sheldon Marsh, turn to any point of the compass, and have a fair chance of finding an interesting bird."

pond into view, and we spied a Green Heron frozen in place on the far shore. Nearer at hand, a Spotted Sandpiper walked the edge of the pond while an Eastern Kingbird surveyed his realm from the top of a stunted tree near the pond.

At about the quarter-mile mark, the trail slips into a dense forest sporting only a thin understory. Most of the large hardwoods stood in pools of dark water and on that May morning the woods were festooned with warblers. Packs of American Redstarts, Yellow-rumped Warblers, Black-and-white Warblers, and Magnolia Warblers moved through the woods. Within a dozen yards, I saw three Ruby-throated Hummingbirds drinking nectar from wildflowers edging the trail and Gray Catbirds everywhere. By their calls it appeared I was surrounded by House Wrens, and when I sat on a old bench to rest for a few minutes I was completely ignored by a wren who was building a nest in a post not five feet from the bench. Resuming my walk, I passed a Chestnut-sided Warbler capering about on a small shrub near enough to the trail that I didn't need binoculars to identify the bird.

I was so intent on searching the wooded swamp to my right that I walked at least 50 yards before noticing the trail bordered a large swamp on the west. Swinging my binoculars to the west and tracing the far side of the marsh revealed two Green Heron and a Great Egret evenly spaced along the edge of the wetlands. At about the half-mile mark on the trail, a secondary trail from the right joins the main trail. A few hundred yards north of the trail intersection, there is a observation deck that presents a great platform for surveying the extensive marsh. A half-hour of looking netted me Forster's, Common, and Black terns, a couple of Great Blue Heron, a Great Black-backed Gull, and only a few ducks. And all the while I was suffering from warbler fever. From the observation deck, it's still at least a quarter-mile walk to the beach, and once there you can walk to the west on the long sand spit. But not today.

Turning my back on possible shorebirds and more gulls, I headed back down the trail to the warbler-infested woods. A Swainson's Thrush crossed the path and sat still long enough for me to ID him on my walk back to the point where the trail from the east meets the main trail. At the intersection, I took the trail coming in from the east hoping I would find some different warblers on the east side of the swamp. I was almost instantly rewarded with a Black-throated Blue Warbler, and a few feet further down the trail I spotted a Rose-breasted Grosbeak perched on a branch directly over the path.

The next several hundred yards took an hour to walk as I spotted both Louisiana and Northern Waterthrushes, a Great Crested Flycatcher, a Veery, and three more varieties of thrushes on dry patches of ground. A golf course borders the east side of the nature preserve, but between the golf course and trail there were several long, narrow marshy areas. These marshy slivers were rife with waterthrushes, Common Yellowthroats, and one Prothonotary Warbler. Sorting through the near jumble of warblers cavorting around one large pool, well off the trail, in the center of the swamp, I found a couple of Black-throated Green Warblers. As I worked my way back to the parking lot and higher ground on the east side trail, I ran out of warblers as I neared the grassy area bordering the east side of the pond but found Chipping Sparrows and Tree Swallows by the hat full. As if to mock me for the shorebirds I turned my back on by deciding not to walk out to the beach, a Killdeer swept past the parking lot as I reached my car. I'd been gone over three hours, and it seemed like it couldn't have been longer than a half-hour since I left the car. I now know how my kids felt after a day at Cedar Point.

Headlands Marsh and Headlands Dunes State Nature Preserves

Nancy M. Csidor, a naturalist at Mentor Marsh, was unequivocal when it came to the Mentor Marsh area and how it stacked up as a birding hot spot against the rest of Ohio's birding sites. According to Csidor, Mentor Marsh and Headlands Dunes Nature Preserves, taken as a whole, is the second best birding area in Ohio, surpassed only by Crane Creek State Park to the west.

I was lucky enough to meet Csidor at Mentor Marsh's Nature/Information Center after a couple of hours birding nearby Headlands Dunes Nature Preserve. She happened to be working at the Nature/Information Center the Saturday afternoon of my visit and after telling her about my research she led me over to a large aerial map and gave me the inside dope on birding the area. Between Csidor and a birding fairy godmother, who turned up twice in the field that day and unerringly directed me to the spots where birds were most active, I was in for a great day of birding.

At the map, Csidor pointed out that Mentor Marsh runs parallel to the southern shore of Lake Erie and is, in fact, an old channel of the Grand River. The river now empties into Fairport Harbor, but long ago the Grand made a sharp U-turn just before hitting the coast at Fairport, headed back inland, and paralleled the shoreline before emptying into Lake Erie some two miles further west than its present mouth. Sometime in the distant past shore erosion and high water caused the Grand River to break through to Lake Erie at the site of the big U-turn at Fairport. The old river channel to the west of the mouth slowly filled in becoming Mentor Marsh.

The marsh and the surrounding woodlands harbor over 50 species of deciduous trees as well as several unique and distinct natural communities. In 1966, Mentor Marsh became one of the first sites in the country to be named a National Natural Landmark. The area has always been rich in birdlife, and birding records for the marsh go back to the 1840s. It has remained a popular birding spot for 150 years and a favorite study area for scientists. A recent ornithology class counted 100 Virginia Rails and Soras in the marsh.

Ms. Csidor said that birding is always better on the north side of the marsh, and generally spring migration peaks here later than the marshes on the western end of Lake Erie. On a good day during spring migration, it's not out of the ordinary for Mentor Marsh and Headlands Dunes to yield 125 bird species to experienced birders. Birding heats up at the two nature preserves in early spring with the arrival of waterfowl and continues unabated through late May.

The two best birding areas in the marsh are at the end of Woodridge Street near the marsh's western end and on the east end of the marsh off Headlands

LOCATION: Mentor, Ohio.

DIRECTIONS: From the junction of I-90 and State Road 44, drive north on State Road 44 for approximately 7 miles to where it ends at the entrance to Headlands Beach State Park. Headlands Dunes Nature Preserve lies in the northeast corner of the state park and is easily reached by following the state park roads to the parking lot next to the beach. To reach the Zimmerman Trail and the birding area around Shipman Pond, turn left at the end of State Road 44, and drive approximately a half-mile to the parking lot on the left at the top of the hill after crossing the pond. The Mentor Marsh Information/Nature Center is reached by turning left on State Route 283 from State Road 44 approximately a quarter-mile before the latter road ends at the entrance to the state park. Drive 0.6 miles west on 283 to Corduroy Road. Turn right on Corduroy and drive a quarter-mile to the Nature/Information Center on the right side of the road.

HOURS: Both Nature Preserves are open year round from dawn to dusk. The Nature/Information Center is open weekends 12 noon-5:00 p.m. from April through October.

BEST TIMES: Birding activity heats up in early spring with the arrival of northbound waterfowl and continues to grow through April until mid May when songbird migration peaks. With well over 100 species nesting in the area, birders will find something of interest even in the summer.

BIRDING HIGHLIGHTS: One of the best places in Ohio during spring migration. More than 250 species have been recorded in just Mentor Marsh. Add in the wooded dunes and beach of Headlands Dunes State Nature Preserve and the open waters of Lake Erie and the shelter waters of Fairport Harbor and you've got incredible birding potential. More than 125 species are regularly seen here at the height of spring migration and 100 species have been recorded on just one trail (Zimmerman) in Mentor Marsh.

FOR MORE INFORMATION: Marsh House, Mentor Marsh State Nature Preserve, 5185 Corduroy Road., Mentor, OH 44060. Phone: (216) 257-0777.

"The area has always been rich in birdlife, and birding records for the marsh go back to the 1840s."

Drive. To reach the western birding area, continue past the Nature Center on Corduroy Road, cross the marsh, take the first left (Woodridge) and drive to the end of the street and walk into the woods. This is an excellent warbler area. There is also a small Mentor Marsh parking lot tucked between houses on Woodridge opposite Wake Robin Road. From the parking lot a trail leads down a hillside to a boardwalk that crosses the marsh.

By far the best birding area is found along the Zimmerman Trail on the marsh's eastern end. From the end of State Route 44 which ends at Headlands Beach State Park turn west on Headlands Drive (no road sign), cross Shipman Pond, and park in the small parking lot at the top of the hill on the left. The area just around the parking lot and pond, as I was to find out, often holds a surprising number of birds. From the back of the parking lot, Zimmerman Trail traces the northern side of the marsh and slips through a variety of habitats. The trail can also be very muddy. On the day I arrived, it was only passable near the trailhead if you were thoughtful enough to wear waterproof hiking boots and weren't afraid of mud. Zimmerman follows the northern edge of the marsh for two miles and

MENTOR MARSH AND HEADLANDS DUNES STATE NATURE PRESERVES FIELD CHECKLIST

The Audubon Society of Greater Cleveland prepared this checklist that includes the greater Cleveland area.
Nearly all the birds on this list have been seen at Mentor Marsh and Headlands Dunes State Nature Preserves.

___ Red-throated Loon	___ Northern Pintail	___ Northern Goshawk	___ Spotted Sandpiper	___ Little Gull
___ Common Loon	___ Blue-winged Teal	___ Red-shouldered Hawk	___ Upland Sandpiper	___ Common Black-headed Gull
___ Pied-billed Grebe	___ Northern Shoveler	___ Broad-winged Hawk	___ Whimbrel	___ Bonaparte's Gull
___ Horned Grebe	___ Gadwall	___ Red-tailed Hawk	___ Hudsonian Godwit	___ Ring-billed Gull
___ Red-necked Grebe	___ Eurasian Wigeon	___ Rough-legged Hawk	___ Marbled Godwit	___ California Gull
___ Eared Grebe	___ American Wigeon	___ Golden Eagle	___ Ruddy Turnstone	___ Herring Gull
___ Northern Gannet	___ Canvasback	___ American Kestrel	___ Red Knot	___ Thayer's Gull
___ Double-crested Cormorant	___ Redhead	___ Merlin	___ Sanderling	___ Iceland Gull
___ American Bittern	___ Ring-necked Duck	___ Peregrine	___ Semipalmated Sandpiper	___ Lesser Black-backed Gull
___ Least Bittern	___ Greater Scaup	___ Ring-necked Pheasant	___ Western Sandpiper	___ Glaucous Gull
___ Great Blue Heron	___ Lesser Scaup	___ Ruffed Grouse	___ Least Sandpiper	___ Great Black-backed Gull
___ Great Egret	___ King Eider	___ Wild Turkey	___ White-rumped Sandpiper	___ Black-legged Kittiwake
___ Snowy Egret	___ Harlequin Duck	___ Northern Bobwhite	___ Baird's Sandpiper	___ Sabine's Gull
___ Little Blue Heron	___ Oldsquaw	___ King Rail	___ Pectoral Sandpiper	___ Caspian Tern
___ Tricolored Heron	___ Black Scoter	___ Virginia Rail	___ Dunlin	___ Common Tern
___ Cattle Egret	___ Surf Scoter	___ Sora	___ Stilt Sandpiper	___ Forster's Tern
___ Green Heron	___ White-winged Scoter	___ Common Moorhen	___ Buff-breasted Sandpiper	___ Least Tern
___ Black-crowned Night-heron	___ Common Goldeneye	___ American Coot	___ Short-billed Dowitcher	___ Black Tern
___ Yellow-crowned Night-heron	___ Bufflehead	___ Sandhill Crane	___ Long-billed Dowitcher	___ Rock Dove
___ Tundra Swan	___ Hooded Merganser	___ Black-bellied Plover	___ Common Snipe	___ Mourning Dove
___ Mute Swan	___ Common Merganser	___ Lesser Golden-plover	___ American Woodcock	___ Black-billed Cuckoo
___ Greater White-fronted Goose	___ Red-breasted Merganser	___ Semipalmated Plover	___ Wilson's Phalarope	___ Yellow-billed Cuckoo
___ Snow Goose	___ Ruddy Duck	___ Piping Plover	___ Red-necked Phalarope	___ Barn Owl
___ Brant	___ Turkey Vulture	___ Killdeer	___ Red Phalarope	___ Eastern Screech-owl
___ Canada Goose	___ Osprey	___ American Avocet	___ Pomarine Jaeger	___ Great Horned Owl
___ Wood Duck	___ Bald Eagle	___ Greater Yellowlegs	___ Parasitic Jaeger	___ Snowy Owl
___ Green-winged Teal	___ Northern Harrier	___ Lesser Yellowlegs	___ Long-tailed Jaeger	___ Long-eared Owl
___ American Black Duck	___ Sharp-shinned Hawk	___ Solitary Sandpiper	___ Laughing Gull	___ Short-eared Owl
___ Mallard	___ Cooper's Hawk	___ Willet	___ Franklin's Gull	___ Northern Saw-whet Owl

often pays off sharp-eyed birders with more than a 100 species in the course of a walk.

Csidor also filled me in on Headlands Dunes Nature Preserve where I had started my day. The state nature preserve encompasses a small point of land nudging into Lake Erie on the eastern edge of Headlands Beach State Park. It is one of the few remaining sand dune-beach ecosystems left in Ohio. The preserve not only protects a fragile and rare ecosystem, it is a haven and resting spot for large numbers of birds. The waters offshore can be counted on for waterfowl and gulls, including loons, grebes, Oldsquaws, and all three species of scoters. The sandy strip of beach draws shorebirds, with rare species often making an appearance at any time from spring through fall. Inland, the shrub and tree covered dunes are adorned with warblers and other songbirds in late April and early May.

I had arrived late in the morning at Headlands Dunes State Nature Preserve and had hardly walked a dozen yards before being greeted by a Solitary Vireo. Gray Catbirds were meowing from almost every bush or thicket, and White-crowned Sparrows were everywhere underfoot. Rounding a wooded dune, I

> *"It's not out of the ordinary for Mentor Marsh and Headlands Dunes to yield 125 bird species to experienced birders."*

___ Common Nighthawk	___ Blue Jay	___ White-eyed Vireo	___ Northern Waterthrush	___ White-throated Sparrow
___ Whip-poor-will	___ American Crow	___ Solitary Vireo	___ Louisiana Waterthrush	___ White-crowned Sparrow
___ Chimney Swift	___ Black-capped Chickadee	___ Yellow-throated Vireo	___ Kentucky Warbler	___ Harris' Sparrow
___ Ruby-throated Hummingbird	___ Tufted Titmouse	___ Warbling Vireo	___ Connecticut Warbler	___ Dark-eyed Junco
___ Belted Kingfisher	___ Red-breasted Nuthatch	___ Philadelphia Vireo	___ Mourning Warbler	___ Lapland Longspur
___ Red-headed Woodpecker	___ White-breasted Nuthatch	___ Red-eyed Vireo	___ Common Yellowthroat	___ Smith's Longspur
___ Red-bellied Woodpecker	___ Brown Creeper	___ Blue-winged Warbler	___ Hooded Warbler	___ Snow Bunting
___ Yellow-bellied Sapsucker	___ Carolina Wren	___ Golden-winged Warbler	___ Wilson's Warbler	___ Bobolink
___ Downy Woodpecker	___ House Wren	___ Tennessee Warbler	___ Canada Warbler	___ Red-winged Blackbird
___ Hairy Woodpecker	___ Winter Wren	___ Orange-crowned Warbler	___ Yellow-breasted Chat	___ Eastern Meadowlark
___ Black-backed Woodpecker	___ Sedge Wren	___ Nashville Warbler	___ Summer Tanager	___ Western Meadowlark
___ Northern Flicker	___ Marsh Wren	___ Northern Parula	___ Scarlet Tanager	___ Yellow-headed Blackbird
___ Pileated Woodpecker	___ Golden-crowned Kinglet	___ Yellow Warbler	___ Northern Cardinal	___ Rusty Blackbird
___ Olive-sided Flycatcher	___ Ruby-crowned Kinglet	___ Chestnut-sided Warbler	___ Rose-breasted Grosbeak	___ Common Grackle
___ Eastern Wood-pewee	___ Blue-gray Gnatcatcher	___ Magnolia Warbler	___ Blue Grosbeak	___ Brown-headed Cowbird
___ Yellow-bellied Flycatcher	___ Eastern Bluebird	___ Cape May Warbler	___ Indigo Bunting	___ Orchard Oriole
___ Acadian Flycatcher	___ Veery	___ Black-throated Blue Warbler	___ Dickcissel	___ Baltimore Oriole
___ Alder Flycatcher	___ Gray-cheeked Thrush	___ Yellow-rumped Warbler	___ Rufous-sided Towhee	___ Pine Grosbeak
___ Willow Flycatcher	___ Swainson's Thrush	___ Black-throated Green Warbler	___ American Tree Sparrow	___ Purple Finch
___ Least Flycatcher	___ Hermit Thrush	___ Blackburnian Warbler	___ Chipping Sparrow	___ House Finch
___ Eastern Phoebe	___ Wood Thrush	___ Yellow-throated Warbler	___ Clay-colored Sparrow	___ Red Crossbill
___ Great Crested Flycatcher	___ American Robin	___ Pine Warbler	___ Field Sparrow	___ White-winged Crossbill
___ Western Kingbird	___ Varied Thrush	___ Palm Warbler	___ Savannah Sparrow	___ Common Redpoll
___ Eastern Kingbird	___ Gray Catbird	___ Bay-breasted Warbler	___ Grasshopper Sparrow	___ Pine Siskin
___ Horned Lark	___ Northern Mockingbird	___ Blackpoll Warbler	___ Henslow's Sparrow	___ American Goldfinch
___ Purple Martin	___ Brown Thrasher	___ Cerulean Warbler	___ LeConte's Sparrow	___ Evening Grosbeak
___ Tree Swallow	___ American Pipit	___ Black-and-white Warbler	___ Sharp-tailed Sparrow	___ House Sparrow
___ Northern Rough-winged Swallow	___ Cedar Waxwing	___ American Redstart	___ Fox Sparrow	
___ Bank Swallow	___ Northern Shrike	___ Prothonotary Warbler	___ Song Sparrow	
___ Cliff Swallow	___ Loggerhead Shrike	___ Worm-eating Warbler	___ Lincoln's Sparrow	
___ Barn Swallow	___ European Starling	___ Ovenbird	___ Swamp Sparrow	

"Without so much as a hello, or how-do-you-do, the silver-haired woman pointed south in the direction of the steep, wooded hillside angling down to the pond and said I would find great birding along the pond's shore. She looked down at my low-cut walking shoes and with a smile told me I'd find the Zimmerman Trail tough going 'in tennis shoes.'"

crossed paths with a pleasant, grandmotherly birder who pointed out a path I should try for both Orchard and Baltimore Orioles. She also said I would probably see a goodly number of Rufous-sided Towhees further up the path.

With a quick thanks, I headed in the direction of her outstretched arm. The orioles were within a dozen feet of where she said I'd find them, and another 50 yards down the trail the towhees could be heard noisily pawing through the leaves and debris under several shrubby thickets. Yellow Warblers, Black-and-white Warblers, and several American Redstarts were also busily searching for morsels amid the tall shrubs and just leafing trees.

Walking east, either along the preserve's beach or through its wooded dunes, you will sooner than later run out of land and hit the west side of Fairport Harbor. The small point of land the preserve encompasses embraces the outer waters of the harbor's west side and should not be overlooked by birders. From early fall to early spring the harbor, when ever and where ever there is open water, plays host to large numbers of waterfowl. Common Loons, and grebes are regular visitors and a few rarities can almost always be sniffed out among all the waterfowl and gulls. Waterfowl numbers and varieties swell during spring migration and during summer storms, water birds, along with boaters, seek shelter in the protected waters of the harbor. Pomarine and Parasitic jaegers, Laughing, Iceland and Glaucous gulls, Roseate Terns, Northern Gannet, and Black and White-winged scoters have all been recorded within the harbor. My haul for scoping the bay included all three species of mergansers, Lesser Scaup, a few Ruddy Ducks, plenty of Mallards and a couple of Spotted Sandpipers working the beach. Later, at the Nature Center, Csidor told me Dunlin had been plentiful the last few days and a Bonaparte's Gull was seen in the harbor earlier in the month.

After talking with Csidor and birding — with little luck — the boardwalk crossing the marsh, I headed for the eastern end of the marsh and Zimmerman Trail. Pulling into the parking lot on top of the hill overlooking Shipman Pond, I parked next to the only other car in the lot. Searching for my Peterson guide and binoculars under the piles of notes, candy wrappers, maps, books, empty pop bottles, and the other detritus that naturally collects in a car on a weekend birding trip, I didn't pay much attention to the other car in the lot. I was a little taken aback when I stepped out of my car to find the woman who had directed me to the orioles and towhees at Headlands Dunes, some four hours earlier, leaning against an old Gremlin — the car, not the elf. Again, without so much as a hello, or how-do-you-do, the silver-haired woman pointed south in the direction of the steep, wooded hillside angling down to the pond and said I would find great birding along the pond's shore. She looked down at my low-cut walking shoes and with a smile told me I'd find the Zimmerman Trail tough going "in tennis shoes."

Without hesitation I made for the hillside and carefully made my way down the wet, slippery, leaf-strewn slope to the overgrown greenery bordering the pond. Along the side of the pond, every bush and small tree held warblers. Black-throated Blue and Black-throated Green warblers, Magnolia Warblers, Ruby-crowned Kinglets, Yellow-rumped Warblers, Gray Catbirds, Blue-gray Gnatcatchers, and Black-and-white Warblers simply over ran the landscape. Here and there among the shrubs I picked out individual Yellow Warblers, and I could see a few Common Yellowthroats flitting among the bushes overhanging the water. Cliff and Barn swallows strafed the open water of the pond while a Great Blue Heron posed like a statue on a partially submerged branch on the far shore. Not to be outdone, a Great Egret struck an equally regal pose farther down the wooded shoreline.

I worked my way north along the wooded shoreline, hit the road and turned east to glass the shoreline from the bridge spanning the pond. A Green Heron crossed the pond north of the bridge, and just as I was lifting the binoculars to scan the pond's northern end a small bird whipped across the road and landed in a small shrub on my side of the road. It was close enough to identify as a Palm Warbler without even lifting my binoculars. Next to grab my attention were several Swamp Sparrows darting in and out of a reedy area near the eastern end of the bridge. After searching the fringes of the pond and not turning up any new species, I headed back to the car along the shoulder of the road and promptly kicked up a Hermit Thrush.

Zimmerman Trail, leading south from the parking lot, drew me in that direction by its reputation alone, but as my "birding fairy godmother" had predicted it was extremely wet and I didn't make it more than 50 yards before I was up to my ankles in mud. But in that short distance I found a Hairy Woodpecker and a Wood Thrush.

Ms. Csidor had invited me on a birding hike, scheduled for next morning that was going to begin at the Zimmerman Trailhead. Unfortunately, I would be down the road checking out another birding hot spot. I did park the car at the corner of State Route 44 and Headlands Drive and walked the fields between State Route 44 and the east side of Shipman Pond. It was another local spot that she vowed was a proven producer of birds during spring migration. A tramp of the area turned up American Goldfinches, a Rose-breasted Grosbeak, and several species of sparrow. I probably would have done better if my birding good luck charm had been there to point me in the right direction.

"My haul for scoping the bay included all three species of mergansers, Lesser Scaup, a few Ruddy Ducks, plenty of Mallards and a couple of Spotted Sandpipers working the beach."

Cuyahoga Valley National Recreation Area

"A not-to-be-missed spectacle is the Great Blue Heron rookery at the south end of the park. It is simply an incredible sight."

LOCATION: Brecksville, Ohio.

DIRECTIONS: From the Ohio Turnpike take exit 12 and drive south on State Road 8 to Road 303. Turn right and follow Road 303 about 1 mile to the Happy Days Visitors Center where you can obtain a map of the recreation area. You can also access the area from I-77 which runs north and south on the west side of the recreation area. From I-77 you can take either Wheatley Road on the south or Chippewa Road on the north and drive east to Riverview Road.

HOURS: Open year-round.

BEST TIMES: Mid-April through mid-June and September and October are the prime birding times but this scenic park has more than enough interesting nesters to make a birding trip worthwhile from spring through fall.

BIRDING HIGHLIGHTS: Especially fine birding for neotropical songbirds in spring and fall. With a wide variety of habitats and ecosystems, the large recreation attracts a wide variety of interesting birds from spring through fall.

FOR MORE INFORMATION: National Park Service, Cuyahoga Valley National Recreation Area, 15610 Vaughn Road, Brecksville, OH 44141. Phone: (216) 650-4636.

From the parking lot at the Ira Trailhead, it was supposed to be only a ten-minute walk to the Beaver Pond and the long boardwalk that crosses it. But I had been on the trail for a half-hour, and I still wasn't in sight of the Beaver Pond. It wasn't that the pond was a greater distance than advertised from the trailhead, it was just that there were too many birds to look at and too much scenery to soak up. The Ira Trailhead was my third stop of the morning in the recreation area, and it was proving to be typical of the first two birding stops. Time is a very relative matter once you slip into Cuyahoga Valley National Recreation Area. Hours can slip by in the blink of a warbler's eye, and a planned schedule has as much chance of being followed here as it would in Alice's Wonderland.

The 22-mile long, 33,000-acre Cuyahoga Valley National Recreation Area is an enchanted river basin of sublime and stunning beauty running north from Akron to the outskirts of Cleveland. Nearly surrounded by urban and suburban sprawl, the recreation area harbors dramatic steep-walled valleys, rolling hills cloaked in dense forests, mesmerizing waterfalls, extensive wetlands, rocky gorges, and sweeping meadows all tied together by a silvery ribbon of blue water that flows through it and from which it takes its name. Adding to the charm is a restored 19th Century farm and the historic Ohio and Erie Canal, opened in 1827 and abandoned in the 1880s. The canal's locks, towpath, buildings, and old stretches of the water-filled ditch still etch the valley's floor. Many of the locks are still plainly visible, and the old canal's towpath now serves as one of the recreation area's main hiking/biking trails.

Scattered within this mix of great natural beauty and quaint history are hiking trails, cross-country and downhill skiing facilities, picnic areas, bike paths, golf courses, museums, beautiful country roads just made for a Sunday drive, and even a covered bridge. Amidst all these heavily used facilities are some of the most productive and scenic birding sites in the state. Most of the people I encountered seemed to be involved in every type of outdoor activity except birding. The trails were packed with fitness walkers, roller bladers, bicyclers, and parents pushing baby carriages.

In the six hours or so of birding, I didn't encounter a dozen other birders; however, Diane Chalfant, Chief of Interpretation and Visitors Services, says the Cuyahoga Valley National Recreation Area is "becoming recognized as one of the leading places to bird in the state of Ohio." You don't have to drive more than a few miles along the park's scenic, winding roads to realize the wide diversity of habitat should hold a wealth of birds. Two hundred thirty-one species of birds have been recorded to date in the areas dense upland forests, floodplain woodlots, meadows, old farmland fields, and extensive wetlands. The checklist includes 38 warbler species and nearly all the other bird families. Chalfant pointed out that the bird checklist is relatively new and expects that the number of species found in the area will continue to grow as more birders visit and habitats continue to diversify. She thinks birders will find good birding any time of the year with the best birding coming during spring and fall migration. Backing up her recommendation is a recent one-day census taken in May that tallied 130 species, of which 28 were warblers.

I arrived at 7:00 a.m. on a beautiful Saturday morning in May eager to explore the prime birding areas recommended by the staff of the recreation area. My first foray into the field was at the Ledges Area on the east side of the recreation area. From the parking lot off Kendall Park Road, west of State Highway 8, a well-worn path led me along the edge of a sandstone cliff shrouded in a mix of hardwoods and evergreens. Mature trees towered over me, and in many places the trail tunneled through a dense understory of younger trees fighting to reach the sunlight. The forest, from the top of the canopy to the leaf-strewn floor, was alive with birds. Eastern Wood-pewees, Black-and-white Warblers, Hermit and Wood thrushes, American Robins, Chestnut-sided Warblers, nuthatches, Brown Creepers, and Black-capped Chickadee's were everywhere. Several Yellow-rumped Warblers were always present, and the high point of the walk came with the sighting of a Black-throated Green Warbler. The ledges are a favorite nesting area of Solitary Vireos, Winter Wrens, and Hooded Warblers. In addition, Ovenbirds, Louisiana Waterthrushes, and Cerulean Warblers often show up here during spring migration. Acadian Flycatchers also frequent the ledges, and I took it on faith that was the identity of the diminutive flycatchers with two wing bars and an eyering that I kept seeing throughout my walk.

A not-to-be-missed spectacle in the Cuyahoga Valley is the Great Blue Heron rookery at the south end of the park. The rookery is simply an incredible sight. The birds have taken up residency in a group of stately hardwoods lying within a dozen yards of Bath Road, between Akron Peninsula Road on the east and Riverview Road on the west. The rookery has proven so popular with visitors that the recreation area installed a wide gravel pull off on Bath Road opposite the nesting birds. I joined a line of parked cars and people who were utterly transfixed by the aviary high-rise apartments. The large trees are packed with enormous nests that seemed precariously balanced (at best) on outstretched limbs. The number of nests per tree varied from 18 to 27. Each nest had at least one parent onboard minding juveniles that were as big as crows. The low clicks and scratchy calls of the birds filled the air, and the sound reminded me of an 19th Century factory I'd visited in historic Greenfield Village where the power was supplied by enormous leather belts running through huge pulleys. The constant slap of belts on pulleys, backed by a continuous chorus of squeaks, and the low hum of machinery was a near pitch-perfect imitation of the sound coming across the road from the hundreds of heron. Every car passing the rookery slowed to a crawl as motorists craned their necks to take in the strange sight. If a car stopped at the side of the road, you could count on it staying there at least 15 minutes as the occupants lost all track of time and destination.

I finally pulled myself away from the rookery and went in search of the first of three birding sites strung along the canal's old towpath, all of which are accessible from a different trailhead. The Ira Trailhead is located on the west side of the Cuyahoga River on Riverview Road just north of Ira Road. From the parking lot, it can't be more than a half-mile to a large wetlands created by some industrious beavers. The beaver pond and marsh is bisected by a new boardwalk, and the pond area is noted for Virginia Rails, Soras, Warbling Vireos, Eastern Bluebirds, Black-billed Cuckoos, Orchard Orioles, and Prothonotary Warblers. The problem is getting there.

Before I even made it out of the parking lot, I stumbled across a Nashville Warbler in marshy wetlands lying in the angle between the parking lot and towpath. Within the next half-hour and maybe 100 feet, I chalked up a Baltimore

"The recreation area harbors dramatic steep-walled valleys, rolling hills cloaked in dense forests, mesmerizing waterfalls, extensive wetlands, rocky gorges, and sweeping meadows all tied together by a silvery ribbon of blue water that flows through it and from which it takes its name."

"The bird checklist is relatively new, and the number of species found in the area will continue to grow as more birders visit and habitats continue to diversify."

Oriole, a Green Heron fishing in the 150 year-old canal, several Yellow Warblers, a pair of Rose-breasted Grosbeaks, and a Common Yellowthroat in addition to another dozen species. All the while I was searching for birds from the side of the trail legions of bikers, joggers and roller bladers whizzed past. After meeting up with an area birder who listed this area as her favorite birding spot in the Cleveland area, we came to a footpath that cut to the east off of the heavily traveled towpath. The little footpath lies at about the halfway mark between the trailhead and the beaver pond. Not only was it pleasant to get away from the heavy traffic on the towpath, but the path leads to dense thickets and a quiet wetlands filled with birds. Besides a noisy Belted Kingfisher flying over the wetlands, the dense thickets yielded Wilson's and Black-and-white warblers and three species of thrushes.

When we rejoined the towpath, we stumbled on another lone birder. The three of us slowly made our way to the Beaver Pond while scoping the trees and vegetation on the far side of the old canal. We continued to pick out more warblers but no new species for the day until the newest member of the trio chanced upon a Magnolia Warbler. By the time we reached the Beaver Pond, 90 minutes had elapsed since I had left the parking lot. We could find none of the more interesting species so often seen around the pond but had added another dozen of the commonly seen species to the day's list. Steeling myself not to stop for any bird, no matter how tempting, I headed back to the parking lot and reached my car in little more than ten minutes.

The next stop recommended by the staff of the recreation area was at Deep Lock Quarry Park, four miles north of the Ira Trailhead on Riverview Road. Again, birding is from the towpath, and the area is one of the better places in the park for warblers during both spring and fall migration. Besides an abundance of warblers, the Deep Lock Quarry area often delights birders with sightings of Scarlet Tanagers and Yellow-throated Vireos. And at half-past noon on a beautiful Saturday, I couldn't find a parking space anywhere in the lot adjacent to the trailhead and nearby picnic area so I continued north.

Vowing to hit Deep Lock Quarry on the way back, I drove to the northern end of the park to the Station Road Bridge area. Chalfant identified it as one of the best locations on the north end of the towpath for birding. The rare Brewster's Warbler, Yellow-throated Warblers, Olive-sided Flycatchers, and Yellow-billed Cuckoos have all been found here. The parking lot for the trailhead is just south of Chippewa Road on Riverview Road. Before I reached the bridge that takes hikers to the east bank of the Cuyahoga River, I got sidetracked by a couple of birders walking back down the railroad tracks on the west side of the river opposite the trail. They told me of spotting a Prothonotary Warbler and a Eastern Screech-owl about a half-mile up the tracks. One of the birders had even jammed a stick with some red ribbon on the end of it opposite the tree where the owl was roosting. I never found the ribbon-bedecked stick or the owl, but the Prothonotary Warbler turned up, as advertised, in some thickets beside the river. The walk also netted several Great Blue Heron, an Indigo Bunting, an Olive-sided Flycatcher, and more Wilson's and Yellow-rumped warblers.

Returning to the parking lot, I detoured to checkout a small patch of wetlands I'd passed near the entrance to the trailhead. It was a circular, water-filled depression in the woods that I thought might attract warblers. The small patch of damp woods turned out to be flooded with birds. Within minutes I ticked off Magnolia, Bay-breasted, Yellow-rumped and Yellow warblers, a dozen Brown Creepers, a Rose-breasted Grosbeak, and several American Redstarts. The busy birds kept me entranced for more than 30 minutes until I realized it was after three o'clock and I should have headed back to Michigan more than an hour earlier.

Deep Lock Quarry would have to wait for another trip. And the Tree Farm Trail on Major Road west of Riverview Road would have to wait for a different season. Chalfant pointed out that the Tree Farm Trail is one of the best spots in the recreation area for winter birding. Red-breasted Nuthatches are abundant there during mid-winter as are Golden-crowned Kinglets. But the biggest winter draw at the Tree Farm Trail are the consistent sightings of Sharp-shinned, Cooper's, and Red-tailed hawks.

If you are unfamiliar with the area, it is best to write the address on page 122 for a map before visiting. With map in hand, it is easy to find all the above sites and plan an itinerary. A schedule, on the other hand, is pretty well pointless once you start birding.

CUYAHOGA VALLEY NATIONAL RECREATION AREA FIELD CHECKLIST

This list was prepared and compiled by the Cuyahoga Valley National Recreation Area.

Common Loon	Rough-legged Hawk	Red-bellied Woodpecker	Northern Mockingbird	Hooded Warbler
Pied-billed Grebe	American Kestrel	Yellow-bellied Sapsucker	Brown Thrasher	Wilson's Warbler
Horned Grebe	Merlin	Downy Woodpecker	American Pipit	Canada Warbler
Double-crested Cormorant	Peregrine Falcon	Hairy Woodpecker	Cedar Waxwing	Yellow-breasted Chat
American Bittern	Ring-necked Pheasant	Black-backed Woodpecker	Northern Shrike	Summer Tanager
Least Bittern	Ruffed Grouse	Northern Flicker	Loggerhead Shrike	Scarlet Tanager
Great Blue Heron	Wild Turkey	Pileated Woodpecker	European Starling	Northern Cardinal
Great Egret	Northern Bobwhite	Olive-sided Flycatcher	White-eyed Vireo	Rose-breasted Grosbeak
Little Blue Heron	Virginia Rail	Eastern Wood-pewee	Solitary Vireo	Indigo Bunting
Cattle Egret	Sora	Yellow-bellied Flycatcher	Yellow-throated Vireo	Rufous-sided Towhee
Green Heron	Common Moorhen	Acadian Flycatcher	Warbling Vireo	American Tree Sparrow
Black-crowned Night-heron	American Coot	Alder Flycatcher	Philadelphia Vireo	Chipping Sparrow
Yellow-crowned Night-heron	Black-bellied Plover	Willow Flycatcher	Red-eyed Vireo	Field Sparrow
Tundra Swan	Semipalmated Plover	Least Flycatcher	Blue-winged Warbler	Vesper Sparrow
Mute Swan	Killdeer	Eastern Phoebe	Golden-winged Warbler	Savannah Sparrow
Snow Goose	Greater Yellowlegs	Great Crested Flycatcher	Brewster's Warbler	Grasshopper Sparrow
Canada Goose	Lesser Yellowlegs	Eastern Kingbird	Lawrence's Warbler	Henslow's Sparrow
Wood Duck	Solitary Sandpiper	Horned Lark	Tennessee Warbler	Fox Sparrow
Green-winged Teal	Spotted Sandpiper	Purple Martin	Orange-crowned Warbler	Song Sparrow
American Black Duck	Upland Sandpiper	Tree Swallow	Nashville Warbler	Lincoln's Sparrow
Mallard	Semipalmated Sandpiper	Northern Rough-winged Swallow	Northern Parula	Swamp Sparrow
Northern Pintail	Least Sandpiper	Bank Swallow	Yellow Warbler	White-throated Sparrow
Blue-winged Teal	Pectoral Sandpiper	Cliff Swallow	Chestnut-sided Warbler	White-crowned Sparrow
Northern Shoveler	Dunlin	Barn Swallow	Magnolia Warbler	Dark-eyed Junco
Gadwall	Common Snipe	Blue Jay	Cape May Warbler	Lapland Longspur
American Wigeon	American Woodcock	American Crow	Black-throated Blue Warbler	Snow Bunting
Canvasback	Bonaparte's Gull	Black-capped Chickadee	Yellow-rumped Warbler	Bobolink
Redhead	Ring-billed Gull	Tufted Titmouse	Black-throated Green Warbler	Red-winged Blackbird
Ring-necked Duck	Herring Gull	Red-breasted Nuthatch	Blackburnian Warbler	Eastern Meadowlark
Greater Scaup	Rock Dove	White-breasted Nuthatch	Yellow-throated Warbler	Yellow-headed Blackbird
Lesser Scaup	Mourning Dove	Brown Creeper	Pine Warbler	Rusty Blackbird
White-winged Scoter	Black-billed Cuckoo	Carolina Wren	Prairie Warbler	Common Grackle
Common Goldeneye	Yellow-billed Cuckoo	House Wren	Palm Warbler	Brown-headed Cowbird
Bufflehead	Barn Owl	Winter Wren	Bay-breasted Warbler	Orchard Oriole
Hooded Merganser	Eastern Screech-owl	Sedge Wren	Blackpoll Warbler	Baltimore Oriole
Common Merganser	Great Horned Owl	Marsh Wren	Cerulean warbler	Pine Grosbeak
Red-breasted Merganser	Snowy Owl	Golden-crowned Kinglet	Black-and-white Warbler	Purple Finch
Ruddy Duck	Barred Owl	Ruby-crowned Kinglet	American Redstart	House Finch
Turkey Vulture	Long-eared Owl	Blue-gray Gnatcatcher	Prothonotary Warbler	Red Crossbill
Osprey	Short-eared Owl	Eastern Bluebird	Worm-eating Warbler	White-winged Crossbill
Bald Eagle	Northern Saw-whet Owl	Veery	Ovenbird	Common Redpoll
Northern Harrier	Common Nighthawk	Gray-cheeked Thrush	Northern Waterthrush	Pine Siskin
Sharp-shinned Hawk	Whip-poor-will	Swainson's Thrush	Louisiana Waterthrush	American Goldfinch
Cooper's Hawk	Chimney Swift	Hermit Thrush	Kentucky Warbler	Evening Grosbeak
Red-shouldered Hawk	Ruby-throated Hummingbird	Wood Thrush	Connecticut Warbler	House Sparrow
Broad-winged Hawk	Belted Kingfisher	American Robin	Mourning Warbler	
Red-tailed Hawk	Red-headed Woodpecker	Gray Catbird	Common Yellowthroat	

Green Lawn Cemetery

"On weekends during spring migration 'The Pit' draws more cars than even the largest funerals."

It was a beautiful spring Sunday morning in downtown Columbus, and I couldn't wait to go and plant myself in Green Lawn Cemetery. I was in the terminal stages of spring birding frenzy and for over two years I'd looked forward to visiting the cemetery billed as "the most famous birding spot in Central Ohio." The claim appears on the Checklist of the Birds of Green Lawn Cemetery and Arboretum, a pamphlet published by the Columbus Audubon Society and Green Lawn Cemetery and available at the cemetery.

The best, yet-to-turn-professional birding guide in the Midwest, Jeff Buecking, and I turned into the cemetery's gate a little after 7:00 a.m. to find only a couple of birders had arrived before us. Our early arrival was rewarded with the glimpse of a Cooper's Hawk coursing through the trees. Jeff was returning to the heart of Buckeye country and eager to revisit some of the great birding sites he regularly birded while working in Columbus for several years. I had a private bet going with myself that we would run into birders he knew within 15 minutes of our arrival. I won the bet within five minutes and we spent the next two hours birding the cemetery in the company of three Columbus birdwatchers who have haunted Green Lawn for years.

The 380-acre park-like cemetery is a pleasing combination of mixed hardwoods, open grassy expanses, brushy areas, and a small, abandoned, water-filled quarry that serves as a pond. The cemetery's bird checklist totals 219 species and, as proof of its fame as a spring migration stopover spot for neotropicals, boasts 38 warbler species, 11 flycatchers, and 7 different vireos. Among the more interesting nesters at the cemetery are Yellow-billed Cuckoos, Great Horned Owls, Carolina Chickadees, Carolina Wrens, Cooper's Hawk, and American Woodcock.

One of the first things I learned from Jeff and the other Columbus birders is that the cemetery has three principle birding areas: "The Pit," "The Bridge," and "The Ridge." The Pit is the most famous and favorite birding spot in the cemetery. The steep-sided, rocky edges of the The Pit suggested the water hole used to be a small quarry. Up until a couple of years ago, this little oasis of water was ringed with thick shrubbery and dense yews. The birds used to pack the shrubbery around the water hole like the Japanese pack a subway, and then the cemetery removed the old, overgrown plantings. Green Lawn management replanted the area surrounding the old quarry, but it will be years before the plantings provide any substantial cover for birds. Birdwatchers feared that one of the great birding spots in the state was ruined, but a local Columbus birder reports the area, "continue[s] to be an excellent birding hot spot. In fact, I would say that the birders were more upset about what was done than the birds seemed to be."

Northern Saw-whet Owls used to be regular visitors to The Pit in March and April, but sightings of the owls have become extremely rare with the removal of the yews. But it's still a great place for warblers, vireos, thrushes, sparrows, kinglets, the odd nuthatch, Brown Thrasher, and Evening Grosbeak. And for a body of water that at best is 30 feet in diameter it attracts a surprising number of waterfowl and shorebirds. Pied-billed Grebes, Blue-winged teal, American Coots, Black-crowned, and Yellow-crowned Night-heron have all been spotted there. By late morning when we left the cemetery it was ringed with birders, but The

LOCATION: Columbus, Ohio.

DIRECTIONS: Drive south out of downtown Columbus on I-71 from the intersection of I-70 and I-71 to the Greenlawn Avenue exit. Go west on Greenlawn for almost 1 mile to where the street ends at the entrance to the cemetery.

HOURS: Open year round from 7:00 a.m.-7:00 p.m.

BEST TIMES: Late April through May with the best birding usually peaking in the second week of May.

BIRDING HIGHLIGHTS: One of the best spots in Ohio, and one of the best urban sites in the Midwest for neotropical songbirds during spring migration. The cemetery also tempts birders with its surprising variety of species from owls to shorebirds. If that's not enough encouragement; how many cemeteries have bird checklists available on the grounds?

FOR MORE INFORMATION: Columbus Audubon Society, P.O. Box 141350, Columbus, Ohio 43214. Phone: (614) 444-1123.

Bridge and The Ridge actually proved to be more productive that Sunday morning. To reach the The Pit, drive through the cemetery gates and head straight for the chapel lying (sorry, I can't resist) dead ahead. As you near the chapel, you will see a mausoleum to the left and behind the chapel. The Pit is directly behind the mausoleum.

The Bridge is an old iron span that crosses a ravine on the south side of the cemetery. The wooded ravine has traditionally been good warbler country and is a constant producer of Hooded, Kentucky and Canada warblers, and Ovenbirds. All of the thrushes can usually be found in the area around the bridge and large pine trees in the area can hold Barn, Barred, Long-eared and Great Horned Owls. Our group spotted a Hooded Warbler just past the bridge and ticked off several thrushes. One particular thrush had the group debating its ancestry and proudly perched on a headstone until the Buckeyes finally decided it was of the Gray-cheeked variety. The Bridge also yielded a Brown Thrasher, an Ovenbird, and Ruby-crowned Kinglets. To reach The Bridge, walk south from The Pit to the first lane going to the right and follow it for about a hundred yards.

From The Bridge we worked our way back to The Ridge which lays across the cemetery like a backbone. The gentle rise is covered with mature oaks and other deciduous trees that can be counted on to hold a wide variety of songbirds. Our wanderings along The Ridge turned up Pine Warblers, a lone Solitary Vireo, Least Flycatchers, a Palm Warbler, Northern Mockingbird, and a Baltimore Oriole. The Ridge is just to the west of the The Pit. You really don't have to worry about finding any of the birding hot spots on weekends in April or May. On weekends during spring migration The Pit draws more cars than even the largest funerals, and there will always be plenty of knowledgeable birders at The Pit to direct you to the other prime biding locations.

Nearly anyplace in the Green Lawn Cemetery will reward birders in late April and early May with the peak of migration coming in the second week of May. Birding remains good through early June. Technically not in the cemetery, but another spot worth checking, is the heavily wooded and brushy area just outside of the cemetery's gates. Rufous-sided Towhees, waterthrushes, and American Woodcock are only a few of the more interesting birds found on the cemetery's doorstep.

After a pleasant morning of birding, and friendly chest-thumping about which state, Michigan or Ohio, offered the best birding, we headed back to The Pit and our cars. But before leaving, I wanted to check out the register of recent sightings kept at the same little wooden kiosk as the bird checklist (it's adjacent to The Pit) to see what we had missed. I also wanted to find the last resting place of James Thurber, one of my favorite authors, who's buried in Green Lawn. Sightings from the last few days included Summer Tanagers, Worm-eating, Cerulean, Black-throated Green, Chestnut-sided, and Blackburnian warblers, Rusty Blackbirds, both cuckoos, a Winter Wren, and a Great Horned Owl. James Thurber's grave turned out to be just a Walter Mitty medicine ball toss to the west of The Pit in the Fisher family plot.

"One particular thrush had the group debating its ancestry and proudly perched on a headstone until the Buckeyes finally decided it was of the Gray-cheeked variety."

GREEN LAWN CEMETERY FIELD CHECKLIST

Published by the Columbus Audubon Society and Green Lawn Cemetery

___ Common Loon
___ Pied-billed Grebe
___ American White Pelican
___ Double-crested Cormorant
___ American Bittern
___ Least Bittern
___ Great Blue Heron
___ Great Egret
___ Little Blue Heron
___ Green Heron
___ Black-crowned Night-heron
___ Yellow-crowned Night-heron
___ Tundra Swan
___ Canada Goose
___ Wood Duck
___ Green-winged Teal
___ American Black Duck
___ Mallard
___ Northern Pintail
___ Blue-winged Teal
___ Northern Shoveler
___ Gadwall
___ American Wigeon
___ Canvasback
___ Redhead
___ Ring-necked Duck
___ Lesser Scaup
___ Common Goldeneye
___ Bufflehead
___ Hooded Merganser
___ Common Merganser
___ Red-breasted Merganser
___ Turkey Vulture
___ Osprey
___ Mississippi Kite
___ Bald Eagle
___ Northern Harrier
___ Sharp-shinned Hawk
___ Cooper's Hawk
___ Red-shouldered Hawk
___ Broad-winged Hawk
___ Red-tailed Hawk
___ Golden Eagle
___ American Kestrel

___ Merlin
___ Peregrine Falcon
___ Ring-necked Pheasant
___ Northern Bobwhite
___ American Coot
___ Killdeer
___ Solitary Sandpiper
___ Willet
___ Spotted Sandpiper
___ Common Snipe
___ American Woodcock
___ Franklin's Gull
___ Ring-billed Gull
___ Herring Gull
___ Common Tern
___ Rock Dove
___ Mourning Dove
___ Yellow-billed Cuckoo
___ Black-billed Cuckoo
___ Barn Owl
___ Eastern Screech-owl
___ Great Horned Owl
___ Snowy Owl
___ Barred Owl
___ Long-eared Owl
___ Northern Saw-whet Owl
___ Common Nighthawk
___ Chuck-will's-widow
___ Whip-poor-will
___ Chimney Swift
___ Ruby-throated Hummingbird
___ Belted Kingfisher
___ Red-headed Woodpecker
___ Red-bellied Woodpecker
___ Yellow-bellied Sapsucker
___ Downy Woodpecker
___ Hairy Woodpecker
___ Northern Flicker
___ Pileated Woodpecker
___ Olive-sided Flycatcher
___ Eastern Wood-pewee
___ Yellow-bellied Flycatcher
___ Acadian Flycatcher
___ Alder Flycatcher

___ Willow Flycatcher
___ Least Flycatcher
___ Eastern Phoebe
___ Great Crested Flycatcher
___ Eastern Kingbird
___ Western Kingbird
___ Purple Martin
___ Tree Swallow
___ Northern Rough-winged Swallow
___ Bank Swallow
___ Cliff Swallow
___ Barn Swallow
___ Blue Jay
___ American Crow
___ Black-capped Chickadee
___ Carolina Chickadee
___ Tufted Titmouse
___ Red-breasted Nuthatch
___ White-breasted Nuthatch
___ Brown Creeper
___ Carolina Wren
___ Bewick's Wren
___ House Wren
___ Winter Wren
___ Sedge Wren
___ Marsh Wren
___ Golden-crowned Kinglet
___ Ruby-crowned Kinglet
___ Blue-gray Gnatcatcher
___ Eastern Bluebird
___ Veery
___ Gray-cheeked Thrush
___ Swainson's Thrush
___ Hermit Thrush
___ Wood Thrush
___ American Robin
___ Gray Catbird
___ Northern Mockingbird
___ Brown Thrasher
___ Cedar Waxwing
___ American Pipit
___ Loggerhead Shrike
___ European Starling
___ White-eyed Vireo

___ Bell's Vireo
___ Solitary Vireo
___ Yellow-throated Vireo
___ Warbling Vireo
___ Philadelphia Vireo
___ Red-eyed Vireo
___ Blue-winged Warbler
___ Golden-winged Warbler
___ Brewster's Warbler
___ Lawrence's Warbler
___ Tennessee Warbler
___ Orange-crowned Warbler
___ Nashville Warbler
___ Northern Parula
___ Yellow Warbler
___ Chestnut-sided Warbler
___ Magnolia Warbler
___ Cape May Warbler
___ Black-throated Blue Warbler
___ Yellow-rumped Warbler
___ Black-throated Green Warbler
___ Blackburnian Warbler
___ Yellow-throated Warbler
___ Pine Warbler
___ Kirtland's Warbler
___ Prairie Warbler
___ Palm Warbler
___ Bay-breasted Warbler
___ Blackpoll Warbler
___ Cerulean Warbler
___ Black-and-white Warbler
___ American Redstart
___ Prothonotary Warbler
___ Worm-eating Warbler
___ Swainson's Warbler
___ Ovenbird
___ Northern Waterthrush
___ Louisiana Waterthrush
___ Kentucky Warbler
___ Connecticut Warbler
___ Mourning Warbler
___ Common Yellowthroat
___ Hooded Warbler
___ Wilson's Warbler

___ Canada Warbler
___ Yellow-breasted Chat
___ Summer Tanager
___ Scarlet Tanager
___ Northern Cardinal
___ Rose-breasted Grosbeak
___ Blue Grosbeak
___ Indigo Bunting
___ Rufous-sided Towhee
___ American Tree Sparrow
___ Chipping Sparrow
___ Clay-colored Sparrow
___ Field Sparrow
___ Vesper Sparrow
___ Savannah Sparrow
___ Fox Sparrow
___ Song Sparrow
___ Lincoln's Sparrow
___ Swamp Sparrow
___ White-throated Sparrow
___ White-crowned Sparrow
___ Harris' Sparrow
___ Dark-eyed Junco
___ Snow Bunting
___ Bobolink
___ Red-winged Blackbird
___ Eastern Meadowlark
___ Rusty Blackbird
___ Common Grackle
___ Brown-headed Cowbird
___ Orchard Oriole
___ Baltimore Oriole
___ Purple Finch
___ House Finch
___ Red Crossbill
___ White-winged Crossbill
___ Common Redpoll
___ Hoary Redpoll
___ Pine Siskin
___ American Goldfinch
___ Evening Grosbeak
___ House Sparrow

Clear Creek Valley Metro Park

For sheer beauty, few drives, hikes, or birding spots in Ohio rival Clear Creek Valley. The narrow, steep-sided, crease in the rolling landscape of central Ohio can almost make visitors believe they have stumbled into a forgotten corner of the Appalachians. At its mouth, the valley is probably about a half-mile wide, but as you travel west on Clear Creek Road, the old farm fields, small woodlots, and meadows are gradually pinched out by the converging walls until there is barely room for Clear Creek and the road at the bottom of the V. For most of its journey, the stream is escorted by two rows of unruly trees and woody vegetation that crowd either side of Clear Creek. Dogwood, redbud, wild plum, sassafras, pitch pine, Kentucky coffee, American beech, and sycamore only hint at the variety of trees guarding the little creek, or finding purchase on the steep hills and near vertical cliffs overlooking the valley floor. Beneath the trees and carpeting the open fields are a plethora of wildflowers, vines, and bushes.

Obviously, you don't have to be a birder to enjoy this pocket of splendid natural beauty. Most of the valley, 3,000 acres, is owned by the Columbus and Franklin County Metropolitan Park District, and much of the park acreage lies within two state nature preserves. Many park visitors come to picnic or hike the well-marked trails that edge Clear Creek, follow small feeder streams into tight little valleys, and climb the steep, heavily wooded hills overlooking the valley. But birders get all of the above thrown in as a bonus when birding one of the best songbird areas in Ohio. Birding heats up at Clear Creek in mid-April with the arrival of the first wave of spring migration, reaches a peak in early May, and continues to be a favorite birding spot into early July because of the numerous species that nest in the valley.

Clear Creek Road hugs the bottom of the steep cliffs lining the north side of the valley, and on weekends during the peak of spring migration you are liable to encounter more birders on the road than cars. The road is narrow, and for most of its run through the valley, there is no shoulder and very few spots to pull off, making birding by car all but impossible. Birders usually leave their cars at the beginning of the valley, at the Creekside Meadows Picnic Area, or at the few roadside spots big enough to hold a car.

Jeff Buecking and I left my car at the entrance to the valley (in a parking lot at the corner of U.S. 33 and Clear Creek Road) and began walking west on Clear Creek Road about 10:30 a.m. on a Sunday morning early in May. In our 90-minute walk we were passed by about a dozen cars and passed nearly 20 birders walking the road in two large groups. I received a great lesson on how a thorough knowledge of bird calls can add to the success of a birding trip. Over half of the more interesting birds encountered and identified that morning in Clear Creek Valley were never eye-balled by either one of us. It was Jeff's expert ear that picked out individual calls from the near constant background chorus of bird calls and matched the call with a species. His familiarity with bird calls added immeasurably to the pleasure of the trip. We might not see them, but it still gave us pleasure knowing that a Yellow-throated Vireo was somewhere in a distant clump of

"From our first step down the road, we were treated to great sights and great birding."

LOCATION: Lancaster, Ohio.

DIRECTIONS: From the junction of U.S. 22 and U.S. 33 in Lancaster drive 9 miles south on U.S. 33 to County Road 116 (Clear Creek Road).

HOURS: Open all year.

BEST TIMES: Birding is very good from mid-April to early July, and fantastic in the first two weeks in May.

BIRDING HIGHLIGHTS: One of the best places in Ohio for songbirds, and one of the most picturesque spots in the state for birding. Not only does the area attract a wide variety of migrating songbirds but many nest here. A very incomplete bird checklist totals 138 species of which the vast majority are songbirds.

"I received a great lesson on how a thorough knowledge of bird calls can add to the success of a birding trip."

trees, and a Carolina Chickadee resided in a dense, stream-side thicket. I can't quite say the same for the Blue-winged Warbler that tantalized us for nearly 15 minutes. It proved more than just a little frustrating to know that somewhere in a narrow patch of shrubs that we fruitlessly searched for a quarter-hour sat a species I'd never seen in my life.

From our first step down the road, we were treated to great sights and great birding. Song and Field sparrows and a variety of swallows were constantly popping into view or swooping over the fields south of the road. Demanding equal attention were warblers, vireos, and other songbirds in the trees and shrubs lining the road and clinging to the cliff face. Jeff also kept scanning the skies and pointing his binoculars at any soaring birds hoping to find at least one of the Black Vultures which frequent this corner of Ohio. Approximately one mile west of U.S. 33, Clear Creek slips between the cliff face on the north and a tall slab of bedrock that cants over the road like the Leaning Tower of Pisa. Some of the more notable birds we saw or heard while walking the road from the parking lot to the tower included: Blue-gray Gnatcatchers, White-eyed Vireos, Common Yellow-throats, Barn, Tree, Cliff, and Northern Rough-winged swallows, a Rufous-sided Towhee, numerous Gray Catbirds, Red-shouldered and Red-tailed hawks, an Eastern Bluebird, a Black-throated Green Warbler, Northern Parula, and a Louisiana Waterthrush.

We walked a quarter-mile past the tower and then retraced our steps to the car. This first mile or so of the Clear Creek Valley is also known for its flycatchers, tanagers, Yellow- and Black-billed Cuckoos, and thrushes; and we kept eyes, and in Jeff's case ears, open for any of these birds on the walk back to the car, but failed to turn up a single one. Back in the car, we drove the road we just walked, and at about the 1.8-mile mark reached Creekside Meadows Picnic Area and its parking lot. Just past the picnic area Starner Road cuts off to the south and crosses Clear Creek on an old iron bridge. According to Jeff, who's birded the Clear Creek Valley several times, the area around the old bridge and the first couple hundred yards of Starner Road south of Clear Creek Road traditionally yields plenty of flycatchers and warblers.

Instead of searching the familiar, we decided to hike one of the trails that departs from the picnic area and climbs the steep hills on the north side of the valley. We spotted a Pileated Woodpecker

CAROLINA WREN

130

perched on a dead tree on a easy stroll along the Creekside Meadows Trail and then worked up a sweat on Hemlock Trail as it took us to the highlands overlooking the valley. It was a beautiful, but tiring walk through a magnificent forest that entailed lots of walking up and staggering down steep hillsides. Several times I was panting so hard I could hardly hold my binoculars steady. The trail added a couple of thrushes to the day's list as well as Yellow-throated Vireo. We were hiking the trail in the heat of mid day. If walked in the morning, this trail should be overrun with birds, especially the first couple of hundred yards where the Hemlock Trail borders and repeatedly recrosses a small brook.

From the Creekside Meadows Picnic Area, the valley narrows dramatically as you head west on Clear Creek Road. Between the picnic area and Written Rock (4.8 miles west of U.S. 33) there is plenty of good birding but few places to park and look for them. Three fishing access sites border the river on this stretch of the road; and they, or any other place where you can get your car off the road, hold something of interest for birders. The area around Written Rock, a roadside slab of sandstone that has inspired graffiti artists for at least 100 years, is home to numerous woodpeckers, warblers, vireos, orioles, and flycatchers.

Visit Clear Creek Valley only once and this special little corner of Ohio will stay with you for a long time. And if you're a birder, you may as well resign yourself to the fact that each succeeding May will arrive with a longing to once again stroll down Clear Creek Road and search out the flycatchers, warblers, and other brilliantly painted songbirds that gently invade this valley every spring.

"You may as well resign yourself to the fact that each succeeding May will arrive with a longing to once again stroll down Clear Creek Road and search out the flycatchers, warblers, and other brilliantly painted songbirds that gently invade this valley every spring."

CLEAR CREEK VALLEY METRO PARK FIELD CHECKLIST

This is a very incomplete checklist drawn from a number of sources.

___ Common Loon	___ Whip-poor-will	___ Red-breasted Nuthatch	___ Northern Parula	___ Hooded Warbler
___ Great Blue Heron	___ Ruby-throated Hummingbird	___ Brown Creeper	___ Tennessee Warbler	___ Wilson's Warbler
___ Green Heron	___ Belted Kingfisher	___ Carolina Wren	___ Nashville Warbler	___ Canada Warbler
___ Canada Goose	___ Red-bellied Woodpecker	___ Bewick's Wren	___ Yellow Warbler	___ Yellow-breasted Chat
___ Wood Duck	___ Downy Woodpecker	___ House Wren	___ Chestnut-sided Warbler	___ Summer Tanager
___ Mallard	___ Hairy Woodpecker	___ Winter Wren	___ Magnolia Warbler	___ Scarlet Tanager
___ Turkey Vulture	___ Northern Flicker	___ Golden-crowned Kinglet	___ Cape May Warbler	___ Northern Cardinal
___ Black Vulture	___ Pileated Woodpecker	___ Ruby-crowned Kinglet	___ Black-throated Blue Warbler	___ Rose-breasted Grosbeak
___ Osprey	___ Eastern Wood-pewee	___ Blue-gray Gnatcatcher	___ Yellow-rumped Warbler	___ Indigo Bunting
___ Sharp-shinned Hawk	___ Acadian Flycatcher	___ Eastern Bluebird	___ Black-throated Green Warbler	___ Rufous-sided Towhee
___ Cooper's Hawk	___ Willow Flycatcher	___ Veery	___ Blackburnian Warbler	___ American Tree Sparrow
___ Red-shouldered Hawk	___ Least Flycatcher	___ Swainson's Thrush	___ Yellow-throated Warbler	___ Chipping Sparrow
___ Broad-winged Hawk	___ Eastern Phoebe	___ Hermit Thrush	___ Pine Warbler	___ Field Sparrow
___ Red-tailed Hawk	___ Say's Phoebe	___ Wood Thrush	___ Prairie Warbler	___ Song Sparrow
___ American Kestrel	___ Great Crested Flycatcher	___ American Robin	___ Palm Warbler	___ White-throated Sparrow
___ Peregrine Falcon	___ Eastern Kingbird	___ Northern Mockingbird	___ Bay-breasted Warbler	___ White-crowned Sparrow
___ Wild Turkey	___ Purple Martin	___ Gray Catbird	___ Blackpoll Warbler	___ Red-winged Blackbird
___ Northern Bobwhite	___ Tree Swallow	___ Brown Thrasher	___ Cerulean Warbler	___ Common Grackle
___ Killdeer	___ Northern Rough-winged Swallow	___ Cedar Waxwing	___ Black-and-white Warbler	___ Orchard Oriole
___ Rock Dove	___ Cliff Swallow	___ European Starling	___ American Redstart	___ Baltimore Oriole
___ Mourning Dove	___ Barn Swallow	___ White-eyed Vireo	___ Worm-eating Warbler	___ Purple Finch
___ Black-billed Cuckoo	___ Blue Jay	___ Solitary Vireo	___ Ovenbird	___ House Finch
___ Yellow-billed Cuckoo	___ American Crow	___ Yellow-throated Vireo	___ Northern Waterthrush	___ Pine Siskin
___ Eastern Screech-owl	___ Carolina Chickadee	___ Warbling Vireo	___ Louisiana Waterthrush	___ American Goldfinch
___ Great Horned Owl	___ Tufted Titmouse	___ Red-eyed Vireo	___ Kentucky Warbler	___ Evening Grosbeak
___ Barred Owl	___ White-breasted Nuthatch	___ Blue-winged Warbler	___ Common Yellowthroat	___ House Sparrow

Killdeer Plains Wildlife Area

To say that Killdeer Plains is 8,000 acres of flat land just does not do justice to this wildlife area's flatness. If you discount the manmade alterations to the landscape, the felt on a pool table has more vertical relief than Killdeer Plains. Add the fact that this vertically challenged landscape lies in a natural basin, and you have an area that's poorly drained at best.

If the area is flat with a tendency to wetness, it's not lacking in diversity. The Ohio Department of Natural Resources has Swiss-cheesed Killdeer Plains with 125 ponds ranging in size from 50 acres down to that of an Olympic-sized swimming pool, built an 800-acre marsh, and created a 285-acre, above-ground reservoir on the wildlife area's western end. The Ohio DNR has also planted trees and shrubs, and manages cropland, woodlots, and meadows to provide food and shelter for migrant waterfowl and upland wildlife. The wildlife area came into being in 1952 when the state began buying land that had originally been part of a vast, 30,000-acre prairie slough that covered much of north central Ohio before it was drained, ditched, tiled, and farmed.

The work has been abundantly rewarded. Eleven thousand Canada Geese, plus a small number of Snow Geese, and 30,000 ducks wing into Killdeer Plains every fall. But that's only a part of the success story at Killdeer Plains. The diversity of habitats has made the wildlife area one of the most interesting and rewarding year-round birding spots in the Midwest.

Jeff Buecking and I arrived on a wet, dismal Saturday afternoon in early May with anything but dampened spirits. We'd made a short detour on the drive from Flint, Michigan to see a Pacific Loon that had somehow mistaken a small, insignificant lake in mid-Michigan for the Pacific West. The loon would prove to be a good omen for the day of birding at Killdeer Plains. Within 15 minutes of arriving at the Ohio wildlife area, we bagged an American Avocet and a pair of Short-eared owls.

Two miles west of Harpster, Ohio on State Highway 294 we turned south on County Road 115 that cuts through the area from north to south. The wildlife area begins immediately on the left. We slowly passed numerous small ponds and flooded fields dotted with Mallard, Wood Ducks, Blue- and Green-winged Teal, and American Black Ducks. Stopping to search the surrounding fields at the junction of CR 115 and CR 71, I followed an Upland Sandpiper as it rocketed past the car while Jeff scanned Pond #6 just to the south of CR 71. Jeff thought he might have seen an American Avocet stalking the edge of the pond. We piled into the car and drove south on CR 115 to the parking lot overlooking the pond. Without even leaving the car, we spotted the avocet. While I was admiring the first of this species I'd seen east of the Mississippi, Jeff spotted a Greater Yellowlegs on the far side of the pond and called my attention to the song of a Savannah Sparrow off to our left.

Just south of Pond #6 is another parking lot from which an active Bald Eagle's nest can be seen by looking due east. We didn't find any eagles on or about the nest, but we had no more than pulled back on CR 115 when I spotted two Short-

LOCATION: Harpster, Ohio.

DIRECTIONS: From the intersection of U.S. 23 and State Highway 294 drive west on State Highway 294 through Harpster, Ohio. Two miles west of Harpster, turn south on CR 115.

HOURS: Open all year.

BEST TIMES: Good birding year-round and excellent birding for raptors in winter.

BIRDING HIGHLIGHTS: One of the finest areas in Ohio for hawks and owls in the winter. The rest of the year offers good to excellent birding for a wide variety of species.

FOR FURTHER INFORMATION: Wildlife District Two Office, 952 Lima Avenue, Box A, Findlay, OH 45840. Phone: (419) 424-5000.

eared Owls leisurely hunting a meadow near the headquarters building. An American Avocet and Short-eared Owls within a quarter-mile is an impressive daily double. The owls didn't seem to be bothered by the slow approach of the car, and we got within thirty or forty yards of the birds as they slowly meandered across the meadow, never more than ten feet above the ground.

Short-eared Owls are just one of the specialty birds that bring birdwatchers to Killdeer Plains. The area is famous for the large concentrations of Black-bellied Plovers and Lesser Golden-plovers that briefly invade the wildlife area every spring on their journey to the far north. Spring also brings lots of warbler activity, plenty of marsh birds, and good numbers of waterfowl. Every season of the year you can count on a sampling of rarities. American White Pelicans, Golden Eagles, Marbled Godwits, Fulvous Whistling-ducks, and the American Avocet that we saw are just a few of the species from Killdeer Plains that have been posted on recent Rare Bird Alerts.

Good birding continues right into summer with Bald Eagles and Short-eared Owls often nesting here. Great Horned and Barred owls, Carolina Chickadees, Sedge Wrens, Warbling Vireos, Prothonotary Warblers, American Bittern, Scarlet Tanagers, and Vesper, Grasshopper and Henslow's sparrows also spend the summer here and are among the birds that lure birders back in the hot summer months. Fall brings large numbers of waterfowl and steady, often spectacular, flights of raptors. Red-tailed Hawks make up most of the large flights of migrating raptors, but there is usually enough variety to keep birders on their toes.

Killdeer Plains Wildlife Area is most famous for its winter birding. Long-eared and Short-eared owls are as regular here in winter as retired Midwesterners are in Florida. Northern Harriers, Cooper's Hawks, Rough-legged Hawks, and American Kestrels all commonly use the area as their winter hunting grounds. Less often seen are Red-shouldered Hawks, Northern Goshawks, and Snowy Owls. There is even a sign posted in the field at the intersection of CR 115 and CR 75 telling motorists that the area is a favorite haunt of the above species. If the fields surrounding the intersection of CR 115 and CR 75 are best for hawks, pine woodlots further west on CR 75, CR 71, and CR 77 in the wildlife area are favored by Barred, Long-eared and Northern Saw-whet owls. Adding to the fun of a winter birding trip to Killdeer Plains are the plentiful Horned Larks and Snow Buntings. The keen-eyed will occasionally be rewarded with the sighting of Lapland Longspurs and Northern Shrikes. And by late winter, Tundra Swans and Snow Geese can sometimes be found on open water.

After watching the owls disappear on the far side of the field, we turned west on CR 75 from CR 115 and headed for the reservoir on the western end of the wildlife area. The road took us through extensive grasslands that are regularly interrupted by brushy fence lines and small woodlots. Killdeer Plains makes for excellent birding by car, but when you do leave the car to do some birding on foot the dikes surrounding some of the wetlands and the mounds left from excavating the ponds make for great observation platforms from which to search the surrounding area.

From atop the impressive earthen impoundment forming the reservoir, we spied Double-crested Cormorants and several Pied-billed Grebes. Through his spotting scope, Jeff found a raft of Ruddy Ducks on the far side of the water. From the reservoir we back-tracked a half-mile, jogged north on Township Road 103, and headed back east on CR 71. We hadn't gone a mile on CR 71 before we came to a spot where open fields, wooded areas, and farm fields all meet at a bend in the road. This intermingling of ecosystems seemed very promising, and we had

"The Ohio Department of Natural Resources has Swiss-cheesed Killdeer Plains with 125 ponds ranging in size from 50 acres down to that of an Olympic-sized swimming pool, built an 800-acre marsh, and created a 285-acre, above-ground reservoir on the wildlife area's western end."

barely parked the car and began walking when a Cooper's Hawk shot across the road. I notched a Hairy Woodpecker in the same clump of young trees in which Jeff found a Great Crested Flycatcher. The area also gave up Yellow-rumped Warblers, White-throated Sparrows, a House Wren, an Eastern Meadowlark, and a Red-tailed Hawk.

We continued east on CR 71 until we came back to CR 115, turned south and retraced our route where we saw an avocet and owls, then at CR 68 turned east. Almost immediately east of the intersection of CR 115 and CR 68, on CR 68 there is a parking area that allows birders to leave their car and walk the short distance to the dike holding back Pond #27. This huge pond extends for almost a mile along the north side of CR 68. Bald Eagles frequent the pond, and we no sooner reached the dike when Jeff spotted one soaring high above the water. We also counted several species of swallows, a Bobolink in a nearby field, and heard the call of a Ring-necked Pheasant. Pond #27 holds large rafts of diving ducks during migration seasons, and mud-flats around the rim of the pond attract shorebirds. There are several parking areas along County Road 68 allowing birders to search nearly the entire length of the pond. A spotting scope is a must here for bringing in distant birds on the north side of the pond.

Another place not to be missed when visiting Killdeer Plains actually lies just south of the wildlife area. Approximately 1.5 miles east of CR 115 on CR 68, Washburn Road heads due south through low, billiard-table-flat farmland. Washburn Road has a well deserved reputation for harboring a wide variety of sparrows. Vesper, Savannah, Grasshopper, Chipping, and Song sparrows have all been recorded as nesting in the area while Horned Larks, Bobolinks, and Dickcissels are regularly seen along the road. Short-eared Owls are often seen here, and in the winter Lapland Longspurs and Snow Buntings frequent the fields. After that impressive list of possibilities, I must sadly report all we saw while driving the road were a few Horned Larks, a Killdeer, and a Savannah Sparrow. Our total for two hours at Killdeer Plains Wildlife Area came to an even 50. As we left the area, I vowed to return in the winter to search for owls, hawks, and Bald Eagles.

Write to the address on page 132 for a detailed map that will aid you in planning a trip to the area.

KILLDEER PLAINS WILDLIFE AREA FIELD CHECKLIST

This checklist was gathered from a number of sources and is far from complete.

___ Pied-billed Grebe	___ Cooper's Hawk	___ American Woodcock	___ Tree Swallow	___ Dickcissel
___ American White Pelican	___ Northern Goshawk	___ Ring-billed Gull	___ Northern Rough-winged Swallow	___ American Tree Sparrow
___ Double-crested Cormorant	___ Red-shouldered Hawk	___ Herring Gull	___ Bank Swallow	___ Chipping Sparrow
___ American Bittern	___ Broad-winged Hawk	___ Rock Dove	___ Barn Swallow	___ Field Sparrow
___ Great Blue Heron	___ Red-tailed Hawk	___ Mourning Dove	___ Blue Jay	___ Vesper Sparrow
___ Great Egret	___ Rough-legged Hawk	___ Black-billed Cuckoo	___ American Crow	___ Lark Sparrow
___ Snowy Egret	___ Golden Eagle	___ Yellow-billed Cuckoo	___ Carolina Chickadee	___ Lark Bunting
___ Cattle Egret	___ American Kestrel	___ Great Horned Owl	___ House Wren	___ Savannah Sparrow
___ Green Heron	___ Peregrine Falcon	___ Snowy Owl	___ Sedge Wren	___ Grasshopper Sparrow
___ Glossy Ibis	___ Ring-necked Pheasant	___ Barred Owl	___ Marsh Wren	___ Henslow's Sparrow
___ Fulvous Whistling-duck	___ Northern Bobwhite	___ Long-eared Owl	___ Eastern Bluebird	___ Sharp-tailed Sparrow
___ Tundra Swan	___ King Rail	___ Short-eared Owl	___ American Robin	___ Song Sparrow
___ Mute Swan	___ Sora	___ Northern Saw-whet Owl	___ Gray Catbird	___ White-throated Sparrow
___ Greater White-fronted Goose	___ American Coot	___ Belted Kingfisher	___ Brown Thrasher	___ Lapland Longspur
___ Snow Goose	___ Sandhill Crane	___ Red-headed Woodpecker	___ Northern Shrike	___ Snow Bunting
___ Canada Goose	___ Black-bellied Plover	___ Red-bellied Woodpecker	___ Loggerhead Shrike	___ Bobolink
___ Wood Duck	___ Lesser Golden-plover	___ Downy Woodpecker	___ European Starling	___ Red-winged Blackbird
___ Green-winged Teal	___ Killdeer	___ Hairy Woodpecker	___ Warbling Vireo	___ Eastern Meadowlark
___ American Black Duck	___ American Avocet	___ Northern Flicker	___ Red-eyed Vireo	___ Common Grackle
___ Mallard	___ Greater Yellowlegs	___ Eastern Wood-pewee	___ Yellow Warbler	___ Brown-headed Cowbird
___ Blue-winged Teal	___ Lesser Yellowlegs	___ Eastern Phoebe	___ Yellow-rumped Warbler	___ American Goldfinch
___ Northern Shoveler	___ Solitary Sandpiper	___ Great Crested Flycatcher	___ Prothonotary Warbler	
___ Turkey Vulture	___ Spotted Sandpiper	___ Eastern Kingbird	___ Common Yellowthroat	
___ Bald Eagle	___ Upland Sandpiper	___ Horned Lark	___ Summer Tanager	
___ Northern Harrier	___ Marbled Godwit	___ Purple Martin	___ Scarlet Tanager	

Spring Valley Wildlife Area

I was so intent on spying an illusive bittern (still haven't seen one) in what I considered prime bittern real estate that I didn't experience the full impact of the marshland until I ran out of boardwalk. No, I didn't fall in, I found myself standing atop a 13-foot-tall observation platform at the end of a 650 foot-long boardwalk that reaches out into the very heart of an 80-acre wetland. It took only one sweep of the surrounding landscape to realize I was at the very epicenter of one of the finest birdwatching areas in Ohio. The marsh surrounding the tower was clogged with a riot of plant life made up of every conceivable color, texture, size, and shape. Narrow watery channels traced black, irregular lines through the thick mat of vegetation. And here and there the vegetation gave way to small pools of quiet water. To the south of the platform, the dense vegetation gradually disappeared and was replaced by 70 acres of open water. Shrubs, grassland, brush, and dense woodland surrounded the other three sides of the marsh, and nearly everywhere I looked there were birds or the promise of birds.

Spring Valley Wildlife Area is, as one would expect, great for marsh birds with King, Virginia, Sora, Yellow, and Black rails, American and Least bitterns, plus a good mix of egrets and heron all noted on the area's checklist. But the real truth is that this wildlife area is a one-stop birding spot for almost every species of bird found in the state. Nearly every common inland bird species seen in Ohio can be seen at Spring Valley, and it is one of the best areas in southwest Ohio for sighting migrant and nesting warblers. Except for sea ducks, almost all waterfowl seen in Ohio have been recorded here. Of the over 230 species recorded at Spring Valley, warblers account for 35 species, with waterfowl representing another 27 species, and marsh and shorebirds chip in over 30 more species. The area does not usually attract great varieties or numbers of shorebirds, but in dry summers when the water level drops low enough to expose mudflats shorebird watching can quickly go from good to excellent. Spring Valley also gets its share of less common birds. A sampling of recent sightings include Purple Gallinule, Red-necked Grebe, Greater White-fronted Goose, Willet, Baird's Sandpiper, Little Blue Heron, Brewster's Warbler, and Worm-eating Warbler.

The area has a reputation for phenomenal spring birding from March through May. Probably the best indication of just how rewarding birding can be here is the fact that the Dayton Audubon Society schedules as many as three birding trips a year to the area. I arrived in early April, just past the peak for waterfowl and several weeks in advance of the major songbird migration, and there were still loads of birds to see. The small ponds within the marsh were saturated with an assortment of ducks, American Coots, Pied-billed Grebes, and Canada Geese. I also had a probable Sora and a Horned Grebe. Both birds kept flirting with me at the very limit of my binoculars. Looking south from the platform, I could see several large rafts of ducks and geese spread across the open water. Closer inspection later in the afternoon showed the rafts to be made up primarily of Ring-necked Ducks, mergansers, Mallards, and American Black Ducks. And I had notched Vesper, Fox, Swamp, and Field sparrows on the walk from the parking

LOCATION: Waynesville, Ohio.

DIRECTIONS: From the intersection of State Road 725 and U.S. 42 in the village of Spring Valley, drive south 1.7 miles on U.S. 42 to Roxanna-New Burlington Road and turn east (left). Drive 1.5 miles to Pence Jones Road, turn right and go 0.3 miles to the unmarked parking lot on the right hand side of the road. This parking lot gives access to the marsh boardwalk. To reach the boat ramp on the south end of the lake, follow Pence Jones another 0.4 miles to its end at Collett Road. Turn right on Collett Road and drive 0.5 miles to the parking lot at the boat launching ramp.

HOURS: Open year-round but the area is open to hunting in the fall. Gary Inwalle, the Spring Valley Wildlife Area Manager, says that a time-sharing pattern has naturally developed over the years at Spring Valley. From September through January 31, most birders go other places while hunting is permitted at the wildlife area. From February through August birders, fishermen, and berry pickers share the wildlife area.

BEST TIMES: March through May.

BIRDING HIGHLIGHTS: One of the best all-round birding spots in Ohio. Spring birding can be phenomenal with large numbers of waterfowl, marsh birds, and songbirds. Extremely good for marsh birds from spring through summer.

FOR MORE INFORMATION: Spring Valley Wildlife Area, 1863 Roxanna-New Burlington Road, Waynesville, OH 45068. Phone: (513) 488-3115.

"The observation deck can quickly seduce an active birder into being a couch potato. There is so much to examine, wonder about, and sort through from your grandstand seat in the middle of the marsh."

lot to the end of the boardwalk.

The observation deck can quickly seduce an active birder into being a couch potato. There is so much to examine, wonder about, and sort through from your grandstand seat in the middle of the marsh that time easily slips away. It doesn't take much encouragement anywhere or anytime for me to become sedentary, but I had the added excuse of witnessing a savage, life-and-death struggle unfold before my eyes. My attention kept being drawn to an enormous snapping turtle that I, at first, thought was basking in the sun. So much of the turtle's body was out of the water that I assumed it was resting on a partially submerged log. But among the little things that seemed wrong with this first impression was the Canada Goose that continuously circled and hissed at the turtle. It wasn't until my third or fourth look at the turtle that I saw the "thing" the snapper was resting on begin thrashing. Over the next few minutes, I came to realize that the snapper had a death grip on a Canada Goose's leg and had somehow climbed up on the goose, while keeping its jaws clenched on the drumstick, in order to drown the bird. Every few minutes the goose would do enough thrashing to gets its head above water and draw another breath then sink below the water under the weight of the turtle. During the 40 minutes I was on the platform, the struggle continued unabated; every time it seemed the goose had drowned, there would be a brief struggle while the bird drew yet another breath. Needless to say, it was hard to concentrate on anything else with this drama playing out before me.

If the marsh boardwalk is the focal point of most birding trips to Spring Valley, there are several other places within the wildlife area that deserve your attention. A wide, well marked, 2.5-mile trail circles the lake and marsh. On the east side of the lake, the trail slips through a mature upland forest that's home to thrushes, woodpeckers, Eastern Wood-pewees, and a variety of warblers. At the extreme southern end of the lake, the trail passes a small boat launching ramp where you can scope the lake for grebes, ducks, geese, and the occasional Tundra Swan. (Canoes or boats with electric motors only are allowed on the lake.) On the north and west sides of the lake/marsh, the trail passes through marshes and flooded woodlands that in May can simply be bursting at the seams with both migratory and nesting birds. Eastern Bluebirds, vireos, Indigo Buntings, Eastern Kingbirds, a variety of flycatchers, woodpeckers, and a wealth of warblers are all found along the northwest section of the trail. Stretches of this trail can be wet, and in addition to birds, you're sure of encountering hungry deer flies from June through August. You'll want to bring insect repellent, waterproof boots, and keep an eye out for massasauga rattlesnakes, another resident of the wildlife area.

Another trail leaves the main trail at the south end of the lake and follows the eastern side of the Little Miami River for about a half-mile. And there is yet another means of locomotion for exploring the western edge of the wildlife area. An old roadbed of the Penn Central Railroad that's been turned into a rails-to-trails pathway runs in a flat, straight line through the wildlife area and edges the western side of the marsh and lake. Walking or riding the roadbed is one sure way of keeping your feet dry on the often wet, west side of the marsh. The bike trail can be accessed from Roxanna-New Burlington Road on the north side of the wildlife area or from the boat ramp's parking lot on the south end of the lake.

SPRING VALLEY WILDLIFE AREA FIELD CHECKLIST

This checklist was compiled for the Spring Valley Wildlife Area
by members of the Dayton Audubon Society.

___ Common Loon
___ Horned Grebe
___ Pied-billed Grebe
___ Double-crested Cormorant
___ Great Blue Heron
___ Green Heron
___ Little Blue Heron
___ Cattle Egret
___ Great Egret
___ Black-crowned Night-heron
___ Yellow-crowned Night-heron
___ Least Bittern
___ American Bittern
___ Mute Swan
___ Tundra Swan
___ Greater White-fronted Goose
___ Canada Goose
___ Snow Goose
___ Mallard
___ American Black Duck
___ Gadwall
___ Northern Pintail
___ Green-winged Teal
___ Blue-winged Teal
___ American Wigeon
___ Northern Shoveler
___ Wood Duck
___ Redhead
___ Ring-necked Duck
___ Canvasback
___ Greater Scaup
___ Lesser Scaup
___ Common Goldeneye
___ Bufflehead
___ Oldsquaw
___ Ruddy Duck
___ Hooded Merganser
___ Common Merganser
___ Red-breasted Merganser
___ Turkey Vulture
___ Black Vulture
___ Northern Goshawk
___ Sharp-shinned Hawk
___ Cooper's Hawk
___ Red-tailed Hawk
___ Red-shouldered Hawk
___ Broad-winged Hawk

___ Rough-legged Hawk
___ Bald Eagle
___ Northern Harrier
___ Osprey
___ Peregrine Falcon
___ American Kestrel
___ Northern Bobwhite
___ Ring-necked Pheasant
___ Sandhill Crane
___ King Rail
___ Virginia Rail
___ Sora
___ Yellow Rail
___ Black Rail
___ Common Moorhen
___ American Coot
___ Semipalmated Plover
___ Killdeer
___ Greater Yellowlegs
___ Lesser Yellowlegs
___ Solitary Sandpiper
___ Spotted Sandpiper
___ American Woodcock
___ Common Snipe
___ Short-billed Dowitcher
___ Semipalmated Sandpiper
___ Least Sandpiper
___ White-rumped Sandpiper
___ Baird's Sandpiper
___ Pectoral Sandpiper
___ Dunlin
___ Herring Gull
___ Ring-billed Gull
___ Bonaparte's Gull
___ Forster's Tern
___ Common Tern
___ Black Tern
___ Rock Dove
___ Mourning Dove
___ Yellow-billed Cuckoo
___ Black-billed Cuckoo
___ Eastern Screech-owl
___ Great Horned Owl
___ Barred Owl
___ Short-eared Owl
___ Common Nighthawk
___ Chimney Swift

___ Ruby-throated Hummingbird
___ Belted Kingfisher
___ Red-headed Woodpecker
___ Red-bellied Woodpecker
___ Yellow-bellied Sapsucker
___ Downy Woodpecker
___ Hairy Woodpecker
___ Northern Flicker
___ Pileated Woodpecker
___ Eastern Kingbird
___ Great Crested Flycatcher
___ Eastern Phoebe
___ Yellow-bellied Flycatcher
___ Acadian Flycatcher
___ Willow Flycatcher
___ Alder Flycatcher
___ Least Flycatcher
___ Eastern Wood-pewee
___ Olive-sided Flycatcher
___ Horned Lark
___ Tree Swallow
___ Bank Swallow
___ Northern Rough-winged Swallow
___ Barn Swallow
___ Cliff Swallow
___ Purple Martin
___ Blue Jay
___ American Crow
___ Black-capped Chickadee
___ Carolina Chickadee
___ Tufted Titmouse
___ White-breasted Nuthatch
___ Red-breasted Nuthatch
___ Brown Creeper
___ House Wren
___ Winter Wren
___ Bewick's Wren
___ Carolina Wren
___ Marsh Wren
___ Sedge Wren
___ Northern Mockingbird
___ Gray Catbird
___ Brown Thrasher
___ Wood Thrush
___ Hermit Thrush
___ Gray-cheeked Thrush
___ Swainson's Thrush

___ American Robin
___ Veery
___ Eastern Bluebird
___ Blue-gray Gnatcatcher
___ Golden-crowned Kinglet
___ Ruby-crowned Kinglet
___ American Pipit
___ Cedar Waxwing
___ European Starling
___ White-eyed Vireo
___ Yellow-throated Vireo
___ Solitary Vireo
___ Red-eyed Vireo
___ Philadelphia Vireo
___ Warbling Vireo
___ Black-and-white Warbler
___ Prothonotary Warbler
___ Golden-winged Warbler
___ Blue-winged Warbler
___ Tennessee Warbler
___ Orange-crowned Warbler
___ Nashville Warbler
___ Northern Parula
___ Yellow Warbler
___ Magnolia Warbler
___ Cape May Warbler
___ Black-throated Blue Warbler
___ Yellow-rumped Warbler
___ Black-throated Green Warbler
___ Cerulean Warbler
___ Blackburnian Warbler
___ Yellow-throated Warbler
___ Chestnut-sided Warbler
___ Bay-breasted Warbler
___ Blackpoll Warbler
___ Pine Warbler
___ Prairie Warbler
___ Palm Warbler
___ Ovenbird
___ Northern Waterthrush
___ Louisiana Waterthrush
___ Kentucky Warbler
___ Connecticut Warbler
___ Mourning Warbler
___ Common Yellowthroat
___ Yellow-breasted Chat
___ Hooded Warbler

___ Wilson's Warbler
___ Canada Warbler
___ American Redstart
___ Worm-eating Warbler
___ Bobolink
___ Eastern Meadowlark
___ Red-winged Blackbird
___ Orchard Oriole
___ Baltimore Oriole
___ Rusty Blackbird
___ Common Grackle
___ Brown-headed Cowbird
___ Scarlet Tanager
___ Summer Tanager
___ Northern Cardinal
___ Rose-breasted Grosbeak
___ Indigo Bunting
___ Dickcissel
___ Purple Finch
___ House Finch
___ Pine Siskin
___ American Goldfinch
___ Rufous-sided Towhee
___ Savannah Sparrow
___ Grasshopper Sparrow
___ Vesper Sparrow
___ Dark-eyed Junco
___ American Tree Sparrow
___ Chipping Sparrow
___ Clay-colored Sparrow
___ Field Sparrow
___ White-crowned Sparrow
___ White-throated Sparrow
___ Fox Sparrow
___ Lincoln's Sparrow
___ Swamp Sparrow
___ Song Sparrow
___ House Sparrow

Accidentals
___ Golden Eagle
___ Purple Gallinule
___ Brewer's Blackbird

Shawnee Lookout and Miami Whitewater Forest Parks

LOCATION: Cincinnati, Ohio.

DIRECTIONS: To reach Miami Whitewater Forest Park take exit 3 from I-74 and drive north on Dry Fork Road approximately 0.5 miles to West Road. Turn east (right) on West Road and drive a few hundred yards to the park entrance and turn left on the first park road, which will lead to the parking area adjacent to Shaker Trace. To reach Shawnee Lookout County Park take exit 21 from I-275 and drive south approximately 1 mile on Kilby Road to U.S. 50. Turn left and drive east on U.S. 50 approximately 2 miles to Mt. Nebo Road in Cleeves, Ohio. Turn right at traffic light onto Mt. Nebo, and drive 3 blocks to River Road. Turn right on River Road, and follow signs 4 miles to park entrance on Lawrenceburg Road.

HOURS: Open all year dawn to dusk.

BEST TIMES: February through May, and August through November.

BIRDING HIGHLIGHTS: Very good all-around birding and excellent for waterfowl, songbirds, shorebirds, and one of the best areas for marsh birds in southwest Ohio.

FOR MORE INFORMATION: Hamilton County Park District, 10245 Winton Road, Cincinnati, Ohio 45231. Phone: (513) 521-7275.

No matter how hard you try to avoid it at these Hamilton County parks, history keeps calling out to you like a carnival barker demanding your attention in spite of how much you want to be left alone to bird. This is especially so at Shawnee County Park where you can't turn around without bumping into history. Prehistoric people left more than just traces of their passing at Shawnee Lookout when they enclosed a 12-acre fort in earthen walls 2,000 years ago, built numerous Indian mounds, and left several prehistoric town sites dotting the park's dramatically beautiful landscape. In more recent times the Shawnee people roamed the area and posted a lookout on the high bluff overlooking the confluence of the Great Miami and Ohio rivers. An archaeological museum explains the precolonial history of the area, and a historical log cabin and school tells of the European settlement of the area. And history cannot be ignored at Miami Whitewater Forest Park just a few miles to the north. During the Civil War, the dashing Confederate cavalryman John Hunt Morgan found shelter in the dense forests of the future park, and from 1824 to 1916 members of the Whitewater Shaker Village quietly went about their spiritual and secular business.

All the above was interesting and absorbing, but what drew me to the two parks was their richness of birdlife and the five-star viewing opportunities for shorebirds, waterfowl, songbirds, and birds of prey. Taken as a whole, the two county parks are not only one of the best birding sites in southwestern Ohio but rate with the best birding sites in the state. There is no authoritative bird checklist for the two parks but a far from complete checklist, put together for this book from a variety of sources, that relies heavily on *Birds of the Oxbow* by David Styer reveals a minimum of 273 species.

If great birding is a given at the two parks, few park visitors at Miami Whitewater on the Easter week I was there evidenced any interest in birds. There were golfers, frisbee golfers, walkers, dog walkers, bikers, joggers, inline skaters, picnickers, campers, sunbathers, paddleboat voyagers, and baby buggy pushers, but I didn't see another soul with a bird book or binoculars. Evidently there were some birders about because within a week of my visit, a Rare Bird Alert for the Cincinnati area listed a wealth of sightings at Miami Whitewater. American Bittern, Sora, both yellowlegs, over 100 Common Snipe, Pectoral Sandpipers, Lesser Golden-plover, American Woodcock, American Wigeon, Gadwall, Northern Shovelers, Ruddy Ducks, Wood Ducks, Horned Grebes, Northern Bobwhite, Red-shouldered Hawks, Cooper's Hawks, White-eyed Vireos, Vesper and Savannah sparrows, and 35 more species were seen in just the park's restored wetlands.

Except for golfers, there were fewer visitors at Shawnee Lookout County Park and I shared the park's trails with only a few fitness walkers and a old Labrador retriever valiantly trying to keep up with its long-legged, arm-pumping mistress. The park occupies a dramatic piece of real estate overlooking the confluence of the Great Miami and Ohio rivers. The park sits at the end of a long, narrow, westward-pointing bluff that forces the two rivers to flow parallel to each other for almost four miles before the Great Miami River slips around the western end of the bluff and joins the mighty Ohio. Dense woods shroud the steep sides of the bluff, and on the Friday morning I was there the woods were bursting with birds.

Three trails depart from the park road that cuts a serpentine path along the top of the bluff. I wasn't even out of the motorhome at the parking lot near the trailheads for Little Turtle and Blue Jacket trails when a Pileated Woodpecker winged past. The Blue Jacket Trail slips down the north side of the bluff and heads toward the Great Miami River. The trail eases through dense, vine-draped woods with plenty of understory softening the forest floor. At two points the 1.25-mile trail passes through open fields before ending in a long loop that presents the hiker with a striking view of the Great Miami River. White-throated and White-crowned sparrows were only outnumbered by Rufous-sided Towhees on the trail. Several Brown Thrashers lurked in the brush and low trees marking the transition zones between the fields and woods, and I counted my first Blue-gray Gnatcatchers and Ruby-crowned Kinglets for the year along the trail.

The 2-mile-long Little Turtle Trail begins on the south side of the park road, directly across from the Blue Jacket Trail, and quickly slips into wooded ravines on the south side of the bluff. Named after a famous Shawnee chief, the trail weaves through mature woodlands, crosses open fields, a creek, and takes hikers to a grand overlook of the Ohio River before looping back to the park road. Once again there were plenty of sparrows and Rufous-sided Towhees. But this trail served up my first Yellow-rumped Warbler and Hermit Thrush of the spring. Both of these trails should be packed with nesting and migrating warblers and other songbirds by late April and early May. The park is known for its plentiful Wild Turkey and is one of the few places in Ohio where Black Vultures nest — unfortunately I saw neither. The third trail departs from the end of the park road and leads visitors to the ruins of the prehistoric fort and plenty of opportunities to mix history with birding.

The next stop at Shawnee Lookout was the boat launching ramp on the Great Miami River. The road to the ramp is directly opposite the park entrance on Lawrenceburg Road. As the road descended into the river's flood plain, I saw that the ramp was still under water from the spring flooding. Water even lapped at the edge of the parking lot just above the ramp. During early spring, the river usually harbors a good selection of waterfowl including Ruddy Ducks, Buffleheads, Lesser Scaup, and Gadwalls. The boat ramp is bracketed on either side by the Uhlmansiek Wildlife Sanctuary, and directly across the river from the ramp is a part of the extensive Oxbow Wetlands that extends into Indiana. A couple of Great Blue Heron lazily flapped across the sky above the boat ramp parking lot, and the day's third Pileated Woodpecker could be seen tattooing a tree in woods just north of the parking lot. Birding along the edges of the wildlife sanctuary and the Oxbow wetlands from the comfort of a boat or canoe should be very good.

Some of the best birding in the area is found in the Oxbow wetlands to the west and north of Shawnee Lookout County Park. The Oxbow wetlands lie within the floodplain of the Great Miami River and is an excellent place for waterfowl and shorebirds. In the past few years White-winged and Surf scoters, Oldsquaw, Horned Grebe, Tundra Swans, and Snow Geese have been all spotted here as well

"The park sits at the end of a long, narrow, westward-pointing bluff that forces the two rivers to flow parallel to each other for almost four miles before the Great Miami River slips around the western end of the bluff and joins the mighty Ohio."

"The Shaker Trace presents one of the best-paved, bike-birding trails in the Midwest. In eight miles it passes through a wide array of fine birding habitat — streams, ponds, meadows, prairies, old growth forest, brushland, farm fields, and restored wetlands."

as the more common waterfowl. The waterfowl show up in February and March and again during fall migration from September to November.

The number and variety of shorebirds found in the Oxbow is directly dependent on water levels. Generally, as spring high water recedes in late April, egret and heron numbers increase, and in late spring, if the water level drops far enough to reveal mudflats, shorebirds begin showing up in great numbers. By August, as shorebirds begin heading south there can be extensive mudflats that attract a wide variety of sandpipers and plovers. American Avocets, Willets, Dunlin, and Long-billed Dowitchers are sometimes part of the passing parade as shorebird activity peaks in September. Before planning a trip aimed at watching shorebirds its best to check with the Cincinnati Rare Bird Alert by calling (513) 521-2847.

With that all said and done, accessing the Oxbow area and the heart of the area, Oxbow Lake, can be difficult, especially from a motorhome, if you're unfamiliar with the area. I am indebted to Ned Keller of Cincinnati for the following directions. To reach Oxbow Lake take exit #16 from I-275 on the west side of Cincinnati. After exiting I-275 turn left onto U.S. 50 at the light. Drive west on U.S. 50 approximately 0.25 miles to the Diary Mart store, turn left on the road just past the store, and proceed up the hill and across the railroad tracks to a cement plant. At the cement plant you can either park your car on a cement pad (all that's left of a gas station), or continue in your car to where the road ends at the cement plant and turn right on a gravel road, then take a left at the next dirt road. There is a large water-filled hole in this road, but the pothole is usually passable. After passing the pothole the road descends a slope and divides. Do not drive your car past the point where the road divides unless it is firm and dry. Timid drivers can leave their cars at the abandoned gas station and follow the above directions on foot — it is not a long walk to where the road divides.

At the divide, the road to the left leads past several water-filled gravel pits and along the edge of Oxbow Lake. This road is low and floods early and stays wet long past when everything else in the area dries out. Mr. Keller warns that when the flood stage reaches 35 feet this area is usually inaccessible. The road to the right is several feet higher and therefore much more accessible. This road also runs along the edge of Oxbow Lake and is also a good vantage point to observe mudflats along the edge of the lake during dry summers. Birders should stay on the roads because much of the area is privately owned or leased to farmers.

Ned Keller also recommends an area behind Gardens Alive during spring floods when the flood stage is around 35 feet. To reach this area drive 1.1 miles past the Dairy Mart and turn right on Rudolph Way. Drive 0.2 miles to Minger Drive, turn right and continue on Minger Drive, past Gardens Alive and follow the gravel road as it bends sharply to the left. Mr. Keller also suggests checking the Lawrenceburg Fair Grounds on U.S. 50, just 0.1 mile beyond Rudolph Way.

Miami Whitewater County Park, a few miles north of Shawnee Lookout, is a vast, sprawling complex of outdoor recreation facilities. Although there are plenty of fine places and trails within the park from which to bird, most of the birding is concentrated at the park's 120 acres of restored wetlands. The wetlands lie on the west side of Shaker Trace Trail, an 8-mile long ribbon of asphalt that scribes a lazy loop through Miami Whitewater's northern acreage. I unlimbered my bike from the back of the motorhome, hung binoculars, bird book, and a notebook from my shoulders and set off in search of birds. Over the phone that morning, a Miami Whitewater naturalist reported American Coots, grebes, Wood Ducks, and a good variety of other waterfowl were plentiful in the wetlands. She suggested the best way to access the wetlands was to bike the Trace to the 2.2-mile maker where a work road led off to the west. If I walked the work road just a few dozen yards to the west, she was sure I would find plenty of birds.

What she didn't tell me was that the mile markers went in a clockwise direction and of course I started out on the Trace pedaling counter-clockwise. My mistake was soon obvious when I passed the 7.5-mile marker, but by then I was coming to the conclusion that the Shaker Trace presents one of the best-paved, bike-birding trails in the Midwest. The Shaker Trace, in eight miles, passes through a wide array of fine birding habitat. Streams, ponds, meadows, prairies, old growth forest, brushland, farm fields, and the restored wetlands all unfold before bikers as they pedal their way around the bike path. After a couple of more miles pedaling against the grain of the mile makers, I reversed course and worked my way around to the west side of the loop and found the work road and walked my bike to the edge of the wetlands. The restored wetlands are visible and birdable from several places along the trace, and no matter how many times I glimpsed the wide expanse of water and marsh they came as a surprise in the high slightly rolling land. They just seemed out of place here in spite of the fact that wetlands covered much of this area before farmers drained and planted the landscape.

A pair of Brown Thrashers greeted me as I neared the edge of the wetlands after turning off the trail. From the edge of the wetlands ducks, grebes, and American Coots dotted the water. I counted Pied-billed and Horned grebes, Ring-necked Ducks, Green-winged Teal, Ruddy Ducks, Northern Shovelers, American Wigeon in the middle distance, but a spotting scope would be needed to identify the most distant birds. Back on the bike path and further pedaling down the bike path brought more views of the wetlands and more birds. From roughly the 2-mile mark to the 3-mile mark there are several opportunities for sweeping the wetlands with binoculars, and I added Hooded and Red-breasted mergansers to the day's tally. On the way back to the parking lot American Tree Sparrows and Barn Swallows swooped across the trail in front of the bike, and to my right a Northern Harrier quartered a meadow. It's also possible to bird the wetlands without indulging in the time and effort it takes to walk or bike the Trace. Instead of turning into the park entrance on Dry Fork Road, continue on Dry Fork Road to its junction with New Haven Road. Continue heading northeast on New Haven Road to Oxford Road. Turn left on Oxford Road and drive a couple hundred yards to Baugham Road. Turn left on Baugham Road and drive approximately a half-mile to a small pond. Park just past the pond, walk back to the pond, and follow the dike to the north.

The Tallgrass, Badlands, and Oakleaf Hiking Trails in the southern half of the park are all shorter than the Shaker Trace and make for good birding as does the Miami Whitewater Lake in the center of the park.

"The park is known for its plentiful Wild Turkey and is one of the few places in Ohio where Black Vultures nest."

SHAWNEE LOOKOUT AND MIAMI WHITEWATER FOREST PARKS FIELD CHECKLIST

This is an incomplete checklist compiled from a variety of sources.

___ Red-throated Loon	___ Bald Eagle	___ Ring-billed Gull	___ Red-breasted Nuthatch	___ Prothonotary Warbler
___ Common Loon	___ Northern Harrier	___ Herring Gull	___ White-breasted Nuthatch	___ Worm-eating Warbler
___ Pied-billed Grebe	___ Sharp-shinned Hawk	___ Iceland Gull	___ Brown Creeper	___ Ovenbird
___ Horned Grebe	___ Cooper's Hawk	___ Glaucous Gull	___ Carolina Wren	___ Louisiana Waterthrush
___ Eared Grebe	___ Red-shouldered Hawk	___ Great Black-backed Gull	___ House Wren	___ Northern Waterthrush
___ Red-necked Grebe	___ Broad-winged Hawk	___ Caspian Tern	___ Winter Wren	___ Kentucky Warbler
___ American White Pelican	___ Red-tailed Hawk	___ Common Tern	___ Sedge Wren	___ Connecticut Warbler
___ Double-crested Cormorant	___ Rough-legged Hawk	___ Forster's Tern	___ Marsh Wren	___ Mourning Warbler
___ American Bittern	___ American Kestrel	___ Least Tern	___ Golden-crowned Kinglet	___ Common Yellowthroat
___ Least Bittern	___ Peregrine Falcon	___ Black Tern	___ Ruby-crowned Kinglet	___ Hooded Warbler
___ Great Blue Heron	___ Ring-necked Pheasant	___ Rock Dove	___ Blue-gray Gnatcatcher	___ Wilson's Warbler
___ Great Egret	___ Wild Turkey	___ Mourning Dove	___ Eastern Bluebird	___ Canada Warbler
___ Snowy Egret	___ Northern Bobwhite	___ Black-billed Cuckoo	___ Veery	___ Yellow-breasted Chat
___ Little Blue Heron	___ King Rail	___ Yellow-billed Cuckoo	___ Gray-cheeked Thrush	___ Summer Tanager
___ Tricolored Heron	___ Virginia Rail	___ Barn Owl	___ Swainson's Thrush	___ Scarlet Tanager
___ Cattle Egret	___ Sora	___ Eastern Screech-owl	___ Hermit Thrush	___ Northern Cardinal
___ Green Heron	___ Purple Gallinule	___ Great Horned Owl	___ Wood Thrush	___ Rose-breasted Grosbeak
___ Black-crowned Night-heron	___ Common Moorhen	___ Snowy Owl	___ American Robin	___ Blue Grosbeak
___ Yellow-crowned Night-heron	___ American Coot	___ Barred Owl	___ Gray Catbird	___ Indigo Bunting
___ White Ibis	___ Sandhill Crane	___ Long-eared Owl	___ Northern Mockingbird	___ Rufous-sided Towhee
___ Tundra Swan	___ Black-bellied Plover	___ Short-eared Owl	___ Brown Thrasher	___ American Tree Sparrow
___ Trumpeter Swan	___ Lesser Golden-plover	___ Northern Saw-whet Owl	___ American Pipit	___ Chipping Sparrow
___ Mute Swan	___ Semipalmated Plover	___ Common Nighthawk	___ Cedar Waxwing	___ Field Sparrow
___ Greater White-fronted Goose	___ Piping Plover	___ Chimney Swift	___ Loggerhead Shrike	___ Vesper Sparrow
___ Snow Goose	___ Killdeer	___ Whip-poor-will	___ European Starling	___ Savannah Sparrow
___ Canada Goose	___ American Avocet	___ Ruby-throated Hummingbird	___ White-eyed Vireo	___ Grasshopper Sparrow
___ Wood Duck	___ Greater Yellowlegs	___ Belted Kingfisher	___ Solitary Vireo	___ Sharp-tailed Sparrow
___ Green-winged Teal	___ Lesser Yellowlegs	___ Red-headed Woodpecker	___ Yellow-throated Vireo	___ Fox Sparrow
___ American Black Duck	___ Solitary Sandpiper	___ Red-bellied Woodpecker	___ Philadelphia Vireo	___ Song Sparrow
___ Mallard	___ Spotted Sandpiper	___ Yellow-bellied Sapsucker	___ Warbling Vireo	___ Lincoln's Sparrow
___ Northern Pintail	___ Willet	___ Downy Woodpecker	___ Red-eyed Vireo	___ Swamp Sparrow
___ Blue-winged Teal	___ Upland Sandpiper	___ Hairy Woodpecker	___ Blue-winged Warbler	___ White-throated Sparrow
___ Northern Shoveler	___ Hudsonian Godwit	___ Northern Flicker	___ Golden-winged Warbler	___ White-crowned Sparrow
___ Gadwall	___ Marbled Godwit	___ Pileated Woodpecker	___ Tennessee Warbler	___ Harris' Sparrow
___ Eurasian Wigeon	___ Semipalmated Sandpiper	___ Olive-sided Flycatcher	___ Orange-crowned Warbler	___ Dark-eyed Junco
___ American Wigeon	___ Western Sandpiper	___ Eastern Wood-pewee	___ Nashville Warbler	___ Lapland Longspur
___ Canvasback	___ Least Sandpiper	___ Yellow-bellied Flycatcher	___ Northern Parula	___ Snow Bunting
___ Redhead	___ White-rumped Sandpiper	___ Acadian Flycatcher	___ Yellow Warbler	___ Bobolink
___ Ring-necked Duck	___ Baird's Sandpiper	___ Willow Flycatcher	___ Chestnut-sided Warbler	___ Red-winged Blackbird
___ Greater Scaup	___ Pectoral Sandpiper	___ Eastern Phoebe	___ Magnolia Warbler	___ Eastern Meadowlark
___ Lesser Scaup	___ Dunlin	___ Great Crested Flycatcher	___ Cape May Warbler	___ Rusty Blackbird
___ Oldsquaw	___ Stilt Sandpiper	___ Eastern Kingbird	___ Black-throated Blue Warbler	___ Brewer's Blackbird
___ Black Scoter	___ Buff-breasted Sandpiper	___ Horned Lark	___ Yellow-rumped Warbler	___ Common Grackle
___ Surf Scoter	___ Ruff	___ Purple Martin	___ Black-throated Green Warbler	___ Brown-headed Cowbird
___ White-winged Scoter	___ Short-billed Dowitcher	___ Tree Swallow	___ Blackburnian Warbler	___ Orchard Oriole
___ Common Goldeneye	___ Long-billed Dowitcher	___ Northern Rough-winged Swallow	___ Yellow-throated Warbler	___ Baltimore Oriole
___ Bufflehead	___ Common Snipe	___ Bank Swallow	___ Pine Warbler	___ Purple Finch
___ Hooded Merganser	___ American Woodcock	___ Cliff Swallow	___ Prairie Warbler	___ House Finch
___ Common Merganser	___ Wilson's Phalarope	___ Barn Swallow	___ Palm Warbler	___ Red Crossbill
___ Red-breasted Merganser	___ Red-necked Phalarope	___ Blue Jay	___ Bay-breasted Warbler	___ Pine Siskin
___ Ruddy Duck	___ Laughing Gull	___ American Crow	___ Blackpoll Warbler	___ American Goldfinch
___ Black Vulture	___ Franklin's Gull	___ Black-capped Chickadee	___ Cerulean Warbler	___ Evening Grosbeak
___ Turkey Vulture	___ Little Gull	___ Carolina Chickadee	___ Black-and-white Warbler	___ House Sparrow
___ Osprey	___ Bonaparte's Gull	___ Tufted Titmouse	___ American Redstart	

ONTARIO

POINT PELEE NATIONAL PARK, 145

HOLIDAY BEACH
CONSERVATION AREA, 150

ST. CLAIR RIVER, 153

Point Pelee National Park

After visiting Point Pelee National Park regularly for over ten years, I've come to the unalterable conclusion that this pie-shaped wedge of land, stretching 12 miles out into Lake Erie, is a place of magic. I've read all the literature and heard all the explanations from scientists and ornithologists as to why Point Pelee is one of the top five birding spots in North America, but all that scientific reasoning simply goes out the window when brought face to face with the wonders encountered at Canada's smallest national park.

Walk the Woodland Trail, like I did a few years ago, and suddenly find yourself surrounded by at least a dozen Ruby-throated Hummingbirds and your mind doesn't register scientific cause and effect. Your heart jumps into your throat, the hairs on the back of your neck stand on end, and you swear there is a tingling, electrical charge in the air as the birds swirl around you like a swarm of bees and zip past at a distance of less than two feet with an unbelievably loud buzz. Time stands still, and while they dart back and forth in front of you two hummingbirds, one right after the other, stop in mid-flight and hovering in the air, stare you in the face from less than three feet away. For half a heart beat you wonder if your looking at Tinker Belle and for the briefest of moments you do believe in faeries.

Or walk Tilden Woods Trail as Jeff and Janet Jones and I did in early May of 1996. It was cold, rainy, and deeply overcast. We rounded a bend in the trail and came to a long stretch of boardwalk crossing a wetland forest area. The boardwalk was jammed shoulder-to-shoulder with excited birders who could hardly believe their eyes. The small, saucer-shaped, water-filled depression, through which the 30-yard-long boardwalk passed, was filled with warblers. Not three feet separated Louisiana and Northern waterthrushes walking the watery edge of the depression. Golden-winged Warblers, Common Yellowthroats, Black-throated Blue, Hooded, Cape May, Chestnut-sided, and Yellow-rumped warblers seemed to be playing tag on the roots and fallen branches rising out of the water. I counted a dozen warbler species packed into the little depression, and all of them were totally oblivious to the crowd of humans. They landed at our feet beside the boardwalk, and even flitted from one side of the boardwalk to the other by passing through, not over, the throng. Ask anybody there on that dank, dark, and dismal morning and each of them would probably swear, as I do, that the birds literally and figuratively lit up that little corner of Tilden Woods. It was unquestionably the brightest spot in the park.

I have stood on the eastern edge of the peninsula and watched a 30- to 40-yard-long parade of Scarlet Tanagers pass in front of me like a regiment of airborne British Redcoats from the 18th century. And there have been mornings at the very tip of Point Pelee when warblers have fallen out of the sky and decorated the trees like it was Christmas in May, and you had to be careful where you walked so as to not accidentally step on a warbler so exhausted from a night of flying it couldn't move out of your way.

I call it magic, but the park staff, experienced birders, and naturalists would have you believe otherwise, that the park is simply the best inland migrant trap

"When the warm front collides with a cold front over Lake Erie, 'fall outs' at Point Pelee can be incredible."

LOCATION: Leamington, Ontario.

DIRECTIONS: From Windsor follow Route 3 to Leamington (about 30 miles) and from Leamington follow the National Park Road signs to the park.

HOURS: Open year-round from 6 a.m-9 p.m. and for three weeks in May the park opens at 5 a.m. There is a small entry fee.

BEST TIMES: Great birding from April to June with the high point of migration being the 2nd and 3rd weeks in May. Also very good birding from late August through October with the best fall birding from late August through September.

BIRDING HIGHLIGHTS: Hands down the best birding site in inland North America. Ranked by all experts as one of the top two or three birding sites in North America. And ranked by your humble author as one of the few places left on this continent that is truly magical.

FOR MORE INFORMATION: Point Pelee National Park, Route 1, Leamington, Ontario N8H 3V4. Phone: (519) 322-2365.

"The warblers landed at our feet beside the boardwalk, and even flitted from one side of the boardwalk to the other by passing through, not over, the throng."

on the North American continent. The reason for this, according to the experts, is that most birds and particularly songbirds, migrate at night. As the sky lightens with dawn the traveling birds look for a place to feed and rest. This is a problem if a bird finds itself in the middle of Lake Erie as the sun comes up. For the weary bird out over the lake, Point Pelee beckons like a green beacon. During spring migration birds converge on the point by the hundreds if not thousands every morning.

But this influx of birds can be magnified ten-fold because migrating birds like to ride northward-moving warm fronts. Migration actually proceeds in waves, as birds wait to ride the warm fronts north, like a surfer waiting for a good wave. When the warm fronts collide with a cold front, the warm air slides up over the colder air and the birds must work harder to fly at higher altitudes. The warm air also cools as it rises, and eventually the cold, exhausted birds must land. Birders call this a "fall out," and when the warm front collides with a cold front over Lake Erie "fall outs" at Point Pelee can be incredible. If rainy weather follows the collision of the two fronts, as it often does, the birds are grounded and the bird-

POINT PELEE NATIONAL PARK FIELD CHECKLIST

This checklist was compiled by Point Pelee National Park and includes areas adjacent to the park and Pelee Island.

___ Red-throated Loon	___ American Black Duck	___ Bald Eagle	___ Lesser Yellowlegs	___ Little Gull
___ Pacific Loon	___ Mallard	___ Northern Harrier	___ Solitary Sandpiper	___ Common Black-headed Gull
___ Common Loon	___ Northern Pintail	___ Sharp-shinned Hawk	___ Willet	___ Bonaparte's Gull
___ Pied-billed Grebe	___ Blue-winged Teal	___ Cooper's Hawk	___ Spotted Sandpiper	___ Mew Gull
___ Horned Grebe	___ Garganey	___ Northern Goshawk	___ Upland Sandpiper	___ Ring-billed Gull
___ Red-necked Grebe	___ Cinnamon Teal	___ Red-shouldered Hawk	___ Whimbrel	___ Herring Gull
___ Eared Grebe	___ Northern Shoveler	___ Broad-winged Hawk	___ Hudsonian Godwit	___ California Gull
___ Western Grebe	___ Gadwall	___ Swainson's Hawk	___ Ruddy Turnstone	___ Thayer's Gull
___ Northern Gannet	___ Eurasian Wigeon	___ Rough-legged Hawk	___ Red Knot	___ Iceland Gull
___ American White Pelican	___ American Wigeon	___ Golden Eagle	___ Sanderling	___ Lesser Black-backed Gull
___ Double-crested Cormorant	___ Canvasback	___ American Kestrel	___ Semipalmated Sandpiper	___ Black-legged Kittiwake
___ American Bittern	___ Redhead	___ Merlin	___ Western Sandpiper	___ Sabine's Gull
___ Least Bittern	___ Tufted Duck	___ Peregrine Falcon	___ Least Sandpiper	___ Caspian Tern
___ Great Blue Heron	___ Ring-necked Duck	___ Gyrfalcon	___ White-rumped Sandpiper	___ Royal Tern
___ Great Egret	___ Greater Scaup	___ Greater Prairie Chicken	___ Baird's Sandpiper	___ Common Tern
___ Snowy Egret	___ Lesser Scaup	___ Ring-necked Pheasant	___ Pectoral Sandpiper	___ Forster's Tern
___ Little Blue Heron	___ Common Eider	___ Wild Turkey	___ Sharp-tailed Sandpiper	___ Least Tern
___ Tricolored Heron	___ King Eider	___ Ruffed Grouse	___ Purple Sandpiper	___ Black Tern
___ Cattle Egret	___ Harlequin Duck	___ Northern Bobwhite	___ Dunlin	___ Black Skimmer
___ Green Heron	___ Oldsquaw	___ Yellow Rail	___ Curlew Sandpiper	___ Thick-billed Murre
___ Black-crowned Night-heron	___ Black Scoter	___ King Rail	___ Stilt Sandpiper	___ Rock Dove
___ Yellow-crowned Night-heron	___ Surf Scoter	___ Virginia Rail	___ Buff-breasted Sandpiper	___ Mourning Dove
___ White Ibis	___ White-winged Scoter	___ Sora	___ Ruff	___ Black-billed Cuckoo
___ Glossy Ibis	___ Common Goldeneye	___ Purple Gallinule	___ Short-billed Dowitcher	___ Yellow-billed Cuckoo
___ Fulvous Whistling-duck	___ Barrow's Goldeneye	___ Common Moorhen	___ Long-billed Dowitcher	___ Barn Owl
___ Tundra Swan	___ Bufflehead	___ American Coot	___ Common Snipe	___ Eastern Screech-owl
___ Mute Swan	___ Hooded Merganser	___ Sandhill Crane	___ American Woodcock	___ Great Horned Owl
___ Greater White-fronted Goose	___ Common Merganser	___ Black-bellied Plover	___ Wilson's Phalarope	___ Snowy Owl
___ Snow Goose	___ Red-breasted Merganser	___ Lesser Golden-plover	___ Red-necked Phalarope	___ Long-eared Owl
___ Ross' Goose	___ Ruddy Duck	___ Semipalmated Plover	___ Red Phalarope	___ Short-eared Owl
___ Brant	___ Black Vulture	___ Piping Plover	___ Pomarine Jaeger	___ Northern Saw-whet Owl
___ Canada Goose	___ Turkey Vulture	___ Killdeer	___ Parasitic Jaeger	___ Lesser Nighthawk
___ Barnacle Goose	___ Osprey	___ American Avocet	___ Long-tailed Jaeger	___ Common Nighthawk
___ Wood Duck	___ American Swallow-tailed Kite	___ Black-necked Stilt	___ Laughing Gull	___ Chuck-will's-widow
___ Green-winged Teal	___ Mississippi Kite	___ Greater Yellowlegs	___ Franklin's Gull	___ Whip-poor-will

watching takes a quantum leap beyond incredible.

The experts also point out that Point Pelee is blessed with an surprising diversity of habitat for such a relatively small area. The park contains one of the largest marshes in the Great Lakes, has forested wetlands, dry woodlands, open grassy expanses, miles of sandy beaches, and is surrounded by the open waters of Lake Erie. And the tree coverage in the park stands in stark relief to the rest of the county, which has been cleared for farmland. Birds who favor woodlands are apt to move into the park to feed and rest if they overshoot Point Pelee or make landfall somewhere else on the north side of Lake Erie.

The park not only attracts a fantastic number and variety of birds, it's almost as if the park goes out of its way to make them easy to find. The cool waters of Lake Erie retards spring foliage. You leave home with leaves bursting forth from every tree and shrub and arrive at the park to find nearly every tree and shrub still bare. Visit Point Pelee in even late May, and there is usually not much for birds to hide behind.

You may choose to believe that all the above facts are very persuasive and more

"I have watched a 30- to 40-yard long parade of Scarlet Tanagers pass in front of me like a regiment of airborne British Redcoats from the 18th century."

___ Chimney Swift	___ Blue Jay	___ Cedar Waxwing	___ Black-and-white Warbler	___ Henslow's Sparrow
___ Ruby-throated Hummingbird	___ Black-billed Magpie	___ Northern Shrike	___ American Redstart	___ LeConte's Sparrow
___ Rufous Hummingbird	___ American Crow	___ Loggerhead Shrike	___ Prothonotary Warbler	___ Sharp-tailed Sparrow
___ Belted Kingfisher	___ Fish Crow	___ European Starling	___ Worm-eating Warbler	___ Fox Sparrow
___ Lewis' Woodpecker	___ Common Raven	___ White-eyed Vireo	___ Swainson's Warbler	___ Song Sparrow
___ Red-headed Woodpecker	___ Black-capped Chickadee	___ Bell's Vireo	___ Ovenbird	___ Lincoln's Sparrow
___ Red-bellied Woodpecker	___ Boreal Chickadee	___ Solitary Vireo	___ Northern Waterthrush	___ Swamp Sparrow
___ Yellow-bellied Sapsucker	___ Tufted Titmouse	___ Yellow-throated Vireo	___ Louisiana Waterthrush	___ White-throated Sparrow
___ Downy Woodpecker	___ Red-breasted Nuthatch	___ Warbling Vireo	___ Kentucky Warbler	___ White-crowned Sparrow
___ Hairy Woodpecker	___ White-breasted Nuthatch	___ Philadelphia Vireo	___ Connecticut Warbler	___ Harris' Sparrow
___ Three-toed Woodpecker	___ Brown Creeper	___ Red-eyed Vireo	___ Mourning Warbler	___ Dark-eyed Sparrow
___ Northern Flicker	___ Carolina Wren	___ Blue-winged Warbler	___ Common Yellowthroat	___ Lapland Longspur
___ Pileated Woodpecker	___ Bewick's Wren	___ Golden-winged Warbler	___ Hooded Warbler	___ Snow Bunting
___ Olive-sided Flycatcher	___ House Wren	___ Tennessee Warbler	___ Wilson's Warbler	___ Bobolink
___ Eastern Wood-pewee	___ Winter Wren	___ Orange-crowned Warbler	___ Canada Warbler	___ Red-winged Blackbird
___ Yellow-bellied Flycatcher	___ Sedge Wren	___ Nashville Warbler	___ Yellow-breasted Chat	___ Eastern Meadowlark
___ Acadian Flycatcher	___ Marsh Wren	___ Virginia's Warbler	___ Summer Tanager	___ Western Meadowlark
___ Alder Flycatcher	___ Rock Wren	___ Northern Parula	___ Scarlet Tanager	___ Yellow-headed Blackbird
___ Willow Flycatcher	___ Golden-crowned Kinglet	___ Yellow Warbler	___ Western Tanager	___ Rusty Blackbird
___ Gray Flycatcher	___ Ruby-crowned Kinglet	___ Chestnut-sided Warbler	___ Northern Cardinal	___ Brewer's Blackbird
___ Least Flycatcher	___ Blue-gray Gnatcatcher	___ Magnolia Warbler	___ Rose-breasted Grosbeak	___ Common Grackle
___ Eastern Phoebe	___ Eastern Bluebird	___ Cape May Warbler	___ Lazuli Bunting	___ Brown-headed Cowbird
___ Ash-throated Flycatcher	___ Mountain Bluebird	___ Black-throated Blue Warbler	___ Indigo Bunting	___ Orchard Oriole
___ Great Crested Flycatcher	___ Townsend's Solitaire	___ Yellow-rumped Warbler	___ Dickcissel	___ Baltimore Oriole
___ Western Kingbird	___ Veery	___ Black-throated Gray Warbler	___ Green-tailed Towhee	___ Pine Grosbeak
___ Eastern Kingbird	___ Gray-cheeked Thrush	___ Townsend's Warbler	___ Rufous-sided Towhee	___ Purple Finch
___ Gray Kingbird	___ Swainson's Thrush	___ Hermit Warbler	___ Bachman's Sparrow	___ House Finch
___ Scissor-tailed Flycatcher	___ Hermit Thrush	___ Black-throated Green Warbler	___ Cassin's Sparrow	___ Red Crossbill
___ Horned Lark	___ Wood Thrush	___ Blackburnian Warbler	___ American Tree Sparrow	___ White-winged Crossbill
___ Purple Martin	___ American Robin	___ Yellow-throated Warbler	___ Chipping Sparrow	___ Common Redpoll
___ Tree Swallow	___ Varied Thrush	___ Pine Warbler	___ Clay-colored Sparrow	___ Hoary Redpoll
___ Northern Rough-winged Swallow	___ Northern Wheatear	___ Kirtland's Warbler	___ Field Sparrow	___ Pine Siskin
___ Bank Swallow	___ Gray Catbird	___ Prairie Warbler	___ Vesper Sparrow	___ American Goldfinch
___ Cliff Swallow	___ Northern Mockingbird	___ Palm Warbler	___ Lark Sparrow	___ Evening Grosbeak
___ Cave Swallow	___ Sage Thrasher	___ Bay-breasted Warbler	___ Lark Bunting	___ House Sparrow
___ Barn Swallow	___ American Pipit	___ Blackpoll Warbler	___ Savannah Sparrow	
___ Gray Jay	___ Bohemian Waxwing	___ Cerulean Warbler	___ Grasshopper Sparrow	

"The park not only attracts a fantastic number and variety of birds, it's almost as if the park goes out of its way to make them easy to find."

than reasonable explanations as to why Point Pelee National Park is one of the best birding sites in North America. Or, like me, you can simply believe there is magic left in this world and it manifests itself at Point Pelee. Just don't make up your mind until you have visited the park in mid-May and run into a squadron of hummingbirds.

As befitting one of the best birding sites in our continent, 357 bird species have been recorded in Point Pelee National Park and another eight have been spotted in areas adjacent to the park. Of that vast number, warblers account for 42 species and several expert birders have tallied 34 warbler species in a single day. No wonder the park is known as the "Warbler Capital of the World." Warblers and other songbirds reach their peak in numbers and diversity in the second and third week in May and so do birders. It's not uncommon for a line of cars to be waiting at the park entrance when it opens at 5:00 a.m. More than 75,000 people, mostly birders, visit the park during May. They are not only treated to a wealth of warblers and songbirds but birds from every family and order. It is not uncommon for even beginners to see a 100 species on an average "magical" day. And as one would expect, rare and uncommon birds regularly put in appearances at Point Pelee. The Visitors Center has a tally board with all recent sightings including rarities and park personnel are always on hand to direct birders to likely spots. The park has become so crowded in May that the staff urge visitors to bird some of the other good birding sites just outside the park. If at all possible during May, it's best to visit the park Monday through Friday and stay away on weekends.

But Point Pelee National Park shouldn't be dismissed the other 11 months of the year. Spring migration starts in March with the arrival of waterfowl and a few songbirds and gains strength in April as shorebirds, terns, raptors, and more songbirds including warblers join the northbound stream. In May the waves of migrants reaches tsunami proportions, but June continues to bring numerous shorebirds and late arriving warblers. The most overlooked birding season at Point Pelee is the fall. From the last week in August through September birding can be just as spectacular as the spring. Extreme rarities are more apt to turn up in the fall than spring, and the tally of individual species can be greater in the fall than the spring.

On many days at Point Pelee you can stop nearly anywhere in the park and find something to capture your interest, but there are several specific trails and locations in the park that are the crème de la crème of birding sites. If you arrive early on a May morning, the place to start is at the very tip of the peninsula. At dawn tired and hungry birds caught out over Lake Erie make a beeline for the nearest land, and in many cases that is Point Pelee. It's not unusual to find the tip of the peninsula — from the transit station where the trackless train drops off birders, south to the narrow sand pit that slips into the lake — packed with birds. Many of the birds will be on the ground and clearly exhausted from their night flight. As the day progresses the birds will spread north through the peninsula to better cover and preferred habitat. The tip is also a favored spot for birders looking for the odd gull, tern, or shorebird blending in among the usual throng of gulls and terns lining the sandy spit that tails off into the lake. In the fall, the best time to hit the point is often in the afternoon as southbound birds funnel into the tip of the peninsula. From April through August and on fall weekends, a trackless train takes birders from the Visitors Center to the tip of the peninsula from 9 a.m. to 9 p.m. In May the train service begins at 6 a.m.

Just to the north and east of the trackless train's turn-around loop, near the end of Point Pelee, is the Sparrow Field. There is very little open space at the peninsula's tip and species preferring grassland pour into this small grassy pocket. Savannah, Chipping, White-crowned, Field, and Song sparrows are all commonly seen here and chances are good of seeing the rarer Henslow's, Grasshopper, and LeConte's sparrows. There is another long, narrow grassy area stretching along the west side of the peninsula south of the Visitors Center that is also popular with sparrows.

The heavily birded Woodland Trail begins on the south side of the Visitors Center and makes two long loops and one very short circle through a picturesque forest. The long, narrow, western loop takes you through dry woodlands, while the eastern loop crosses a series of boardwalks and passes through a beautiful wooded wetlands. I always seem to run into a band of hummingbirds on the western loop, while the eastern loop, for four years in a row, faithfully presented me with a new, personal, never-before-seen bird. Before and/or after walking the Woodland Trail, a stop in the Visitors Center is de rigueur. Park staff are always on had to answer questions and point you in the right directions. The Center is always warm and dry, when it's cold and wet outside, and restroom facilities are always a major draw. There is a fine gift shop offering everything from souvenir doodads to the latest in birding optics, including an impressive collection of books on birding.

Tilden Woods Trail begins on the east side of the Visitors Center parking lot, and many birders will tell you it's their favorite birding trail in the entire park. At barely more than a half-mile long, the trail passes through an astonishing array of habitats including mature forests, grasslands, pockets of cattails, wooded wetlands, and dry forested ridges. As you would suspect, the different habitats attract a wide diversity of birds, and the trail is famous for its warblers and vireos. Golden-winged, Kentucky, Prothonotary, and Hooded warblers as well as Northern and Louisiana waterthrushes all make regular appearances along the trail and often share the spotlight with each other. The Tilden Woods Trail is always worth a look-see.

The two remaining birding hotspots are farther north on the peninsula. The De Laurier Trail circles through the open fields and orchards of an old homestead before heading east and slipping into woodlands and edges a marsh before returning to the homestead. The wetlands area often yields warblers; and the orchard and open fields are favorite locations for spotting sparrows, Eastern Bluebirds, and Bobolinks. The Marsh Boardwalk, still further north on the peninsula, will take you on a 1-mile walk into the heart of a vast marsh. The boardwalk passes through a huge expanse of cattails, here and there dotted with small, quiet pools of water. Marsh Wrens, Swamp Sparrows, Common Yellowthroats, Virginia Rails, and Sora are all seen from the boardwalk with the shy and retiring Least and American bitterns less often observed. A detailed park map is presented to all birders entering the park, and all the above trails are marked on the map

Onion fields border the northern boundary of the park and the black, moist soil draws gulls, terns, and shorebirds in both spring and fall. Dunlins, Ruddy Turnstones, and plenty of sandpipers and plovers are all commonly seen probing the fields for food. Further afield, but worth a trip if you have the time, is Hillman Marsh Conservation Area. The marsh is only a few miles to the northeast of the park and features a large wetlands penetrated by a 3-mile long trail. Hillman Marsh can be counted on for large congregations of waterfowl and shorebirds. Yellow-headed Blackbirds, King Rails, Sedge Wrens, and Prothonotary Warblers all nest here; and the area receives more than its fair share of rarities.

"Your heart jumps into your throat, the hairs on the back of your neck stand on end, and you swear there is a tingling, electrical charge in the air as the birds swirl around you like a swarm of bees and zip past at a distance of less than two feet with an unbelievably loud buzz."

Holiday Beach Conservation Area

"You only have to go there once to realize that it is a place where you experience the annual flow and current of bird migration with the same tactile sense as stepping in the water and wading out into the current of a fast-moving creek."

LOCATION: Essex, Ontario.

DIRECTIONS: Approximately 25 miles south of the Ambassador Bridge on Highway 18 turn right on County Road 18 in Malden Centre, and go south about 1.5 miles to Holiday Beach Conservation Area.

HOURS: Open all year.

BEST TIMES: September through November.

BIRDING HIGHLIGHTS: One of the great spots in North American for experiencing the fall hawk migration. The movement of songbirds can also be impressive.

FOR MORE INFORMATION: Essex Region Conservation Authority, 360 Fairview Avenue. West, Essex, Ontario N8M 1Y6. Phone: (519) 736-3772.

On the best of fall days when you climb the three-story, hawk-watching tower at Holiday Beach Conservation Area it's the equivalent of sticking your finger in a wall socket. There may be other sites that witness heavier flights of migrating hawks and songbirds, but there is no other place in the Midwest that gives you the feeling of being literally plugged into the migration.

It's one thing to marvel at the huge concentrations of waterfowl that fly into an area to rest and feed while either heading north or south, but from atop the tower at Holiday Beach you are up in the birds' element. Sharp-shinned Hawks, American Kestrels, and an occasional Cooper's Hawk barrel past at or near eye-level. At higher altitudes, echelons of Turkey Vultures fill the sky and stream past like the Eighth Air Force heading toward Germany. Take your eyes from the heavens and you'll find Eastern Bluebirds, Blue Jays, American Goldfinches, and other songbirds chattering past you either at eye-level or lower. And while you're lost in amazement looking down at a flight of 150 American Goldfinches, the hawk spotter next to you calls attention to a Red-shouldered Hawk to the right and a Cooper's Hawk coming over the tree line on the left. And before you get either one of those focused in your binoculars, someone else calls out a probable Bald Eagle soaring high and in front. Being atop the observation tower at Holiday Beach is simply one of the most electrifying experiences you can have birding.

Holiday Beach, in southern Ontario, lies at the small end of a huge fall migratory bird funnel formed by Lake Huron on the north and Lakes Erie and Ontario on the south. Generally, many bird species and especially raptors do not like to cross large bodies of water. Birds of prey use thermals when migrating and thermals are only created over land. So when southbound raptors from Canada hit the northern shore of Lakes Erie or Ontario they follow the shoreline south to the Detroit River. Ornithologists believe birds also use shorelines as navigation landmarks. You only have to look at a map of southern Ontario to see that Holiday Beach is in a near perfect position from which to observe the fall bird migration, especially raptors. This has been no secret to local birders who have been coming to the Holiday Beach for years to marvel at and document the fall passage of birds.

The years of careful observation and record keeping make it abundantly clear that Holiday Beach is an uncommonly good birding spot. But you only have to go there once to realize that it is a place where you experience the annual flow and current of bird migration with the same tactile sense as stepping in the water and wading out into the current of a fast-moving creek. The current at Holiday Beach is at full flow from early August through the end of November. In an average year 40,000 Broad-winged Hawks, 10,000 Turkey Vultures, 100 Ospreys, 45 Golden and 30 Bald eagles will be among the three-quarter million birds that stream pass Holiday Beach every fall.

Jeff Jones and I arrived there on a beautiful, warm Saturday in early October. As we pulled into the parking lot next to the observation tower, banders were giving an impromptu hawk identification class and using a Sharp-shinned Hawk and a Cooper's Hawk they had just captured and banded. Amazing how different they look from each other at ten feet and how similar, except to the trained eye, at anything over 100 feet.

After the birds were released I joined about 30 people on the observation tower. There was always something to look at whether it was a Sharp-shinned Hawk or American Kestrel winging past at the same altitude as I was or watching a huge kettle of Turkey Vultures in the distance reach the top of a thermal, form loose Vs and soar past the tower at great height without a single wing flap. Someone in the group was always calling attention to a raptor, and everybody kept an ear tuned to the official hawk counter who either confirmed someone else's sighting or announced new birds. This is a great place for the beginning birder to learn raptor identification. Nearly every bird is identified and pointed out to everybody on the tower, and the hawk counter is very good about pointing out the characteristics and clues as to a distant bird's identity.

Even more impressive were the Blue Jays. Yes, Blue Jays. In the two hours I was atop the tower, Blue Jays were constantly moving past. There simply was not a period of time longer than a minute when you couldn't pick out a group of jays in the area surrounding the tower heading west. In the first full hour I was there 2,040 Blue Jays were tallied. Sparrows were also on the move, and every now and then a noisy troop of American Goldfinches whipped by. If it wasn't for the fact that the hawk counter called his counterpart at Lake Erie Metro Park in Michigan every hour and ticked off the sightings at Holiday Beach, you could loose all sense of time as birds endlessly stream by the platform. I hadn't been on the tower a half-hour before the hawk watcher was reporting that 37 Turkey Vultures, 12 Sharp-shinned Hawks, one each of Cooper's and Red-shouldered hawks, 10 Red-tailed, and 2 Broad-winged hawks had been counted in the last hour. The next hour was to prove even more active as American Kestrels and Bald Eagles joined the list, and the number of birds seen in the previous hour doubled then tripled.

As much as I was enjoying the day I tried to keep in mind that this was just a normal day, and I wondered what it would be like to experience those rare oc-

"Being atop the observation tower is simply one of the most electrifying experiences you can have birding."

COOPER'S HAWK

"Someone in the group was always calling attention to a raptor, and everybody kept an ear tuned to the official hawk counter who either confirmed someone else's sighting or announced new birds."

casions when the stream of birds becomes a flood. Like the day 95,000 Broad-winged Hawks were seen and more than 50,000 were counted in 60 minutes. Other daily high counts include 50,000 Blue Jays; 9,700 Turkey Vultures; 200 hummingbirds; 825 Eastern Bluebirds; and over 1,000 Sharp-shinned Hawks. Really good viewing days usually occur on days when the wind is out of the northwest.

You have a pretty fair chance of predicting what you will see by the time of the year you visit. Fall migration begins in late August with the arrival of waterfowl, marsh birds, shorebirds, and warblers. Warbler viewing is best in the brush and shrubs on either side of a causeway that lies about halfway between the entrance gate and the tower, or in the woods near the park store. Warblers move through the area in large groups that can contain better than half-a-dozen species. When water level recedes enough to expose mudflats adjacent to the causeway, a good sampling of sandpipers and plovers call at the conservation area.

Early September brings Ospreys, American Kestrels, Sharp-shinned Hawks, and hummingbirds. It's not uncommon for over a thousand raptors to be seen daily in September, especially by mid-month when Broad-winged Hawks join the southward flow of birds. Traditionally one of the days between September 9 and 20 sees the largest numbers of hawks at Holiday Beach. Mid-month also sees the arrival of Northern Harriers. By late September when the ranks of Broad-winged Hawks begin to thin, Turkey Vultures, Merlins, and Peregrine Falcons begin to appear. In early October Bald Eagles join the passing parade, and by mid-month Red-tailed and Red-shouldered Hawks are seen as Turkey Vulture numbers peak. Late October sees the arrival of a few Northern Goshawks and Golden Eagles. Golden Eagles and Red-tailed Hawks continue to be seen in early November and are joined by Rough-legged Hawks. November is the best bet for seeing Golden Eagles with November 10, 1991 holding the record for most Golden Eagles in a single day — 24. By mid-November Northern Saw-whet and Short-eared Owls are the main points of interest.

It only takes one visit to Holiday Beach to convince even the skeptical that the place is one of the great hawk-watching sites in North America. Novice hawk watchers should plan on visiting during one of the three weekends in September when raptor identification classes, guided hawk watching tours, live raptor displays, and banding demonstrations add to the fun. For exact dates and times call the number on page 150.

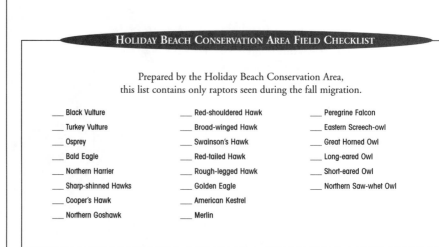

HOLIDAY BEACH CONSERVATION AREA FIELD CHECKLIST

Prepared by the Holiday Beach Conservation Area,
this list contains only raptors seen during the fall migration.

___ Black Vulture	___ Red-shouldered Hawk	___ Peregrine Falcon
___ Turkey Vulture	___ Broad-winged Hawk	___ Eastern Screech-owl
___ Osprey	___ Swainson's Hawk	___ Great Horned Owl
___ Bald Eagle	___ Red-tailed Hawk	___ Long-eared Owl
___ Northern Harrier	___ Rough-legged Hawk	___ Short-eared Owl
___ Sharp-shinned Hawks	___ Golden Eagle	___ Northern Saw-whet Owl
___ Cooper's Hawk	___ American Kestrel	
___ Northern Goshawk	___ Merlin	

St. Clair River

It was six degrees above zero at nine in the morning with the wind coming off Lake Huron at a good enough clip to make the wind-chill factor the equal of standing naked on the far side of the moon. Jeff Buecking and I stood on Point Edward, at the southern end of Lake Huron with the cold tearing our eyes when Jeff observed, "You got to be crazy to stand out here in this cold." I couldn't help but agree with him, and we jumped back into the warm truck. But within minutes we were confirming Jeff's earlier diagnosis with both of us back out in the wind and cold scoping the open water between the ice floes funneling into the St. Clair River and searching open patches of water in the lake for ducks and gulls.

Jeff and I were going to make a day of it, by birding one of the best winter birdwatching areas in the Midwest: Sarnia Airport and the St. Clair River from its mouth at Point Edward to Port Lambdon in the south. The airport is known for attracting wintering owls and the river can always be counted on for waterfowl. There is usually open water in the St. Clair River between Sarnia and Port Lambdon even during the coldest winters. This open water draws a large numbers of wintering waterfowl and gulls to the river, and nearly every year amidst the more common and abundant Redhead, Canvasback and mergansers are found occasional Oldsquaw, Barrow's Goldeneye, King and Common eiders, Harlequin Ducks, and White-winged Scoters. Usually each winter also finds a few Glaucous, Iceland and Thayer's gulls mixed in with the ubiquitous Ring-billed and Herring gulls.

It's true that birding can be equally good on the Michigan side of the river from Port Huron to Algonac, but we'd chosen the Canadian side for two reasons. On the east side of the St. Clair River the sun is at the birder's back in the morning whereas on the U.S. side birders are looking into the sun until late in the morning. Secondly, the farming country east of the river is excellent hawk and Snowy Owl territory, and Sarnia Airport, due east of town, should be considered a must stop in late afternoon for several winter specialties. Many winter birders will bird both sides of the river starting at Point Edward in the morning, working their way south to Sombra by late morning and crossing the ferry at Sombra to Marine City and working their way back up river to Port Huron in the afternoon. The only problem with this plan is the possible suspension of ferry service at Sombra due to thick ice on the river.

At first glance from the parking lot at Point Edward, the lake and river appeared c-c-c-cold and lifeless. As Jeff searched the open pools of water among the vast ice sheets out in the lake, my attention was drawn to the mouth of the St. Clair River. It's not until you witness the speed with which the ice is drawn into and flows down the river that you become fully aware of the speed of the current. It was the fascination with watching the current that led to the first good sighting of the day. Intent on watching the ice flowing into the mouth of the river, I spotted a Horned Grebe riding the current south. Jeff in the meantime had ticked off Common and Hooded mergansers and a Greater Black-backed Gull. Two weeks earlier from this very spot Jeff had counted 50 Oldsquaws out on the lake.

Point Edward is not only the natural starting point for winter birding the St. Clair River but is probably the best observation post in the province from which

"The St. Clair River Parkway borders the river and provides a number of places where drivers can pull off the road to study the river and its bird life."

LOCATION: Sarnia, Ontario.

DIRECTIONS: The following directions are complicated by the fact that construction is ongoing in the area of the Bluewater Bridge. All the right and left hand turns are within two or three blocks of each other. To reach the rest of the sites covered in the tour backtrack to Venetian Boulevard and follow directions in the text. The following directions are for getting to Point Edward. After crossing the Bluewater Bridge into Canada, take the first exit on the right after customs and turn right on Venetian Boulevard. Venetian will take you back under the bridge to Alexandra Street. Turn right on Alexandra and drive to Monk Street. Turn left on Monk and drive to Michigan Street. Turn left on Michigan and drive to Livingston Street. Turn right on Livingston and drive to Victoria Street. Turn right on Victoria and drive to Fort Street where you will make a left which will lead you to the parking lot at Point Edward.

HOURS: Open all year.

BEST TIMES: Late December through February.

BIRDING HIGHLIGHTS: Very good birding for waterfowl and winter specialties.

"I slowed down to investigate what appeared to be a large, white, plastic bag caught in the top of a roadside tree. My heart rate nearly doubled when the plastic bag turned into a Snowy Owl."

to watch the fall migration of sea birds. In late autumn jaegers, Sabine's Gulls, Brant, all three scoters, Red-throated Loons and Black-legged Kittiwake have all been seen from the point. Both binoculars and a spotting scope are musts for birding Point Edward.

From Point Edward we drove back under the Bluewater Bridge and south on Venetian Boulevard to Exmouth Street, turned right on Exmouth and drove less than a quarter-mile to Harbour Road. A left turn on Harbour brought us to a park overlooking Sarnia Bay. Jeff who regularly birds the St. Clair River corridor in the winter and was serving as my guide said the small little harbor was a prime area for ducks and gulls if there was open water. Instead of open water and birds a large oval was being carved in the bay's ice by a motorcycle.

Harbour Street appropriately enough ends at Sarnia Harbour where the road makes a 90-degree right turn and becomes Seaway. Seaway ends in less than a half-mile in a small parking lot surrounded by great lake freighters. Looking around the bow of a freighter that was less than 50 yards away and towered over us, we had a good view of the St. Clair River. In years past Jeff had found this area a great place for spotting diving ducks, gulls, and on a few memorable occasions, Snowy Owls and Peregrine Falcons perched on the grain elevators to the right of us. That was not to be today, but it was still worth a trip to the end of Seaway for the close-up view of the freighters that were waiting out winter berthed along the river and looking even larger because they rode so high in the water.

Leaving Sarnia Harbour and working our way through downtown Sarnia to the St. Clair River Parkway, Jeff proved he deserves to be ranked with the elite of birding guides by leading me unerringly to a Tim Horton's Donut Shop. To reach the St. Clair River Parkway back track to Exmouth, turn right and drive to Christina Street. Turn right and follow Christina Street through town until it ends south of town at Clifford Street. Turn left on Clifford Street and drive a block to Vidal Street and turn right. Vidal Street is County Road 33 and becomes the St. Clair River Parkway south of town.

For most of its length between Sarnia and Port Lambton, the St. Clair River Parkway borders the river and provides a number of places where drivers can pull off the road to study the river and its bird life. It would be almost suicidal to bird this road without a spotter riding shotgun. The road gently twists and turns as it follows the course of the river, and with all the possible bird life and opportunities for spotting something rare a lone birder would put a car in the river or into a tree within a few miles. Guthrie Park just south of the Chemical Valley area and Willow Park in front of the Lambton Power Plant are traditionally good places to stop and scope the river. We spent a half-hour at each park and paused at a number of other spots on the drive and added Common Goldeneye, Canvasbacks, Redheads, Greater Scaup, American Black Ducks, Buffleheads, and Ring-necked Ducks to the day's tally.

South of Port Lambton we turned east on a country road that led us through farmland and a search for hawks and owls as we made our way back to Sarnia and Sarnia Airport. Within less than a mile we found ourselves paralleling a Northern Harrier as it skimmed over a farm field. The road also offered up Snow Buntings, Mourning Doves, American Trees Sparrows, a Red-tailed Hawk and Horned Larks before we hit Highway 40 where we turned north and drove back to Sarnia. Highway 40 was proving to be the quietest birding stretch of the day until I slowed down to investigate what appeared to be a large, white, plastic bag caught in the top of a roadside tree. My heart rate nearly doubled when the plastic bag turned into a Snowy Owl.

Still excited about the Snowy Owl we returned to Sarnia following Highway 40 to Canada Highway 401, turned east and drove to exit 9. From exit 9 we drove north less than a mile to Sarnia Airport. The airport has traditionally been a wintering ground for Short-eared Owls, and Rough-legged Hawks have often been seen here as well. We arrived at the airport in the late afternoon with a good hour of sunlight left and drove around the east and north sides of the airport on Tefler Road and Michigan Avenue. Stopping on Michigan Avenue Jeff caught sight of two Short-eared Owls casting across distant fields and pointed out their characteristic moth-like flapping of wings. Turning around we slowly drove back to Tefler Road and were treated to the sight of a Short-eared Owl perched on a fence post not 40 feet from the car. The bird sat and let Jeff unpack his camera and take a half-dozen exposures before tiring of our attention. The owl lifted off the post, on what seemed like disproportionately large wings in relation to its body, and flew away doing a pretty good imitation of a flying rag doll. It was the perfect close to a great day of birding.

"At first glance the lake and river appeared c-c-c-cold and lifeless."

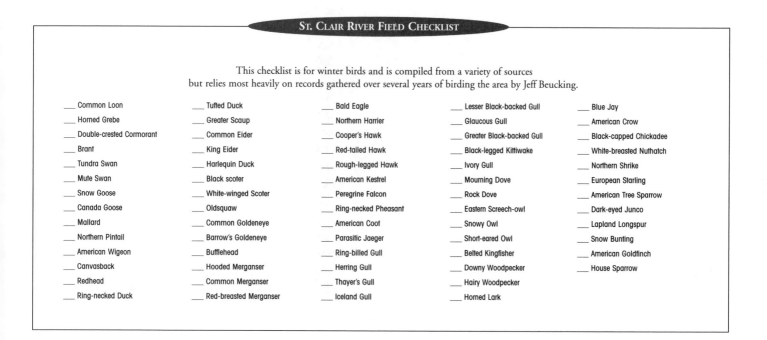

ST. CLAIR RIVER FIELD CHECKLIST

This checklist is for winter birds and is compiled from a variety of sources
but relies most heavily on records gathered over several years of birding the area by Jeff Beucking.

___ Common Loon	___ Tufted Duck	___ Bald Eagle	___ Lesser Black-backed Gull	___ Blue Jay
___ Horned Grebe	___ Greater Scaup	___ Northern Harrier	___ Glaucous Gull	___ American Crow
___ Double-crested Cormorant	___ Common Eider	___ Cooper's Hawk	___ Greater Black-backed Gull	___ Black-capped Chickadee
___ Brant	___ King Eider	___ Red-tailed Hawk	___ Black-legged Kittiwake	___ White-breasted Nuthatch
___ Tundra Swan	___ Harlequin Duck	___ Rough-legged Hawk	___ Ivory Gull	___ Northern Shrike
___ Mute Swan	___ Black scoter	___ American Kestrel	___ Mourning Dove	___ European Starling
___ Snow Goose	___ White-winged Scoter	___ Peregrine Falcon	___ Rock Dove	___ American Tree Sparrow
___ Canada Goose	___ Oldsquaw	___ Ring-necked Pheasant	___ Eastern Screech-owl	___ Dark-eyed Junco
___ Mallard	___ Common Goldeneye	___ American Coot	___ Snowy Owl	___ Lapland Longspur
___ Northern Pintail	___ Barrow's Goldeneye	___ Parasitic Jaeger	___ Short-eared Owl	___ Snow Bunting
___ American Wigeon	___ Bufflehead	___ Ring-billed Gull	___ Belted Kingfisher	___ American Goldfinch
___ Canvasback	___ Hooded Merganser	___ Herring Gull	___ Downy Woodpecker	___ House Sparrow
___ Redhead	___ Common Merganser	___ Thayer's Gull	___ Hairy Woodpecker	
___ Ring-necked Duck	___ Red-breasted Merganser	___ Iceland Gull	___ Horned Lark	

WISCONSIN

GREEN BAY, 157

GEORGE W. MEAD
WILDLIFE AREA, 161

NECEDAH NATIONAL
WILDLIFE REFUGE, 164

HORICON MARSH NATIONAL
WILDLIFE REFUGE, 168

WYALUSING STATE PARK, 172

TREMPEALEAU
NATIONAL WILDLIFE REFUGE, 174

CREX MEADOWS
WILDLIFE AREA, 177

Green Bay

In 1634 French explorer Jean Nicolet stepped ashore at the future site of Green Bay, Wisconsin dressed to the nines in a robe of fine China damask beautifully decorated with colorful flowers and birds. Nicolet's sartorial splendor was intended to suitably impress the Chinese and gain entry to their emperor. Obviously he didn't find any Chinese — he was only half a continent and the Pacific Ocean short of his goal — but he did see and made note of the incredible number of birds that inhabited the lower end of Green Bay. Three and a half centuries later, Barb and I didn't make the same mistake. We came to Green Bay looking for birds, not China; and we didn't over dress for the occasion.

Of course, much has changed in Green Bay in 350 years, but Nicolet would probably still be impressed by the bird life in the area. The southern end of the bay collects huge numbers of birds during spring and fall migration, and there are enough species nesting in the area to make summer birding interesting. The presence of Snowy Owls, rare gulls, winter finches, and large numbers of geese and ducks overwintering in the area make birding a year-round activity in Green Bay. The current checklist for the county totals a whopping 365 species and includes 30 species of waterfowl, 17 different birds of prey, 43 species of shorebirds, and 35 species from the warbler family. Simply put, the Green Bay area is one of the best all-around birding spots in the Midwest.

If there are plenty of birds, there are also a lot of spots from which to observe them. The following five locations all ring the southern end of the bay and taken together, not only represent a good cross section of the area's habitat but consistently produce most of the 365 species to be found in Brown County. Barb and I started on the eastern edge of Green Bay and worked our way to the west. All but the last site, Barkhausen Waterfowl Preserve, can easily be accessed from Interstate 43 which parallels the shoreline in downtown Green Bay.

The Cofrin Arboretum at the University of Wisconsin Green Bay is a 290-acre greenbelt encircling the campus. Even if it wasn't a great birding site, it would still warrant a visit for its scenic beauty. The west side of the arboretum touches the bay while the east side climbs the steep sides of the Niagara Escarpment. A tower atop the escarpment presents visitors a stunning view of the campus, the surrounding countryside, and Green Bay. The widely diverse habitat — a half-mile of Green Bay shoreline, an upland forest, cedar swamp, restored prairie, wetlands, and a stream — within the circular arboretum attracts over 200 bird species. Fifty species have been documented as nesting in the area. A 5-mile-long trail, which is very popular with walkers and joggers, gives access to all the various habitats; but local birders have found the most productive locations, especially during spring migration, are the shoreline and Mahon Woods, adjacent to each other, in the southwest quadrant of the circle.

The parking lot most convenient to the lakeshore is on the left-hand side of Nicolet Drive, 100 yards or so past the Main entrance to the campus. The shoreline section of the trail begins immediately on the south side of the parking lot. Within a few steps the birder is briefly enveloped in a hardwood forest with a dense understory that quickly gives way to the shrub-lined beach. I spotted a Brown Thrasher, Wood Thrush, and a Red-eyed Vireo along the trail before hitting the shoreline and caught sight of a Green Heron lifting off from a small pond

LOCATION: Green Bay, Wisconsin.

DIRECTIONS: To reach Cofrin Arboretum head east on Highway 54/57 from its junction with I-43 for about a half-mile to the intersection of 54-57 and Nicolet Drive. Turn left (north) on Nicolet Drive and drive another half-mile to the campus of University of Wisconsin Green Bay.

Bay Beach Wildlife Sanctuary is reached by exiting I-43 at Webster Avenue/East Shore Drive in downtown Green Bay and driving northeast a half-mile.

The Fox River mouth is reached by taking the same exit off I-43 as the Bay Beach Wildlife Sanctuary. From the exit travel east 0.2 mile to Irwin Avenue and turn left. Stay on Irwin Avenue as it turns into Bay Beach Road and ends at the boat launching ramp on the river.

The Ken Euers Nature Area is reached by exiting I-43 at Atkinson Road (exit 189). Drive north to the first intersection and turn left on Hulbert. Follow Hulbert west as it parallels the expressway. Hulbert becomes Military Road as it turns to the north. Follow Military Road to the parking area.

To reach Barkhausen Waterfowl Preserve drive north from the junction of U.S. 41/141 and I-43 on 41/141 about 2 miles to Lineville Road. Turn right on Lineville Road and drive 0.5 mile to Lakeview. Turn north (left) and drive 0.5 mile to the preserve entrance.

HOURS: All sites are open all year. Daily hours vary, but most are open by 8 a.m. and close between 5 p.m. and dusk.

BEST TIMES: Birding is good year-round and excellent in April/May and August/September.

BIRDING HIGHLIGHTS: Green Bay is one of the most productive birding areas in the Midwest. More than 360 species are included in the Brown County bird checklist, and nearly all those species have been seen in the Green Bay area.

FOR MORE INFORMATION: Bay Beach Wildlife Sanctuary, 1660 East Shore Drive, Green Bay, WI 54302.

"The cottonwoods and willows act like a huge magnet for the songbirds."

just back from the beach. After about a quarter-mile, the trail turns to the left, crosses Nicolet Drive and enters Mahon Woods. I tallied 18 species in an hour's walk, and had hoped, but failed, to bag a Gray Partridge, either an Alder or a Willow flycatcher, or a Warbling Vireo, all of which nest in the area.

The next stop, just a couple of miles to the west, is not just a birding spot, it's a tourist attraction. Green Bay's Bay Beach Wildlife Sanctuary boasts an architecturally spectacular nature center, manmade lagoons that attract thousands of waterfowl, an outside aviary featuring several members of the owl family, a wolf pack, a nocturnal animal display, and several miles of trails that cut through bird rich woodlands and wetlands. "Where to start?" you ask. Well, we started at the guest register in the Nature Center to see what kind of company we were keeping. A quick scan of the last few pages showed visitors from Edinborough, Madrid, Bahrain, Germany, and London.

Before hitting the trails, we strolled around the Nature Center, took in the displays and exhibits, and kept an eye on the many feeders hung just outside the Center's windows. In addition to the Black-capped Chickadees, nuthatches, and sparrows coming for handouts was a Rose-breasted Grosbeak. Even in early summer the lagoons near the Nature Center were packed with waterfowl. The sanctuary is home to 3,000 resident Branta Canadensis Maxima or giant Canada

GREEN BAY FIELD CHECKLIST

___ Red-throated Loon	___ American Black Duck	___ Red-tailed Hawk	___ Spotted Sandpiper	___ Little Gull
___ Common Loon	___ Mallard	___ Rough-legged Hawk	___ Upland Sandpiper	___ Bonaparte's Gull
___ Pied-billed Grebe	___ Northern Pintail	___ Golden Eagle	___ Whimbrel	___ Ring-billed Gull
___ Horned Grebe	___ Blue-winged Teal	___ American Kestrel	___ Long-billed Curlew	___ Herring Gull
___ Red-necked Grebe	___ Cinnamon Teal	___ Merlin	___ Hudsonian Godwit	___ Iceland Gull
___ Eared Grebe	___ Northern Shoveler	___ Peregrine Falcon	___ Marbled Godwit	___ Glaucous Gull
___ Western Grebe	___ Gadwall	___ Gyrfalcon	___ Ruddy Turnstone	___ Great Black-backed Gull
___ American White Pelican	___ Eurasian Wigeon	___ Gray Partridge	___ Red Knot	___ Caspian Tern
___ Double-crested Cormorant	___ American Wigeon	___ Ring-necked Pheasant	___ Sanderling	___ Common Tern
___ American Bittern	___ Canvasback	___ Ruffed Grouse	___ Semipalmated Sandpiper	___ Forster's Tern
___ Least Bittern	___ Redhead	___ Wild Turkey	___ Western Sandpiper	___ Arctic Tern
___ Great Blue Heron	___ Ring-necked Duck	___ Northern Bobwhite	___ Least Sandpiper	___ Black Tern
___ Great Egret	___ Greater Scaup	___ Yellow Rail	___ White-rumped Sandpiper	___ Rock Dove
___ Snowy Egret	___ Lesser Scaup	___ King Rail	___ Baird's Sandpiper	___ Mourning Dove
___ Little Blue Heron	___ Oldsquaw	___ Virginia Rail	___ Pectoral Sandpiper	___ Black-billed Cuckoo
___ Tricolored Heron	___ White-winged Scoter	___ Sora	___ Dunlin	___ Yellow-billed Cuckoo
___ Cattle Egret	___ Common Goldeneye	___ Common Moorhen	___ Stilt Sandpiper	___ Groove-billed Ani
___ Green Heron	___ Ruddy Duck	___ American Coot	___ Buff-breasted Sandpiper	___ Eastern Screech-owl
___ Black-crowned Night-heron	___ Bufflehead	___ Sandhill Crane	___ Ruff	___ Snowy Owl
___ Yellow-crowned Night-heron	___ Hooded Merganser	___ Black-bellied Plover	___ Short-billed Dowitcher	___ Burrowing Owl
___ Tundra Swan	___ Common Merganser	___ Lesser Golden-plover	___ Long-billed Dowitcher	___ Barred Owl
___ Trumpeter Swan	___ Red-breasted Merganser	___ Semipalmated Plover	___ Common Snipe	___ Long-eared Owl
___ Mute Swan	___ Turkey Vulture	___ Piping Plover	___ American Woodcock	___ Short-eared Owl
___ Greater White-fronted Goose	___ Osprey	___ Killdeer	___ Wilson's Phalarope	___ Northern Saw-whet Owl
___ Snow Goose	___ Mississippi Kite	___ American Avocet	___ Red-necked Phalarope	___ Common Nighthawk
___ Ross' Goose	___ Bald Eagle	___ Greater Yellowlegs	___ Red Phalarope	___ Whip-poor-will
___ Canada Goose	___ Northern Harrier	___ Lesser Yellowlegs	___ Pomarine Jaeger	___ Chimney Swift
___ Wood Duck	___ Sharp-shinned Hawk	___ Solitary Sandpiper	___ Laughing Gull	___ Ruby-throated Hummingbird
___ Green-winged Teal	___ Broad-winged Hawk	___ Willet	___ Franklin's Gull	___ Belted Kingfisher

Geese, the largest of a dozen subspecies of Canada Geese. The big birds are almost twice the size of their smaller cousins, are non-migratory, were thought to be extinct at one time, and decoy another 7,000 geese into the sanctuary every winter. Several of the lagoons are kept ice-free in the winter as an additional enticement for waterfowl. A stroll around the lagoons revealed a variety of ducks mixed in with the geese.

A couple of hours easily slipped away as we strolled among the nearly tame ducks and geese, got close-up looks at Barred, Snowy, Short-eared and Great Horned owls at the outdoor aviary, and watched a pack of wolves in a large wooded enclosure. Making a determined effort to get some birding done, we dragged ourselves away from the wolves only to run into a fascinating nocturnal animal exhibit in a nearby building that chewed up another 20 minutes. The sorry truth is we had two hours of great birding and nature study and hardly made it 200 yards down any one of the trails that wind through the far reaches of the sanctuary.

If we'd been a little more disciplined, there is no telling what we might have run into in the sanctuary's back country. Its checklist contains 210 regularly observed species and another 34 species listed as rarities. A birder can hardly fail to find something of interest at any time of the year, but spring can bring excep-

"The presence of Snowy Owls, rare gulls, winter finches, and large numbers of geese and ducks overwintering in the area make birding a year-round activity."

___ Red-headed Woodpecker	___ Red-breasted Nuthatch	___ White-eyed Vireo	___ Ovenbird	___ Lincoln's Sparrow
___ Red-bellied Woodpecker	___ White-breasted Nuthatch	___ Solitary Vireo	___ Northern Waterthrush	___ Swamp Sparrow
___ Yellow-bellied Sapsucker	___ Brown Creeper	___ Yellow-throated Vireo	___ Louisiana Waterthrush	___ White-throated Sparrow
___ Downy Woodpecker	___ Carolina Wren	___ Warbling Vireo	___ Kentucky Warbler	___ White-crowned Sparrow
___ Hairy Woodpecker	___ Bewick's Wren	___ Philadelphia Vireo	___ Connecticut Warbler	___ Harris' Sparrow
___ Northern Flicker	___ House Wren	___ Red-eyed Vireo	___ Mourning Warbler	___ Dark-eyed Junco
___ Pileated Woodpecker	___ Winter Wren	___ Blue-winged Warbler	___ Common Yellowthroat	___ Lapland Longspur
___ Olive-sided Flycatcher	___ Sedge Wren	___ Golden-winged Warbler	___ Hooded Warbler	___ Snow Bunting
___ Eastern Wood-pewee	___ Marsh Wren	___ Tennessee Warbler	___ Wilson's Warbler	___ Bobolink
___ Yellow-bellied Flycatcher	___ Golden-crowned Kinglet	___ Orange-crowned Warbler	___ Canada Warbler	___ Red-winged Blackbird
___ Acadian Flycatcher	___ Ruby-crowned Kinglet	___ Nashville Warbler	___ Yellow-breasted Chat	___ Eastern Meadowlark
___ Alder Flycatcher	___ Blue-gray Gnatcatcher	___ Northern Parula	___ Scarlet Tanager	___ Yellow-headed Blackbird
___ Willow Flycatcher	___ Eastern Bluebird	___ Yellow Warbler	___ Summer Tanager	___ Rusty Blackbird
___ Least Flycatcher	___ Townsend's Solitaire	___ Chestnut-sided Warbler	___ Western Tanager	___ Brewer's Blackbird
___ Eastern Phoebe	___ Veery	___ Magnolia Warbler	___ Northern Cardinal	___ Common Grackle
___ Great Crested Flycatcher	___ Gray-cheeked Thrush	___ Cape May Warbler	___ Rose-breasted Grosbeak	___ Brown-headed Cowbird
___ Western Kingbird	___ Swainson's Thrush	___ Black-throated Blue Warbler	___ Indigo Bunting	___ Orchard Oriole
___ Eastern Kingbird	___ Hermit Thrush	___ Yellow-rumped Warbler	___ Rufous-sided Towhee	___ Baltimore Oriole
___ Horned Lark	___ Wood Thrush	___ Black-throated Green Warbler	___ American Tree Sparrow	___ Pine Grosbeak
___ Purple Martin	___ American Robin	___ Blackburnian Warbler	___ Chipping Sparrow	___ Purple Finch
___ Tree Swallow	___ Varied Thrush	___ Pine Warbler	___ Clay-colored Sparrow	___ House Finch
___ Northern Rough-winged Swallow	___ Gray Catbird	___ Palm Warbler	___ Field Sparrow	___ Red Crossbill
___ Bank Swallow	___ Northern Mockingbird	___ Bay-breasted Warbler	___ Vesper Sparrow	___ White-winged Crossbill
___ Cliff Swallow	___ Brown Thrasher	___ Blackpoll Warbler	___ Savannah Sparrow	___ Common Redpoll
___ Barn Swallow	___ American Pipit	___ Cerulean Warbler	___ Grasshopper Sparrow	___ Hoary Redpoll
___ Blue Jay	___ Bohemian Waxwing	___ Black-and-white Warbler	___ Henslow's Sparrow	___ Pine Siskin
___ American Crow	___ Cedar Waxwing	___ American Redstart	___ LeConte's Sparrow	___ American Goldfinch
___ Common Raven	___ Northern Shrike	___ Prothonotary Warbler	___ Fox Sparrow	___ Evening Grosbeak
___ Black-capped Chickadee	___ European Starling	___ Worm-eating Warbler	___ Song Sparrow	___ House Sparrow

"The sorry truth is we had two hours of great birding and nature study and hardly made it 200 yards down any one of the trails that wind through the far reaches of the sanctuary."

tional numbers of songbirds and warblers while the winter brings waterfowl rarities mixed in with the resident geese, Snowy Owls, and winter finches.

We found fewer distractions at the next site, the mouth of the Fox River. The river, bay, and even the adjacent parking lot are prime spots for viewing gulls, terns, and migrating shorebirds. Renard Island, just offshore and east of the mouth of the Fox River, is a nesting ground for Double-crested Cormorants, Black-crowned Night-heron, Cattle and Snowy egrets as well as Caspian, Forster's, and Common terns. Many of the birds come to the mouth of the river to feed, and others can be seen flying along the coast. From the parking lot next to the boat ramp, we spotted a Great Blue Heron and a Great Egret knee-deep in the bay and a Caspian Tern paralleling the shoreline. Scattered along the river a few semi-domesticated teal, mergansers, and Mallards paddled along with an eye out for handouts from people along the shore. We saw all the above with either the naked eye or binoculars, but a spotting scope is really essential for best results.

During migration periods, shorebirds can often be seen on and along the edges of the parking lot, but you have to get there early in the morning before they are disturbed and move on. Winter birding can be very good here, because the mouth of the Fox River is often the only open water in the area and collects waterfowl, gulls, Snowy Owls, and the occasional Bald Eagle. Iceland and Glaucous gulls have been regularly spotted in the area, especially in late winter and early spring when the ice breaks up.

Farther to the west and only a few minutes by car is the Ken Euers Nature Area. Before being diked and partially filled, this area was one of the great marshes in the Great Lakes. In spite of years of abuse, there are still extensive marshes, periodic mudflats, sedge marshes, small groves of willow and cottonwood all sitting next to the open waters of Green Bay. It is one of the finest all-around birding areas in the area, especially for waterfowl and shorebirds. There have been 35 species of shorebirds counted at the marshes including Wilson's and Red-necked phalaropes, Whimbrel, both dowitchers and various tribes of sandpipers. Redheads, Ruddy Ducks, Gadwall, Yellow-headed Blackbirds, Virginia and King rails, and Sora all nest in the area. The best times for seeing the shorebirds are either May and June or August and September when they can arrive in huge numbers.

An added inducement for a Spring trip is the arrival of warblers in late April and early May. The cottonwoods and willows act like a huge magnet for the songbirds. The area is also excellent for gulls. And it can not be ignored in the winter. Snowy Owls, Rough-legged Hawks, and Northern Shrikes are regularly spotted in the area when the snow flies.

From the parking lot at the end of Military Avenue easily walked dikes give access to two sides of the marsh and are great platforms for viewing the extensive marshes, pools, and open water of the bay. An old landfill near the parking lot presents a great panoramic view of the area. On the late June afternoon we called at the marsh, the open pools were etched by duck weed and cattails and contained Canvasbacks, Green-winged Teal, Common Goldeneye, Northern Shovelers, and scaup. Black Terns swooped over the marsh and a variety of shorebirds were busy all across the area. Birds were plentiful everywhere we looked, but a spotting scope is needed to pick species out in the farthest reaches of the marsh.

The last stop of the day was at the Barkhausen Waterfowl Preserve, a 900-acre wetland, on the west side of the bay. The preserve's cattail marshes, lagoons, ponds, and lowland hardwoods provide resting, feeding, and nesting habitat for a plethora of birds. Gulls, terns, and waterfowl can all be seen along the lakeshore and lagoons, while the lowland hardwoods collect impressive numbers of warblers, flycatchers, and other songbirds during spring migration. The marshes and lagoons draw a fine array of shorebirds and marsh species. Waterfowl seem especially fond of the preserve and congregate here in large groups in the fall, and shorebird numbers can be equally impressive when they pass through in late summer.

Nine miles of trails lace the preserve. The trails begin at the Interpretive Center which houses restrooms, nature exhibits, and birding information. The winding drive from the Preserve back to the highway passes by several pools and a small wetlands area. The drive is a great place to bird from the car. Along the short drive, we found several species of sparrow, a variety of songbirds, ducks as well as egrets, and heron fishing from the edges of the pools.

George W. Mead Wildlife Area

I felt like Forrest Gump. The temperature was somewhere above 95 degrees in the shade. If the humidity was any higher I'd need an aqualung to breathe. The mosquitoes and black flies were about to carry me off, and I had more insect bites than bird sightings. But I kept remembering what my mama always said, "Good things come to those who wait." I should have listened to Forrest's mother, "Stupid is as stupid does."

I hadn't given up and returned to the car to scratch my bites because I was at the George W. Mead Wildlife Area described by a Wisconsin Department of Natural Resources publication as "a paradise for birds and birders." So I had roamed, hiked, and glassed the area for over two hours. I stood beside ponds, lost my way on a false trail, soaked my pants, shoes and socks when skirting some wetlands, and been broiled to a fine medium-rare by the blazing sun while walking along high dikes bordering large floodings that were supposed to be packed with birds.

Barb was smart enough to stay at the headquarters building, find some shade, and read a book while she kept an eye on the Eastern Bluebird tending a nest in a box in front of the building. She could follow my progress out in the field by watching the large black cloud of flies and mosquitoes that slowly advanced and retreated across a blast furnace masquerading as a wildlife area.

I finally had to face the awful truth. Except for a snipe, a female Wood Duck nervously shepherding a curious clutch of ducklings, a Pied-billed Grebe, an assortment of sparrows, kingbirds, a lone flicker, a Yellow Warbler and a Gray Catbird that seemed to mock my every step, the birds were smarter than I and, even though it was only midmorning, had retreated to the deep shade and were staying quiet in the oppressive heat.

This forlorn trip was a great reminder that even the most highly-touted birding hotspots are going to have off days when it's just not worth making the trip and uncasing the binoculars. And the 28,000-acre George W. Mead Wildlife Area is certainly one of Wisconsin's best birding spots.

The Little Eau Pleine River flows through the heart of the area, and the Wisconsin Department of Natural Resources has constructed miles of ditches and dikes to create flowages, planted food patches, encouraged aquatic food plants, created artificial nesting sites, and planted nesting seed coverage. In addition to the man-made improvements, the area also includes a good variety of natural habitats including wetlands, upland fields, forests, and bogs. The result is an area bird checklist that boasts nearly 220 species.

Wildlife Technician Beth Arthur reports that "some of the more interesting species include Trumpeter Swans, Double-crested Cormorants, Great Blue Heron and Black-crowned Night-heron rookeries, Northern Goshawks, Osprey, and LeConte's Sparrow." Other occasional sightings of interest include Peregrine Falcons, Common Moorhens, Black-necked Stilts, Hudsonian Godwits, Red-necked Phalaropes, Blue-winged Warblers, Bonaparte's Gulls, Golden Eagles and Marbled Godwits. All of which, it goes without saying, I failed to observe. The area is especially well known for its resident Greater Prairie Chickens, and two

"The area is especially well known for its resident Greater Prairie Chickens, and two blinds are available for viewing their dancing during mating season in the spring."

LOCATION: Milladore, Wisconsin.

DIRECTIONS: From Milladore, Wisconsin take U.S. 10 west approximately 1 mile to County Road S. Turn north and drive 7 miles to the headquarters.

HOURS: Open all year. Some areas restricted from September 1 through December 10 due to hunting season.

BEST TIMES: Glorious wildlife viewing most of the year with the best birding time being April and May.

BIRDING HIGHLIGHTS: The area contains the largest man-made cormorant rookery in the state, and its bird checklist boasts more than 200 species. Prairie chickens are a sure bet. The area offers spectacular numbers and varieties of waterfowl during spring and fall migrations and is equally good for marsh and shorebirds.

FOR MORE INFORMATION: George W Mead Wildlife Area, S2148 County Highway S, Millador, WI 54454. Phone: 715-359-4522.

"The Little Eau Pleine River flows through the heart of the area, and the Wisconsin Department of Natural Resources has constructed miles of ditches and dikes to create flowages, planted food patches, encouraged aquatic food plants, created artificial nesting sites, and planted nesting seed coverage."

blinds are available for viewing their dancing during mating season in the spring. Reservations should be made for the blinds by calling the wildlife area. Arthur recommends April and May as the prime birding months but said anytime of the year can bring satisfying results.

There are four general areas that usually bring good to great results. The Townline Reservoir and Berkhahn Flowage lie on the eastern edge of the wildlife area and can be reached from a road (open to foot traffic only) that begins behind the headquarters building. The road cuts through a field swept by swallows, kingbirds and sparrows, passes through a wooded area and finally edges the marshes and open waters of the reservoir and flowage. A one-way trip is 2.5 miles. The rewards for this lengthy walk are many. The east end of Berkhahn Flowage shelters a large rookery of Great Blue Heron, Double-crested Cormorants and Black-crowned Night-heron. The area also usually contains several active Osprey nests. A wide variety of waterfowl, shorebirds and songbirds are also observable on the walk.

Almost directly opposite the headquarters building a dirt road (open to vehicular traffic) leads birders to an extensive system of walkable dikes that extend for several miles alongside pools and flowages. From the parking lot, its only a quarter-mile walk to the dikes which offer excellent viewing of the open pools and marshes that are usually home to grebes, ducks, geese, coots, bitterns, Black Terns, Yellow-headed Blackbirds and, when the water is low, numerous waders.

One mile north of the headquarters building on the west side of County Road S is a small parking lot adjacent to Teal Flowage. Although the area can be scoped from the road, it is well worth leaving the car and hiking into the interior on a dike that borders the southern edge of the flowage. Plenty of marsh birds and waterfowl can be spotted along the trail.

The last major birding area can be reached by traveling 1 mile north on County Road S to County Road C and turning west and driving approximately 3 miles to Smokey Hill Road. Turn south and drive 1 mile to the Rice Lake and Smokey Hill Flowage. Birding can be spectacular here during spring and fall migrations producing large numbers and unusual sightings of waterfowl. In the summer months the turnout of shorebirds can be equally impressive. This area also contains a restored tall grass prairie that is a favorite spot for Sandhill Cranes and Bobolinks.

GEORGE W. MEAD WILDLIFE AREA FIELD CHECKLIST

Compiled by the George W. Mead Wildlife Area.

___ Common Loon	___ Cooper's Hawk	___ Yellow-billed Cuckoo	___ Brown Creeper	___ Wilson's Warbler
___ Horned Grebe	___ Red-tailed Hawk	___ Black-billed Cuckoo	___ House Wren	___ Canada Warbler
___ Pied-billed Grebe	___ Broad-winged Hawk	___ Eastern Screech-owl	___ Marsh Wren	___ American Redstart
___ Double-crested Cormorant	___ Rough-legged Hawk	___ Great Horned Owl	___ Sedge Wren	___ House Sparrow
___ Great Blue Heron	___ Golden Eagle	___ Snowy Owl	___ Gray Catbird	___ Bobolink
___ Green Heron	___ Bald Eagle	___ Barred Owl	___ Brown Thrasher	___ Eastern Meadowlark
___ Cattle Egret	___ Northern Harrier	___ Long-eared Owl	___ American Robin	___ Western Meadowlark
___ Great Egret	___ Osprey	___ Short-eared Owl	___ Wood Thrush	___ Yellow-headed Blackbird
___ Black-crowned Night-heron	___ Peregrine Falcon	___ Northern Saw-whet Owl	___ Hermit Thrush	___ Red-winged Blackbird
___ Yellow-crowned Night-heron	___ American Kestrel	___ Whip-poor-will	___ Veery	___ Baltimore Oriole
___ Least Bittern	___ Ruffed Grouse	___ Common Nighthawk	___ Eastern Bluebird	___ Rusty Blackbird
___ American Bittern	___ Greater Prairie Chicken	___ Chimney Swift	___ Ruby-crowned Kinglet	___ Brewer's Blackbird
___ Wood Stork	___ Sharp-tailed Grouse	___ Ruby-throated Hummingbird	___ American Pipit	___ Common Grackle
___ Tundra Swan	___ Northern Bobwhite	___ Belted Kingfisher	___ Cedar Waxwing	___ Brown-headed Cowbird
___ Canada Goose	___ Ring-necked Pheasant	___ Northern Flicker	___ Golden-crowned Kinglet	___ Scarlet Tanager
___ Snow Goose	___ Sandhill Crane	___ Pileated Woodpecker	___ Northern Shrike	___ Northern Cardinal
___ Mallard	___ Virginia Rail	___ Red-headed Woodpecker	___ Starling	___ Rose-breasted Grosbeak
___ American Black Duck	___ Sora Rail	___ Yellow-bellied Sapsucker	___ Yellow-throated Vireo	___ Indigo Bunting
___ Gadwall	___ Common Moorhen	___ Hairy Woodpecker	___ Solitary Vireo	___ Evening Grosbeak
___ Northern Pintail	___ American Coot	___ Downy Woodpecker	___ Red-eyed Vireo	___ Purple Finch
___ Green-winged Teal	___ Lesser Golden-plover	___ Eastern Kingbird	___ Warbling Vireo	___ Pine Grosbeak
___ Blue-winged Teal	___ Semipalmated Plover	___ Great Crested Flycatcher	___ Black-and-white Warbler	___ Common Redpoll
___ American Wigeon	___ Killdeer	___ Eastern Phoebe	___ Golden-winged Warbler	___ Pine Siskin
___ Northern Shoveler	___ American Woodcock	___ Alder Flycatcher	___ Tennessee Warbler	___ American Goldfinch
___ Wood Duck	___ Common Snipe	___ Least Flycatcher	___ Orange-crowned Warbler	___ Rufous-sided Towhee
___ Redhead	___ Greater Yellowlegs	___ Eastern Wood-pewee	___ Nashville Warbler	___ Savannah Sparrow
___ Ring-necked Duck	___ Lesser Yellowlegs	___ Olive-sided Flycatcher	___ Northern Parula	___ Vesper Sparrow
___ Canvasback	___ Spotted Sandpiper	___ Horned Lark	___ Yellow Warbler	___ Dark-eyed Junco
___ Greater Scaup	___ Pectoral Sandpiper	___ Tree Swallow	___ Magnolia Warbler	___ American Tree Sparrow
___ Lesser Scaup	___ Baird's Sandpiper	___ Bank Swallow	___ Cape May Warbler	___ Chipping Sparrow
___ Common Goldeneye	___ Dunlin	___ Northern Rough-winged swallow	___ Yellow-rumped Warbler	___ Clay-colored Sparrow
___ Bufflehead	___ Wilson's Phalarope	___ Barn Swallow	___ Black-throated Green Warbler	___ Field Sparrow
___ Ruddy Duck	___ Solitary Sandpiper	___ Cliff Swallow	___ Blackburnian Warbler	___ White-throated Sparrow
___ Hooded Merganser	___ Herring Gull	___ Purple Martin	___ Chestnut-sided Warbler	___ Fox Sparrow
___ Common Merganser	___ Ring-billed Gull	___ Blue Jay	___ Bay-breasted Warbler	___ Swamp Sparrow
___ Red-breasted Merganser	___ Bonaparte's Gull	___ Common Raven	___ Blackpoll Warbler	___ Song Sparrow
___ Red-shouldered Hawk	___ Common Tern	___ American Crow	___ Palm Warbler	___ Lapland Sparrow
___ Turkey Vulture	___ Black Tern	___ Black-capped Chickadee	___ Ovenbird	___ Snow Bunting
___ Northern Goshawk	___ Rock Dove	___ Tufted Titmouse	___ Mourning Warbler	
___ Sharp-shinned Hawk	___ Mourning Dove	___ White-breasted Nuthatch	___ Common Yellowthroat	

Necedah National Wildlife Refuge

LOCATION: Necedah, Wisconsin.

DIRECTIONS: To reach Necedah National Wildlife Refuge drive either 5 miles west from Necedah on Highway 21, or 16 miles east on Highway 21 from its intersection with I-94. To reach Sandhill Wildlife Demonstration Area drive approximately 18 miles north of Necedah on Highway 80. One mile south of Babcock turn left on County Road X and drive 0.5 mile to the entrance.

HOURS: Necedah National Wildlife Refuge is open year round, the headquarters building is open weekdays 7:30 a.m.-4:00 p.m. Sandhill Wildlife Demonstration Area is open from mid-April to mid-November.

BEST TIMES: Spring and fall at both sites to view Sandhill Cranes and large concentrations of waterfowl. Sandhill Crane numbers peak at both sites in late October. Good songbird viewing from mid-May through summer at both sites.

BIRDING HIGHLIGHTS: Extraordinary gathering of sandhill cranes in spring and fall. Upwards of 1,000 of the giant birds can be seen at Necedah while Sandhill Wildlife Demonstration Area boasts the largest concentration of cranes in Wisconsin with up to 5,000 on hand in late October. Both sites also offer very good waterfowl viewing and good numbers of songbirds.

FOR MORE INFORMATION: Necedah National Wildlife Refuge, W7996 29th Street West, Necedah, WI 54646. Phone: (608) 565-2551. Superintendent, Sandhill-Meadow Valley Work Unit, Box 156, Babcock, WI 54413. Phone: (715) 884-2437.

I've never been a patient person and after walking for more than 15 minutes and not seeing a single bird, I was close to counting the huge horsefly that had been following, make that pestering, me as a hummingbird. As it buzzed around my head it began to assume the proportions of a hummingbird or maybe it just appeared larger than normal because it was the only other creature besides myself to be seen in the vast backyard of Necedah's headquarters building. I had left my car in a small parking lot next to the headquarters and followed signs to a trail that led through a small pocket of woods before presenting me with a view that halted me in mid-stride. In front of me was just a remnant of Great Central Wisconsin Swamp that at one time covered over 7,000 square miles of the state. If only a remnant, it was still a huge, tabletop flat expanse of marsh and meadow that stretched almost to the horizon to the north and was fringed by far-off trees to the east and west.

Turning left, I followed a work road along the edge of the vast sea of grass and kept eyes peeled for the abundance of bird and animal life that is supposed to inhabit the refuge. But in the first quarter-hour my only sighting was the, umm, "hummingbird." Trudging along the road my attention was finally drawn to a solitary tree bordering the marsh and two birds that kept circling above it and taking turns diving into the branches on the tree's north side. Intrigued by both the birds and their strange behavior I raised my binoculars and discovered a scene that made the trip to Necedah worthwhile, even if I didn't spot another bird for the rest of the day. Two Eastern Kingbirds were harassing a Great Horned Owl. For over five minutes the two flycatchers took turns dive-bombing the huge owl. Through it all, the owl sat stoically on a large branch with only its head turning slowly as it followed my progress down the road. Whether it was the much smaller birds' incessant pestering or my presence, the owl finally took flight and left the field to the aptly named kingbirds.

Returning to the car I drove to the observation platform to the east of the headquarters for a better view of the refuge and hopefully an elevated chance of seeing more birds. The two-story platform overlooks vast wetlands and Rynearson Pool and presents a markedly different perspective of the marsh than one gets from ground level. From the top of the observation deck I could see low sand ridges snaking across the landscape, open patches of water within the vast expanse of green, occasional clumps of trees rising from small islands of higher ground, and birds. A dozen Sandhill Cranes were scattered across the marsh. A Wood Duck nosed around the open water of a nearby pool, and a Northern Harrier could be seen skimming low over the marsh close to the nearest tree line.

The sight of even these few birds restored my confidence in the many claims for Necedah National Wildlife Refuge as a prime birdwatching area. Established in 1939, the logged-over and farmed-out land was "reserved and set apart as a refuge and breeding ground for migratory birds and other wildlife." A tally board at the entrance of the refuge notified visitors that over 26,000 geese, 20,000 ducks, and 751 Sandhill Cranes had been counted in the refuge the previous fall.

The refuge is a way station every spring and fall for huge numbers of migrating waterfowl, and some years as many as 50,000 ducks make a stopover here. Also, each fall usually brings Bald Eagles, Greater White-fronted Geese, and numerous Tundra Swans. The best spot from which to view all this activity is the observation deck.

The refuge's checklist numbers 221 species including 23 members of the waterfowl family, a good selection of woodpeckers, and 13 different birds of prey. The refuge is not noted for shorebirds, but late spring often finds both species of yellowlegs, several varieties of sandpipers, and occasional phalaropes and dowitchers at Rynearson Pool. Warbler and songbird traffic in spring and fall can be heavy, especially in the pine/oak forest on the east side of the refuge. This area is accessible from Main Dike Road three miles north of the village of Necedah at the spot where the road crosses the second drainage ditch north of town. Park at the ditch and walk north on the trail next to the ditch.

Among the many other birds commonly sighted throughout the refuge are Wild Turkey, Common Loons, Scarlet Tanagers, Rose-breasted Grosbeaks, Indigo Buntings, heron, bitterns, Caspian and Black terns, Red-headed Woodpeckers, and both Eastern and Western meadowlarks. Necedah is also home to one of the largest concentrations of Sandhill Cranes on any national wildlife refuge in the country with sometimes more than a 1,000 of them in residence in the spring and fall. Peak numbers are usually reached in mid-October. If more than 1,000, 4-foot tall birds isn't spectacle enough, they put on a show-stopping performance each spring with their mating dances. Gathering in large circles and spreading their 7-foot wingspans they leap into the air and break loose with eerie calls that can be heard all across the refuge.

While I stood on the observation deck trying to imagine what 1,000 hormone-overloaded cranes would look like, a Belted Kingfisher flew past and broke the spell. Even though the afternoon was winding down and there was much more of the vast 43,000-acre refuge to explore, the scene from the observation deck was too beautiful to turn my back on. I sat down on the deck, dangled my feet over the edge, leaned on a corner post, and contemplated the view. In the next 20 minutes a Red-headed Woodpecker and a Pileated Woodpecker winged past me at eye level. Tree Swallows flitted in and out of the edge of the woods, the soft calls of Cedar Waxwings drifted across the marsh, and a Red-tailed Hawk cut lazy circles in the afternoon thermals.

Finally rousing myself, I returned to the car and set out to explore the rest of the refuge on its 13-mile self-guided auto tour. A brochure with numbered paragraphs explain the natural features of the refuge and tell a bit of its history. Admittedly I was too taken with the views to read the brochure until that night. I had driven less than a mile before passing a flooded area with a white-tailed deer, hip deep in the water, browsing on the vegetation. When I stopped the car to admire the deer, a Marsh Wren working the brush near the shoulder of the road grabbed my attention. Scanning the rest of the surrounding wetlands turned up a Green-winged Teal, a multitude of Red-winged Blackbirds and a Green Heron. After passing through a variety of habitats, from pine plantations and sedge meadows to old farm fields returning to the wild, the auto tour arrives at Sprague-Mather Pool. This vast pool is another fine spot for observing ducks and geese, especially during spring and fall migrations. A dike bordering the north side of Sprague-Mather Road makes a convenient hiking trail. Be sure and check the edges of the dike for rails and wrens. Driving west on Sprague Mather Road from its intersection with Speedway Road will bring you to Bewick Trail. Turning

"If more than 1,000 4-foot-tall birds isn't spectacle enough, they put on a show-stopping performance each spring with their mating dances."

"The refuge's checklist numbers 221 species including 23 members of the waterfowl family, a good selection of woodpeckers, and 13 different birds of prey."

north on this road will take you out into the heart of Sprague-Mather Pool and wonderful viewing opportunities from the comfort of your car.

Birding can also be very good here in the winter. The auto tour follows township roads that are kept open in all but the worst winter storms. Horned Larks, Snow Buntings, American Tree Sparrows, Common Redpolls, American Goldfinches, Evening Grosbeaks, and Rough-legged Hawks are all commonly sighted while driving the roads. No matter the season, be sure and stop at the headquarters and pick up a map of the refuge, a bird checklist, and a brochure for the auto tour.

Sandhill Crane Wildlife Area, 20 miles north of Necedah, both the village and refuge headquarters, hosts the largest gathering of cranes in the entire state. Each fall between 3,000 and 5,000 convene at the 9,000-acre state wildlife area before heading south for the winter. A 14-mile self-guided auto tour wanders through a 260-acre prairie restoration area (complete with buffalo), hardwood forests, floodings, and sedge meadows. Three observation towers on the tour offer excellent views of the surrounding area and the bird life. Late October finds the largest concentrations of cranes. The best viewing is from the observation tower overlooking Gallagher Marsh, either just before sunrise or an hour before sunset. Besides cranes, the area provides food and a resting area for geese, Mallards, teal, Wood Ducks, and other waterfowl in the spring and fall.

Though best known for its cranes, the area also offers excellent birding for a variety of species from spring through summer. Warbler migration peaks in mid-May, and good songbird viewing continues throughout the summer. Chestnut-sided and Golden-winged warblers, Least and Great Crested flycatchers, Soras, rails, Ruffed Grouse, thrushes, vireos, and several species of sparrows are all regularly sighted.

In addition to the auto tour, birders can leave their cars in the parking area near the marsh observation tower and walk the road, bird by foot from atop a dike, or explore the marsh from a hiking trail that edges out into the wetlands.

NECEDAH NATIONAL WILDLIFE REFUGE FIELD CHECKLIST

___ Common Loon	___ Peregrine Falcon	___ Eastern Screech-owl	___ Marsh Wren	___ American Redstart
___ Horned Grebe	___ Merlin	___ Great Horned Owl	___ Sedge Wren	___ Bobolink
___ Pied-billed Grebe	___ American Kestrel	___ Snowy Owl	___ Gray Catbird	___ Eastern Meadowlark
___ Double-crested Cormorant	___ Ruffed Grouse	___ Barred Owl	___ Brown Thrasher	___ Western Meadowlark
___ Great Blue Heron	___ Sharp-tailed Grouse	___ Great Gray Owl	___ American Robin	___ Yellow-headed Blackbird
___ Green Heron	___ Northern Bobwhite	___ Long-eared Owl	___ Wood Thrush	___ Red-winged Blackbird
___ Cattle Egret	___ Ring-necked Pheasant	___ Short-eared Owl	___ Hermit Thrush	___ Baltimore Oriole
___ Great Egret	___ Wild Turkey	___ Northern Saw-whet Owl	___ Swainson's Thrush	___ Rusty Blackbird
___ Snowy Egret	___ Sandhill Crane	___ Whip-poor-will	___ Gray-cheeked Thrush	___ Brewer's Blackbird
___ Black-crowned Night-heron	___ Virginia Rail	___ Common Nighthawk	___ Veery	___ Common Grackle
___ Least Bittern	___ Sora	___ Chimney Swift	___ Eastern Bluebird	___ Brown-headed Cowbird
___ American Bittern	___ Common Moorhen	___ Ruby-throated Hummingbird	___ Blue-gray Gnatcatcher	___ Scarlet Tanager
___ Tundra Swan	___ American Coot	___ Belted Kingfisher	___ Golden-crowned Kinglet	___ Northern Cardinal
___ Canada Goose	___ Semipalmated Plover	___ Northern Flicker	___ Ruby-crowned Kinglet	___ Rose-breasted Grosbeak
___ Greater White-fronted Goose	___ Killdeer	___ Pileated Woodpecker	___ Bohemian Waxwing	___ Indigo Bunting
___ Snow Goose	___ Lesser Golden-plover	___ Red-bellied Woodpecker	___ Cedar Waxwing	___ Rufous-sided Towhee
___ Mallard	___ Black-bellied Plover	___ Red-headed Woodpecker	___ Northern Shrike	___ Savannah Sparrow
___ American Black Duck	___ American Woodcock	___ Yellow-bellied Sapsucker	___ Loggerhead Shrike	___ Grasshopper Sparrow
___ Gadwall	___ Common Snipe	___ Hairy Woodpecker	___ European Starling	___ Henslow's Sparrow
___ Northern Pintail	___ Upland Sandpiper	___ Downy Woodpecker	___ Yellow-throated Vireo	___ Vesper Sparrow
___ Green-winged Teal	___ Spotted Sandpiper	___ Eastern Kingbird	___ Solitary Vireo	___ Dark-eyed Junco
___ Blue-winged Teal	___ Solitary Sandpiper	___ Great Crested Flycatcher	___ Red-eyed Vireo	___ American Tree Sparrow
___ American Wigeon	___ Greater Yellowlegs	___ Eastern Phoebe	___ Warbling Vireo	___ Chipping Sparrow
___ Northern Shoveler	___ Lesser Yellowlegs	___ Yellow-bellied Flycatcher	___ Black-and-white Warbler	___ Clay-colored Sparrow
___ Wood Duck	___ Pectoral Sandpiper	___ Alder Flycatcher	___ Golden-winged Warbler	___ Field Sparrow
___ Redhead	___ White-rumped Sandpiper	___ Least Flycatcher	___ Tennessee Warbler	___ Harris' Sparrow
___ Ring-necked Duck	___ Baird's Sandpiper	___ Eastern Wood-pewee	___ Orange-crowned Warbler	___ White-crowned Sparrow
___ Canvasback	___ Least Sandpiper	___ Olive-sided Flycatcher	___ Nashville Warbler	___ White-throated Sparrow
___ Greater Scaup	___ Dunlin	___ Horned Lark	___ Northern Parula	___ Fox Sparrow
___ Lesser Scaup	___ Short-billed Dowitcher	___ Tree Swallow	___ Yellow Warbler	___ Lincoln's Sparrow
___ Common Goldeneye	___ Long-billed Dowitcher	___ Bank Swallow	___ Magnolia Warbler	___ Swamp Sparrow
___ Bufflehead	___ Stilt Sandpiper	___ Northern Rough-winged Swallow	___ Cape May Warbler	___ Song Sparrow
___ Ruddy Duck	___ Semipalmated Sandpiper	___ Barn Swallow	___ Black-throated Blue Warbler	___ Lapland Longspur
___ Hooded Merganser	___ Western Sandpiper	___ Cliff Swallow	___ Blackburnian Warbler	___ Snow Bunting
___ Red-breasted Merganser	___ Wilson's Phalarope	___ Purple Martin	___ Chestnut-sided Warbler	___ Evening Grosbeak
___ Turkey Vulture	___ Herring Gull	___ Gray Jay	___ Bay-breasted Warbler	___ Purple Finch
___ Northern Goshawk	___ Ring-billed Gull	___ Blue Jay	___ Blackpoll Warbler	___ Pine Grosbeak
___ Sharp-shinned Hawk	___ Bonaparte's Gull	___ Common Raven	___ Pine Warbler	___ Common Redpoll
___ Cooper's Hawk	___ Forster's Tern	___ American Crow	___ Palm Warbler	___ Pine Siskin
___ Red-tailed Hawk	___ Common Tern	___ Black-capped Chickadee	___ Ovenbird	___ American Goldfinch
___ Red-shouldered Hawk	___ Caspian Tern	___ Tufted Titmouse	___ Northern Waterthrush	___ Red Crossbill
___ Broad-winged Hawk	___ Black Tern	___ White-breasted Nuthatch	___ Connecticut Warbler	___ White-winged Crossbill
___ Rough-legged Hawk	___ Rock Dove	___ Red-breasted Nuthatch	___ Mourning Warbler	___ House Sparrow
___ Golden Eagle	___ Mourning Dove	___ Brown Creeper	___ Common Yellowthroat	
___ Northern Harrier	___ Yellow-billed Cuckoo	___ House Wren	___ Wilson's Warbler	
___ Osprey	___ Black-billed Cuckoo	___ Winter Wren	___ Canada Warbler	

Horicon Marsh National Wildlife Refuge

"A Marsh Wren flitted across the gently rocking boards close enough to untie my shoelaces, found a perch just above the water, and welcomed us to the magnificent marsh with his throaty call."

LOCATION: Horicon, Wisconsin.

DIRECTIONS: Wisconsin Highways 28 and 49 border the marsh on the north and south. The area is approximately 40 miles northeast of Madison and the same distance northwest of Milwaukee.

HOURS: Open dawn to dusk year-round. Special hours and seasons for the auto tour and Dike Road.

BEST TIMES: March and September/October concentrations of geese is one of the great natural spectacles in the Midwest. Spring and fall migrations offer exceptional birding and resident waterfowl and a good number of shore- and marsh birds keep things interesting in the summer.

BIRDING HIGHLIGHTS: Spectacular concentrations of geese and waterfowl in spring and fall. Very good shore- and marsh bird viewing. More than 248 species have been recorded in the area, half of which are nesters, and many rarities have also been sighted.

FOR MORE INFORMATION: Horicon National Wildlife Refuge, Route 2, Mayville, WI 53050. Phone: (414) 387-2658.

We could hear them long before we saw them. As my wife and I walked out on the floating boardwalk into Horicon Marsh, the largest cattail marsh in the United States, Virginia Rails sent up loud complaints. Whether they were directed at their young or us, it sure sounded like someone was being scolded. The calls became so harsh and strident that our attention was drawn away from the Black-crowned Night-heron, egrets, Black Terns and Pied-billed Grebes who seemed to be taking our intrusion into their world with a much more laid-back attitude.

Then as I looked down to make sure of my footing while crossing from one section of the floating walkway to another, a brazen rail stepped onto the boardwalk and preceded me for a dozen feet before stepping back off the path and seemingly walked on water and into the rushes. With his appearance the area came alive with rails. We were surrounded by the calling birds as they crossed and recrossed the boardwalk or paralleled our progress in the cattails. As quickly as they appeared they disappeared. Then to punctuate my amazement, a Marsh Wren flitted across the gently rocking boards close enough to untie my shoelaces, found a perch just above the water, and welcomed us to the magnificent Horicon Marsh with his throaty call.

It was the high point of our day and clearly eclipsed the stunning view of the marsh from the top of a hill on Wisconsin Highway 49. To read that it's the largest such marsh in America and to see it are two entirely different things. Topping the hill the view is simply jaw-dropping. The last glacial incursion into Wisconsin sculpted out a huge shallow lakebed nearly five miles wide and more than twice as long. Over the eons the lake filled in with cattails and created one of the prime birding habitats in the Midwest. The sea of moving cattails fills your view, and the wide expanse of green is dotted by large pools of open water. The hills ringing the marsh are occupied by large, neat farms that make a beautiful counterpoint to the sea of grass. I thought this view alone was worth the trip until Barb and I stepped out in the marsh on the floating Egret Trail.

Settlers in the 1840s dammed the Rock River, which flows through the center of the marsh, but after protests from other farmers who watched their farms sink under the waters, the dam was removed in the 1860s. The upper two-thirds of the marsh was designated a National Wildlife Refuge in 1941, and the bottom one-third of the marsh is a Wisconsin Department of Natural Resources Wildlife Area. Taken altogether it presents both experienced and novice birders a multitude of opportunities for fantastic birding.

In the spring and fall, upwards of 200,000 Canada Geese call at the marsh during their biannual migrations and attract so many people to the spectacle that there have been 10-mile-long traffic jams on Highway 49, the only public road that crosses the marsh and the best spot from which to be awed by the congregating geese. The marsh is also home to one of the largest Great Blue Heron rookeries in the Midwest and is the largest nesting area of Redhead Ducks east of the Mississippi. The 31,000-acre area is mainly composed of wetlands with a lesser extent of upland grasses and an almost insignificant 500 acres of woodland. More than 248 bird species have been recorded in the area and nearly half that number nest here.

Starting from the northwest corner of the marsh where the National Wildlife Refuge has built a 3-mile-long auto tour (open 8:00 a.m.-3:00 p.m. daily) and moving in a clockwise direction around the marsh there are a number of excellent sites from which to enjoy the resident birdlife. Located at the eleven o'clock position the auto tour takes motorists through a variety of habitat and excellent birding spots from the comfort of your car. Additionally, six miles of hiking trails web the same area and include the Egret Trail. The upland meadows hold a variety of sparrows including Savannah, Field, and occasionally Henslow's and Grasshopper. Both Eastern and Western Meadowlarks can be found here as well as Bobolinks. A small woodlot is a magnet for migrating songbirds during spring migration and summer residents include: Indigo Bunting, Great Crested and Willow flycatchers, flickers and Eastern Wood-pewees. There are seven pull-offs or stops on the auto trail including the not-to-be-missed Egret Trail. Heron, terns, kingbirds, coots, rails, Soras, and a wealth of ducks are sure bets on the 0.4-mile trail as well as some pleasing surprises. From the same pull-off, birders can also access the half-mile Red Fox Trail that offers a sampling of several micro habitats.

Highway 49 which cuts across the north end of the marsh is located at twelve o'clock straight up position on the marsh clock face. In spite of this being a major east/west highway with semis and cars speeding past at 55 mph plus, the shoulders of the road are packed bumper-to-bumper with cars in March and October/November when the geese invade the refuge and put on one of the great nature spectacles in the Midwest as they fly in and out of the refuge each morning and evening. The Fish and Wildlife Service has named it as one of the outstanding photographic opportunities in the entire national wildlife refuge system.

The roadway presents excellent viewing points for several large pools that can contain Mallards, Ruddy Ducks, American Black Ducks, Northern Shovelers, Blue and Green-winged teal, Redhead, Lesser Scaup, Ring-necked Ducks, and hundreds of coots. Black and Forster's terns, Yellow-headed Blackbirds, Eared and Red-necked grebes, and bitterns are also frequently spotted from the highway.

At the intersection of Highway 49 and County Road Z on the northeastern corner (at the one o'clock position) of the marsh the National Wildlife Refuge has constructed a scenic overlook. Ample parking, restrooms and a great view of the marsh can be had away from the traffic on the highway. The overlook presents a panoramic view of the northern end of the marsh and is a fine vantage point from which to view the waterfowl show in spring and fall.

Approximately 1.5 miles south of the intersection of County Road Z and Highway 49, Ledge Road heads west from County Road Z into the heart of the northern section of the marsh. The road borders Strooks Drain and edges a half-mile out into the marsh and ends in an overlook. The road is a proven producer of birds and most of the marsh birds that reside or visit the area can, at one time or another, be spotted here. The road is also the point from which the state's only known sighting of White-faced Ibis occurred.

The National Wildlife Refuge headquarters is at the three o'clock position on County Road Z. The headquarters building has detailed maps of the area, birdlists and personnel can direct visitors to the seasonal hotspots.

Just a short distance south of the headquarters, a bare half-hour on the clock face is Dike Road which forms a 3-mile arrow-straight platform into the heart of

"In the spring and fall, upwards of 200,000 Canada Geese call at the marsh during their biannual migrations and attract so many people to the spectacle that there have been 10-mile-long traffic jams on the only public road that crosses the marsh."

VIRGINIA RAIL

the marsh. Open to the public from April 15 to September 15, Dike Road is the only way to experience the interior of the marsh from terra firma. Cattails and several large pools reach to within a couple of feet of the elevated roadway and keep motorists eagerly craning their necks to the right and left for a wide variety of waterfowl, marsh birds and shorebirds. The last mile of the road is especially good in late summer if water levels have gone down. When conditions are right shorebirds by the hundreds gather here and can include Red-necked Phalaropes, Black-necked Stilts and other Wisconsin rarities. A small clump of woods at the end of the road and another near the entrance to the dike are great for songbirds during spring and fall migrations.

About a mile south of Dike Road, Greenhead Road ends at the Rock River and a boat landing from which a canoe can be launched. Canoeing may be the best means of birding the marsh, and from the landing it's an hour's trip to Fourmile Island Heron Rookery. In late April and early May hundreds of Great Blue Heron, Great Egrets, Black-crowned Night-heron and Double-crested Cormorants nest on the island. The island is closed to visitors, but the view is memorable from the water. Canoes can be rented in the City of Horicon. Only the state-owned part of the marsh is open to canoeists.

Further south at the five o'clock position is the state Department of Natural Resources headquarters. The building sits on top of a low hill at the end of Palmatory Road, reached from Highway 28 on the east side of the town of Horicon, and presents one of the best views of the marsh to be found anywhere. Birders with spotting scopes can spend hours here searching the open pools for birds. A 1.5-mile hiking trail decamps from a parking lot just short of the headquarters building and cuts through a stand of timber before bordering the marsh. This and the other small woodlots surrounding the marsh are wonderful concentrators of warblers and other song birds during spring migration in May.

In the town of Horicon a half-mile trail pushes out into the marsh from the boat landing at the end of Nebraska Street. The Horicon Marsh Boat Tours operates out of the town and takes sightseers and birders on one and two-hour tours of the marsh aboard a pontoon raft. They also rent canoes. For more information and prices call (414) 485-4663.

On the west side of the marsh Burnett Ditch Road (at the eight o'clock position) extends three-quarters of a mile into the marsh and provides access to canoes. The short drive features bitterns, rails, Soras, and a wide variety of shore and water birds.

In addition to all the above mentioned access points the county roads surrounding the marsh and especially County Road Z, are not only pleasant and scenic but offer motorists views of sandhill cranes feeding in farm fields or egrets, heron, and hawks on wing in the skies above.

HORICON MARSH NATIONAL WILDLIFE REFUGE FIELD CHECKLIST

Compiled and published by the wildlife refuge.

___ Pied-billed Grebe	___ Virginia Rail	___ Yellow-bellied Flycatcher	___ Yellow-rumped Warbler	___ American Goldfinch
___ Horned Grebe	___ Sora	___ Alder Flycatcher	___ Black-throated Green Warbler	___ Evening Grosbeak
___ American White Pelican	___ Common Moorhen	___ Willow Flycatcher	___ Blackburnian Warbler	___ House Sparrow
___ Double-crested Cormorant	___ American Coot	___ Least Flycatcher	___ Pine Warbler	
___ American Bittern	___ Sandhill Crane	___ Eastern Phoebe	___ Palm Warbler	ACCIDENTALS
___ Least Bittern	___ Black-bellied Plover	___ Great Crested Flycatcher	___ Bay-breasted Warbler	___ Common Loon
___ Great Blue Heron	___ Lesser Golden-plover	___ Eastern Kingbird	___ Blackpoll Warbler	___ Red-necked Grebe
___ Great Egret	___ Semipalmated Plover	___ Horned Lark	___ Black-and-white Warbler	___ Western Grebe
___ Snowy Egret	___ Killdeer	___ Purple Martin	___ American Redstart	___ Little Blue Heron
___ Cattle Egret	___ Greater Yellowlegs	___ Tree Swallow	___ Ovenbird	___ Glossy Ibis
___ Green Heron	___ Lesser Yellowlegs	___ Northern Rough-winged Swallow	___ Northern Waterthrush	___ White-faced Ibis
___ Black-crowned Night-heron	___ Solitary Sandpiper	___ Bank Swallow	___ Louisiana Waterthrush	___ Mute Swan
___ Yellow-crowned Night-heron	___ Spotted Sandpiper	___ Cliff Swallow	___ Connecticut Warbler	___ Ross' Gull
___ Tundra Swan	___ Semipalmated Sandpiper	___ Barn Swallow	___ Mourning Warbler	___ Brant
___ Trumpeter Swan	___ Least Sandpiper	___ Blue Jay	___ Common Yellowthroat	___ Cinnamon Teal
___ Greater White-fronted Goose	___ White-rumped Sandpiper	___ American Crow	___ Wilson's Warbler	___ Black Scoter
___ Snow Goose	___ Baird's Sandpiper	___ Black-capped Chickadee	___ Canada Warbler	___ Oldsquaw
___ Canada Goose	___ Pectoral Sandpiper	___ Red-breasted Nuthatch	___ Scarlet Tanager	___ Golden Eagle
___ Wood Duck	___ Buff-breasted Sandpiper	___ White-breasted Nuthatch	___ Northern Cardinal	___ Northern Goshawk
___ American Black Duck	___ Dunlin	___ Brown Creeper	___ Rose-breasted Grosbeak	___ Merlin
___ Mallard	___ Stilt Sandpiper	___ House Wren	___ Indigo Bunting	___ Northern Bobwhite
___ Northern Pintail	___ Short-billed Dowitcher	___ Winter Wren	___ Dickcissel	___ Wild Turkey
___ Green-winged Teal	___ Long-billed Dowitcher	___ Sedge Wren	___ Rufous-sided Towhee	___ American Avocet
___ Blue-winged Teal	___ Common Snipe	___ Marsh Wren	___ American Tree Sparrow	___ Willet
___ Northern Shoveler	___ American Woodcock	___ Golden-crowned Kinglet	___ Chipping Sparrow	___ Ruddy Turnstone
___ Gadwall	___ Wilson's Phalarope	___ Ruby-crowned Kinglet	___ Clay-colored Sparrow	___ Black-necked Stilt
___ American Wigeon	___ Red-necked Phalarope	___ Blue-gray Gnatcatcher	___ Field Sparrow	___ Upland Sandpiper
___ Canvasback	___ Bonaparte's Gull	___ Eastern Bluebird	___ Vesper Sparrow	___ Marbled Godwit
___ Redhead	___ Ring-billed Gull	___ Veery	___ Savannah Sparrow	___ Hudsonian Godwit
___ Ring-necked Duck	___ Herring Gull	___ Gray-cheeked Thrush	___ Grasshopper Sparrow	___ Sanderling
___ Greater Scaup	___ Forster's Tern	___ Swainson's Thrush	___ Henslow's Sparrow	___ Ruff
___ Lesser Scaup	___ Black Tern	___ Hermit Thrush	___ Fox Sparrow	___ Caspian Tern
___ Common Goldeneye	___ Rock Dove	___ Wood Thrush	___ Song Sparrow	___ Common Tern
___ Bufflehead	___ Mourning Dove	___ American Robin	___ Lincoln's Sparrow	___ Saw-whet Owl
___ Hooded Merganser	___ Black-billed Cuckoo	___ Gray Catbird	___ Swamp Sparrow	___ Whip-poor-will
___ Common Merganser	___ Yellow-billed Cuckoo	___ Brown Thrasher	___ White-throated Sparrow	___ Tufted Titmouse
___ Red-breasted Merganser	___ Eastern Screech-owl	___ Cedar Waxwing	___ White-crowned Sparrow	___ Carolina Wren
___ Ruddy Duck	___ Great Horned Owl	___ Northern Shrike	___ Harris' Sparrow	___ Northern Mockingbird
___ Turkey Vulture	___ Snowy Owl	___ European Starling	___ Dark-eyed Junco	___ Loggerhead Shrike
___ Osprey	___ Barred Owl	___ Solitary Vireo	___ Lapland Longspur	___ Bell's Vireo
___ Bald Eagle	___ Long-eared Owl	___ Yellow-throated Vireo	___ Snow Bunting	___ Prothonotary Warbler
___ Northern Harrier	___ Short-eared Owl	___ Warbling Vireo	___ Bobolink	___ Cerulean Warbler
___ Sharp-shinned Hawk	___ Common Nighthawk	___ Philadelphia Vireo	___ Eastern Meadowlark	___ Black-throated Blue Warbler
___ Cooper's Hawk	___ Chimney Swift	___ Red-eyed Vireo	___ Western Meadowlark	___ Worm-eating Warbler
___ Red-shouldered Hawk	___ Ruby-throated Hummingbird	___ Blue-winged Warbler	___ Red-winged Blackbird	___ Yellow-breasted Chat
___ Broad-winged Hawk	___ Belted Kingfisher	___ Golden-winged Warbler	___ Yellow-headed Blackbird	___ Lark Sparrow
___ Red-tailed Hawk	___ Red-headed Woodpecker	___ Tennessee Warbler	___ Rusty Blackbird	___ Pine Siskin
___ Rough-legged Hawk	___ Red-bellied Woodpecker	___ Orange-crowned Warbler	___ Brewer's Blackbird	___ Pine Grosbeak
___ American Kestrel	___ Yellow-bellied Sapsucker	___ Nashville Warbler	___ Common Grackle	
___ Peregrine Falcon	___ Downy Woodpecker	___ Northern Parula	___ Brown-headed Cowbird	
___ Gray Partridge	___ Hairy Woodpecker	___ Yellow Warbler	___ Baltimore Oriole	
___ Ring-necked Pheasant	___ Northern Flicker	___ Chestnut-sided Warbler	___ Purple Finch	
___ Yellow Rail	___ Olive-sided Flycatcher	___ Magnolia Warbler	___ House Finch	
___ King Rail	___ Eastern Wood-pewee	___ Cape May Warbler	___ Common Redpoll	

Wyalusing State Park

"From the views atop the bluff, to the lush bottomland bordering the Mississippi and the forest-clad ravines, to the open meadows and upland forests back from the rivers, the park pleases the eye in every direction and seems absolutely stuffed to capacity with birds of every size and description."

No matter how dedicated a birder you are, the first priority at this 2,600-acre state park in the southwest corner of Wisconsin is a visit to the bluffs overlooking the confluence of the Wisconsin and Mississippi rivers. The jaw-dropping view from 500 feet above the two rivers is one of the most spectacular sights in the Midwest.

As I sat in contemplation of the magnificent scenery and the fact that I was looking at the spot where Father Marquette and Louis Joliet became the first Europeans to be borne on the back of the Father of Waters, a sparrow lit on a nearby branch and joined me for the view. In 1673, the two explorers floated down the Wisconsin River and discovered the Mississippi. I was impressed, but I can't say the same for the sparrow, or the huge Broad-winged Hawk that flashed through the trees and out over the dropoff, or the numerous hawks and Turkey Vultures soaring on the updrafts kicked up by the long line of bluffs bordering the two rivers.

The park is a feast for the eyes. From the views atop the bluff, to the lush bottomland bordering the Mississippi and the forest-clad ravines, to the open meadows and upland forests back from the rivers, the park pleases the eye in every direction and seems absolutely stuffed to capacity with birds of every size and description.

Yes, the park is more than just a pretty face, it's a birder's paradise. Over 90 species nest within the park, and another 100 pass through during spring and fall migrations. Birding is great anytime of year, and the park is one of the great birding spots during the dog days of summer.

I hit the park in mid-July and the bird activity was simply feverish. As promised by the park ranger at the office, the boat landing area at the end of Long Valley Road offered the best all around birding in the park. Just back from the boat landing, the road crosses a double set of railroad tracks. As I stood on the shoulder of the road near the tracks, one bush yielded two Baltimore Orioles, a Prothonotary Warbler, a Red-eyed Vireo, and a male and female American Redstart in only ten minutes.

Turning from the bush an Indigo Bunting perched in the sun across the tracks, and just a few steps along the Sugar Maple Trail which begins near the tracks, a family of Eastern Phoebes busily went about feeding. Further along the trail a Yellow-bellied Sapsucker disrupted the quiet of the woods as he began mining a nearby tree. All this in the first 20 minutes after leaving the car! It was going to be a great day.

Based on all available evidence, there are a lot of great days for birders at Wyalusing, and plenty of spots within the park that call for attention. Long Valley Road is a favorite haunt for Kentucky Warblers. Although Wyalusing marks the northern edge of their range, these hipsters of the warbler family, with their long black sideburns who look like they're wearing yellow glasses, regularly nest in the park. They can usually be heard, if not seen along Long Valley Road. A slow drive, or better yet, a walk along the tree-crowded lane will likely produce plenty of other woodland birds in addition to Kentucky Warblers. During spring migration, the road is often chock-a-block full of warblers, flycatchers, and other passerines.

Along the bluff line, from both the picnic grounds and the campground, nu-

LOCATION: Bagley, Wisconsin.

DIRECTIONS: From U.S. 18 five miles east of Prairie du Chein turn right on County Highway C and drive to County Highway X. The park entrance is right 1 mile on County Highway X. Signs from U.S. 18 lead motorists to the park.

HOURS: The park is open year-round from dawn-11:00 p.m. Only registered campers are allowed in the park after 11:00 p.m.

BEST TIMES: Spring through fall.

BIRDING HIGHLIGHTS: Noted for Wild Turkeys and Kentucky Warblers. Great summer birding with nearly 100 species nesting in the park.

FOR MORE INFORMATION: Wyalusing State Park, 13342 County Highway C, Bagley, WI 53801 Phone:(608) 996-2261.

WYALUSING STATE PARK FIELD CHECKLIST

___ Horned Grebe	___ Osprey	___ Downy Woodpecker	___ Cedar Waxwing	___ Bobolink
___ Pied-billed Grebe	___ Merlin	___ Eastern Kingbird	___ Loggerhead Shrike	___ Eastern Meadowlark
___ Double-crested Cormorant	___ American Kestrel	___ Great Crested Flycatcher	___ European Starling	___ Western Meadowlark
___ Great Blue Heron	___ Ruffed Grouse	___ Eastern Phoebe	___ Bell's Vireo	___ Red-winged Blackbird
___ Green Heron	___ Northern Bobwhite	___ Acadian Flycatcher	___ Yellow-throated Vireo	___ Baltimore Oriole
___ Great Egret	___ Wild Turkey	___ Least Flycatcher	___ Solitary Vireo	___ Rusty Blackbird
___ Black-crowned Night-heron	___ Gray Partridge	___ Eastern Wood-peewee	___ Red-eyed Vireo	___ Brewer's Blackbird
___ American Bittern	___ Sandhill Crane	___ Olive-sided Flycatcher	___ Warbling Vireo	___ Common Grackle
___ Canada Goose	___ American Coot	___ Horned Lark	___ Black-and-white Warbler	___ Brown-headed Cowbird
___ Snow Goose	___ Killdeer	___ Tree Swallow	___ Prothonotary Warbler	___ Scarlet Tanager
___ Mallard	___ Upland Sandpiper	___ Bank Swallow	___ Worm-eating Warbler	___ Northern Cardinal
___ American Black Duck	___ Greater Yellowlegs	___ Northern Rough-winged Swallow	___ Golden-winged Warbler	___ Rose-breasted Grosbeak
___ Gadwall	___ Lesser Yellowlegs	___ Barn Swallow	___ Blue-winged Warbler	___ Indigo Bunting
___ Northern Pintail	___ Solitary Sandpiper	___ Cliff Swallow	___ Tennessee Warbler	___ Common Redpoll
___ Green-winged Teal	___ Spotted Sandpiper	___ Purple Martin	___ Orange-crowned Warbler	___ Dickcissel
___ Blue-winged Teal	___ American Woodcock	___ Blue Jay	___ Nashville Warbler	___ Evening Grosbeak
___ American Wigeon	___ Common Snipe	___ American Crow	___ Northern Parula	___ Purple Finch
___ Northern Shoveler	___ Least Sandpiper	___ Black-capped Chickadee	___ Yellow Warbler	___ American Goldfinch
___ Wood Duck	___ Pectoral Sandpiper	___ Tufted Titmouse	___ Magnolia Warbler	___ Rufous-sided Towhee
___ Redhead	___ Herring Gull	___ White-breasted Nuthatch	___ Cape May Warbler	___ Savannah sparrow
___ Ring-necked Duck	___ Forster's Tern	___ Red-breasted Nuthatch	___ Black-throated Blue Warbler	___ Grasshopper Sparrow
___ Canvasback	___ Rock Dove	___ Brown Creeper	___ Yellow-rumped Warbler	___ Henslow's Sparrow
___ Lesser Scaup	___ Mourning Dove	___ House Wren	___ Black-throated Green Warbler	___ Vesper Sparrow
___ Common Goldeneye	___ Yellow-billed Cuckoo	___ Winter Wren	___ Cerulean Warbler	___ Lark Sparrow
___ Bufflehead	___ Black-billed Cuckoo	___ Bewick's Wren	___ Blackburnian Warbler	___ Dark-eyed Junco
___ Ruddy Duck	___ Eastern Screech-owl	___ Marsh Wren	___ Chestnut-sided Warbler	___ American Tree Sparrow
___ Hooded Merganser	___ Great Horned Owl	___ Sedge Wren	___ Bay-breasted Warbler	___ Chipping Sparrow
___ Common Merganser	___ Barred Owl	___ Gray Catbird	___ Blackpoll Warbler	___ Field Sparrow
___ Red-breasted Merganser	___ Whip-poor-will	___ Brown Thrasher	___ Palm Warbler	___ Harris' Sparrow
___ Turkey Vulture	___ Common Nighthawk	___ American Robin	___ Ovenbird	___ White-crowned Sparrow
___ Sharp-shinned Hawk	___ Chimney Swift	___ Wood Thrush	___ Northern Waterthrush	___ White-throated Sparrow
___ Cooper's Hawk	___ Ruby-throated Hummingbird	___ Hermit Thrush	___ Louisiana Waterthrush	___ Fox Sparrow
___ Red-tailed Hawk	___ Belted Kingfisher	___ Swainson's Thrush	___ Kentucky Warbler	___ Lincoln's Sparrow
___ Red-shouldered Hawk	___ Northern Flicker	___ Gray-cheeked Thrush	___ Mourning Warbler	___ Swamp Sparrow
___ Broad-winged Hawk	___ Pileated Woodpecker	___ Veery	___ Common Yellowthroat	___ Song Sparrow
___ Rough-legged Hawk	___ Red-bellied Woodpecker	___ Eastern Bluebird	___ Wilson's Warbler	___ Snow Bunting
___ Bald Eagle	___ Red-headed Woodpecker	___ Blue-gray Gnatcatcher	___ Canada Warbler	
___ Northern Harrier	___ Yellow-bellied Sapsucker	___ Golden-crowned Kinglet	___ American Redstart	
___ Peregrine Falcon	___ Hairy Woodpecker	___ Ruby-crowned Kinglet	___ House Sparrow	

merous trails lead down the steep incline toward the river and offer excellent birding. The trails can be difficult walking but return the hard work with splendid scenery and prime birding, especially for warblers.

Birders who come equipped with canoes or boats shouldn't pass up the opportunity to search for egrets, heron, and waterfowl in the backwater sloughs of the Mississippi immediately adjacent to the boat landing.

Back from the bluffs several trails cut through open fields and skirt or cut through upland woods. The Turkey Hollow Trail and the Walnut Springs Trail both depart from a parking area on the main entrance road about halfway between the entrance and the park office. Both trails hold promise for sighting Eastern and Western meadowlarks, Bobolinks, Henslow's Sparrows, Wild Turkeys, Bell's Vireo, and other species that like open fields and upland forests.

An equally good way to bird the park is just to slowly drive the many paved roads. On any of the scenic byways birds are constantly flitting in front of your windshield or singing from shrubs at the edge of the pavement. Midsummer seems especially good for birding by auto with every other roadside bush holding young fledglings begging their parents for food. Traffic is usually light enough and the shoulder wide enough in most places to pull off for closer looks when an unusual bird is sighted or you hit a hot spot.

Wyalusing State Park is also worth a visit in the winter when Bald Eagles can be observed from the bluffs as they soar above the Mississippi. In March the park is witness to great waterfowl passages as the birds make their way north along the Mississippi flyway.

Trempealeau National Wildlife Refuge

"The drive offers great birding from the comfort of a car, but many places are so inviting that it is almost impossible not to stop and search for birds on foot."

LOCATION: Trempealeau, Wisconsin.

DIRECTIONS: Drive west of Centerville, Wisconsin on State Highway 35 to West Prairie Road and turn south. The entrance to the refuge is approximately 1 mile south on West Prairie.

HOURS: Open all year sunrise to sunset.

BEST TIMES: Spring and fall for migrating waterfowl, March for Bald Eagles and mid-May for warblers and songbirds.

BIRDING HIGHLIGHTS: Each season at Trempealeau offers special attractions. Large numbers of Bald Eagles funnel into the refuge in early March waiting for the ice to break up on the upper Mississippi. Good concentrations of waterfowl arrive in early spring and the refuge offers some of the best warbler and songbird viewing in the region. There is good birding here for a wide variety of birds throughout late spring and summer, and the year culminates with spectacular concentrations of waterfowl in October.

FOR MORE INFORMATION: Trempealeau National Wildlife Refuge, Rt. 1, Box 1602, Trempealeau, WI 54661. Phone: (608) 539-2311

I assumed that water would be one of the dominating factors at this national wildlife refuge that lay between the Trempealeau and Mississippi rivers, but this was more than I bargained for. Barb and I arrived in late March. Turning into the refuge's entrance, we were stopped in our tracks. The Trempealeau River had overflowed its banks and was washing over the refuge's entrance road. At first glance it looked like it would be a very brief trip to what the refuge's brochure bragged is "one of Wisconsin's best kept secrets!"

The 5,700-acre Trempealeau National Wildlife Refuge lies in the lowland Mississippi River corridor and through nature's design and the accidental hand of man, it has become an extremely inviting place for birds. The sloughs, marshes, and old oxbow lakes bordering the Mississippi have attracted birds from time immemorial, and the coming of railroads in the 1800s serendipitously preserved the habitat from further destruction. The tracks of three railroads enclose the refuge. The railroad beds, acting as dikes, have preserved the refuge from both siltation and pollution. The refuge's bird list, which totals 251 species, attests to the importance of the area as a resting and breeding ground for birds. But it looked like the Trempealeau River was going to keep Trempealeau a well-guarded secret, at least from us, until we spotted a small sign directing visitors to a back entrance to the refuge.

Marshland Road, a couple of miles west of the main entrance, carried us over the flooded bottomland forest of the refuge and eventually led to the headquarters where Doug Damberg, Assistant Refuge Manager, tantalized us with stories about the richness of bird life here and highlighted a refuge map with the best places to bird. The morning of our arrival Damberg had counted 35 Bald Eagles in the refuge, and only a couple of weeks earlier 138 eagles were counted just from the refuge's observation deck. The refuge is an annual gathering place for eagles as they await the ice breakup on the upper Mississippi, and early March usually finds the eagle population peaking in the refuge. The highest one-day total for the year was 160. The best places to spot the birds are either from the observation deck or the boat launching ramp and the lagoon that nearly encloses it. Later in the morning when we visited the boat launching ramp it was not hard to see why eagles favored the place; dead carp were stacked like cord wood along the nearby shore. We disturbed three eagles that had been enjoying the feast.

In addition to eagles, Damberg had also spotted Sandhill Cranes, an Eastern Meadowlark, several Great Blue Heron, and a wide variety of waterfowl the morning we arrived. Our appetites thoroughly whetted, we set off to explore the refuge. Our first stop was the observation platform overlooking a vast wetlands bordering the Mississippi. An area that in a few short weeks would hold Yellow-headed Blackbirds, cormorants, terns, bitterns, and Osprey was solidly iced over and the only bird in sight was a Bald Eagle perched on a distant tree.

To the right of the observation deck and the small parking area are two of the best birding walks in the refuge. The Pine Creek Dike, an abandoned railroad bed, cuts a straight line into the wetlands and borders several oxbow lakes that are favored by numerous ducks. Near the junction of the refuge road and Pine Creek Dike, the Woodland Trail meanders through a dense stand of hardwoods. Damberg recommends Pine Creek Dike and the Woodland Trail as not only the best place in the refuge for spotting warblers in mid-May but the best place in the entire region for warblers and other songbirds. A short walk on the dike flushed a variety of waterfowl from small patches of open water, including Northern Shovelers, Wood Ducks, Mallards, mergansers, and what I think was a briefly glimpsed Common Goldeneye.

A half-mile drive to the east of the observation deck on Marshland Road a narrow drive leads to the boat launching ramp and parking lot. From the parking lot, birders have only a short walk to Kiep's Island, the second best warbler viewing area in the refuge, via a narrow causeway. It was too early in the spring to hope for any warblers, but a 20-minute walk scared up a Northern Harrier, an immature Bald Eagle, a noisy gaggle of grackles, a Great Blue Heron, and a Sandhill Crane. The small island features hardwoods, wooded swamps, and plenty of brush; it should be a great place for spotting songbirds later in the spring. In October large numbers of Tundra Swans, American White Pelicans and a wide variety of waterfowl can be seen from both Kiep's Island and the observation deck.

Back in the car we continued to explore the refuge on a 5-mile long wildlife drive that takes the birder through open prairies, alongside marshes and hardwood floodplains and edges the Mississippi backwaters. We heard but couldn't spot an Eastern Meadowlark, checked off several sparrows and caught sight of Wood Ducks, Mallards and the teal drifting in the flooded woodlands. The drive offers great birding from the comfort of a car, but many places are so inviting that it is almost impossible not to stop and search for birds on foot. One of the most inviting is where the entrance road crosses the Trempealeau River. A small parking lot south of the Trempealeau River allows visitors to sweep a wide expanse of prairie to the south, investigate the wooded edge of the river, and on our visit, get a close-up look at the river pouring over the entrance road.

Mr. Damberg also recommends Delta Road on the western edge of the refuge for terns, heron and egrets later in the spring and through the summer. The road is closed to vehicles but is easily walked. No matter where we drove, Turkey Vultures could be seen cutting slow circles in the sky. Only slightly less plentiful were the Red-tailed and Broad-winged Hawks that dotted any quarter of the sky we cared to search.

"The refuge is an annual gathering place for eagles as they await the ice breakup on the upper Mississippi, and early March usually finds the eagle population peaking in the refuge. The highest one-day total for the year was 160."

TREMPEALEAU NATIONAL WILDLIFE REFUGE FIELD CHECKLIST

___ Common Loon
___ Pied-billed Grebe
___ Horned Grebe
___ American Bittern
___ Least Bittern
___ Great Blue Heron
___ Great Egret
___ Green Heron
___ Black-crowned Night-heron
___ Yellow-crowned Night-heron
___ Tundra Swan
___ Snow Goose
___ Wood Duck
___ Green-winged Teal
___ American Black Duck
___ Mallard
___ Northern Pintail
___ Northern Shoveler
___ Gadwall
___ American Wigeon
___ Canvasback
___ Redhead
___ Ring-necked Duck
___ Greater Scaup
___ Lesser Scaup
___ White-winged Scoter
___ Common Merganser
___ Red-breasted Merganser
___ Turkey Vulture
___ Osprey
___ Bald Eagle
___ Northern Harrier
___ Red-shouldered Hawk
___ Broad-winged Hawk
___ Red-tailed Hawk
___ Rough-legged Hawk
___ American Kestrel
___ Merlin
___ Peregrine Falcon
___ Ring-necked Pheasant
___ Ruffed Grouse
___ Wild Turkey
___ Northern Bobwhite
___ Virginia Rail
___ Sora
___ Common Moorhen
___ American Coot
___ Sandhill Crane

___ Black-bellied Plover
___ Lesser Golden-plover
___ Semipalmated Plover
___ Killdeer
___ Greater Yellowlegs
___ Lesser Yellowlegs
___ Solitary Sandpiper
___ Willet
___ Spotted Sandpiper
___ Upland Sandpiper
___ Sanderling
___ Semipalmated Sandpiper
___ Least Sandpiper
___ White-rumped Sandpiper
___ Baird's Sandpiper
___ Pectoral Sandpiper
___ Dunlin
___ Stilt Sandpiper
___ Short-billed Dowitcher
___ Long-billed Dowitcher
___ Common Snipe
___ American Woodcock
___ Wilson's Phalarope
___ Franklin's Gull
___ Bonaparte's Gull
___ Ring-billed Gull
___ Herring Gull
___ Caspian Tern
___ Common Tern
___ Forster's Tern
___ Black Tern
___ Rock Dove
___ Mourning Dove
___ Black-billed Cuckoo
___ Yellow-billed Cuckoo
___ Eastern Screech-owl
___ Great Horned Owl
___ Snowy Owl
___ Barred Owl
___ Long-eared Owl
___ Short-eared Owl
___ Northern Saw-whet Owl
___ Common Nighthawk
___ Whip-poor-will
___ Chimney Swift
___ Ruby-throated Hummingbird
___ Belted Kingfisher
___ Red-headed Woodpecker

___ Red-bellied Woodpecker
___ Yellow-bellied Sapsucker
___ Downy Woodpecker
___ Hairy Woodpecker
___ Northern Flicker
___ Pileated Woodpecker
___ Olive-sided Flycatcher
___ Eastern Wood-pewee
___ Yellow-bellied Flycatcher
___ Alder Flycatcher
___ Willow Flycatcher
___ Least Flycatcher
___ Eastern Phoebe
___ Great Crested Flycatcher
___ Scissor-tailed Flycatcher
___ Eastern Kingbird
___ Horned Lark
___ Purple Martin
___ Tree Swallow
___ Northern Rough-winged Swallow
___ Bank Swallow
___ Cliff Swallow
___ Barn Swallow
___ Blue Jay
___ American Crow
___ Black-capped Chickadee
___ Tufted Titmouse
___ Red-breasted Nuthatch
___ White-breasted Nuthatch
___ Brown Creeper
___ House Wren
___ Winter Wren
___ Sedge Wren
___ Marsh Wren
___ Golden-crowned Kinglet
___ Ruby-crowned Kinglet
___ Blue-gray Gnatcatcher
___ Eastern Bluebird
___ Veery
___ Gray-cheeked Thrush
___ Swainson's Thrush
___ Wood Thrush
___ American Robin
___ Gray Catbird
___ Northern Mockingbird
___ Brown Thrasher
___ Cedar Waxwing
___ Northern Shrike

___ Loggerhead Shrike
___ European Starling
___ White-eyed Vireo
___ Bell's Vireo
___ Solitary Vireo
___ Yellow-throated Vireo
___ Warbling Vireo
___ Philadelphia Vireo
___ Red-eyed Vireo
___ Blue-winged Warbler
___ Golden-winged Warbler
___ Tennessee Warbler
___ Orange-crowned Warbler
___ Nashville Warbler
___ Northern Parula
___ Yellow Warbler
___ Chestnut-sided Warbler
___ Magnolia Warbler
___ Cape May Warbler
___ Yellow-rumped Warbler
___ Black-throated Green Warbler
___ Blackburnian Warbler
___ Palm Warbler
___ Bay-breasted Warbler
___ Blackpoll Warbler
___ Cerulean Warbler
___ Black-and-white Warbler
___ American Redstart
___ Ovenbird
___ Northern Waterthrush
___ Louisiana Waterthrush
___ Mourning Warbler
___ Common Yellowthroat
___ Wilson's Warbler
___ Canada Warbler
___ Yellow-breasted Chat
___ Scarlet Tanager
___ Northern Cardinal
___ Rose-breasted Grosbeak
___ Indigo Bunting
___ Dickcissel
___ Rufous-sided Towhee
___ American Tree Sparrow
___ Chipping Sparrow
___ Clay-colored Sparrow
___ Field Sparrow
___ Vesper Sparrow
___ Savannah Sparrow

___ Grasshopper Sparrow
___ LeConte's Sparrow
___ Fox Sparrow
___ Song Sparrow
___ Lincoln's Sparrow
___ Swamp Sparrow
___ White-throated Sparrow
___ White-crowned Sparrow
___ Harris' Sparrow
___ Dark-eyed Junco
___ Snow Bunting
___ Bobolink
___ Red-winged Blackbird
___ Eastern Meadowlark
___ Western Meadowlark
___ Yellow-headed Blackbird
___ Rusty Blackbird
___ Brewer's Blackbird
___ Common Grackle
___ Brown-headed Cowbird
___ Baltimore Oriole
___ Pine Grosbeak
___ Purple Finch
___ House Finch
___ Red Crossbill
___ Common Redpoll
___ Hoary Redpoll
___ Pine Siskin
___ American Goldfinch
___ Evening Grosbeak
___ House Sparrow

Rare or accidental species
___ Mute Swan
___ Parasitic Jaeger
___ Glaucous Gull
___ Black-legged Kittiwake
___ Western Kingbird
___ Worm-eating Warbler
___ Trumpeter Swan
___ Cinnamon Teal
___ Red Knot
___ Least Tern
___ Common Raven
___ Western Grebe
___ Glossy Ibis

Crex Meadows Wildlife Area

The best way to bird Crex Meadows Wildlife Area, one of the finest wildlife viewing areas in Wisconsin, is from a specially designed and expensive portable blind. Before you ask where you can get one, how much do they cost, or just say the hell with it, about the only way to get to Crex Meadow is in a probable blind. Forty miles of good roads meander through the area, 18 of them atop dikes that border flowages, pothole ponds, and vast marshy areas. The roads make great platforms for viewing the birds, and your car is the perfect moveable blind from which to observe the birds, sometimes at almost arms length.

In spite of the aforementioned, after a 2-hour drive to Crex Meadows, I was in the mood to stretch my legs and do some birding afoot, even if the temperature was over 90 degrees and the humidity could have reduced Melba toast to porridge in five minutes. I parked in the observation area overlooking the south end of Phantom Lake and decided to look for songbirds in the surrounding woods before going in search of waterfowl. Within minutes the black flies disabused me of the idea.

A birder may have entered the woods, but less than three minutes later what emerged looked more like a Whirling Dervish who was dancing himself into a state of ecstasy. Turning in circles to confront the assault coming from every quarter, stamping feet to dislodge flies from socks, and frantically beating the air around my head, I stumbled back to the 4 x 4. Barb looked up from the book she was reading in the comfort and seclusion of an air-conditioned pickup and said, "Done already?"

Not hardly! If the black flies had more than scratched my surface, we had not done the same at this 30,000-acre wildlife area. This vast network of prairies, marshes, open water and forests makes up the largest state wildlife area in Wisconsin. It is a superb haven for a multitude of birds and animals and, strangely enough, owes some of its success to the introduction and popularity of linoleum.

The vast marshes of Crex Meadows were created when a string of shallow, ice-age lakes slowly filled with vegetation. The uplands surrounding the marshes developed into equally game-rich brush prairies. Then Europeans came, drained the marshes, and tried to farm the area. The draining of the land destroyed the wetlands, and created vast, dry sedge marshes filled with wire grass. It proved to be poor farming country, but the wire grass made great grass rugs. In 1912 the area was bought up by the Crex Carpet Company, and the grass was harvested and sent to Minneapolis to be woven into carpets. But the Great Depression, drought, and the preference for linoleum over grass rugs doomed the Crex Carpet Company. In 1946 the state took over the area and began restoration efforts that continue today. The upland brush prairies are once again flourishing, and an elaborate system of dikes has returned 11,000 acres of the wildlife area to marsh habitat. And the birds love it.

The wildlife area's checklist contains 260 species including 24 species of ducks, 28 members of the sandpiper family, 16 different birds of prey, and 27 species of

LOCATION: Grantsburg, Wisconsin.

DIRECTIONS: At the intersection of State Highway 70 and Pine Street (Highway 48/87) in Grantsburg turn north on Pine Street and drive through the business district to the post office. At the post office turn west (left) and drive one block, then turn north on Oak St. Drive north about a half-mile to the end of Oak Street. Turn right (east) for one block then take a left (north) and drive about a half-mile to Crex Avenue/County Road D. Turn right on Crex Avenue, Crex Meadows Wildlife Area headquarters will be on the left just a short distance down the road.

HOURS: The refuge is open all year. Visitors Center Hours: weekends 10 a.m.-4 p.m.; week days 8 a.m.-4:30 p.m.

BEST TIMES: Outstanding birding all year. April and May bring the largest diversity of birds while the fall migration, September through November, brings the largest number of birds as ducks and geese by the thousands descend on the area. Late summer and early fall can be very good for shorebirds.

BIRDING HIGHLIGHTS: Extraordinary waterfowl and shorebird viewing. Sharp-tailed Grouse and Greater Prairie Chicken nest in the area and blinds are available for viewing their spring mating dances. Sandhill Cranes, Osprey, swans, Bald and Golden eagles, occasional American White Pelicans, Snow Geese, White-fronted Geese and a wide variety of songbirds are only some of the 260 bird species that draw over 100,000 birding enthusiasts every year to the area.

FOR MORE INFORMATION: Crex Meadows Wildlife Area, Box 367, Grantsburg, WI 54840. Phone: (715) 463-2896.

"This vast network of prairies, marshes, open water and forests is a superb haven for a multitude of birds and animals and, strangely enough, owes some of its success to the introduction and popularity of linoleum."

warblers. But a recitation of the checklist hardly does the area justice. Both Sharp-tailed Grouse and Greater Prairie Chicken nest in the refuge and Crex Meadows is only one of two locations in Wisconsin with a self-sustaining prairie chicken population. Dancing grounds are maintained for both birds, and two blinds are available by reservation for viewing their fantastic spring mating dance.

Yellow-headed Blackbirds, Sandhill Cranes, Ospreys, Bald and Golden eagles, Common Loons, Snow Geese, and Trumpeter Swans are all commonly sighted. Spring brings the greatest diversity of birds as ducks, geese, swans, Osprey and songbirds arrive at Crex Meadows to either rest on their northward journey or nest. Late summer and early fall witness the peak of shorebird activity as the birds come to feed on the exposed mud flats. September and October mark the largest number of birds in the area as ducks and geese by the thousands funnel through Crex Meadows on their way south.

Safe from the blood thirsty black flies in our Chevrolet bird blind, Barb and I decided to make a grand circuit of Crex beginning at Phantom Lake, widely regarded as the wildlife area's prime birding spot. The vast marsh and open waters of the lake are bordered on the west by Phantom Lake Road. The wide, well-maintained road is an excellent observation platform, and we had barely driven a 100 yards before spotting Horned and Pied-billed grebes within yards of the road. Red-winged Blackbirds seemed to be everywhere, but Yellowed-headed Blackbirds, which also nest in the area, would elude us the entire day. Within a mile we added a Black Tern and Great Blue Heron to the day's sightings along with a lone female Wood Duck.

Turning east on the Main Dike Road, we crossed the northern loop of Phantom Lake on our way to the wildlife refuge in the heart of Crex Meadows. Canada Geese lolled about in the open patches of water bordering the road. Before reaching the refuge, Main Dike Road passes through some of the 6,000 acres of restored brush prairie in Crex Meadows. This stretch of the road was lined with Cedar Waxwings, Eastern Kingbirds, Mourning Doves, and an occasional Lark Sparrow.

The high point of the trip came at the southern edge of the wildlife refuge where the road curves around a series of open pools in the a marsh. The first pool held a magnificent Trumpeter Swan. In the next pool, not 50 yards down the road, a Common Loon with two chicks on board drifted across the wind rippled water. Other pools in the area were staked out by Blue-winged Teal, Ring-necked Ducks, Buffleheads, and Mallards. This south edge of the refuge, bordering Main Dike Road is even more productive in the fall when thousands of ducks, Greater White-fronted, Snow and Canada geese pack themselves into the marsh. Upwards of two dozen Bald Eagles are also drawn to this part of Crex Meadows each fall.

Turning back west and retracing our steps on Main Dike Road, we turned north on West Refuge Road. West, North and East Refuge Roads took us around the last three sides of the refuge and the last road delivered us back near the starting point of our circumnavigation of the area. All of the roads are wide enough to permit birders to pull over and glass birds from the car, or park and bird on foot. As we followed the refuge boundary roads, we spotted Northern Harriers lazily strafing the marsh while American Kestrels perched atop low shrubs in the upland prairies. Stopping to glass birds too distant to identify with the naked eye rewarded us with sightings of Yellow and Yellow-rumped warblers, a Yellow-billed Cuckoo, and a variety of sparrows.

On North Refuge Road, at about the halfway point of circling Crex Meadows, a rest area with grills, fire rings, pit toilets, drinking water and picnic tables occupies a low hill overlooking the northern end of the refuge. It is a perfect place to setup a spotting scope and sweep the vast expanse of brush prairie and Reisinger Lake. Snow Geese and Sandhill Cranes congregate here every October and a wide variety of sparrows including Vesper, Grasshopper, Savannah and Clay-colored inhabit the brush prairie. Chances are also good for spotting Sharp-tailed Grouse, Upland Sandpipers, Yellow-headed Blackbirds and Horned Larks. Camping is permitted at the rest area from September 1 through December 31 each year.

A number of old logging trails, firebreaks, and maintenance trails meander through the area and although they are not open to vehicular traffic, birders are welcome to walk them. They are identified by the sign "Hunter Walking Trails". In fact, foot travel is allowed anywhere on the property except the refuge. Two trails within the wildlife area were designed specifically for hikers or cross-country skiers. A mile-long trail that begins about a 100 yards east of the Visitors Center cuts through a wooded area and leads to a observation platform overlooking Hay Creek Flowage. The second and longer trail consists of four loops totaling 3.7 miles and can be accessed from East Refuge Road, south of North Refuge Road. The trail is groomed for cross-country skiing.

A detailed map of the Crex Meadows Wildlife Area that leads visitors to all the area's nooks and crannies is available at the Visitors Center on Highway D. A self-guided auto tour pamphlet, a visitor's guide to Crex Meadows, and a bird checklist can also be picked up while you ask about the most recent sightings and seasonal hot spots. The Center also houses displays of mounted birds and animals, and exhibits relating the story of Crex Meadows. If the Center is closed, all pamphlets can be found in a rack next to the door.

COMMON LOON

CREX MEADOWS WILDLIFE AREA FIELD CHECKLIST

The following checklist was compiled by Crex Meadows Wildlife Area.

___ Arctic Loon	___ Northern Harrier	___ Wilson's Phalarope	___ Black-capped Chickadee	___ Common Yellowthroat
___ Red-throated Loon	___ Sharp-shinned Hawk	___ Northern Phalarope	___ Red-breasted Nuthatch	___ Wilson's Warbler
___ Common Loon	___ Cooper's Hawk	___ Parasitic Jaeger	___ White-breasted Nuthatch	___ Canada Warbler
___ Pied-billed Grebe	___ Northern Goshawk	___ Franklin's Gull	___ Brown Creeper	___ Scarlet Tanager
___ Horned Grebe	___ Red-tailed Hawk	___ Bonaparte's Gull	___ House Wren	___ Northern Cardinal
___ Red-necked Grebe	___ Red-shouldered Hawk	___ Ivory Gull	___ Winter Wren	___ Rose-breasted Grosbeak
___ Eared Grebe	___ Broad-winged Hawk	___ Ring-billed Gull	___ Sedge Wren	___ Evening Grosbeak
___ Western Grebe	___ Swainson's Hawk	___ Herring Gull	___ Marsh Wren	___ Indigo Bunting
___ American White Pelican	___ Rough-legged Hawk	___ Forster's Tern	___ Golden-crowned Kinglet	___ Dickcissel
___ Double-crested Cormorant	___ American Kestrel	___ Caspian Tern	___ Ruby-crowned Kinglet	___ Rufous-sided Towhee
___ American Bittern	___ Merlin	___ Common Tern	___ Blue-gray Gnatcatcher	___ Pine Grosbeak
___ Least Bittern	___ Peregrine Falcon	___ Black Tern	___ Eastern Bluebird	___ Purple Finch
___ Great Blue Heron	___ Ring-necked Pheasant	___ Rock Dove	___ Veery	___ Red Crossbill
___ Great Egret	___ Ruffed Grouse	___ Mourning Dove	___ Gray-cheeked Thrush	___ White-winged Crossbill
___ Snowy Egret	___ Greater Prairie Chicken	___ Black-billed Cuckoo	___ Swainson's Thrush	___ Common Redpoll
___ Cattle Egret	___ Sharp-tailed Grouse	___ Boreal Owl	___ Hermit Thrush	___ Pine Siskin
___ Tricolored Heron	___ Northern Bobwhite	___ Eastern Screech-owl	___ American Robin	___ American Goldfinch
___ Green Heron	___ Yellow Rail	___ Great Horned Owl	___ Gray Catbird	___ American Tree Sparrow
___ Black-crowned Night-heron	___ King Rail	___ Snowy Owl	___ Northern Mockingbird	___ Chipping Sparrow
___ Tundra Swan	___ Virginia Rail	___ Barred Owl	___ Brown Thrasher	___ Clay-colored Sparrow
___ Trumpeter Swan	___ Sora	___ Great Gray Owl	___ Water Pipit	___ Field Sparrow
___ Greater White-fronted Goose	___ Common Moorhen	___ Long-eared Owl	___ Bohemian Waxwing	___ Vesper Sparrow
___ Snow Goose	___ American Coot	___ Short-eared Owl	___ Cedar Waxwing	___ Lark Bunting
___ Brant	___ Sandhill Crane	___ Northern Saw-whet Owl	___ Northern Shrike	___ Savannah Sparrow
___ Canada Goose	___ Lesser Golden-plover	___ Whip-poor-will	___ Loggerhead Shrike	___ Baird's Sparrow
___ Wood Duck	___ Black-bellied Plover	___ Common Nighthawk	___ European Starling	___ Henslow's Sparrow
___ Green-winged Teal	___ Semipalmated Plover	___ Chimney Swift	___ Solitary Vireo	___ LeConte's Sparrow
___ Blue-winged Teal	___ Killdeer	___ Ruby-throated Hummingbird	___ Yellow-throated Vireo	___ Sharp-tailed Sparrow
___ American Black Duck	___ Avocet	___ Belted Kingfisher	___ Warbling Vireo	___ Fox Sparrow
___ Mallard	___ Greater Yellowlegs	___ Red-headed Woodpecker	___ Red-eyed Vireo	___ Song Sparrow
___ Northern Pintail	___ Lesser Yellowlegs	___ Red-bellied Woodpecker	___ Golden-winged Warbler	___ Lincoln's Sparrow
___ Northern Shoveler	___ Solitary Sandpiper	___ Yellow-bellied Sapsucker	___ Tennessee Warbler	___ Swamp Sparrow
___ Gadwall	___ Willet	___ Downy Woodpecker	___ Orange-crowned Warbler	___ White-throated Sparrow
___ American Wigeon	___ Spotted Sandpiper	___ Hairy Woodpecker	___ Nashville Warbler	___ White-crowned Sparrow
___ Eurasian Wigeon	___ Upland Sandpiper	___ Northern Flicker	___ Northern Parula	___ Harris' Sparrow
___ Canvasback	___ Long-billed Curlew	___ Pileated Woodpecker	___ Yellow Warbler	___ Dark-eyed Junco
___ Redhead	___ Hudsonian Godwit	___ Olive-sided Flycatcher	___ Chestnut-sided Warbler	___ Lapland Longspur
___ Ring-necked Duck	___ Marbled Godwit	___ Eastern Wood-pewee	___ Magnolia Warbler	___ Snow Bunting
___ Greater Scaup	___ Whimbrel	___ Alder Flycatcher	___ Cay May Warbler	___ Bobolink
___ Lesser Scaup	___ Ruddy Turnstone	___ Least Flycatcher	___ Black-throated Blue Warbler	___ Red-winged Blackbird
___ Oldsquaw	___ Red Knot	___ Great Crested Flycatcher	___ Yellow-rumped Warbler	___ Western Meadowlark
___ Surf Scoter	___ Sanderling	___ Western Kingbird	___ Black-throated Green Warbler	___ Eastern Meadowlark
___ White-winged Scoter	___ Semipalmated Sandpiper	___ Eastern Kingbird	___ Blackburnian Warbler	___ Yellow-headed Blackbird
___ Common Goldeneye	___ Least Sandpiper	___ Horned Lark	___ Pine Warbler	___ Brewer's Blackbird
___ Bufflehead	___ White-rumped Sandpiper	___ Purple Martin	___ Palm Warbler	___ Common Grackle
___ Hooded Merganser	___ Baird's Sandpiper	___ Tree Swallow	___ Bay-breasted Warbler	___ Brown-headed Cowbird
___ Common Merganser	___ Pectoral Sandpiper	___ Northern Rough-winged Swallow	___ Blackpoll Warbler	___ Baltimore Oriole
___ Red-breasted Merganser	___ Dunlin	___ Bank Swallow	___ Black-and-white Warbler	___ House Sparrow
___ Ruddy Duck	___ Stilt Sandpiper	___ Cliff Swallow	___ American Redstart	
___ Wild Turkey	___ Buff-breasted Sandpiper	___ Barn Swallow	___ Prothonotary Warbler	
___ Osprey	___ Short-billed Dowitcher	___ Blue Jay	___ Ovenbird	
___ Mississippi Kite	___ Long-billed Dowitcher	___ Gray Jay	___ Northern Waterthrush	
___ Bald Eagle	___ Common Snipe	___ American Crow	___ Connecticut Warbler	
___ Golden Eagle	___ American Woodcock	___ Common Raven	___ Mourning Warbler	

RARE BIRD ALERTS

Rare Bird Alerts are recorded telephone messages that list birds of special interest that have been seen in a general area or on a statewide basis. The messages are usually updated weekly. They can be a great help in letting you know when migration is in full swing in specific areas, and also let you know of unusual sightings in your state or general area.

RARE BIRD ALERTS IN THE GREAT LAKES AREA

ILLINOIS
Central Illinois (217) 785-1083
Chicago (847) 265-2118
Dupage (630) 406-8111
Northwestern (815) 965-3095

INDIANA
Statewide (317) 259-0911

MICHIGAN
Statewide (616) 471-4919
Detroit (810) 477-1360
Sault Ste. Marie (705) 256-2790

OHIO
Cincinnati (513) 521-2847
Cleveland (216) 526-2473
Columbus (614) 221-9736
Southwest Ohio (937) 277-6446
Northwest Ohio (419) 877-9640

ONTARIO
Sault Ste. Marie (705) 256-2790
Windsor/Point Pelee (519) 252-2473

WISCONSIN
Statewide (414) 352-3857
Madison (608) 255-2476
Green Bay (414) 434-4207

The Internet can be even more valuable for tracking bird migrations and letting you know of unusual sightings in your area, your state, or in the Midwest. Many of the above Rare Bird Alerts are also posted on the Internet on a weekly basis and printing the list is much easier than trying to either take notes or simply remember what you heard. There are two World Wide Web sites that give access to regional Rare Bird Alerts:

The National Birding Hotline Cooperative at **http://www.nbhc.com/**

and

The American Birding Association home page at **http://www.americanbirding.org**

Notes

Notes

THE AUTHOR

Tom Powers' interest in birding began innocently enough with the feeding of birds in his backyard. As so many others have discovered, a backyard bird feeder is often the first perilous step down a long road leading to a lifetime of addiction. After the bird feeder came a trip to Point Pelee National Park in Canada, then a visit to Tawas Point State Park and so on and so on. Within two years the author found himself buying more and more bird identification books, starting a life list, wanting better binoculars, craving a spotting scope, and scrutinizing L.L. Bean catalogs for birding apparel. Powerless in the face of an urge to drop everything and go birding, the author joined the Audubon Society under the mistaken notion the organization was a 12-step program that would help him break his birding addiction. Today, alas, Tom Powers is treasurer of his local Audubon club and writes press releases for the club's monthly meetings, luring more people down a road from which there is no return.

Powers is the author of three previous books — *Michigan State and National Parks: A Complete Guide*, *Natural Michigan, A Nature Lover's Guide to 228 Attractions*, and *Michigan in Quotes*. The author also created the world's first and only Mime Radio Show and dismisses accusations that the show was instrumental in causing a radio station's demise.

When not involved with the above activities the author loves to travel, camp, cook, read, and is a fanatical fan of blues music and ice hockey. The other passions in his life are his wife Barbara, their two children and their spouses, and four grandchildren. When time permits, Powers is the Head of Adult Services at the Flint Public Library where he has been employed for the past 30 years.